MOVING LIBRARY COLLECTIONS

MOVING LIBRARY COLLECTIONS

A Management Handbook

Second Edition

Elizabeth Chamberlain Habich

Libraries Unlimited Library Management Collection
Gerard B. McCabe, Series Editor

Libraries Unlimited
An Imprint of ABC-CLIO, LLC

A B C 🞄 C L I O

Santa Barbara, California • Denver, Colorado • Oxford, England

Copyright 2010 by Libraries Unlimited

All rights reserved. No part of this publication may be reproduced, stored in a retrieval system, or transmitted, in any form or by any means, electronic, mechanical, photocopying, recording, or otherwise, except for the inclusion of brief quotations in a review, without prior permission in writing from the publisher.

Library of Congress Cataloging-in-Publication Data

Habich, Elizabeth Chamberlain, 1955-
  Moving library collections : a management handbook / Elizabeth Chamberlain Habich. — 2nd ed.
      p. cm. — (Libraries Unlimited library management collection)
  Includes bibliographical references and index.
  ISBN 978-1-59158-670-8 (pbk. : acid-free paper)
  1. Library moving. 2. Library moving—United States. I. Title.
  Z703.5.H29 2010
  025.8'1—dc22   2009041734

14 13 12 11 10   1 2 3 4 5

This book is also available on the World Wide Web as an eBook.
Visit www.abc-clio.com or details.

ABC-CLIO, LLC
130 Cremona Drive, P.O. Box 1911
Santa Barbara, California 93116-1911

This book is printed on acid-free paper ∞
Manufactured in the United States of America

Foreword by Lee B. Brawner and Chapter 11 by Joyce Frank Watson from *Moving Library Collections: A Management Handbook* by Elizabeth Chamberlain Habich. Westport, CT: Greenwood Press. Copyright © 1998 by Elizabeth Chamberlain Habich. Reproduced with permission of ABC-CLIO, LLC.

CONTENTS

CONTENTS

IV. Doing the Move Yourself

V. Special Topics

FOREWORD

Moving a library—the furnishings, shelving, equipment, and collection— across the hall or across town is a mammoth task that requires precise, long-range planning. Moving the library's collection is particularly demanding and requires a specialized methodology. This book focuses on moving the library collection and provides a sequential guide and decision path for planning and executing successful relocations and moves.

The book will be a godsend to library directors, administrators, and managers who typically assume direct responsibilities for planning and supervising a collection move. It details the planning that must precede the primary decisions regarding the types, size, and relationships of collection space requirements for new or expanded library buildings. These data are included in the building program for the new space and are subsequently incorporated into the long-range moving plan. This process calls for determining the present and projected size for each collection, the shelving and floor space requirements, and the collection layout within the overall floor plan. It includes the use of allocations providing for expansion or "growth joints." In addressing these needs, the author provides guidance in how to integrate the existing collection into the new space using spreadsheet collection allocation models, techniques for sampling and measuring the collection holdings, and criteria for calculating linear shelving footage.

The book addresses the broad range of planning processes and issues associated with a move. What collections will be relocated? Does the collection have surplus materials that should be weeded or sold prior to the move? Are plans for multiple and interim move locations needed? Will the collection be reorganized in the new space? Will portions of the collection be converted into new microform or electronic formats? How reliable are the current holdings records? What are the conversion formulas for determining linear shelving space for the various material formats? These issues and questions emphasize the need to begin planning for the move early in the building project and to generate an accurate inventory of existing and projected collection holdings. Moving companies will estimate their costs and fees by converting the library's inventory holdings records into the number of moving containers, time, and labor to accomplish the move.

The book focuses at length on whether the library should handle the move itself or engage a moving company. It describes how to write a Request for Proposal (RFP) for choosing and contracting with a mover. The criteria include experience, references, project managers and other personnel, availability, basic and optional services, methodology, schedule for the move, time frame for completing the job, pre-move orientation walk-throughs, access to the collection during the move, the designated moving route, equipment (boxes, carts, dollies, trucks), description of the owner's role including building maintenance staff and security staff, handling of special materials, and legal conditions. Many of these same specifications and factors should also be incorporated into the plan of work if the library chooses to move itself.

Some libraries use library staff and students or volunteers to move the collection, especially for short moves. This way the move can usually be achieved for about half the cost of contracting with a moving company. Most libraries, however, do not have access to the labor and specialized equipment necessary to handle the move. Larger libraries may also contract with a library moving consultant to guide the planning process and to serve as the owner's agent on the job to inspect the work. My experience has shown me that all but the smallest libraries contract with moving companies. Large libraries may opt to engage two moving companies: a specialized firm to move the collection and another firm to move the furnishings, shelving, and equipment. Libraries that handle the physical move with staff, students, and volunteers must be diligent about the risk factors for injuries and accidents and the liability involved; provision of appropriate insurance is necessary. Commercial moving companies provide this insurance along with optional coverage for handling archival collections, works of art, and other specialized library materials.

A successful move, with or without a moving company, hinges on allowing a lot of lead time, accurately determining the location of individual materials or collections in the new space, and assigning staff responsibilities for the move. The methodology to identify individual shelf locations is described in this book, accompanied by steps for preparing a documented plan of the existing space and the new layout, with labels identifying each stack and shelf. Color-coded labels can be used to distinguish formats, specific collections, or building locations. The labels are designed to peel off and travel with the boxed or carted materials to the new location. Whether the library moves itself or hires a moving company, designated staff members must be oriented, trained, and scheduled to supervise

FOREWORD

every hour of the move. The move time frame may include evenings and weekends, with allowances for emergencies such as elevator or other equipment failure or inclement weather.

Even the best planned and executed moves are disruptive and may create morale and stress problems among the staff, inconvenience for customers, and negative public relations. Elizabeth Habich candidly addresses these issues with sound guidance for planning a successful move that incorporates effective communications with the staff and the public and generates positive public relations for the library.

The preplanning, orientation, training, and documentation methods described in this book draw on the experience of many libraries and can save a library money, time, and frustration when moving its collections.

Lee B. Brawner
Executive Director, Metropolitan Library System, Oklahoma City, OK
and Library Building Consultant

PREFACE

This new edition of *Moving Library Collections* incorporates several changes. Temporary moves and moves to storage facilities have become more frequent as libraries cope with space pressures and the impact of shifting to electronic journals, and these moves are all addressed in more detail.

The needs of public libraries and smaller libraries are also better addressed. Small moves and simplified planning are both covered in more detail. A new section detailing the average widths of public library materials has been added to Appendix A, to aid in planning shelf space requirements. An expanded section on moving archives is also included.

Appendix B, a list of moves reported in the English-language literature, has been brought up to date to let move planners easily find key facts and articles on moves similar to those they are planning.

The spreadsheets will be available for download at www.elizabethhabich. com. This will make it considerably easier (and faster) to use these valuable planning tools. Although the examples given are in U.S. Customary System (USCS) measurements (e.g., inches, feet, and pounds), librarians in countries using the International System of Units (SI) can substitute metric figures to get the results they require.

For most of us, moving a library is something that occurs once in our professional lives. It's a huge task, and how well it's planned and executed can make a big difference in the cost, time required, cleanup required, staff morale, and public support. For all of these reasons, it's worth doing well.

PREFACE

In the late 1980s I was responsible for managing the Northeastern University Libraries' planning for a new, central building. As an extension of this work, I was asked to take responsibility for planning and managing the 1990 move from the old main Dodge Library, three branch libraries, and the contents of a storage facility into the new Snell Library, with the help of an able committee. I quickly found that there was no one source in which I could find the answers to the many questions that arose, nor one guide that walked the move planner through all of the logical steps of preparing for a complex move. How much material does the library have now? How much will have to be accommodated? How should it be arranged? Should the library perform the move itself? Should volunteers be used? How long will the move take? How much will it cost? What needs to be included in an RFP? The questions went on and on, and as the date of the move got closer, not only did the questions became more numerous and more detailed, but finding answers to them (the correct answers!) became more urgent. With lots of analysis, sweat, and teamwork with the staff of William B. Meyer, library movers, the move was completed successfully with minimal complications.

This book is, I hope, the comprehensive guide to planning and managing library collection moves I wanted when planning our move. It is divided into five sections. Part I addresses issues related to planning collection space. It answers the questions: How much material does the library have? (Chapter 1); How much space must be allowed for future collections? (Chapter 2); and How should the material be arranged (Chapter 3)? This section will be useful both to those planning to move into new collection space and to collection managers considering the best use of space in an existing facility.

Part II and Chapter 4 discuss general considerations in planning the collection move: What are the advantages and disadvantages of using library staff, volunteers, or a moving company to plan and carry out the move? How long might the move take? How should materials be packed and moved? How can public relations best be handled? What special problems are posed by temporary moves?

Part III focuses on issues related to managing a move that will be carried out by a moving company. Chapter 5 considers library and mover responsibilities from the librarian's and the mover's perspective, with a contribution by Michael J. Kent of William B. Meyer, Inc. Chapter 6 is a detailed guide to preparing a Request for Proposal (RFP), and Chapter 7 deals with selecting a mover through the RFP process, including how to organize a pre-bid conference and tour, and approaches to evaluating RFP responses. Chapter 8 follows up with methods for working effectively with a mover during the actual execution of a move.

Part IV is primarily for libraries planning to carry out a move without a moving company, but will also be of general interest to libraries working with a moving company. Chapter 9 addresses planning move logistics, including development of a planning calendar (how early should the planning start?); discusses differences in planning requirements for small- and larger-scale moves; and shows the move planner how to create a work breakdown structure (WBS), perform detailed analyses of move operation planning using PERT and Gantt techniques, and prepare the master schedule and budget. Chapter 10 deals with the nitty-gritty issues involved in executing a move yourself: how to recruit workers, whom to recruit, and how to train and supervise them; various move methods and their pros and cons (why a book brigade generates good public relations, but is bad for the collections); pre-move setup steps; facilities issues (why elevators **must** be in good working order and an elevator repair service on call during the move); daily operations; monitoring progress and resolving problems; security and health and safety issues; maintaining service during the move; and communicating with the public.

Part V covers several special and difficult situations that may not be a part of every move. Chapter 11, by Joyce Watson, discusses when and how to clean whole collections of bound volumes other than rare materials. Chapter 12 deals with moving from disorganized conditions: what to do when lack of staff or space over a period of time has led to materials being "shelved" on the floor, in out-of-order sequences, and in more extreme conditions of disorder.

Appendix A provides charts of the average width of library materials in both academic and public libraries, with widths of monograph and bound periodical volumes broken out by class or category. This will be of particular interest to planners with large collections who seek a means of accurately assessing the linear footage requirements for various segments of the collection.

Appendix B summarizes data for 200 library moves reported in the English-language literature from 1929 to 2006. This chart shows for each move the number of items moved, duration, approximate date, container type, means of transportation, type of labor, special problems encountered, and a brief citation to the article(s) in which the move was reported.

The extensive Annotated References section lists English-language books, articles, and reports from 1929 to the present and includes brief annotations highlighting the usefulness of each item to the move planner. Although a number of the books are out of print, and the articles listed go back a number of years, most can be easily obtained through interlibrary loan.

ACKNOWLEDGMENTS

To Sue Easun and Jerry McCabe at Greenwood, many thanks for their interest in a new edition.

To my colleagues in the LLAMA Moving Libraries Discussion Group and Facilities Discussion Group, thanks for your suggestions and comments.

At Northeastern University, thanks to Ed Warro, William Wakeling, and Lesley Milner for their support; to Roxanne Palmatier for her expert advice on government documents practice for both this and the original edition; and to the superb resource-sharing group, led by Brian Greene, for making it possible to get most of the articles I needed without leaving my desk. Thanks also to Toby Bernstein, Debra Mandel, and Anne Moore for their expert advice on matters relating to oversized practice and AV terminology in the first edition.

At the Flint Memorial Library, the public library of North Reading, Massachusetts, thanks to director Helena Minton and library staff for letting me make the measurements used to expand Appendix B.

At Thompson Scientific, many, many thanks to Peter Travis, customer technical support representative and file wizard extraordinaire, who migrated my ten-year-old ProCite files to EndNote and saved me from having to re-create them from scratch.

To Mike Kent for his contribution to this and the first edition, and to my late colleagues Lee Brawner, Joyce Watson, and Agnes Quigg for their contributions to the first edition.

ACKNOWLEDGMENTS

And finally, huge thanks (and pie) to Mike Habich, who drew several of the original figures, and for this edition converted all of them to the required format.

It is my hope that with this book in hand, the move planner and manager will have the tools necessary to plan and carry out a successful move.

Elizabeth Chamberlain Habich
North Reading, MA

I

PLANNING COLLECTION SPACE

Every library needs to move its collections at some point. The move may be a simple internal collection shift, needing just a few days, or a large, complex project involving multiple locations and classifications that will take several weeks or longer. The occasion may be a happy one, the opening of a new building, or sad, closing a library and dispersing its collections. It may be executed by a library moving company, by the library itself, by volunteers, or by a combination of these.

Each move has its own challenges, but all moves share similar goals and planning issues. In each case, we want every item to end up where it is supposed to be, with no items lost or damaged; we want the work to be completed on time, on or under budget; and we want staff, library users, and the people we report to all be satisfied with the process and the outcome.

The key to a successful outcome is detailed and accurate planning and clear communication. Planning takes time and effort, but as reports in the literature confirm, time invested in planning WILL prevent problems and save time during the move. Well-done planning will reduce the likelihood of missing books, damaged materials, and anxiety during the move, and pay dividends in the years after the move by minimizing the need to continuously shift collections to free up open space.

Part I addresses the steps that are fundamental to any successful move:

1. Determine the size of the current collections, taking into account any one-time changes planned in association with the move, such as weeding and merging collections.

2. Estimate net annual growth rate and identify the number of years of growth to be accommodated.

3. Determine how the collection will be housed and the amount of shelving required.

4. Determine how the collections will be arranged.

Professionals use various terms to refer to shelving and building elements. The following conventions are used throughout this work: One section of shelving is the shelving between two adjacent uprights or vertical dividers. A typical section of shelving is 36 inches wide, with one fixed (base) shelf and five or six movable shelves.

A section of shelving may be either *single faced (SF)* or *double faced (DF)*. Most commonly, single-faced shelving is installed against a wall. Double-faced shelving (which has shelving on both sides) is freestanding and has twice the capacity of single-faced shelving of the same height and with the same number of shelves (e.g., 2 SF = 1 DF or 1 SF = .5DF). Many library planners work in DF units and convert any SF units to .5 DF. I prefer the simplicity of working in whole units only and have chosen to work in SF equivalent units. This also eliminates the need to worry about introducing rounding error to section counts.

A *range of shelving* comprises multiple connected sections of either SF or DF shelving units.

A *shelving row* is the space between two ranges of shelving, and is used to access material on the shelf.

A *column* is a structural element of building construction.

A *bay* is the area within four columns.

1 DETERMINING THE SIZE OF EXISTING COLLECTIONS

INTRODUCTION

Most of the time, when librarians talk about collection size, we mean the number of titles, items, or volumes, or the amount of information we can access. Sometimes we think about the number of sections of shelving or the amount of space that shelving occupies. However, to plan an effective and efficient collection move, we need to think of the collection in different terms: the linear inches it occupies on a shelf.

The collection's linear measurement is critical in determining whether it will fit in a new location, whether more empty space can be left on each shelf, if the collection needs to be weeded in order to fit, and how much time and effort will be needed to move it. As with the unsound foundation of a building, a collection measurement done with insufficient accuracy can cause a move to develop cracks or crumble: material may take up more or less space on the shelf in the new location than anticipated; the shelves may end up closer to capacity than planned; more people or more days (and therefore more money) may be required for the move; the move may have to be halted to rework a collection layout plan; or back shifting may be required after the move is theoretically done to even out growth space. In short, time invested now in measuring the collection saves aggravation later during the move.

For the purposes of planning a collection move, it is necessary to know both the linear measurement of both the collection as a whole and of each part of the collection that will be shelved separately. These collection parts will be determined by the nature of the collection, the library, and its users. For instance, parts of a music library's collections might include circulating and reference

3

monographs (regular and oversized); bound periodical volumes; several sizes of scores; recordings in multiple formats (CDs, LP or 33 rpm records, laser discs, videotapes, reel-to-reel tapes); and reserve or restricted access collections. A children's collection might have a section for preschool children, including picture and pop-up books, toys, and games; an area for elementary school students including reference, fiction, nonfiction, and biography sections; and reference, fiction, and nonfiction for older students. A university library might have regular and oversized monographs and bound periodicals, reference monographs, abstracts and indexes, ready reference, government documents, microforms, current periodicals, archives, special collections, and various formats of video and audio recordings, and in addition might establish different cutoff points for oversized material in various subject classifications. To further complicate matters, libraries with the same types of collections may arrange or segment them differently to best serve their users' specific needs. From the move planner's perspective, the important thing is to identify and measure separately each segment of the collection that will be shelved separately.

At this point, before taking any measurements, it is important to think carefully about whether to undertake any major changes in the current arrangement of the collections. For instance, can bound journals now covered by JSTOR be moved to storage? Should recordings be moved from a media center to open shelving? If periodicals have been shelved by title, should they be reclassified and interfiled with monographs? Will the oversized cutoff be increased to allow more materials to be shelved together? The important point is to identify any changes that will affect how the collections are segmented.

If, for instance, bound periodicals have been maintained in a separate sequence, shelved alphabetically by title, and the new plan calls for them to be classified and integrated into the call number sequence with monographs on a title-by-title basis, then the collection measurements will have to be more detailed than if the current arrangement were to be maintained. By thinking carefully at this point about how the collections should be arranged, you will save yourself the time and aggravation of having to redo measurements and planning work later on.

Likewise, this is the last practical opportunity to think about whether to maintain or change the type of collection housing used. For instance, if the library has stored its compact discs in cabinets and has decided to instead place them on shelves or in display bins, that decision should be made now, so that capacity calculations may be done for the new type of housing. Will paperbacks that have been shelved with other circulating collections be placed in display shelving? Will recordings' jackets be placed in display bins and a second set of shelving be maintained in a staff-controlled area for the recordings themselves? Does the library want to create special-interest collection areas (such as career or job seeker resources) by pulling materials from the general collection and housing them on an index table that has both seating and shelving? All these sorts of questions need to be identified and answered at this point, so that measurements of the existing collections can be done for the relevant segments of the collection and projections of collection space required can be done for the type of housing that will be used.

SOURCES AND TYPES OF COLLECTION MEASUREMENTS

Once you have decided how the collection will be segmented, it's time to measure. Collection measurements may be estimated or actual. Estimates may be based on inspection of the stacks, the shelflist, and online catalog records; measurements may draw from stack maintenance records or be done specifically for move planning. Each approach has advantages and disadvantages.

When to Estimate and When to Measure

The first decision is whether to estimate or use measurements. Estimates are good when the collection is relatively small, for preliminary planning, or when the consequences of an error are relatively minor (for instance, the new stack location has considerable excess capacity). Some estimates can be constructed relatively quickly and with minimal calculation. The downside is that estimates are an approximation, and the degree of accuracy will depend on the assumptions made. If collection measurements are kept for stack maintenance purposes, these may be a useful compromise, though there are several caveats, discussed below.

When the collection is large, the arrangement complex, the space and time tight, or the existing information not reliable, invest the time and effort in measuring the collections specifically for the move—you'll thank yourself later.

Estimates Based on Inspection of the Stacks

A fairly accurate, fairly quick approximation of a collection's linear measurement can be made as follows:

1. Determine the percentage of the shelves you wish to measure (e.g., 5 percent or every twentieth shelf). Measure the material, recording both the linear inches of material and the width of the shelves measured:

Nominal Shelf-Width	Material on Shelf	Total Inches of Materials	Number of Shelves Measured	Average Inches of Material per Shelf
36 in.	34 in., 34 in., 32 in., 35 in., 35 in., 35 in., 33 in., 33 in., 35 in., 34 in., 33 in., 32 in., 34 in., 34 in., 32 in., 35 in.	540 in.	16	33.75 in.
30 in.	29 in.	29 in.	1	29.0 in.
24 in.	22 in., 23in.	45 in.	2	22.5 in.

PLANNING COLLECTION SPACE

2. Calculate the average fill ratio (the percentage of the shelf occupied by material) for the sample, as follows:

   a. Add up the total inches of materials in the sample set:

      540 in. + 29 in. + 45 in. = 614 in. of material

   b. Add up the linear measurement of actual shelf space in the sample set:

      (35.5 in./shelf x 16 shelves) + (29.5 in./shelf x 1 shelf) + (23.5 in./shelf x 2 shelves) = 644.5 in. actual shelf space

   c. Divide the total inches of material by the total inches of shelf space in the sample set:

      614 in. of material/644.5 in. of shelf space = 95.3% fill ratio

3. Next, determine the actual linear measurement of all shelving in the area under consideration. First, count the number of single-faced (SF) equivalent sections of shelving of each width and height, and record the number of shelves in each. Measure the actual inside measurement of each nominal width, type, and brand of shelving. The typical inside measurement of a 36-inch nominal width cantilever steel shelf is 35.5 inches; however, there is variation between case and cantilever type shelving, between different manufacturers' products, and even some among shelves of the same model from the same manufacturer. Then add up the number of sections of each width with the identical number of shelves per section, for example:

Nominal Width	Actual Size	No. of Shelves/SF	Total SF
36 in.	35.5 in.	7	168
30 in.	29.5 in.	7	2
24 in.	23.5 in.	7	12

4. And calculate the shelving's total linear measurement:

   (168 SF sections x 7 shelves/section x 35.5 in./shelf) +

   (2 SF sections x 7 shelves/section x 29.5 in./shelf) +

   (12 SF sections x 7 shelves/section x 23.5 in./shelf) = 44,135 in. shelf space

5. Finally, use the fill ratio of the sample set (from no. 2c, above) and the total actual shelf (from no. 4, above) to calculate the estimated linear measurement of the collection:

44,135 in. shelf space x .953 fill ratio = 41,266 in. occupied by collections

This measurement may be checked by calculating the average width of an item in the sample set, dividing the estimated inches occupied by the collection by the average number of inches per item, and then comparing the resulting estimate item count with the library's current estimate of its holdings in number of volumes.

For example, if the average width of an item in the collection above were 1.25 inches, then the approximate number of items should be:

41,266 in. collection size/(1.25 in./item) = 33,012 items

Another Method of Estimating Collection Size Based on Stack Inspection

An alternate method of estimating the measurement of a collection has been detailed by P. G. Peacock (1983, 152–55):

1. Inspect each shelf.

2. Estimate how full it is to the nearest 25 percent (e.g., .25, .50, .75, or 1.0 full).

3. Enter the amount on a handheld calculator and cumulatively sum the fractional shelf amounts at the end of a range or the end of a classification, as preferred.

4. Multiply the shelf-equivalents by the linear measurements of a shelf to convert the shelf-equivalent measurement to a linear measurement.

Although this "quick and dirty" method may be tempting, it's not clear whether it yields a time savings, and the rough estimate it yields may be too rough to be truly useful. Its claimed advantage is speed: Peacock reports that one person can collect data on 16,000 shelves in two days. Peacock also argues that this method results in at most a discrepancy of up to 45 out of 8,117 full equivalent shelves (Peacock 1983, 153), or .5 percent. Although this seems like a very small error, consider that in a collection of 16,000 three-foot shelves, the linear extent of the error would be 88 shelves, or 12.5 seven-shelf SF sections. This method also assumes that all shelves are a standard length, although most libraries have some shelves of nonstandard length to accommodate columns and other architectural features. The claimed time saving may not be much of an advantage, either. Kurkul (1983, 229) reports that actual measurement of 1,200 shelves with yardsticks took two people two hours, or about 600 shelves/hour, versus Peacock's 1,000 shelves/hour (assuming his reported "two days" equaled 16 hours total).

Other methods of estimating material on shelves rely on measuring empty space on a shelf, rather than collection material. The accuracy of measurements using these methods may also be compromised by unnoticed variations in shelf length.

Estimates from Shelflist or Online Catalog

Online catalogs and paper shelflists may also provide information on the existing collection's size. Before using either, you will need to determine how accurate or complete each is and whether information on the size of constituent segments of the collection can be easily obtained. Matt Roberts (1966, 104–5) argues persuasively that,

> One of the most serious mistakes that can be made in planning a move, especially if locations must be predetermined, is to accept the established figure as to the number of books in the collection. . . . [S]uch figures are usually based on an inaccurate estimate, and become more inaccurate as the years go by. . . . [T]he only method for determining the average number of volumes per linear foot is by a random sample. . . . To do this we must determine the total number of shelves in the book stack; therefore an accurate count of shelves is necessary. . . . [I]t is my considered opinion that comprehensive measuring involves but little more work and results in far greater accuracy than any of the sampling techniques.

For online catalogs, determine whether all holdings are included, or certain types or ages of material are accounted for elsewhere (e.g., documents, archives, AV materials, specialized collections such as tests or kits). Are missing and lost items included? Can a report be easily generated that provides the number of items (as opposed to bibliographic records) in each segment of the collection?

If working from a paper shelflist, what portion of the collection does it represent? Is there overlap with the online catalog? Are the records segmented into the collection divisions required, or are they arranged in broader groupings?

If the answers are satisfactory, the next step is to convert the shelflist's bibliographic data into an estimated volume count by measuring the shelflist cards, as follows:

1. Estimate the number of bibliographic records (i.e., the number of shelflist cards) by counting the number of cards in one inch and multiplying by the total number of inches of records.

2. Sample the records to estimate the average number of physical items per bibliographic record. For comparison, the rule of thumb is "one inch of shelf list cards for 100 volumes" (McDonald 1994, 15). See

Fraley and Anderson (1990, 45–47) for more detailed instructions on measuring the shelflist to estimate collection size.

3. Multiply the total number of records by the average number of physical items per bibliographic record.

4. Estimate the total linear measurement of the collection by multiplying the item count by the average width of an item (use Appendix A of this book, or construct a local average), thus:

linear measurement of the collection = number of items x linear measurement/item

Examples of collections where this simplified approach might be appropriate include adult fiction or a specialized subject collection comprised entirely of one type of material. For relatively small collections, measuring the whole collection may involve less work than constructing and measuring a sample set.

Stack Maintenance Measurements

Stack maintenance measurements of linear collection size can be very useful, but only if the measurements are current, complete, and done for the entire collection at close to the same point in time. If such records exist in sufficient detail for the collection in question, then it is a relatively straightforward matter to add information on material in circulation, material considered missing, and material added to the collection since the measurement was done. There are, however, some potential problems in using stack maintenance measurements.

In a large collection, stack maintenance measurements of a collection may be made on a rolling basis, so that the entire collection is measured perhaps once or twice a year. The progressive nature of most stack maintenance measurements makes it harder to develop an accurate measure of the collections on move day, because data for items in circulation, missing, and so on must be found for (at least approximately) the same day the collections were measured, and an estimate of material added to that part of the collection must be made since the time it was measured. This means making a series of counts, which is a complicated and time-consuming task. Accurately hitting this moving target requires so much detail that the planner is at some point likely to become frustrated and yield to the temptation to oversimplify. Because oversimplification can lead to inaccuracies and unpleasant surprises when moved books are actually being put on their new shelves, this approach is not recommended.

Measurements Taken for Move Planning

Exact measurements take much more time to construct, but may be necessary for moves involving large, non-homogenous collections, for collections where the shelflist and/or online catalog records are incomplete or unreliable, the space into which the collection is being moved is relatively modest, the collection is being broken into numerous smaller segments, or significant change is planned in the ordering of the collection (for example, if integration of previously separate collections is planned).

If there is any question about whether the entire collection should be measured, try estimating the size of one part of the collection and compare the results to an actual measurement. Generally, the results will tell you whether the estimate is close enough.

If you have determined that the collection should be measured, two questions arise: How precise must the measurements be, and what is the best way to organize and carry out the project?

Precision

Collection measurements must be precise enough to prevent significant cumulative error, but easy enough that they can be completed with the available labor and time. So how exactly do we determine what's precise enough? This will vary with the size of the collection.

For example, consider a collection of 100 single-faced equivalent sections of shelving, each with seven shelves: a total of 700 shelves. Assume the shelf contents are measured to the nearest 1 inch, rounding up for measurements of greater than ½ inch and rounding down for measurements of ½ inch or less. To assess the maximum possible impact of cumulative rounding error, assume a rounding error of ½ inch per shelf. The cumulative rounding error would be:

100 SF sections x (7 shelves/SF) x (½-in. rounding error/shelf) = 350 in.

Is this acceptable? If the collection actually measures 23,607 inches, the percentage error is:

350-in. cumulative rounding error/23,607 inches actual measurement = 1.48%

Given an actual shelf-width of 35.5 linear inches and a hypothetical fill ratio of .75, the actual collection would require:

23,607 in./((35.5 in./shelf) x (7 shelves/SF) x .75 fill ratio) = 127 SF sections

The cumulative rounding error is the equivalent of:

350-in. cumulative rounding error/(35.5 in./shelf x .75 fill ratio) = 13.15 shelves or 1.88 SF sections

Over a total of 127 SF sections of shelving, this might be acceptable. It could be absorbed by accepting a higher fill ratio throughout (though this would require considerable back shifting), or just near the end (requires less back shifting, but means the higher fill ratio sections will fill sooner than the rest of the collections, thus pushing the problem into someone else's lap at a future time).

For larger collections, even small percentages become large actual amounts. For instance, given the same assumptions and a collection housed in 5,000 SF sections, a ½-inch rounding error per shelf results in a cumulative error of 93.9 SF sections:

5,000 SF sections x (7 shelves/SF) x (½ in. rounding error/shelf) = 17,500 in. possible cumulative rounding error

17,500 linear in. cumulative rounding error/(35.5 in./shelf x.75 fill ratio) = 657.3 shelves

657.3 shelves /(7 shelves/SF section) = 93.9 SF sections

This is a large enough error in terms of the absolute number of sections to lead to problems in purchasing or arranging new shelving and in calculating how the collection will be arranged relative to specific shelving locations. If the error were discovered only while placing collections on the shelf during the move (when overly optimistic assumptions and oversights made in the planning phase do get discovered), this would require a significant change in the planned layout.

In this instance, requiring measurement to the nearest ½ inch would reduce the possible cumulative error to 46.9 SF sections

5,000 SF sections x 7 shelves/SF x ¼-in. maximum rounding error/shelf = 8,750 in. maximum cumulative rounding error

8,750 in. max. cum. rounding error/(35.5 in./shelf x .75 fill ratio) = 328.6 shelves

328.6 shelves/(7 shelves/SF) = 46.9 SF sections

and requiring measurement to the nearest ¼ inch would further reduce the possible cumulative error to 23.5 sections:

5,000 sections x 7 shelves/SF x ⅛ in. maximum rounding error/shelf = 4,375 in. maximum cumulative rounding error

4,365 max. cum. rounding error/(35.5 inches/shelf x .75 fill ratio) = 164.3 shelves

164.3 shelves/(7 shelves/SF) = 23.5 SF sections

Although absolute accuracy is a lofty goal, it is also important to recognize that in practice, there are limits to the degree of precision that can be expected from people carrying out a collection measurement project. Despite good intentions at the outset, a project team charged with measuring to the nearest $\frac{1}{8}$ inch is effectively being asked to measure to the nearest $\frac{1}{16}$ inch and to round up or down as appropriate. As a practical matter, $\frac{1}{16}$ inch markings on most tape measures are difficult to distinguish with a degree of speed, and the rounding of book spine edges increases this difficulty. Measuring to the nearest $\frac{1}{2}$ inch balances an acceptable level of precision with reasonable ease in measuring. In addition, time pressure, boredom, and physical fatigue all reduce the accuracy of measurements.

It is therefore desirable, particularly in larger collections, where the effect of cumulative rounding errors may be substantial in absolute terms, to allow a modest amount of shelf space in the new collection layout to compensate for errors in the measurement, or to budget time and money to adjust the collection layout after the move is formally completed.

ORGANIZING AND CARRYING OUT A COLLECTION MEASUREMENT PROJECT

Measuring the collection requires simple tools: a plan of the collection that accurately shows the number and location of book stacks (including the sections in each range), an accurate tape measure, a pen or pencil, and a recording device, such as the form shown in Figure 1.1.

The process itself is also straightforward:

1. Record the collection segment and location being measured. The Stack block, Row, and Section columns in Figure 1.1 are location identifiers, keyed to a map of the stacks to describe the location of materials being measured.

2. Record the date the collection is being measured.

3. Record the individual(s) measuring the collection (helpful in uncovering systematic errors due to individual technique or misunderstood directions, in case handwriting proves illegible, and if notes made on the measurement collection form need later clarification).

4. Adjust the material on the shelf so that it is uniformly compressed.

5. Measure the material on the shelf.

6. Record the measurement.

Figure 1.1
Collection Measurement Form

First call number:	In circulation:
Last call number:	In preshelving:
Date measured:	At bindery:
Team members:	Missing:
	Total:

Stack block	Row	Section	Shelf	Length (to nearest 1/2")	Loose volumes (Inches)	Problems? (s) shelving (b) binding
			1			
			2			
			3			
			4			
			5			
			6			
			7			
			1			
			2			
			3			
			4			
			5			
			6			
			7			
			1			
			2			
			3			
			4			
			5			
			6			
			7			

Step 4 is important because a collection that is in daily use will likely have small gaps and loose pockets where individual volumes have been removed. Because the objective is to measure the book material, not the gaps, you want to have the material on the shelf compressed uniformly. Achieving uniformity can be a challenge. Demonstrating the desired technique to the whole group of measurers at one time should help achieve consistency. A practical verbal description might be to compress the volumes to the left side of the shelf, using enough pressure that no obvious gaps remain between adjacent volumes but not so much pressure that the volumes are obviously compressed (e.g., "enough but not too much").

In Step 5, the objective is to measure the actual width of the volumes as if they were shelved next to each other in a manner consistent with good preservation practice, so that a volume can be easily removed by pushing in the spines of left- and right-adjacent volumes, then grasping the desired volume with fingers on either side of its spine, rather than the spine-damaging method of hooking a finger into the volume's hinge.

Steps 4 and 5 may pose a problem if the shelving is at more than 100 percent capacity, with volumes jammed into the shelves, lying horizontally on top of the vertically shelved material, or on the floor in the aisles. In this case, remove material until the desired degree of compression is achieved, and then record the width of the loose volumes that should be on that shelf.

Team Composition

Although one person can do collection measurement, teams of two generally work better for several reasons:

1. There are two distinct tasks, measuring and recording, each of which requires different tools. It is more efficient for one person to work with each set of tools. When one person performs both tasks, motion (and time) is wasted picking up and putting down the tools.

2. Two individuals may trade tasks, reducing boredom and the potential errors that come with it.

3. Two individuals may consult about the best approach to resolving problems that arise. This advantage can be maximized if the team is comprised of a more knowledgeable person, perhaps a member of the permanent library staff, and a less knowledgeable person, perhaps a student employee.

Estimating the Amount of Time Required

It is important to estimate the time required for the collection measurement project, so that the move planner and library management know what to expect, an accurate estimate can be made of any additional direct labor costs, and staff who may be asked to participate and their supervisors have a realistic expectation of the time commitment required. At one college, cited previously, measuring 1,200 shelves took two people two hours (Kurkul 1983, 229). At another, estimating the occupancy of 16,000 shelves took one person two days (Peacock 1983, 152).

A practical way of estimating the time required is to do a pilot or test run of one to two hours, using individuals with the same skill level as those who will be performing the actual measurement. The larger the pilot project, the more reliable the estimate will be, particularly if several teams of individuals with different degrees of skills can be assembled to provide a truly average estimate of the rate at which work may progress. It's important that the move planner not be the sole tester. Because the move planner will be more familiar with the measuring methods and more motivated, he or she will probably measure at a more rapid rate than others recruited for the project, yielding an unrealistically low estimate of the time required.

It's useful to estimate the range of time it may take to complete the measuring project, based on faster and slower test runs, and this can be readily done via a spreadsheet, as shown in Figure 1.2 (p. 16). Constructing this spreadsheet before the measuring project begins also gives you benchmarks to monitor the progress of the project: if a majority of the measurement teams are operating slower or faster than initially estimated, the spreadsheet will let you know how this will affect the overall completion time, without having to resort to time-consuming recalculations.

Determining Team Assignments

Team assignments may be developed by separating the collection into blocks of equal numbers of sections of shelving. This won't result in a completely even division of labor, because some areas of the collection will be more crowded or in greater states of disorder; however, it does provide an objective and understandable approach. Figure 1.3A and B (pp. 17–18) shows a spreadsheet used for this purpose.

Team Training and Instructions

Before the measuring teams begin work, hold a briefing session, which all team members are required to attend. Explain both *what* the measurers are expected to do and *why*, so that if questions arise and team members improvise without asking the move planner for advice, there will be a greater likelihood that their decisions will be made within the appropriate context.

Provide each team member with a brief, clearly written set of key instructions (the reverse side of the tally sheet is good), so that as the measuring progresses and questions arise, everyone is working from a common set of directions.

15

Figure 1.2
Range of Time Estimates for Hypothetical Collection Measurement Project

Classification	Number of SF at 5 shelves per section	Number of SF at 6 shelves per section	Number of SF at 7 shelves per section	Total number of shelves	Estimated time in minutes at 30 seconds per shelf	Estimated time in minutes at 45 seconds per shelf	Estimated time in minutes at 60 seconds per shelf
A	1	20	5	160	80.0	120.0	160.0
B	0	8	15	153	76.5	114.8	153.0
C	0	2	6	54	27.0	40.5	54.0
D	0	1	7	55	27.5	41.3	55.0
E				0	0.0	0.0	0.0
F				0	0.0	0.0	0.0
G	0	0	2	14	7.0	10.5	14.0
H	2	10	30	280	140.0	210.0	280.0
J				0	0.0	0.0	0.0
K				0	0.0	0.0	0.0
L	0	2	4	40	20.0	30.0	40.0
M	5	8	3	94	47.0	70.5	94.0
N	4	4	6	86	43.0	64.5	86.0
P	0	2	40	292	146.0	219.0	292.0
Q	2	16	29	309	154.5	231.8	309.0
R	4	19	24	302	151.0	226.5	302.0
S	3	4	15	144	72.0	108.0	144.0
T	5	15	23	276	138.0	207.0	276.0
V	0	1	2	20	10.0	15.0	20.0
Z	0	3	8	74	37.0	55.5	74.0
Total time (in minutes)					1,176.5	1,764.8	2,353.0
Total time (in hours)					19.6	29.4	39.2

16

Figure 1.3A
Collection Measurement Project: Collection Segmentation and Team Assignments

Classification	Total number of shelves	Estimated time in minutes at 45 seconds per shelf	Cumulative shelves assigned	Team assignments (using 7 teams)	
A	160	120.0	313.0	Team 1	
B	153	114.8	336.0	Team 1	Team 1: Shelves 1-20	Team 2: Shelves 21 - 54
C	54	40.5	89.0	Team 2	
D	55	41.3	89.0	Team 2	
E	0	0.0	89.0	Team 2	
F	0	0.0	89.0	Team 2	
G	14	10.5	103.0	Team 2	
H	280	210.0	336.0	Team 2: Shelves 1-233	Team 3: Shelves 234-280
J	0	0.0	47.0	Team 3	
K	0	0.0	47.0	Team 3	
L	40	30.0	87.0	Team 3	
M	94	70.5	181.0	Team 3	
N	86	64.5	267.0	Team 3	
P	292	219.0	336.0	Team 3: Shelves 1-69	Team 4: Shelves 70-292
Q	309	231.8	336.0	Team 4: Shelves 1-113	Team 5: Shelves 114-309
R	302	226.5	336.0	Team 5: Shelves 1-140	Team 6: Shelves 141-302
S	144	108.0	306.0	Team 6	
T	276	207.0	336.0	Team 6: Shelves 1-30	Team 7: Shelves 31-276
V	20	15.0	266.0	Team 7	
Z	74	55.5	340.0	Team 7	
Total shelves	2,353	1,764.8 Total minutes			
		29.4 Total hours			

17

Figure 1.3B
Minutes per Team

Minutes per Team

Number of teams	Minutes per team	Hours per team	Shelves per team
5	363.0	5.9	470.6
6	294.1	4.9	392.2
7	252.1	4.2	336.1
8	220.6	3.7	294.1
9	196.1	3.3	261.4
10	176.5	2.9	235.3

As the measuring progresses, check periodically with each measuring team to monitor progress, to see whether problems or questions have arisen, and to determine whether the teams have discovered improvements on the technique described in the training session.

Asking about improvements in techniques can serve two purposes. Some teams may develop real improvements, while other teams may make changes that have unintended (and undesired) consequences. Asking about improvements lets the move planner both identify true improvements and share them with other teams, improving the overall efficiency of the project, and identify well-intentioned but counterproductive practices, providing the opportunity to educate others involved in the project.

Finally, consider matters of morale and motivation. Those participating in the measuring project should be exempt from the usual dress standards, because there will be significant dust and dirt in all but the best-cleaned collections. Consider providing T-shirts with the library's logo or with a new logo or humorous slogan ("Library Collection Measurement Swat Team"; "We Came, We Saw, We Measured"), either for the duration of the project or as a reward for successful completion of the project. Food can also be a good motivator, provided either in a break area or at the conclusion of the project. Finally, don't forget genuine praise and appreciation.

Be careful not to base any rewards solely on the time required to complete the assigned work. First, you want to encourage accurate work, and fast work is not necessarily accurate. Second, some parts of the collection will be more difficult to measure, whether because the stack aisles are narrower, or because more loose items must be separately measured.

Segmenting the Collection

Areas of the collection where the average width of material varies will have to be measured in more detail. Examples include most nonfiction collections, in which the average physical dimensions of books varies somewhat with subject material; audio and video collections, which include multiple formats; and reference collections, which include reference monographs, abstracts and indexes, and nonprint formats.

Physical formats that must be separately measured include

1. monographs, segmented by regular and oversized (however defined by the library);

2. bound periodicals (with any local height distinctions);

3. current periodicals;

4. reference collections, broken down at least into

   a. monographs and
   b. abstracts and indexes;

5. government documents;

6. microfiche, distinguishing between those filed

   a. with envelopes and
   b. without envelopes;

7. microfilms;

8. audio and video recordings, segmented by format (e.g., compact discs, vinyl records (33 rpm, 45 rpm, 78 rpm), DVDs, videocassettes, 16 mm films, etc.);

9. CD-ROMs;

10. archival materials, with separate measurements for each different format, e.g.

    a. Hollinger boxes,
    b. bound volumes, and
    c. realia;

11. special collection materials, distinguishing each special collection;

12. juvenile literature;

13. children's picture books;

14. children's pop-up books; and

15. children's toys and games;

This list is not intended to be exhaustive, but suggests the wide variety of types of material found in a typical library, and is meant to encourage the move planner to look critically at the materials to be moved.

PLANNING COLLECTION SPACE

Material Not on the Shelf

Once the collection has been measured, this information must be collated, and an allowance must be made for items not on the shelf at the time of measurement. These include items that are in circulation or in preshelving areas, on display, at the bindery or in repair, missing, or on reserve.

Another approach is to assume that some material will always be in circulation, at the bindery, and so on, and to measure at a point when the minimum amount of material is in circulation. A potential problem with this approach is that the amount of material in circulation from specific areas of the collection at the selected time may not be representative or average, thus requiring later shifting. Of course, the disadvantage of assuming that shelf space for all material in circulation needs to be provided is that, except in very unusual circumstances, there is always some portion of the collection in use, thus leading to over provision of shelf space. Unless the expense involved is great, though, it's probably better to err on the side of caution.

This information must be collected for each part of the collection that was measured separately; recording it on the collection measurement sheet is a useful check. Measure items that are on hand in the library; for instance, those in preshelving areas, on reserve, or on display. Count items that are not on hand; for instance, in circulation or at the bindery. Decide whether to plan space for missing items.

With a measurement of material on the shelf and a count of material not on the shelf in hand, an accurate estimate of the collection's linear measurements can be calculated, as in the spreadsheet shown in Figure 1.4. Measurements for all items on hand are summed together. The counts of all items not on hand are also summed together and converted to inches of material by multiplying the number of items by an average figure for inches per item. The total inches of items on the shelf and the estimated total inches of material in circulation, at the bindery, etc., are then added together to provide the estimated total inches of material.

The difference between the total linear inches of material on the shelf (column A) and the estimated total inches of material (column K) illustrates the importance of accounting for items that are not on the shelf.

SIMPLIFIED MEASURING METHODS

Measuring, recording, and adding up the measurements of thousands of individual shelves is time consuming and subject to errors in rounding, recording, and adding. The three methods discussed below offer alternative approaches.

University of Oregon Method

This method is a variation on that described by Shirien Chappell (2006) as part of her excellent Web site, Moving Library Collections, Planning Shifts of

Figure 1.4
Summation of Collection Measurements

Class	Material on hand (inches)					Items not on hand				Average inches/item	Estimated inches (i x j)	Total inches (estimated) (e+k)
	On shelf	In preshelving	On reserve	On display	Total (a+b+c+d)	In circulation	At bindery	Missing	Total (f+g+h)			
	(a)	(b)	(c)	(d)	(e)	(f)	(g)	(h)	(i)	(j)	(k)	(l)
A	200.0	2.0	2.0	0.0	204.0	0	5	1	6	0.98	5.9	209.9
B	400.0	30.0	45.0	0.0	475.0	6	2	10	18	0.92	16.6	491.6
C	125.0	23.0	44.0	0.0	192.0	10	0	0	10	1.02	10.2	202.2
D	450.0	60.0	15.0	0.0	525.0	8	0	1	9	1.02	9.2	534.2
E	600.0	75.0	50.0	30.0	755.0	16	0	2	18	1.11	20.0	775.0
F	450.0	40.0	25.0	13.0	528.0	12	0	0	12	1.07	12.8	540.8
G	125.0	0.0	0.0	0.0	125.0	0	0	0	0	1.13	0.0	125.0
H	700.0	65.0	50.0	0.0	815.0	24	2	4	30	1.09	32.7	847.7
Total	3,050.0	295.0	231.0	43.0	3,619.0	76	9	18	103		107.3	3,726.3

Library Collections. It uses a two-person team working with a string and a tally sheet to measure the number of shelf-widths of material in an area of the collection. (Chappell describes measuring empty shelf space; I recommend measuring collections on the shelf, to avoid measuring errors resulting from random sections of shelving that are nonstandard widths.)

Make the measuring string:

1. Determine the exact inside measurement of your shelves (e.g., 35½ inches). This is measurement X.

2. Cut a length of string at least 6 inches longer than that.

3. On one end, tie a metal nut or washer. Mark the knot between the metal nut and the string. This is knot A.

4. From A, measure X inches, and make a second knot. This is knot B.

5. Take your string to a shelf and check that the distance between A and B is *exactly* the inside width of a shelf. The accuracy of your measurements depends on this, so be careful!

Using the measuring string:

1. This procedure is done by two people. One person measures with the string, and the second person tallies the measurements. Set up a tally sheet with columns for the range number, starting call number, ending call number, and hatch marks.

2. Position knot A carefully at the left side of the first item on the shelf and hold it in place.

3. Extend the string to the right, along all the material on the shelf.

4. At the right side of the last item on the right-hand side of the shelf, pinch the string securely between thumb and forefinger. The pinched point on the string is point C.

5. *Still pinching the string securely and being very careful not to let the string move,* proceed to the next shelf and position point C (i.e., your pinching thumb and forefinger) on the left side of the material.

6. Hold the string (point C) in place on the left side of the material and extend the string to the right.

7. When you reach the knot on the right side of the string (knot B), the measurer announces "Hatch" or "Mark" or "One," and the recorder makes a hatch mark on the tally sheet.

8. Move knot A to the exact position of knot B, and continue in the same manner.

At the end of the process, you will have a tally of the number of shelf-widths of material in the range measured. To determine the linear measurement of the material, multiply the number of hatch marks by the distance from knot A to knot

B. *Note:* The string will stretch, so check the distance from knot A to knot B at least once a day, and reposition knot B when necessary.

"Magic String" Method

Snow (2004, 60–61) suggests a similar method using a fixed length of string, say 20 feet. (Snow recommends using a 50-foot length of string, but also notes that this length makes tangles inevitable; hence my recommendation to work with a shorter length.) Using the same approach described above, the measurer progresses through the stacks, moving from left to right, and from top to bottom, tallying the number of lengths of string comprising the collections. Take care to measure the string accurately and to accurately tally the string-lengths that have been counted.

One-Person, Cloth Tape Method

Don Kelsey (2005) describes a one-person version of this approach using a ten-foot cloth tape with knots at the "0" and 10-foot marks and a handheld counter, of the sort used to tally attendance. The counter may be held in the palm of one hand and clicked once when the measurer reaches the end of the ten-foot cloth tape. This method depends critically on the accuracy of the measurer, but with practice has been used to measure a collection of 500,000 volumes in fewer than three days. Kelsey has conducted three trials comparing measurements taken in this way with those taken with a metal tape measure and found a discrepancy of +/- 0.5 percent or less.

The present author suggests using a nonwoven tape measure from a sewing supply store. It is designed to resist stretching and is premarked with measurements. Also, there is no ambiguity about where "0" is located.

With accurate assessment of the current collections' linear measurements in hand, the next step is to consider factors that affect shelving capacity.

DIMENSIONAL CHARACTERISTICS OF LIBRARY MATERIAL AND SHELVING AFFECTING SHELVING CAPACITY

Bound volumes of print material, audio and video recordings, and some storage media for electronic information all have specific physical characteristics that affect the vertical and horizontal space needed to house them in shelving.

To estimate the number of sections of shelving needed to house a collection requires knowing the linear measurement of the collection, the actual internal measurement of each type of shelving to be used, how full the shelves should be immediately after the move and at the end of the planning horizon, and how many shelves will be used within each section of shelving. For instance, shelving may be set up with seven shelves per section for standard monographs, six shelves per section for bound periodicals and oversized material, and at five or fewer shelves/section for taller material.

Dimensional Characteristics of Library Materials

In addition to the linear measurement of a collection, the average height and depth of items in the collection will affect the selection, setup, and capacity of the shelving. Height, as well as whether a library elects to shelve some materials in a separate "oversized" or "folio" area (and the cutoff point for "oversized" designation), will determine the number of shelves used per section of shelving.

The average depth of the materials will likely drive shelf depth, which in combination with the aisle width and column placement will determine the number of sections of shelving that can fit into a given amount of floor space.

Width/Item

Appendix A lists average width/item measurements for a variety of print, audio, video, and electronic media, measured by the author at Northeastern University in 1996, and adult, YA, juvenile, large print, AV, and other public library collections measured at the Flint Memorial Library (North Reading, MA) in 2008. Other tables appear in Brawner and Beck (1996, 123), "Conversion Factors" (1981, 14), Ellsworth (1973, 110–11, 118), Klasing (1991, 98), Kurth and Grim (1966, 198), Leighton and Weber (1999, 730), Roberts (1984, 306–14), Spyers-Duran (1965, 3), and Wittenborg and Camp 1977, 14). The move planner may use these tables to convert an estimated volume count into an estimate of linear footage; however, it is important to consider potential pitfalls:

1. The composition of the collection upon which the measurement was based may be substantively different than yours. For example, the proportion of thick volumes may be larger in a research-oriented library than in a library primarily serving recreational needs, and the average width of juvenile fiction and nonfiction will likely be less than that of adult fiction and nonfiction.

2. Collection arrangement practices may affect the reported average volume width. For example, in a university library that interfiles bound periodical runs on a title by title basis with monographs, the generally wider measurements of these bound periodical volumes might be averaged with the generally narrower width of monographs and one figure reported for the classification as a whole.

3. Storage containers for microform (stored in paper sleeves or not?), audiovisual (stored in plastic cases? jewel boxes? etc.), and electronic media will affect the average width per item, as will the percentage of multi-item sets (e.g., in a music collection, the number of boxed sets of operas, song-cycles, etc.) versus single disc recordings.

Height/Item

The library probably already has an established shelf spacing practice in the collection to be moved. It may already be standard practice to use seven shelves/section in the general collection area, six shelves/section in areas of bound periodicals and in most oversized areas, with more generous spacing in a few places as needed. If the arrangement of the collections after the move will be essentially the same as before, it may be satisfactory (and expedient) to simply accept prior practice.

Leighton and Weber (1999, 729) state that spacing shelves 12 inches apart on center "is adequate for books that are 11 inches tall or less, which . . . includes 90 percent of the books in a typical collection . . . . It is suggested that most of the remaining 10 percent will be concentrated in a comparatively few subjects, that 70 percent of this 10 percent will be between 11 and 13 inches, and that six shelves 14 inches on centers will provide for them."

If the arrangement of the collection will change substantially, it is probably worth taking time to reassess current practice. Examples include a bound periodical collection that is to be integrated title-by-title with monographs, and decisions to integrate a larger percentage of oversized materials with "regular" height materials or to store AV materials on shelves instead of in cabinets.

Item Depth

Though the average depth of collection materials will not affect the linear footage of the collection that needs to be shelved, it will affect the depth of the shelving needed (and the amount of floor space needed for the shelving). Shelves that are 14 inches deep may be needed to accommodate LP phonograph discs, whereas 8-inch-deep shelves may be entirely adequate for a collection of compact discs. Nominal 8-inch and 9-inch shelves are frequently used for general print collections, with 10-inch- and 12-inch-deep shelves frequently used for reference collections. The operative concern is how much of the physical item must be supported by the shelf, and whether is it acceptable for a portion of the physical item to extend beyond the actual shelf.

Making Your Own Tables

When to Make Your Own Tables

Studies have concluded that calculations of a single average width per library volume "are not readily transferable from one library to another" (Daehn 1982a, 37) and that although figures for monographs may be transferable if they are calculated for a closely defined subject area, the same is not true for bound periodical volumes (Roberts 1984, 310–11). This makes sense, considering that there is variation in the width of volumes in difference subject areas and in the relative size of different subject collections in each library.

If you are considering using an existing table, first try to find one that mirrors the composition of your collection. Then, spot-check its accuracy in areas where there are most likely to be divergences. If a table were to give figures for "biomedical sciences" for instance, and your collection had substantial separate collections for nursing, biology, medicine, pharmacy, etc. (or conversely, only one for the broader category of science), sample these collection areas to see whether the figures reported in the table mirror those in your collection. If your figures and the tables' figures agree, you can then use the table with greater confidence; if not, you will have a rationale for undertaking the additional work of constructing your own tables.

How to Construct Your Own Tables

If you have determined that it's desirable to construct your own tables of average width/item or average height/item, first decide how finely to segment the subject areas to be measured. Consider the following:

1. Divisions in the proposed collection layout plan. Will all fiction be shelved in one uninterrupted sequence and all nonfiction in a second uninterrupted sequence? Will the collection be segmented by broad LC classification? Will broad groupings of the collection be shelved on separate floors? Will bound periodical volumes be shelved separate from monographs? Integrated in subject blocks? On a title-by-title basis?

2. Are there known concentrations of differently sized materials within the collection? Does the collection include a particularly strong collection of sets? Is it particularly strong in specific subject areas? In illustrated volumes or "coffee-table books"?

3. Are there particular areas of the collection where spot checking shows that figures in published tables don't mirror the characteristics of the collection?

4. Does something not "feel right" about the published tables with respect to your collection?

The objective is to divide the collection into fine enough segments that the information you collect will help create an accurate collection layout plan without requiring the investment of unnecessary time and effort, and this requires an element of professional judgment.

Dimensional Characteristics of Library Shelving

The dimensions of library shelving vary from type to type, and within type, from manufacturer to manufacturer; manufacturers may also occasionally change the dimensions of a specific model of shelving (e.g., "legal" depth). It is therefore important to determine the actual physical characteristics of the type(s) of shelving that will receive collection materials being moved. Three critical dimensions are the actual available internal width of the shelf, the clear vertical space between adjacent shelves, and shelf depth. Figure 1.5 illustrates these and other dimensions of interest.

Figure 1.5
Dimensional Characteristics of Library Shelving

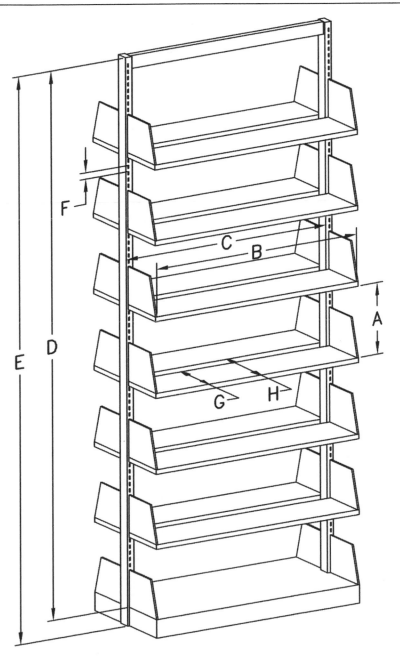

Measurement A is the vertical space available between shelves.

Measurement B is the horizontal clear space.

Measurement C is the shelf's nominal width, and is the repeat dimension of a section of shelving. Note that measurement B is typically about .5 inch *less* than measurement C.

Measurement D, from the top surface of the shelving unit's base (fixed shelf) to the top of the shelving upright, is the total amount of space available for division into vertical shelving space and is less than measurement E, the total height of the shelving unit.

Note also that measurement F, the spacing between slots in the uprights (into which shelves are inserted), governs the flexibility with which shelves can be spaced, and is usually 1 inch.

Measurement G is the actual shelf depth, that is, the actual dimension of the shelf material, whereas measurement H is the nominal shelf depth, measured from the center point of the upright to the outer edge of the shelf.

Measurement H is larger than G, by perhaps 1 inch; in double-faced cantilever shelving, it includes half the air space between the back edges of horizontally adjacent shelves.

Actual and Nominal Shelf-Widths

In cantilever shelving the upright occupies space, which reduces the effective available width of shelving upon which materials may sit. The nominal width of shelving typically refers to its **repeat** dimension, measured from the center point of one upright to the center point of the adjacent upright, rather than the shelf space on which material may be placed. For instance, for a specific manufacturer's 36-inch nominal width shelving, the effective internal shelf space may be 35.5 inches. Similarly, actual and nominal shelf-width differ in four-post and case-type shelving. For any one shelf, this may not make much difference, but it adds up.

Lest this be doubted, consider that for any 100 single-faced (SF) section of shelving (for simplicity, counts are given in equivalent single-faced sections, rather than mixing SF and double-faced sections), each with seven shelves, the overall difference in capacity will be:

.5-in./shelf x 7 shelves/SF section x 100 SF sections = 350 in.

or the equivalent of 1.41 SF sections of shelving:

350inches/(7 shelves/SF section x 35.5-in. capacity/shelf)

For each 1,000 SF sections of shelving, then, the impact will be 14.1 SF sections, and for an area of 5,000 SF sections of shelving, the difference in capacity will be 70.5 SF sections of shelving.

Slotted shelves fitted with supporting dividers or panels are very useful for thin materials such as compact discs, LP records, pamphlets, and documents; however, the usable width of the shelf is reduced slightly by the cumulative width of the dividers, and a calculation of the actual usable shelf space must be made.

Vertical Clearance Between Shelves

It is common practice for libraries to separate larger than usual volumes into one or more oversized categories and shelf them apart from other volumes in the same classification sequence. However, a library may choose different cutoff points for the oversized designation for different physical types of material or for different subject areas within a library's collection.

Setting the oversized cutoff at different heights in different areas of the collection can allow fuller integration of materials into the main collection sequence in subject areas where a large percentage of the collections may be typically published in a large format. In these areas, shelving may be adjusted to provide greater vertical clearance per shelf, reducing the number of shelves per section from seven to six or five. By limiting the portion of the stacks where this is done, the overall reduction in collection capacity is also limited.

Bound periodical volumes, music scores, photography books, and biology texts come to mind as specific adult collection areas that may well benefit from a higher oversized cutoff, but this will likely vary somewhat from collection to collection. Choice of oversized cutoff will affect the number of shelves accommodated within each section of shelving, which in turn will affect the capacity of each area's shelving.

The range of adjustment in vertical spacing between adjacent shelves is limited by the spacing of the slots in the shelving upright into which shelves are inserted. This spacing is typically 1 inch. If the library is moving into a new building and has the option of establishing a new oversized cutoff point, first determine the vertical spacing possible with your specific shelving, then sample the collection to determine the percentage of materials that would be considered oversized if the shelves were spaced differently.

In calculating the vertical space available for distribution among shelves within a section of shelving, it is important to remember that both the shelving base and each shelf have height. So, for a hypothetical 90-inch-high section of shelving, with a 3-inch base and six movable shelves each .75 inches thick, the vertical space available for allocation would be

90-in. height – 3-in. base – (6 movable shelves x .75-in./movable shelf) = 82.5 in. usable height

Divided among seven shelf spaces, this would theoretically allow

82.5 in. usable height/7 shelf spaces = 11.8 in. height/shelf space

However, because shelf placement is governed by the spacing of the notches in the shelving uprights, it isn't possible to divide the available space evenly. In the example above, the most evenly divided spacing would provide two 11-inch shelf spaces plus five 12-inch shelf spaces. See also Kurth and Grim (1966, 107 and 109), Figure 17, "Spacing Between Shelves on 90 Inch Upright" and Table 16, "Distance Between Shelves with Differing Number of Shelves per Section and Height of Shelves from Floor."

Another important factor to consider is the height of the top shelf in relation to an average person's reach. Comfortable high reach height for the 50th percentile of males in the United States is 80.0 inches; for the 50th percentile of females it is 74.9 inches. For the 97.5th percentile of males, the comfortable high reach is 86.1 inches, and for females it is 80.6 inches. For the 2.5th percentile, the corresponding figures are 74.1 inches for adult males and 69.6 inches for adult females (Ramsey and Sleeper 1994, 4). Will users require step stools to reach the top shelf, and is that acceptable in the context of the library's access philosophy?

Also, library shelving can be provided with or without a canopy. For a nominal 90-inch-high section of shelving without a canopy, it would be theoretically possible to locate the top shelf at, say, 86 inches from the floor. This could increase either the number of shelves accommodated within the section of shelving or the height per shelf, but reaching the top shelf would require most people to use a step stool.

Figure 1.6 (pp. 32–33) presents in tabular form the cumulative height required for various shelf spacing options, assuming a 3-inch base, ¾-inch-thick shelves, and 1-inch fixed shelf adjustment increments. This table may be used to identify the number of shelves that can be positioned in a section of shelving given a specific vertical spacing, upright height, and top shelf height requirement. For instance, given a requirement for 11.25-inch-clear vertical space on each shelf, and a 90-inch shelving standard, then either seven or eight shelves could be positioned on the upright. If seven shelves were used, the top shelf would be positioned at 75 inches from the floor, and the shelving space would extend to 86.25 inches. If eight shelves were used, the top shelf would be positioned at 87 inches from the floor, and the shelving space would extend to 98.25 inches. If canopies are to be used with the shelving, and they are attached to the top of the shelving unit, then use of the air space above the upright is not possible, and only the seven-shelf option could be considered.

High-Density Shelving

The capacity of compact shelving and extra-tall book shelving may be calculated using the same approach as used for typical cantilever or case-type library shelving. The dimensions are different, but the configuration is similar.

However, calculating the capacity of high-density storage using an automated retrieval system is based on the number of bins and their dimensions. In a Harvard-model high-density storage facility, books to be stored are sorted according to height and stored in trays that closely match that height. The trays are housed on shelves spaced to provide the minimum necessary headroom. Material is bar-coded and retrieved by an automated warehouse-style inventory picker. Calculating the capacity of each bin is fairly straightforward, but has to take into account height as well as length and width. Libraries considering this type of facility should consult Danuta Nitecki and Curtis Kendrick's 2001 book, *Library Off-Site Shelving*.

Working Capacity and Fill Ratio

The amount of material initially placed on each shelf (its initial fill ratio) and the point at which a shelf is considered full (its working capacity) will also affect the capacity at the time of the move and the capacity available for growth. Leighton and Weber suggest a maximum working capacity of 86 percent to allow for ease in shelving operations (1999, 182–83). Adopting this as the point at which shelves are considered full for planning purposes requires adjusting planning figures accordingly:

35.5-in. actual available space x 86% maximum working capacity = 30.5-in. adjusted available space per shelf

For a group of 100 single-faced sections of shelving, each with seven shelves/SF section, the reduction in capacity would therefore be

100 SF sections of shelving x (35.5-in. available/shelf – 30.5-in. maximum working capacity/shelf) x (7 shelves/SF section) = 3,500 in. less linear shelf space

or the equivalent of

3,500-in. linear shelf space/((7 shelves/SF section) x 30.5-in. maximum working capacity/shelf) = 16.4 SF fewer sections shelving

For 1,000 SF sections of shelving, this reduction amounts to 163.9 SF sections, and for 5,000 SF sections of shelving, 819.7 SF sections of shelving.

Not all libraries may be able to afford the additional space required for ease in shelving; however, making these calculations can help one make an informed decision.

Fill Ratio

The choice of initial fill ratio will affect the number of sections of shelving over which the collection is spread at the time of the move and the number of

Figure 1.6
Shelf Spacing Options

Shelf number	6.25" spacing		7.25" spacing		8.25" spacing		9.25" spacing		10.25" spacing	
	Unit height	Cumulative height	Unit height	Cumulative height	Unit height	Cumulative height	Unit height	Cumulative height	Unit height	Cumulative height
13	6.25	93.25								
	0.75	87.00								
12	6.25	86.25								
	0.75	80.00								
11	6.25	79.25	7.25	90.25						
	0.75	73.00	0.75	83.00						
10	6.25	72.25	7.25	82.25	8.25	92.25				
	0.75	66.00	0.75	75.00	0.75	84.00				
9	6.25	65.25	7.25	74.25	8.25	83.25	9.25	92.25		
	0.75	59.00	0.75	67.00	0.75	75.00	0.75	83.00		
8	6.25	58.25	7.25	66.25	8.25	74.25	9.25	82.25	10.25	90.25
	0.75	52.00	0.75	59.00	0.75	66.00	0.75	73.00	0.75	80.00
7	6.25	51.25	7.25	58.25	8.25	65.25	9.25	72.25	10.25	79.25
	0.75	45.00	0.75	51.00	0.75	57.00	0.75	63.00	0.75	69.00
6	6.25	44.25	7.25	50.25	8.25	56.25	9.25	62.25	10.25	68.25
	0.75	38.00	0.75	43.00	0.75	48.00	0.75	53.00	0.75	58.00
5	6.25	37.25	7.25	42.25	8.25	47.25	9.25	52.25	10.25	57.25
	0.75	31.00	0.75	35.00	0.75	39.00	0.75	43.00	0.75	47.00
4	6.25	30.25	7.25	34.25	8.25	38.25	9.25	42.25	10.25	46.25
	0.75	24.00	0.75	27.00	0.75	30.00	0.75	33.00	0.75	36.00
3	6.25	23.25	7.25	26.25	8.25	29.25	9.25	32.25	10.25	35.25
	0.75	17.00	0.75	19.00	0.75	21.00	0.75	23.00	0.75	25.00
2	6.25	16.25	7.25	18.25	8.25	20.25	9.25	22.25	10.25	24.25
	0.75	10.00	0.75	11.00	0.75	12.00	0.75	13.00	0.75	14.00
Base: 1	6.25	9.25	7.25	10.25	8.25	11.25	9.25	12.25	10.25	13.25
	3.00	3.00	3.00	3.00	3.00	3.00	3.00	3.00	3.00	3.00

Figure 1.6 (Cont.)

Shelf number	11.25" spacing Unit height	11.25" spacing Cumulative height	12.25" spacing Unit height	12.25" spacing Cumulative height	13.25" spacing Unit height	13.25" spacing Cumulative height	14.25" spacing Unit height	14.25" spacing Cumulative height	15.25" spacing Unit height	15.25" spacing Cumulative height	16.25" spacing Unit height	16.25" spacing Cumulative height
8	11.25	98.25										
	0.75	87.00										
7	11.25	86.25	12.25	93.25	13.25	100.25						
	0.75	75.00	0.75	81.00	0.75	87.00						
6	11.25	74.25	12.25	80.25	13.25	86.25	14.25	92.25	15.25	98.25		
	0.75	63.00	0.75	68.00	0.75	73.00	0.75	78.00	0.75	83.00		
5	11.25	62.25	12.25	67.25	13.25	72.25	14.25	77.25	15.25	82.25	16.25	87.25
	0.75	51.00	0.75	55.00	0.75	59.00	0.75	63.00	0.75	67.00	0.75	71.00
4	11.25	50.25	12.25	54.25	13.25	58.25	14.25	62.25	15.25	66.25	16.25	70.25
	0.75	39.00	0.75	42.00	0.75	45.00	0.75	48.00	0.75	51.00	0.75	54.00
3	11.25	38.25	12.25	41.25	13.25	44.25	14.25	47.25	15.25	50.25	16.25	53.25
	0.75	27.00	0.75	29.00	0.75	31.00	0.75	33.00	0.75	35.00	0.75	37.00
2	11.25	26.25	12.25	28.25	13.25	30.25	14.25	32.25	15.25	34.25	16.25	36.25
	0.75	15.00	0.75	16.00	0.75	17.00	0.75	18.00	0.75	19.00	0.75	20.00
Base: 1	11.25	14.25	12.25	15.25	13.25	16.25	14.25	17.25	15.25	18.25	16.25	19.25
	3.00	3.00	3.00	3.00	3.00	3.00	3.00	3.00	3.00	3.00	3.00	3.00

33

years of growth space. In addition to space left on each shelf for shelving ease, probably the most important factor in selecting a fill ratio is the amount of growth space to be provided within the collection. This is discussed further in Chapter 2; however, to illustrate the point briefly, assume you wish to provide 5 inches of growth space per shelf, and that you have identified your maximum working capacity as 86 percent: the space available per shelf to hold materials at the time of the move is developed as follows:

1. Calculate the maximum working capacity in inches:

   35.5 in. actual available space per shelf x 86 percent maximum working capacity = 30.5 in. maximum working capacity per shelf

2. Subtract from the maximum working capacity the shelf space to be allocated for collection growth:

   30.5 in. maximum working capacity per shelf – 5 in. per shelf allowance for collection growth = 25.5 in. per shelf available for shelving materials at the time of the move

3. Divide the result by the actual width of the shelf to obtain the fill ratio:

   25.5 in. usable shelf space/35.5 in. actual shelf space = 72% fill ratio

Calculating Available Shelving Space in Cabinets and Display Shelving

The approach detailed for calculating the extent of linear space available on traditional shelving may also be used for cabinets and display shelving. By treating each drawer as a "shelf" and measuring the linear storage space available within each drawer, comparable figures can be developed. For instance, in a hypothetical five-drawer cabinet 30 inches deep, with 29 inches of actual clear storage depth, designed to accommodate six rows of compact discs, the shelf space per drawer would be

29 in. clear space/row x 6 rows/drawer = 174 in. shelf space/drawer
174 in. shelf space/drawer x 5 drawers/cabinet = 870 in. shelf space/cabinet

If the library is purchasing new cabinets, the manufacturer's promotional literature will probably provide a capacity figure in terms of the number of items that can be accommodated, though you might want to verify its accuracy.

The same approach may be used for display shelving and bins; however, the planner will want to make an adjustment based on how full the display is intended to be. In most cases, the point of display shelving is to allow browsing, and this requires leaving some space empty, perhaps 25–33 percent of the available depth. Thus, if a hypothetical display rack had 100 inches of shelf space, the planner might want to assume only 66–75 inches of it would be filled.

2   PLANNING FOR GROWTH

The wide acceptance of, and indeed preference for, Web-accessible journals and reference material is changing the face of library services, organizations, and facilities, particularly those in larger academic libraries. Off-site, remote, high-density, and compact shelving options are increasingly being used to house print material now available through services such as JSTOR and less-used monographs—even as services such as WorldCat and Google Scholar are beginning to make available the bibliographic records for "the long tail," rare items of intense interest to a few scattered readers, potentially increasing demand for these items, which were formerly known of only by those at the institution that owned them.

In addition, the pressure of rapidly increasing journal prices, in tandem with undiminished user desire for access to journal articles, has led many libraries to focus on resource sharing via interlibrary loan: a shift to providing just-in-time access instead of just-in-case ownership.

At colleges and universities, campus administrators, faced with increased demand for computing, faculty, and student support space and with finite budgets, may see space occupied by library collections as an opportunity waiting to be harvested and be reluctant to provide additional library space. In the public arena, interest has increased in facilities shared by public libraries and either school or college libraries.

In the past, library collections were generally moved because they outgrew their old space. Increasingly, they are being moved because they are available in e-format and the space is needed for another purpose, or because of consolidation. In planning collection space, the librarian must now be much more aware of and take into account opportunities for negative collection growth, for example through the transfer of less-used items to off-site or high-density facilities, where items are most often arranged by size for maximum space efficiency rather than ease of browsing, and retrieved based on highly accurate location records.

One thing has not changed: each time a collection needs to be moved or shifted, time and money are expended, and user access is disrupted. In planning the layout of a collection in its new location, then, it is important to plan an amount of space that will allow collections to remain in place for the longest reasonable period of time.

GROSS LEVEL PLANNING

At the most basic level, planning for growth in the collection requires estimating the net number of volumes that will be added to the collection each year (net annual acquisitions), determining the number of years the new space is to accommodate collection growth (the planning horizon), and multiplying these two factors:

net annual acquisitions (volumes/year) x planning horizon (years) = predicted collection growth (in volumes)

By converting the predicted collection growth (in volumes) into an estimated linear footage and adding it to the linear footage of the current collections, the total linear footage the collection will occupy at the end of the planning horizon is obtained:

Current collection (in linear in. or ft.) +
Predicted collection growth (in linear in. or ft.) =
Total collection space required (in linear in. or ft.)

The years of growth, or planning horizon, selected by the library should take into account the next likely opportunity to add collection space through either new construction or conversion of existing space.

The net annual acquisitions rate will depend on anticipated collection budget, collection development policies, publishing trends, and changes in technology, and must take into account not only items the library purchases, but also those it receives without charge (e.g., government publications and gifts) and deselection and loss rates. Other factors include targeted weeding in specific areas; planned transfer of collections to storage; conversion of print to electronic formats; and branch library growth, consolidation, or elimination (Black and Bahrenfus 1988, 39).

Gross Versus Detailed Planning and Why Detailed Planning Is Needed

For all but the smallest, most homogenous collections, a detailed approach to planning is necessary. Physical growth does not usually occur evenly across a collection. For instance, if a hypothetical collection had ten subject divisions, and

36

1,000 items were added to the collection each year, it is unlikely that 100 items would be added to each subject division, or that each item added would have the same physical characteristics. It is more likely that collection development policies and practices, guided by past use, future need, and budgetary considerations, would result in some subject divisions getting more than 100 volumes and others getting fewer than 100 volumes. It is also likely that if two of the subject divisions were, for example, engineering and poetry, the individual engineering volumes would be thicker and taller, and the individual poetry volumes shorter and thinner. Similarly, targeted weeding, or moving to storage journal runs now available electronically, will result in uneven reductions in the amount of shelf space required.

Identifying Collection Segments

The key consideration in developing a detailed collection growth model is to identify the smallest relevant unit of the collection, based on its proposed physical arrangement. This will be governed by the nature of the collection and how it is arranged.

The segments identified must include both those in the current collection and those that will be added to the collection, because the need for collection space is determined by adding together the linear measurements required by current collections plus those required by future collections. In some instances, there will be segments in which there are no collections currently (for instance, when the library intends to begin collecting in a new subject area or format, or when there may be no future collections, such as when a collection is inactive or the library intends to stop collecting in a specific subject area or material format.

For example, if a public library proposed to shelve all adult fiction alphabetically by author in a single continuous block of shelving on one floor, it might be sufficient to consider the adult fiction as a single segment. If mysteries, science fiction, Westerns, and romances were shelved separately, growth in these areas would have to be considered separately. If a university library proposed to interfile its bound periodicals in several large blocks among related LC classes of monographs, then growth within each block of bound periodicals and monographs would have to be considered separately. Because growth space for individual bound periodical titles occurs at the end of each run, it must be calculated on a title-by-title basis, taking into account which titles are current, ceased, and planned for acquisition.

The same principle applies to microform, audiovisual, and storage media for electronic information. If AV collections are shelved by format, growth must be considered separately for each format—say compact discs, DVDs, videotapes, and so on—with the important caveat that planned discontinuation of dead and dying formats also has to be taken into account. For example, if the library by policy collects new audio recordings only in compact disc format, it may also have collections of LP or 45 rpm records that it intends to retain and preserve until the same recording becomes available in compact disc format. In this case, the annual acquisitions for these formats might be 0 items/year, or perhaps a negative number (if some number of LP or 45 rpm records are replaced annually with CDs and withdrawn from the collection).

In planning for government documents growth, consider the increasing proportion of materials available via the Internet and any changes planned in the types of documents the library accepts.

In planning for academic course reserve collections, consider the extent to which the library has been able to implement electronic reserves and whether the total number of print items on reserve will be relatively static, with the items changing from semester to semester.

In planning for picture book, toy, and game collections for preschool children, consider whether the number of items added to the collection annually will equal, exceed, or be less than the number that are worn out and must be discarded.

In planning for archives growth, consider historical growth trends, collecting initiatives, any upcoming historical milestones that may elicit gifts, and, if a records management program is in place, the likely annual linear footage of files to be received and retained.

For special collections growth, consider the historical pattern of gifts, any gifts that may be pending or possible, the budget available for purchases, and appropriate collections that may become available for purchase.

In planning space for journal collections, consider whether the library wishes to move into storage the backfiles of journals available in electronic format, such as those available through JSTOR. In instances when the electronic version is available after a period of five years (a "moving wall") , and the library has decided to move to storage those issues available electronically, shelf space need only be planned for the most current five years, provided the oldest year is consistently removed and sent to storage each year.

In planning space for monographs, consider whether a large-scale weeding plan is contemplated, either to move lesser-used items to storage or to discard duplicates.

Detailed Planning Method

Once you have identified the smallest relevant collection segment, the next step is to determine net annual growth in number of volumes or items within each segment, convert it to a linear measurement, and add it to the linear measurement of the segment's current collections. The calculation is:

(Current number of items + (Average number of items added per year x number of years)) x average width per item = linear in. of collection space needed

Figure 2.1 shows a spreadsheet that calculates these figures.

Figure 2.1
Calculating the Linear Footage of Current Collections and Growth

Type of material	Current number items	Est'd or actual?	Est'd net annual growth (items)	15 years' growth (items) (15 x c)	Planned total (items) (a + d)	Linear inches per item (from appendix)	Linear inches needed (e x f)	Shelves used per SF section shelving	Maximum working capacity this type material (percent)	Maximum working capacity per SF this type material (inches) (h x i x 35.5)	Number SF sections needed (g/j)	Rounded number SF sections needed
	(a)	(b)	(c)	(d)	(e)	(f)	(g)	(h)	(i)	(j)	(k)	(l)
Reference												
Books	554	est.	15	225	779	1.61	1,254	6	86%	183	6.8	7.0
Abstracts & indexes	1,011	est.	70	1,050	2,061	1.87	3,854	6	86%	183	21.0	22.0
Monographs												
LC	310,108	est.	11,480	172,200	482,308	0.98	472,662	7	86%	214	2,219.1	2,220.0
LC oversize	2,131	actual	0	0	2,131	1.04	2,216	5	86%	153	14.5	15.0
Dewey	3,211	mix	0	0	3,211	0.98	3,147	7	86%	214	14.7	15.0
Dewey oversize	164	actual	0	0	164	1.04	171	5	86%	153	1.1	2.0
Bound periodicals												
LC	103,611	est.	1,160	17,400	121,011	1.77	214,189	6	86%	183	1,173.2	1,174.0
Dewey	756	actual	0	0	756	1.77	1,338	6	86%	183	7.3	8.0
Recordings												
33 rpm discs	5,713	est.	0	0	5,713	0.30	1,725	6	95%	202	8.5	9.0
Audio cassettes	233	actual	0	0	233	0.93	218	10	95%	337	0.6	1.0
Compact discs	1,951	actual	500	7,500	9,451	0.59	5,590	11	95%	371	15.1	16.0
Video cassettes	86	actual	25	375	461	1.15	528	10	95%	337	1.6	2.0
DVD's	0	actual	10	150	150	0.30	45	6	95%	202	0.2	1.0
Total	429,529		13,260	198,900	628,429		706,938				3,483.9	3,492.0

Note that in Figure 2.1, collections to which no more material will be added, such as the DDC monographs and bound periodicals, 33 rpm recordings, and audio cassettes, all have estimated annual growth rates of 0 items. The laser disc collection, just being started, has estimated annual growth, but 0 current items. Also note that column C is net annual growth. Additional columns could be inserted listing items added and removed from the collection annually and calculating the net acquisition by subtracting removals from additions.

Identifying Material to Remove to Remote Storage

Selecting material to be moved from a library's general collections to remote storage (this term will be used generically to refer to any shelving or storage option other than the main shelving area) is a collection management decision and is discussed here only in summary. Items to consider include the following:

1. *Items for which there is a stable, electronic version*, for instance abstracts and index volumes now covered by databases, and journals available in JSTOR (i.e., those beyond the moving wall).

2. *Duplicate items*, when it is desirable to maintain backup copies (e.g., classic works).

3. *Material that has not been used since date x*, when x is an agreed upon date, for instance, twenty years before the present.

4. *Blocks of material that as a whole have been determined to be lesser used*, for instance bound journal volumes prior to a certain date. (Carpenter and Horrell [chapter 10] and Powell [chapter 11], both in Nitecki and Kendrick 2001)

Access and preservation criteria mean that items should be moved only when there is an accurate record in the online catalog and only when they can be moved without damage.

Because items moved to remote storage may not be inspected for long periods of time, it is important to prepare them carefully for transfer. This includes "wiping or vacuuming materials and weeding out any that show evidence of mold, insect infestations, or sticky accretions. In addition, . . . [removing] any bookmarks, forms, paper clips, sticky notes, or rubber bands that may have been left in the item by staff or users. . . . And deciding whether fragile, brittle, or unbound materials need to be tied, wrapped, enveloped, or encased" (George, in Nitecki and Kendrick 2001, 144). Additional work is required to adjust the holdings locations records. This description only hints at the work required. Libraries seriously considering remote storage will wish to study Danuta Nitecki and Curtis Kendrick's *Library Off-Site Shelving* (2001).

MODELS FOR SHELVING MATERIAL

The critical first question to ask in considering how growth space should be allocated is how the collection will be arranged. Will material be separated by format, or will formats be integrated within a shelving sequence? Will oversized materials be shelved separately, and if so, what height will be the cutoff for considering an item oversized? In the case of a storage facility, will items be shelved by size?

Overall Models

Answers to these questions will most likely be determined within the context of each library's collection access philosophy and space considerations, and many variations are possible. Frequently found variations and their basic space planning advantages and disadvantages include the following:

1. *Separating collections by format and height*: bound monographs, bound periodicals, various microformats, various audio and video formats, etc., are each shelved separately. Oversized materials are shelved separately from smaller materials. Significantly oversized materials may be further separated, for instance, into a folio grouping. The main space planning advantage of this approach is that it maximizes shelving capacity by reducing waste vertical space within each section of shelving: the ratio of cubic collection material to cubic shelf space is high. The main disadvantage is that it increases the difficulty of users' browsing and finding tasks by creating multiple locations where material on a given topic may be found; however, this difficulty can be lessened with good bibliographic control and signage.

2. *Separating collections by broad subject content*: fiction, nonfiction, biographies, and so on are each shelved separately, and materials are also separated by the age of the intended audience. For example, materials for adults are shelved separately from those for preschool children, elementary school children, and junior high students. Like the preceding model, this one tends to separate material by height, although this separation is a by-product of the arrangement, rather than its primary purpose. However, hardcover adult fiction tends to be published in a relatively consistent physical format, as are adult hardcover biographies and so forth. The most variation is likely to occur within the nonfiction collections, and use of an oversized cutoff within nonfiction can reduce the demand for space.

Bound Periodicals Models

A special concern for libraries with large collections of bound periodicals is how to shelve them. There are at least three broad approaches:

1. *Shelve bound periodicals in a single sequence separate from monographs, arranged either by call number or alphabetically by title.* Shelving by call number may confer some slight space planning advantage, because journals within a particular broad discipline may tend to be more homogenous in size (e.g., English literature periodicals tend to be short;

41

engineering periodicals tend to be tall). This may work reasonably well for a relatively small periodical collection. With large periodical collections, however, this approach may widely separate materials in a particular discipline, particularly if shelved by title, and make the subject seeker's browsing and finding tasks tedious and cumbersome.

2. *Shelve blocks of bound periodicals, arranged by subject classification, within the monograph shelving sequence.* In this scenario, English literature periodicals might be shelved together as a block, and within the block, individual journal titles would be arranged either by call number or alphabetically by title. The question with this arrangement is how broadly or finely to delineate the blocks, and this choice should probably be determined by the nature of the specific collection and its users. This arrangement has the space planning advantage of separating the bound periodicals, which are likely to require more vertical space per shelf, from monographs, which typically can accept a tighter vertical spacing. From an access perspective, it has the advantage of placing related monographs and bound periodicals in some proximity to each other and can help facilitate subject browsing.

3. *Integrate bound periodicals within the monograph shelving sequence on a title-by-title basis.* This places bound periodicals in immediate proximity to related monographs, so that, for example, both the monographs and journals dealing with Shakespeare's work are in the same sections of shelving. However, it may require additional linear footage of shelving and square footage of floor space, as the number of shelves that can be used within a section of shelving will be governed by the larger format material, that is, the bound periodicals.

Audio and Video Materials Models

Audio and video materials pose their own challenges.

1. *In libraries where these materials are available for public browsing, there may be a need to have one shelving area to display record jackets, videotape cases, and other outer covers, and a second shelving area to house the actual recordings.* In this case, for ease of user access, the browsing display may be arranged loosely by subject or genre and alphabetically by the primary access point (that is, compact discs might be divided by type of music, then arranged alphabetically by artist or composer; videotapes might be divided by genre and arranged alphabetically by movie title), whereas the actual recordings, accessible only to library staff, might be arranged by accession number.

2. *Some libraries may choose to place all material, regardless of format, in a single integrated shelving sequence.* This would, for instance, place monographs, bound periodicals, microforms, videotapes, and compact discs dealing with the same subject next to each other on the same

shelf. As with title-by-title integration of bound periodicals, this has the access advantage of placing all related material together, easing the users' browsing and finding tasks. However, it can require extra space, particularly for inclusion of large format materials, such as LP records, which typically require deeper shelves and greater headroom. (For instance, if LPs and oversized material are shelved with print materials, their taller height might require using five shelves per section of shelving, a loss in capacity of about 28 percent compared to a more typical arrangement of seven shelves per section.)

3. *In a closed-access AV collection, materials may easily be separated by format and arranged in accession number order, if there is good bibliographic control.* For AV materials, separation by format is the most space efficient arrangement, particularly because there is great variation between the shelf depth and headroom required for different formats.* However, this limits user access and prevents browsing.

Oversized Models

Handling of oversized material and some space implications are discussed in Chapter 1. The two broad options for its shelving arrangement are full integration of oversized material and the establishment of an oversized shelving area, defined by a uniform height threshold.

1. *Full integration of oversized material will require the same linear footage of shelving as would be needed if the material were shelved in a separate sequence,* but that linear footage will occupy more square feet of floor space because the vertical space requirements of the interspersed oversized volumes will mean the shelving must be set up with fewer shelves per section.

2. *Full separation of oversized material increases the number of items that can be accommodated per square foot of floor space,* but increases the number of locations where a user must look to find an item. Further separation of oversized material by size accentuates both of these factors: it's more space efficient and less user-friendly.

3. *An alternative is to vary the oversized cutoff point by subject area,* so that in specific areas of the collection, for instance music or photography, where there may be a high percentage of tall items, there may be a

---

*Providing different depth shelves for different formats may maximize space utilization. For example, provide 8-inch-deep shelves for compact discs and videotapes, while using 14-inch-deep shelves for LP records. By using the shallowest depth shelving appropriate to the physical format, less floor space is used, and the number of items accommodated per square foot of floor may be maximized. The challenge in this approach for AV materials is to accurately predict the trends in changing formats within the context of the library's collection development policies: if you purchase and install a significant number of 14-inch-deep shelving units, then discontinue an LP collection, efficient space planning would suggest the 14-inch units should be removed and replaced with 8-inch-deep units.

policy of considering only items above 43 cm to be oversized, whereas in other areas, for example English literature or psychology, a cutoff of 28 cm might apply. This approach has the advantage of flexibly responding to the physical formats common to specific subject areas. The net effect may be that in each subject area, the percentage of the materials considered oversized is relatively constant, whereas if a uniform cutoff height were used, the percentage of items considered oversized might vary considerably from discipline to discipline, placing users of some subject areas at greater disadvantage in browsing.

4. *Another alternative is to use the bottom of each section of shelving for oversized material.* This has the advantage of placing the oversized materials in close proximity to regular-sized material, with the space advantage of requiring the greater vertical spacing on only one shelf per section. This approach can work if the proportion of oversized material to other material is such that the oversized shelf is more or less evenly filled. However, this does not predictably occur in most collections. As a result, oversized materials on the bottom shelf may migrate out of sequence with those in the shelves above (if the sequence of oversized material is continued on adjacent shelves), or, if the attempt is made to shelve oversized material within the section of shelving where related regular-sized materials are shelved, some bottom shelves may be underutilized (when there is less oversized material), or more than one shelf per section of shelving may be needed to accommodate the oversized material.

Shelving by Size

1. *In storage areas where materials are retrieved by staff (either with or without an automated picking system), greater space efficiency may be obtained by shelving material by size.* For instance, shelving or trays may be designated for materials that are less than 7 inches tall, less than 8 inches tall, less than 9 inches tall, and so forth. In this model, retrieving material relies on highly accurate location records.

MODELS FOR ALLOCATING GROWTH SPACE

The gross estimate of growth space identifies the amount of linear footage required to accommodate the growth of a whole collection over a period of years. The detailed estimate identifies the amount of linear footage needed in each relevant segment of the collection. Beyond this, there is the question of how to arrange the growth space allocated to each segment of the collection. There are several possible models.

Growth Space All in One Area

The growth space could be left in one area. This is in effect what is done when plans call for a later addition to a building or for conversion to stack space of an area currently used for another purpose, but it could also be done by leaving an entire block of shelving empty. The disadvantage of this approach is that it requires substantial collection shifting at some point.

Even Allocation

Growth space can be left evenly throughout the collection, with an equal amount of growth space left on each shelf. This works well within a homogenous collection, say a collection of fiction, where the growth rate is expected to be even throughout. For example: assume a collection now measures 12,000 linear inches, is expected to grow 1,200 inches per year, and has a planning horizon of 10 years, then the total collection to be accommodated would equal

Current collections	12,000 linear in.
Future collections (1,200 linear in./year x 10 years)	<u>12,000 linear in.</u>
Total collection to be accommodated	24,000 linear in.

Further assume shelf space amounting to 120 SF sections, each with seven shelves having an actual inside measurement of 35.5 inches, providing a total of 29,820 linear inches. At the outset, then, each shelf should be filled as follows:

Current collection	12,000 linear in.
divided by ($\div$)	
Total shelf space available	29,820 linear in.
equals	40.2% fill ratio
which becomes	35.5 in./shelf x .402 = 14.3 in. per shelf

So, in this case, to spread growth space evenly throughout the collection, each shelf would be filled 14.3 inches, and the remaining 21.2 inches would be left empty. Figure 2.2 (p. 46) shows how a section of shelving with this fill ratio would look right after the move, with 14.3 inches occupied and 21.2 inches left empty for future growth.

Figure 2.3 (p. 47) shows the same section of shelving at the end of ten years, assuming growth followed the predicted rate and was exactly even throughout the collection. Each shelf would be 82.5 percent full, with collection material occupying 28.6 inches of each shelf and 6.9 inches still empty, as follows:

Total collection to be accommodated:	24,000 linear in.
divided by	
Total shelf space available:	29,820 linear in.
equals	80.5% fill ratio
which becomes	28.6 in. per shelf

Because growth rates across a large collection will generally not be exactly even, the need for later shifting may be minimized by calculating different fill ratios for each significant segment of the collection. Figure 2.4 shows how to set up a spreadsheet to make these calculations.

Figure 2.2
Even Allocation of Growth Space: Opening Day Distribution of
Collection

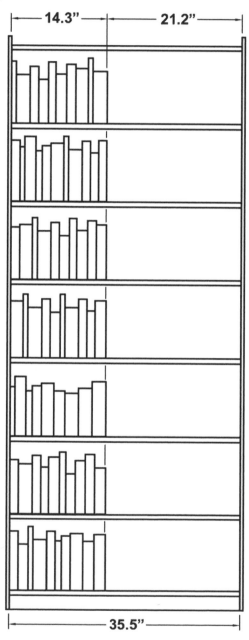

Figure 2.3
Even Allocation of Growth Space: Collection Distribution after Ten Years

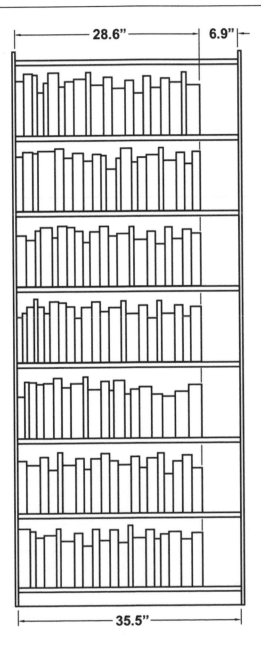

Note that in Figure 2.4 (p. 49) it is assumed each collection segment will begin on a new section of shelving, the number of sections required for each segment is rounded up, and both the initial and eventual fill ratios are calculated on the rounded number of sections of shelving. This yields a range of fill ratios within each segment at the end of ten years. If the fill ratio calculations were based on the total sections needed in ten years (column L) rather than the rounded number of sections needed (column M), the fill ratios would be essentially the same in each collection segment.

Growth Space for Bound Periodicals

Planning growth space for runs of bound periodicals presents a special problem. Unless backfiles are purchased or missing volumes replaced, generally no growth occurs *within* a run of backfiles. Growth occurs only at the *end* of the run, where each new year's volumes are shelved. Because the number of inches added per year varies considerably among journals, minimizing the need for later shifting means calculating the shelf inches of growth space required for each title per year and multiplying that by the planning horizon.

Figure 2.5 (p. 50) shows how to set up a spreadsheet to calculate growth space and total space required for seven sequentially shelved, hypothetical periodical titles. Note that Title F has ceased publication and therefore has no anticipated growth, whereas Title G is a new title, and the library's current number of volumes equals 0.

If this collection were allocated evenly across three sections of shelving, each with six shelves per section and an actual internal measurement of 35.5 inches, or available linear space of 639 linear inches, then the fill ratio would be

Total current collection:	316.5 linear in.
divided by	
Total available shelf space:	639 linear in.
equals a fill ratio of	49.5%, which equals 17.6 in. filled per shelf

Figure 2.6 (p. 51) illustrates the way this collection would look initially. However, this arrangement would result in inadequate provision of growth space at the end of each title. As the collection grew, this arrangement would require ongoing shifting to reposition the growth space at the end of each title. Note that growth space for each title occurs out of sequence. In practice, this would be corrected by shifting, but Figure 2.7 (p. 52) illustrates the extent of shifting that would be required.

Instead, to avoid the ongoing labor cost of shifting, each shelf within the backfile should be filled to the maximum working capacity set by the library, and growth space for each title should be left in a single block after its most recently bound volume. For example, if the library has decided to use a maximum working capacity of 31.1 inches within bound periodical collections, the titles illustrated above would be arranged as calculated in Figure 2.8 (p. 53) and illustrated in Figure 2.9 (p. 54). This arrangement assumes the use of six shelves in each section.

Figure 2.4
Calculating Initial Fill Ratios for Monograph Collection Segments with Different Growth Rates

LC class	Current volumes (items)	Linear inches per volume	Current linear inches (a x b)	Anticipated average net annual growth (volumes)	Planning horizon (years)	Anticipated total growth (volumes) (d x e)	Anticipated growth (inches) (f x b)	Anticipated total collection (inches) (e + g)	Shelves used per SF section	Maximum working capacity	Working linear inches per SF section (i x j x 35.5)	Total SF sections needed in 10 years (h /k)	Rounded number of SF sections	Total linear inches available (i x m x 35.5)	Initial fill rate (c/n)	Fill rate in 10 years (h/n)
	(a)	(b)	(c)	(d)	(e)	(f)	(g)	(h)	(i)	(j)	(k)	(l)	(m)	(n)	(o)	(p)
A	150	0.98	147.0	2	10	20	19.6	166.6	7	86%	213.7	0.8	1	248.5	59%	67%
B	125	0.92	115.0	15	10	150	138.0	253.0	7	86%	213.7	1.2	2	497.0	23%	51%
C	50	1.11	55.5	2	10	20	22.2	77.7	7	86%	213.7	0.4	1	248.5	22%	31%
D	25	1.11	27.8	1	10	10	11.1	38.9	7	86%	213.7	0.2	1	248.5	11%	16%
E	25	1.11	27.8	1	10	10	11.1	38.9	7	86%	213.7	0.2	1	248.5	11%	16%
F	10	1.07	10.7	1	10	10	10.7	21.4	7	86%	213.7	0.1	1	248.5	4%	9%
G	35	1.13	39.6	3	10	30	33.9	73.5	7	86%	213.7	0.3	1	248.5	16%	30%
HA	125	1.09	136.3	10	10	100	109.0	245.3	7	86%	213.7	1.1	2	497.0	27%	49%
HB	110	0.97	106.7	25	10	250	242.5	349.2	7	86%	213.7	1.6	2	497.0	21%	70%
HC-HD	60	0.97	58.2	15	10	150	145.5	203.7	7	86%	213.7	1.0	1	248.5	23%	82%
HE	190	0.97	184.3	22	10	220	213.4	397.7	7	86%	213.7	1.9	2	497.0	37%	80%
HF	225	0.97	218.3	45	10	450	436.5	654.8	7	86%	213.7	3.1	4	994.0	22%	66%
HG-HZ	75	0.97	72.8	14	10	140	135.8	208.6	7	86%	213.7	1.0	1	248.5	29%	84%
J	50	0.99	49.5	4	10	40	39.6	89.1	7	86%	213.7	0.4	1	248.5	20%	36%
K	75	1.10	82.5	3	10	30	33.0	115.5	7	86%	213.7	0.5	1	248.5	33%	46%
L	65	0.82	53.3	6	10	60	49.2	102.5	7	86%	213.7	0.5	1	248.5	21%	41%
M	50	1.11	55.5	22	10	220	244.2	299.7	7	86%	213.7	1.4	2	497.0	11%	60%
N	75	0.98	73.5	26	10	260	254.8	328.3	7	86%	213.7	1.5	2	497.0	15%	66%
P	325	0.98	318.5	35	10	350	343.0	661.5	7	86%	213.7	3.1	4	994.0	32%	67%
Q	90	1.00	90.0	5	10	50	50.0	140.0	7	86%	213.7	0.7	1	248.5	36%	56%
QA	180	1.00	180.0	30	10	300	300.0	480.0	7	86%	213.7	2.2	3	745.5	24%	64%

Figure 2.5
Calculating Growth Space for Periodicals on a Title-by-Title Basis

	Current number of volumes	Current total linear inches	Anticipated annual growth (volumes)	Planning horizon (years)	Anticipated total growth (volumes) (c x d)	Linear inches per volume	Anticipated total growth (inches) (e x f)	Total space needed (inches) (b + g)
	(a)	(b)	(c)	(d)	(e)	(f)	(g)	(h)
Title A	30	30.0	1	10	10	1.00	10.0	40.0
Title B	20	50.0	4	10	40	2.50	100.0	150.0
Title C	67	100.5	2	10	20	1.50	30.0	130.5
Title D	31	31.0	2	10	20	1.00	20.0	51.0
Title E	36	45.0	4	10	40	1.25	50.0	95.0
Title F	40	60.0	0	10	0	1.50	0.0	60.0
Title G	0	0.0	2	10	20	1.75	35.0	35.0
Total		316.5					245.0	561.5

Figure 2.6
Even Allocation of Growth Space in a Periodicals Collection: Titles A–G on Day One

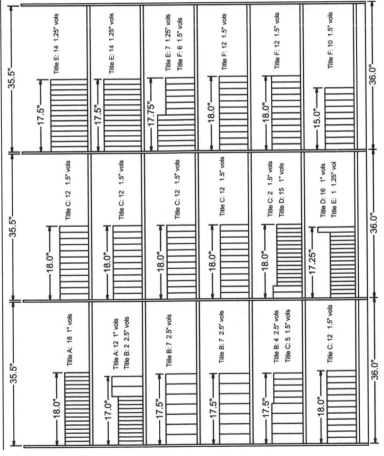

The theoretical fill ratio is 49.5%, or 17.6" per shelf. Actual space occupied on each shelf varies slightly because specific titles' widths vary.
Note that no space is used for new Title G, for which there are no backfiles.

51

Figure 2.7
Even Allocation of Growth Space in a Periodicals Collection: Titles A–G at End of Year Ten

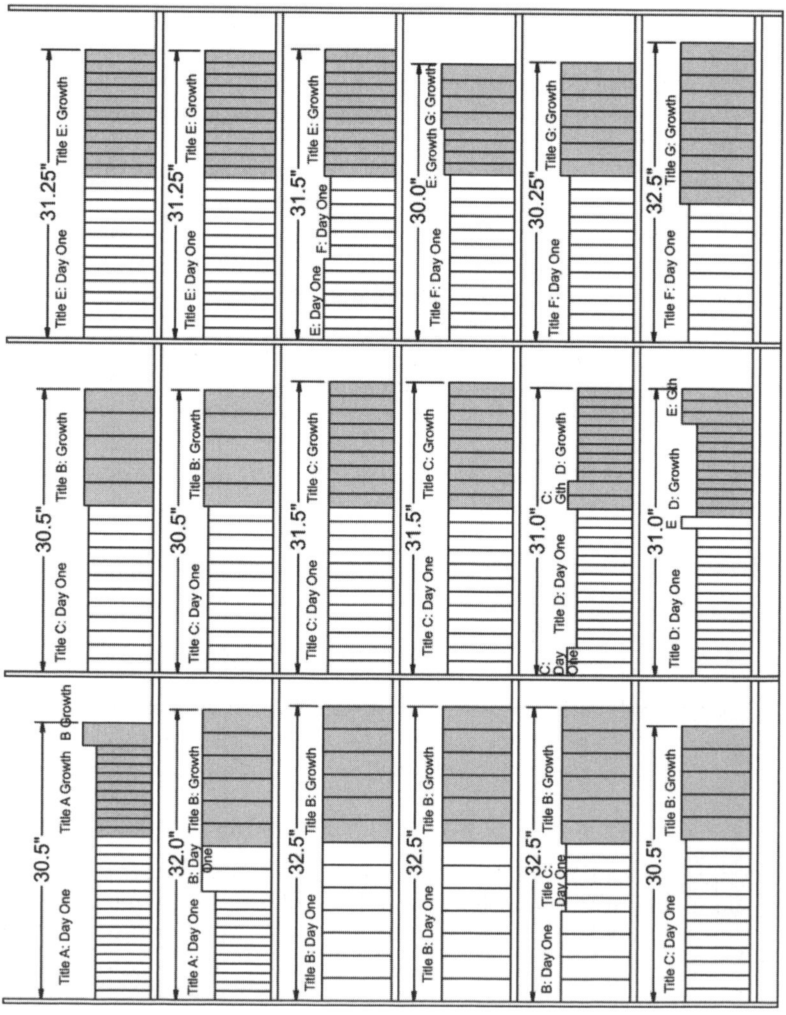

Figure 2.8
Calculating Shelf Space for Titles A–G

Section	Shelf	Theoretical capacity (inches)	Title	Inches per volume	This shelf — Backfile Volumes	Backfile (Inches)	Growth Volumes	Growth (Inches)	Inches of material	Cumulative Backfile (Volumes)	Cumulative Growth (Volumes)	Title
One	top	31.1	A	1.00	30	30.00	2	2.00	32.00	30	2	Title A
	2	31.1	A	1.00	0	0.00	8	8.00	8.00	30	**10**	**Title A**
		31.1	B	2.50	9	22.50	0	0.00	30.50	9	0	Title B
	3	31.1	B	2.50	11	27.50	1	2.50	30.00	20	1	Title B
	4	31.1	B	2.50	0	0.00	13	32.50	32.50	20	14	Title B
	5	31.1	B	2.50	0	0.00	13	32.50	32.50	20	27	Title B
	bottom	31.1	B	2.50	0	0.00	13	32.50	32.50	20	**40**	**Title B**
Two	top	31.1	C	1.50	21	31.50	0	0.00	31.50	21	0	Title C
	2	31.1	C	1.50	21	31.50	0	0.00	31.50	42	0	Title C
	3	31.1	C	1.50	21	31.50	0	0.00	31.50	63	0	Title C
	4	31.1	C	1.50	4	6.00	17	25.50	31.50	67	17	Title C
	5	31.1	C	1.50	0	0.00	3	4.50	4.50	67	**20**	**Title C**
		31.1	D	1.00	27	27.00	0	0.00	31.50	27	0	Title D
	bottom	31.1	D	1.00	4	4.00	20	20.00	24.00	31	**20**	**Title D**
		31.1	E	1.25	5	6.25	0	0.00	30.25	5	0	Title E
Three	top	31.1	E	1.25	25	31.25	0	0.00	31.25	30	0	Title E
	2	31.1	E	1.25	6	7.50	19	23.75	31.25	36	19	Title E
	3	31.1	E	1.25	0	0.00	21	26.25	26.25	36	**40**	**Title E**
		31.1	F	1.50	3	4.50	0	0.00	30.75	3	0	Title F
	4	31.1	F	1.50	21	31.50	0	0.00	31.50	24	0	Title F
	5	31.1	F	1.50	16	24.00	0	0.00	24.00	40	**0**	**Title F**
		31.1	G	1.75	0	0.00	4	7.00	31.00	0	4	Title G
	bottom	31.1	G	1.75	0	0.00	16	28.00	28.00	0	**20**	**Title G**
Total (inches)						316.50		245.00	648.25			

Figure 2.9
Growth Space Placed at End of Each Title in a Periodicals Collection: Titles A–G at the End of Year Ten

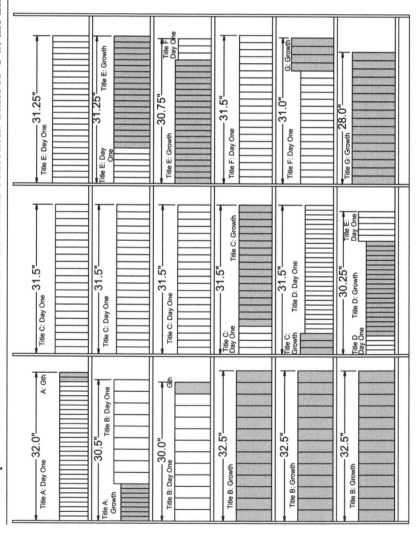

Collecting data on individual titles will be easier if a standard form is used. The form shown in Figure 2.10 draws on Lumb (1972, 262), Johnson (1980, 131), Uzelac (1969, 457–58), and Seiler and Robar (1987, 330–32).

Figure 2.10.
Periodical Data Collection Form

Current title: _____

Previous/variant titles: _____

_____

Call number: _____

Present location: _____

Proposed location: _____

Current number of volumes: ___ volumes

Current linear inches: ___ linear inches

Linear inches for last year's bound volumes: ___ linear inches

Last year bound (date):   20__

Height of tallest bound volume: ___ inches

This title is (circle one):   active
                                              ceased
                                              planned (subscription to start):_____ (date)

                                              retained for ___ year(s) only

---

Note the following when using the periodical data collection form:

1. Record the data for each title on a separate page or card. Consider getting a list from the online catalog of all periodical titles and holdings, to use as a starting point. Edit to reflect actual holdings in the old location. Then, after the move, check the edited list against items on the shelf in the new location to make sure everything was moved (Brinkman and Whiteside 2002, 14).

2. If the library's catalog system includes a report writer, look into having a report of journal holdings run as a starting point.

3. Once the data have been gathered, enter the information into a spreadsheet or database for easier manipulation.

4. For periodicals with variant or changed titles, consider collecting data under each title, for more precise manipulation of the data (Lumb 1972, 262).

5. Similarly, collect data separately for duplicate runs held in different locations, for example, when several collections are being merged, particularly if binding decisions have been made separately in each location.

6. Height of the tallest volume is included so that appropriate shelf spacing may be planned ahead of time (Seiler and Robar 1987, 331; Uzelac 1969, 457).

Growth Joints

An alternate growth space allocation approach is to leave empty sections of shelving between major segments of the collection. This may be most practical when there is significant spare capacity and the technique is combined with another approach or approaches. It may be particularly useful when shelving blocks of bound periodicals within a run of monographs, especially when collection development parameters and/or funding levels may be changing, or when changing patterns of acquisitions may create the need to make significant changes in the arrangement of the collections. In these circumstances, the inclusion of growth joints can help reduce the need for later large-scale stack shifts. For the move itself, it can also provide insurance against one section of the collection encroaching on the next as a result of miscalculation. The disadvantage of growth joints is that they interrupt the flow of a collection sequence and can lead to user confusion, although this may be reduced with good signage.

To illustrate, consider a collection comprising three blocks of monographs and bound periodicals requiring total shelf space of 91,000 inches or 442 SF sections of shelving (calculations shown in Figure 2.11)

Also consider an area of shelving comprising the equivalent of 500 SF sections. Assume that two-thirds of these sections will be set up with seven shelves/section to accommodate monographs and the remaining third set up with six shelves/section to accommodate bound periodical volumes. Its linear capacity will therefore be 118,321 linear inches, as calculated in Figure 2.12 (P. 58).

This provides 57 SF sections (500 SF available – 443 SF used) of spare shelving capacity beyond what will be needed within the monograph and bound periodical sections to accommodate their collections' growth. This could be divided into growth joints, either among each of the six collection segments identified in Figure 2.10, or after each of the three groups.

Figure 2.11
Calculating Shelving Requirements for Collection A

	Current holdings (inches)	Anticipated growth (inches)	Total (inches) (a +b)	Shelves used per section	Inches available per shelf	Ending fill ratio	Available inches per section (d x e x f)	Sections needed Current (a / g)	Growth (b / g)	Total (h + i)
	(a)	(b)	(c)	(d)	(e)	(f)	(g)	(h)	(i)	(j)
Bound periodicals group A	6,500	1,000	7,500	6	35.5	90%	191.7	33.9	5.2	39.1
Monographs group A	11,000	6,000	17,000	7	35.5	86%	213.7	51.5	28.1	79.5
Bound periodicals group B	7,500	5,000	12,500	6	35.5	90%	191.7	39.1	26.1	65.2
Monographs group B	27,500	7,000	34,500	7	35.5	86%	213.7	128.7	32.8	161.4
Bound periodicals group C	7,000	3,500	10,500	6	35.5	90%	191.7	36.5	18.3	54.8
Monographs group C	5,000	4,000	9,000	7	35.5	86%	213.7	23.4	18.7	42.1
	64,500	26,500	91,000					313.1	129.1	442.2

Figure 2.12
Calculating Capacity of an Area with Mixed Shelf Spacing

| 500 sections of shelving | x ⅔ set up for monographs | = 333 sections |
| | x ⅓ set up for bound periodicals | = 167 sections |

   333 sections of shelving set up for monographs
x   7 shelves/section
x 35.5 in./shelf
82,750 linear in. of shelf space

   167 sections of shelving set up for bound periodicals
x   6 shelves/section
x 35.5 in./shelf
35,571 linear in. of shelf space

  82,750 linear in. of shelf space (monographs)
+ 35,571 linear in. of shelf space (bound periodicals)
 118,321 linear in. of shelf space

The amount of the spare capacity to be allocated to each growth joint can be figured in one of several ways:

A. **In proportion to the anticipated growth within each preceding block.** This approach probably makes the most sense from a space planning perspective, since the purpose of the growth joint is primarily to serve as a buffer against unforeseen changes in collection growth patterns. In this case, assuming three growth joints are planned following each of the bound periodical blocks, the spare capacity would be allocated as follows:

1. Calculate the percentage of growth anticipated in each monograph and bound periodical block in proportion to the total:

Block A $\dfrac{7{,}000 \text{ linear in. anticipated growth}}{26{,}500 \text{ linear in. anticipated overall growth}} = 26.4\%$

Block B $\dfrac{12{,}000 \text{ linear in. anticipated growth}}{26{,}500 \text{ linear in. anticipated overall growth}} = 45.3\%$

Block C $\dfrac{7{,}500 \text{ linear in. anticipated growth}}{26{,}500 \text{ linear in. anticipated overall growth}} = 28.3\%$

2. Allocate the spare capacity according to these percentages, rounding so that growth joints comprise whole SF sections of shelving:

Available spare shelving = 57 SF sections

Allocate following Block A:

57 SF sections x .264 = 15.05 SF sections, rounded to 15 SF sections

Allocate following Block B:

57 SF sections x .453 = 25.8 SF sections, rounded to 26 SF sections

Allocate following Block C:

57 SF sections x .283 = 16.1 SF sections, rounded to 16 SF sections

B. In proportion to the total collection size of each preceding block This approach biases the allocation of growth space toward past collecting patterns rather than future collecting patterns. Particularly for bound periodicals, where publications cease or change title (and sometimes, therefore, location), this approach may result in an allocation of space that may require premature stack shifts.

Block A $\dfrac{24{,}500 \text{ linear in. total in Block A}}{91{,}000 \text{ linear in. total in Collection A}} = 26.9\%$

Block B $\dfrac{47{,}000 \text{ linear in. total in Block B}}{91{,}000 \text{ linear in. total in Collection A}} = 51.7\%$

Block C $\dfrac{19{,}500 \text{ linear in. total in Block C}}{91{,}000 \text{ linear in. total in Collection A}} = 21.4\%$

Allocate 26.9 percent following Block A:

57 SF sections x .269 = 15.3 sections, rounded to 15 SF sections

Allocate 51.7 percent following Block B:

57 SF sections x .517 = 29.5 F sections, rounded to 30 SF sections

Allocate 21.4 percent following Block C:

57 SF sections x .214 = 12.2 SF sections, rounded to 12 SF sections

C. **Evenly, without regard to the size of the preceding block** If time is of the essence, this may be an expedient way to divide spare capacity. It has the advantage of being easy to calculate:

57 SF sections spare capacity/3 growth joints = 19 SF section per growth joint.

However, compare the space thus allocated to the allocations arrived at by more closely modeling predicted growth, and it will become apparent that the relatively small amount of calculation time saved will result in early and extensive stack shifting, not a good trade-off!

Empty Top and/or Bottom Shelves

Another way of allocating spare capacity is to leave the top and/or bottom shelves of each section empty. These mini-growth joints leave expansion space evenly through the collection, and so don't have the advantage of being in proportion to anticipated growth, but they do make it easier for library users to reach material, at least during the initial years after the move.

Figure 2.13 shows the number of SF sections of shelving that would be required to accommodate the hypothetical collection discussed above in this manner.

Combination Approaches

Several of these approaches may be combined. For example, in a library with considerable spare capacity, it might be desirable to use growth joints, empty top and bottom shelves, and growth space within each collection. The spreadsheet shown in Figure 2.14 illustrates how this would be calculated.

It is important to think about the trade-off between having more space on the shelves and more space on the library floor implicit in the choice of fill ratio and number of shelves used per section of shelving. Consider, for instance, that 40.2 SF sections of shelving will hold 10,000 inches of collections if each section if seven shelves are used in each section and each shelf is completely filled (not good for shelving operations or for preservation, but sometimes necessary). The same 10,000 inches of collections requires 55.2 SF sections of shelving if a fill ratio of 85 percent and six shelves per section are used. A fill ratio of 60 percent and use of only five shelves per section yields a requirement of 93.9 SF sections of shelving. Figure 2.15 (p. 62) calculates the single-face equivalent sections of shelving required to house 10,000 linear inches of material, assuming various fill ratios and number of sections used per section of shelving.

Figure 2.13
Shelving Capacity Required for Collection A (Top and Bottom Shelves Left Empty)

	Current holdings (inches)	Anticipated growth (inches)	Total (inches) (a + b)	Shelves used per section*	Available inches per shelf	Ending fill ratio	Inches used per shelf (e x f)	Inches used per section (d x g)	Sections Needed Current (a /h)	Sections Needed Growth (b / h)	Sections Needed Total (i +j)
	(a)	(b)	(c)	(d)	(e)	(f)	(g)	(h)	(i)	(j)	(k)
Bound periodicals group A	6,500	1,000	7,500	4	35.5	90%	32.0	127.8	50.9	7.8	58.7
Monographs group A	11,000	6,000	17,000	5	35.5	86%	30.5	152.7	72.1	39.3	111.4
Bound periodicals group B	7,500	5,000	12,500	4	35.5	90%	32.0	127.8	58.7	39.1	97.8
Monographs group B	27,500	7,000	34,500	5	35.5	86%	30.5	152.7	180.2	45.9	226.0
Bound periodicals group C	7,000	3,500	10,500	4	35.5	90%	32.0	127.8	54.8	27.4	82.2
Monographs group C	5,000	4,000	9,000	5	35.5	86%	30.5	152.7	32.8	26.2	59.0
	64,500	26,500	91,000						449.3	185.7	635.0

* Assumes shelving is set up with 7 shelves/SF in monograph areas, and 6 shelves/SF in bound periodical areas.

Figure 2.14
Shelving Capacity Required for Collection A (Top and Bottom Shelves Left Empty; Growth Joints Added)

	Current holdings (inches)	Anticipated growth (inches)	Total (inches) (a + b)	Shelves used per section*	Available inches per shelf	Ending fill ratio	Inches used per shelf (e x f)	Inches used per section (d x g)	Sections needed Current (a /h)	Sections needed Growth (b / h)	Sections needed Growth joint	Sections needed Total (i + j + k)
	(a)	(b)	(c)	(d)	(e)	(f)	(g)	(h)	(i)	(j)	(k)	(l)
Bound periodicals group A	6,500	1,000	7,500	4	35.5	90%	32.0	127.8	50.9	7.8		58.7
Monographs group A	11,000	6,000	17,000	5	35.5	86%	30.5	152.7	72.1	39.3		111.4
Growth joint											11.0	11.0
Bound periodicals group B	7,500	5,000	12,500	4	35.5	90%	32.0	127.8	58.7	39.1		97.8
Monographs group B	27,500	7,000	34,500	5	35.5	86%	30.5	152.7	180.2	45.9		226.0
Growth joint											18.0	18.0
Bound periodicals group C	7,000	3,500	10,500	4	35.5	90%	32.0	127.8	54.8	27.4		82.2
Monographs group C	5,000	4,000	9,000	5	35.5	86%	30.5	152.7	32.8	26.2		59.0
Growth joint											12.0	12.0
	64,500	26,500	91,000						449.3	185.7	41.0	676.0

* Assumes shelving is set up with 7 shelves/SF in monograph areas and 6 shelves/SF in bound periodical areas.

Figure 2.15
Shelving Requirements for 10,000 Inches of Collections, Given Various Fill Ratios and Numbers of Shelves Used Per Section (Assumes 35.5-inch Clear Space per Shelf)

Fill ratio	Number of shelves used per section	Inches used per shelf (a x 35.5)	Inches used per section (b x c)	SF equivalent sections required (10,000 / d)
(a)	(b)	(c)	(d)	(e)
100%	5	35.5	177.5	56.3
	6	35.5	213.0	46.9
	7	35.5	248.5	40.2
	8	35.5	284.0	35.2
95%	5	33.7	168.6	59.3
	6	33.7	202.4	49.4
	7	33.7	236.1	42.4
	8	33.7	269.8	37.1
90%	5	32.0	159.8	62.6
	6	32.0	191.7	52.2
	7	32.0	223.7	44.7
	8	32.0	255.6	39.1
85%	5	30.2	150.9	66.3
	6	30.2	181.1	55.2
	7	30.2	211.2	47.3
	8	30.2	241.4	41.4
80%	5	28.4	142.0	70.4
	6	28.4	170.4	58.7
	7	28.4	198.8	50.3
	8	28.4	227.2	44.0
75%	5	26.6	133.1	75.1
	6	26.6	159.8	62.6
	7	26.6	186.4	53.7
	8	26.6	213.0	46.9
70%	5	24.9	124.3	80.5
	6	24.9	149.1	67.1
	7	24.9	174.0	57.5
	8	24.9	198.8	50.3
65%	5	23.1	115.4	86.7
	6	23.1	138.5	72.2
	7	23.1	161.5	61.9
	8	23.1	184.6	54.2
60%	5	21.3	106.5	93.9
	6	21.3	127.8	78.2
	7	21.3	149.1	67.1
	8	21.3	170.4	58.7
55%	5	19.5	97.6	102.4
	6	19.5	117.2	85.4
	7	19.5	136.7	73.2
	8	19.5	156.2	64.0
50%	5	17.8	88.8	112.7
	6	17.8	106.5	93.9
	7	17.8	124.3	80.5
	8	17.8	142.0	70.4

3   PREPARING A COLLECTION LAYOUT PLAN

When you're crunching numbers, don't let the calculator or the spreadsheet convince you against your better judgment.

—Shirien Chappell (2006)

A collection layout plan is the "road map" showing where and how material is to be shelved when the move is done. It consists of two parts: a spreadsheet detailing the fill ratio to be used for shelving each segment of the collection and a plan of the shelving, marked up to show where specific parts of the collection start and end. Together, these two documents tell where to shelve each part of the collection and how many inches of each shelf are to be filled during the move.

Preparing an accurate, detailed collection layout plan is important for several reasons:

1. It saves time during the move: everyone involved knows where everything should end up.

2. It forces the move planner to calculate how many sections of shelving will be required for each part of the collection and how full each section should be at the time of the move, and to map out the results of these calculations onto a plan, greatly increasing the chance that errors in calculation or stack counts will be found and can be corrected before the move itself.

3. It provides an opportunity to discuss and resolve ahead of time any questions concerning how the collections should be arranged. Collection layout options can be discussed much more effectively

when reviewing a layout in plan form instead of in the abstract. Forming a consensus about the layout ahead of time through this process also helps reduce stress at the time of the move, valuable because a move is itself inherently stressful.

4. It provides a necessary tool for walking through the move on paper later on, which gives the move planners time to identify and resolve logistical problems before the move actually takes place.

Before preparing the collection layout plan, the size of the collection and the capacity of the available shelving must be determined. Chapter 1 describes how to determine the physical size of existing collections, and Chapter 2 discusses planning for collection growth. This chapter describes how to determine the capacity of the available shelving and integrate that with the information on current and future collections developed in Chapters 1 and 2 to prepare the collection layout plan.

DETERMINING SHELVING CAPACITY

Shelving Inventory

To start, prepare a physical inventory of the shelving. For both the inventory and the move, you will need a method of uniquely identifying each section of shelving. If the library's stack signage already assigns each range a unique number, this can be combined with a numbering system for each section of shelving in the range. If no such system is currently in use, an identification system must be developed to assure that each section of shelving is inventoried once and only once.

Before starting the inventory, make a reduced-scale plan of the stack areas to be inventoried and label it for reference during and after the inventory. Identify blocks of shelving, each side of each range, and each section of shelving, so that each side of each DF section of shelving (e.g., each SF equivalent section) can be uniquely identified.

If no numbering scheme is in use, consider using the following hierarchical scheme:

floor	number
block	letter
range face	number
section	number

A block of stacks may be defined in any way that is logical for a library's floor plan; natural dividing lines include walls, major aisles, and large blocks of seating interspersed in a stack area. A range face is one side of a double-sided range of shelving. Using the scheme outlined above, for example, 3 A 2-8 indicates the eighth single-faced section of shelving on Floor 3, stack block A, range face 2. An advantage of this scheme is that it allows easy conversion of inventory information to a rough estimate of sections of shelving in a block of stacks by multiplying number of range faces by number of sections. (Though keep in mind this provides only a crude estimate, because it does not take into account variations in the width of shelving sections. For instance, where 36-inch nominal width sections are the norm, and every nth range engrosses a column, filler sections of, say, 24-inch width may be included. The gross estimate would not account for these smaller width sections, resulting in a somewhat inflated capacity estimate.)

The reduced-scale plan will also be used later in preparing the collection layout plan. Preparation of the plan may require several iterations, so it is helpful to have a master and several copies. The scale of the plan should be large enough that labels for each side of individual ranges may be legibly recorded and read, but small enough to be physically manageable. For a large library, this may mean using full-sized architectural plans or separately enlarging portions of full-sized architectural plans; however, the determining factors should be legibility and ease of handling. Figure 3.1 (p. 66) shows a sample stack plan labeled using the hierarchical scheme discussed above, and Figure 3.2 (p. 67) shows a sample shelving inventory data collection form.

The shelving collection form illustrated in Figure 3.2 is designed to collect information on single-faced equivalent sections of shelving. Although most shelving used in libraries is double-faced or double-sided, that is, shelving facing two aisles, shelves on double-sided shelving can be individually adjusted, and it is therefore necessary to record separately information for each half of a double-sided section.

If reuse of existing shelving is planned, the inventory must also collect information on the manufacturer, style, dimensions, color, end panel type and dimensions, and any refinishing that should be done (Fraley and Anderson 1990, 33–38).

Note that it is important to measure the *inside* dimension of each section of shelving. This is the unobstructed space between a shelving section's uprights, the width on which material can be shelved. For shelving with a nominal 36-inch width, this inside dimension will be typically less than 36 inches because the uprights and fixtures that attach the shelves to the uprights all occupy some amount of width. Figure 3.3 (p. 68) illustrates the dimension to measure.

Particularly in libraries that have added shelving over a period of years, it is important to not assume that all sections of shelving have the same width; efforts to maximize shelving capacity often result in the use of a variety of widths of shelving. In addition, different manufacturers' shelving may have slightly different inside dimensions, which can cumulatively make a significant difference in the available capacity. If the library has more than one type of shelving, photograph each for quick reference during the inventory and planning process.

Figure 3.1
Reduced-scale Stack Layout, with Blocks, Rows, and Sections Labeled

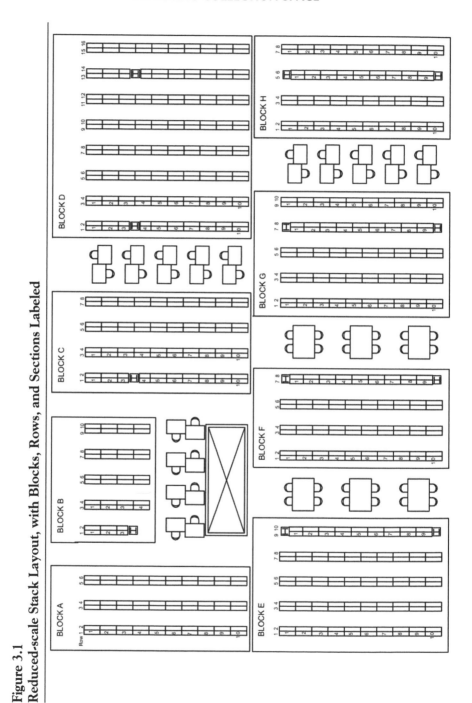

Figure 3.2.
Sample Shelving Inventory Data Collection Form

Type of shelving	
Manufacturer	

Location:	
Floor	
Block	

Shelving:	
Material	
Color/finish	
Height	
Nominal depth	

End panels:	
Material	
Color/finish	
Dimensions	

Inventoried by:	
Date:	
Notes:	

Block	Row	Sections	Number of sections	Number of shelves per section	Inside dimension of shelf	Notes

Figure 3.3
Clear Inside Dimension of Shelf

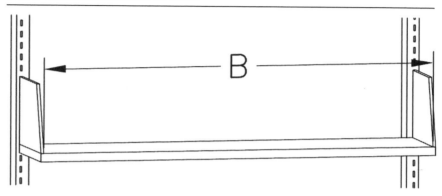

In a library where new shelving has been installed, the inventory task may be considerably easier. For instance, it may be possible to have the shelving manufacturer or installer provide as-built plans of the shelving, from which tentative calculations may be made. However, the move planner must still verify the accuracy of any such plan, as site conditions not infrequently require an installer to make unplanned modifications not reflected on the plans, and if these aren't discovered until the move is underway, they can cause unpleasant surprises.

Calculate Stack Capacity

Once the shelving inventory is complete, next calculate the stack capacity and prepare a summary list of shelving characteristics, referencing the locations noted on the reduced scale plan of the stacks. Figure 3.4 shows a sample completed stack characteristic summary for hypothetical stack block 3C.

The capacity calculations are straightforward. For each shelving configuration (or unique combination of width and number of shelves within a section of shelving), the calculation is

> (number of shelves/SF section) x (inside or clear in. per shelf) =
> linear capacity per SF section

For example,

> (7 shelves/SF section) x (35.5 in./shelf) = 248.5 in./SF section

or

> (6 shelves/SF section) x (35.5 in./shelf) = 213.0 in./SF section

Figure 3.4
Sample Shelving Inventory Data Collection Form, Completed

Type of shelving	cantilever
Manufacturer	Library Bureau

Location:	
Floor	3
Block	3C

Shelving:	
Material	metal
Color/finish	sand beige (paint)
Height	90"
Nominal depth	9"

End panels:	
Material	wood
Color/finish	oak
Dimensions	20"w x 90"h

Inventoried by:	Ann Jones and Jeremy Johnson
Date:	April 10, 2008
Notes:	needs shelf-reading

Block	Row	Sections	Number of sections	Number of shelves per section	Inside dimension of shelf	Notes
3C	1	1-3	3	6	35.5	
	1	4	1	7	35.5	
	1	5-8	4	6	35.5	
	2	1-6	6	6	35.5	
	2	7-8	2	7	35.5	
	3	1-8	8	7	35.5	
	4	1-8	8	7	35.5	
	5	1	1	7	23.5	3 brown shelves
	5	2-8	7	7	35.5	
	6	1	1	7	23.5	
	6	2-8	7	7	35.5	
	7	1-5	5	7	35.5	
	7	6-8	3	8	35.5	
	8	1-7	7	7	35.5	
	8	8	1	3	35.5	consultation desk and chair
	9	1	1	6	35.5	base shelf missing
	9	2-8	6	7	35.5	
	10	1-8	8	7	35.5	shelves have movable dividers
	11	1-8	8	7	35.5	shelves have movable dividers
	12	1-8	8	7	35.5	shelves have movable dividers
	13	1-2	2	6	35.5	shelves have movable dividers
	13	3-8	6	7	35.5	shelves have movable dividers

The capacity of a row is calculated by totaling the number of sections with each configuration within a range and multiplying by that configuration's linear capacity; for example, for a range of six SF 36-inch nominal width sections using six shelves/SF and two SF 36-inch nominal width sections using seven shelves/SF:

(6 SF sections using 6 shelves) x (213 in./SF)	= 1,278.0 in.
(2 SF sections using 7 shelves) x (248.5 in./SF)	= 497.0 in.
Row total	= 1,775.0 in.

Total capacity for a block of rows or for a floor is then calculated by adding up the capacity of the rows within the block. Figure 3.5 illustrates capacity calculations for the hypothetical stack block inventoried in Figure 3.4.

Figure 3.5
Calculating Shelving Capacity from Shelving Inventory Data Collection Form

Block	Row	Number of sections (a)	Number of shelves per section (b)	Clear inside shelf dimension (c)	Linear inches capacity per SF (b xc)	Linear inches capacity this row & configuration (a x d)	Linear inches capacity this row
3C	1	7	6	35.5	213.0	1,491.0	
	1	1	7	35.5	248.5	248.5	1,739.5
	2	6	6	35.5	213.0	1,278.0	
	2	2	7	35.5	248.5	497.0	1,775.0
	3	8	7	35.5	248.5	1,988.0	1,988.0
	4	8	7	35.5	248.5	1,988.0	1,988.0
	5	1	7	23.5	164.5	164.5	
	5	7	7	35.5	248.5	1,739.5	1,904.0
	6	1	7	23.5	164.5	164.5	
	6	7	7	35.5	248.5	1,739.5	1,904.0
	7	5	7	35.5	248.5	1,242.5	
	7	3	8	35.5	284.0	852.0	2,094.5
	8	7	7	35.5	248.5	1,739.5	
	8	1	3	35.5	106.5	106.5	1,846.0
	9	1	6	35.5	213.0	213.0	
	9	6	7	35.5	248.5	1,491.0	1,704.0
	10	8	7	35.5	248.5	1,988.0	1,988.0
	11	8	7	35.5	248.5	1,988.0	1,988.0
	12	8	7	35.5	248.5	1,988.0	1,988.0
	13	2	6	35.5	213.0	426.0	
	13	6	7	35.5	248.5	1,491.0	1,917.0
				Total		24,824.0	24,824.0

Remember that this is a provisional calculation, which will have to be adjusted when areas requiring different shelf spacing have been identified, for example, to accommodate oversized monographs, bound periodical volumes, or scores.

PLANNING COLLECTION MERGERS

Chapter 2 describes a model for integrating information on the linear extent of existing collections and the anticipated linear extent of collection growth, and Figure 2.1, repeated here as Figure 3.6 (p. 72), shows how to calculate this information in a spreadsheet.

In preparing the collection layout plan, it's important to consider not only the total linear measurement of the existing collections, but also where they are being moved from. If several collections are being merged, you will need to calculate how many inches of material from each collection will be placed on the shelves in each area.

To do this, you'll first need measurements of each segment of the collection in each location, and the total for the merged collection. The spreadsheet in Figure 3.7 (p. 73) illustrates these calculations for an academic library merging collections from a main building and four subject branches. Figure 3.8 (p. 74) illustrates these calculations for a public library merging adult fiction shelved by genre from a main library and two branches.

Because materials are usually moved from each old location in sequence, the fill ratio, or amount of material on each shelf, after the addition of each successive collection must be calculated and documented. Figures 3.9A and B (pp. 75–76) and 3.10 (p. 77) show these calculations for the two mergers shown in Figures 3.7 and 3.8.

The merger of periodical backfiles poses special problems. First, if duplicate holdings exist, the library will have to decide whether to place all copies in the same stack area, put one or more copies in a storage area, or discard the duplicates. Because growth occurs after the most recently bound volume and not within the run (unless missing volumes are being replaced), merging backfiles from several locations requires creation of a master list of the titles, arranged in the planned shelving order, showing the collection from which they are being moved, with the start and stop points keyed to specific shelving locations, and with allowance made for growth space.

Figures 3.11 through 3.14 show the development of this type of list. Figure 3.11 (p. 78) shows a listing of titles at each location. Note the overlap in holdings for Title C (both the Main Library and Branch A receive copies) and Title J (Main Library and Branch B). Also note that Title F has ceased publication, thus requiring no growth space, and that Title G is a new publication, requiring no space for backfiles. Figure 3.12 (p. 78) shows a merged list, with notes indicating that the library intends to cancel the duplicate subscriptions to Titles C and J and interfile each title's backfiles. Figure 3.13 (p. 79) calculates the inches of shelf space needed for each title, and Figure 3.14 (pp. 81–82) translates the number of inches of shelf space needed into the number of shelves needed and a starting point for each title.

Figure 3.6
Calculating Linear Footage for Current Collections and Growth

Material Type	Current number items	Est'd or actual?	Est'd net annual growth (items)	15 Years' Growth (# items) (15 x c)	Planned total (# items) (a + d)	Linear inches per item (from appendix)	Total linear inches needed (e x f)	Shelves used per SF section shelving	Maximum working capacity this type material (percent)	Maximum working capacity per SF this type material (inches) (h x i x 35.5)	Number SF sections needed (g /j)	Rounded number SF sections needed
	(a)	(b)	(c)	(d)	(e)	(f)	(g)	(h)	(i)	(j)	(k)	(l)
Reference												
Books	554	est.	15	225	779	1.61	1,254	6	86%	183	6.9	7.0
Abstracts & indexes	1,011	est.	70	1,050	2,061	1.87	3,854	6	86%	183	21.1	22.0
Monographs												
LC	310,108	est.	11,480	172,200	482,308	0.98	472,662	7	86%	213	2,219.1	2,220.0
LC Oversize	2,131	actual	0	0	2,131	1.04	2,216	5	86%	152	14.6	15.0
Dewey	3,211	mix	0	0	3,211	0.98	3,147	7	86%	213	14.8	15.0
Dewey oversize	164	actual	0	0	164	1.04	171	5	86%	152	1.1	2.0
Bound Periodicals												
LC	103,611	est.	1,160	17,400	121,011	1.77	214,189	6	86%	183	1,173.2	1,174.0
Dewey	756	actual	0	0	756	1.77	1,338	6	86%	183	7.3	8.0
Recordings												
33 rpm discs	5,713	est.	0	0	5,713	0.30	1,725	6	95%	202	8.5	9.0
Audio cassettes	233	actual	0	0	233	0.93	218	10	95%	337	0.6	1.0
Compact discs	1,951	actual	500	7,500	9,451	0.59	5,590	11	95%	371	15.1	16.0
Video cassettes	86	actual	25	375	461	1.15	528	10	95%	337	1.6	2.0
DVD's	0	actual	10	150	150	0.30	45	6	95%	202	0.2	1.0
Total	429,529		13,260	198,900	628,429		706,938				3,484.1	3,492.0

Figure 3.7 Merging Collections of an Academic Main Library and Four Branch Libraries

LC class	Main Current number items (a)	Main Est'd annual growth (items) (b)	BRANCH A Current number items (c)	BRANCH A Est'd annual growth (items) (d)	BRANCH B Current number items (e)	BRANCH B Est'd annual growth (items) (f)	BRANCH C Current number items (g)	BRANCH C Est'd annual growth (items) (h)	BRANCH D Current number items (i)	BRANCH D Est'd annual growth (items) (j)	Total current items (a+c+e+g+i) (k)	Total annual growth items (b+d+f+h+j) (l)	Ten years' growth (items) (l x 10) (m)	Total Items (k + m) (n)	Linear inches per item (o)	Total linear inches (n x o)
A	5,000	150									5,000	150	1,500	6,500	0.98	6,370.0
B	7,000	225									7,000	225	2,250	9,250	1.03	9,527.5
C-G	10,000	500									10,000	500	5,000	15,000	1.02	15,300.0
H-HJ	6,000	350									6,000	350	3,500	9,500	0.97	9,215.0
HM-HX	5,000	100			10,000						15,000	600	6,000	21,000	0.97	20,370.0
J	6,600	270									6,600	270	2,700	9,300	0.99	9,207.0
K	1,500	55									1,500	55	550	2,050	1.10	2,255.0
L	1,000	10			17,500	500					18,500	510	5,100	23,600	0.82	19,352.0
M	15,000	325			100	10					15,100	335	3,350	18,450	1.11	20,479.5
N	3,000	70	25,000	1,000	100	10					28,100	1,080	10,800	38,900	0.98	38,122.0
P-PM	14,000	200									14,000	200	2,000	16,000	0.95	15,200.0
PN-PZ	55,000	775			2,000	75					57,000	850	8,500	65,500	0.99	64,845.0
Q-QA10.3, 101-939	4,000	350					100	10			4,100	360	3,600	7,700	0.92	7,084.0
QA75.5-76.95	1,000	150					3,500	350			4,500	500	5,000	9,500	1.00	9,500.0
QB-QC	6,000	175									6,000	175	1,750	7,750	1.06	8,215.0
QD	10,000	300							3,000	100	13,000	400	4,000	17,000	0.96	16,320.0
QE-QR	20,000	275									20,000	275	2,750	22,750	1.05	23,887.5
R	8,000	200									8,000	200	2,000	10,000	0.97	9,700.0
S	1,400	125									1,400	125	1,250	2,650	0.96	2,544.0
T	27,000	500	250	10			350	15			27,600	525	5,250	32,850	1.02	33,507.0
U-V	1,000	15									1,000	15	150	1,150	0.92	1,058.0
Z	1,400	45									1,400	45	450	1,850	0.89	1,646.5
TOTAL	208,900	5,165	25,250	1,010	29,700	1,095	3,950	375	3,000	100	270,800	7,745	77,450	348,250		343,705.0

Figure 3.8 Merging Adult Fiction Collections of a Public Library plus Two Branches

	MAIN LIBRARY		BRANCH A		BRANCH B		Total number current items (a + c + e)	Total annual growth (items) (b + d + f)	Ten years' growth (items) (h x 10)	Planned total (items) (g + i)	Linear inches per item	Total linear inches (j x k)
	Current number items	Est'd annual growth (items)	Current number items	Est'd annual growth (items)	Current number items	Est'd annual growth (items)						
	(a)	(b)	(c)	(d)	(e)	(f)	(g)	(h)	(i)	(j)	(k)	
Adult Fiction												
General	15,000	375	2,000	75	3,500	100	20,500	550	5,500	26,000	0.98	25,480.0
Mysteries	750	75	300	20	350	30	1,400	125	1,250	2,650	0.98	2,597.0
Science Fiction	200	20	0	0	100	10	300	30	300	600	0.98	588.0
Westerns	150	10	0	0	0	0	150	10	100	250	0.98	245.0
Romance	400	50	250	30	300	25	950	105	1,050	2,000	0.98	1,960.0
Total	16,500	530	2,550	125	4,250	165	23,300	820	8,200	31,500		30,870

Figure 3.9A Calculating Successive Fill Ratios for Collection Merger of the Academic Library and Four Branch Libraries Illustrated in Figure 3.7

LC class	Current number of items — Main Library (a)	Branch A (b)	Branch B (c)	Branch C (d)	Branch D (e)	Total current items (a+b+c +d+e) (f)	Planned total items (from Fig. 3.7) (g)	Linear inches per item (h)	Total linear inches (g x h) (h)	Shelves used per SF section shelving (i)	Maximum working capacity this type material (percent) (k)	Maximum working capacity per SF this type material (inches) (j x k x 35.5) (l)	Number SF sections needed (m) (h / l)	Rounded number SF sections shelving needed (n)
A	5,000					5,000	6,500	0.98	6,370.0	7	86%	213.7	29.8	30
B	7,000					7,000	9,250	1.03	9,527.5	7	86%	213.7	44.6	45
C-G	10,000					10,000	15,000	1.02	15,300.0	7	86%	213.7	71.6	72
H-HJ	6,000					6,000	9,500	0.97	9,215.0	7	86%	213.7	43.1	44
HM-HX	5,000	10,000				15,000	21,000	0.97	20,370.0	7	86%	213.7	95.3	96
J	6,600		10,000			16,600	9,300	0.99	9,207.0	7	86%	213.7	43.1	44
K	1,500					1,500	2,050	1.10	2,255.0	7	86%	213.7	10.6	11
L	1,000		17,500			18,500	23,600	0.82	19,352.0	7	86%	213.7	90.6	91
M	15,000		100			15,100	18,450	1.11	20,479.5	6	86%	183.2	111.8	112
N	3,000	25,000	100			28,100	38,900	0.98	38,122.0	6	86%	183.2	208.1	209
P-PM	14,000					14,000	16,000	0.95	15,200.0	7	86%	213.7	71.1	72
PN-PZ	55,000		2,000			57,000	65,500	0.99	64,845.0	7	86%	213.7	303.4	304
Q-QA10.3, 101-939	4,000			100		4,100	7,700	0.92	7,084.0	7	86%	213.7	33.1	34
QA75.5-76.95	1,000			3,500		4,500	9,500	1.00	9,500.0	7	86%	213.7	44.5	45
QB-QC	6,000					6,000	7,750	1.06	8,215.0	7	86%	213.7	38.4	39
QD	10,000				3,000	13,000	17,000	0.96	16,320.0	7	86%	213.7	76.4	77
QE-QR	20,000					20,000	22,750	1.05	23,887.5	7	86%	213.7	111.8	112
R	8,000					8,000	10,000	0.97	9,700.0	7	86%	213.7	45.4	46
S	1,400					1,400	2,650	0.96	2,544.0	7	86%	213.7	11.9	12
T	27,000	250		350		27,600	32,850	1.02	33,507.0	7	86%	213.7	156.8	157
U-V	1,000					1,000	1,150	0.92	1,058.0	7	86%	213.7	5.0	5
Z	1,400					1,400	1,850	0.89	1,646.5	7	86%	213.7	7.7	8
Total	208,900	25,250	29,700	3,950	3,000	270,800	348,250		343,705.0				1,654.0	1,665

75

Figure 3.9B

LC Class	Inches Shelving Available (n x j x 35.5) (o)	Eventual Fill Ratio Merged Collections (h /o) (p)	Inches Filled Per Shelf (p x 35.5) (q)	Opening Day Fill Ratio Merged Collections ((f x h)/o) (r)	Inches Filled Per Shelf (r x 35.5) (s)	Main Library Initial Fill Ratio (a x b)/o (t)	Inches Filled Per Shelf (t x 35.5) (u)	Main + Branch A Initial Fill Ratio ((a+b)xh)/o (v)	Inches Filled Per Shelf (v x 35.5) (w)	Main + Branches A,B Initial Fill Ratio ((a+b+c) x h) / o (x)	Inches Filled Per Shelf (x x 35.5) (y)	Main + Branches A,B,C Initial Fill Ratio (((a+b+c+d) x h) / o (z)	Inches Filled Per Shelf (z x 35.5) (aa)
A	7,455.0	85.4%	30.3	65.7%	23.3	65.7%	23.3	65.7%	23.3	65.7%	23.3	66%	23.3
B	11,182.5	85.2%	30.2	64.5%	22.9	64.5%	22.9	64.5%	22.9	64.5%	22.9	64%	22.9
C-G	17,892.0	85.5%	30.4	57.0%	20.2	57.0%	20.2	57.0%	20.2	57.0%	20.2	57%	20.2
H-HJ	10,934.0	84.3%	29.9	53.2%	18.9	53.2%	18.9	53.2%	18.9	53.2%	18.9	53%	18.9
HM-HX	23,856.0	85.4%	30.3	61.0%	21.7	20.3%	7.2	20.3%	7.2	61.0%	21.7	61%	21.7
J	10,934.0	84.2%	29.9	59.8%	21.2	59.8%	21.2	59.8%	21.2	59.8%	21.2	60%	21.2
K	2,733.5	82.5%	29.3	60.4%	21.4	60.4%	21.4	60.4%	21.4	60.4%	21.4	60%	21.4
L	22,613.5	85.6%	30.4	67.1%	23.8	3.6%	1.3	3.6%	1.3	67.1%	23.8	67%	23.8
M	23,856.0	85.8%	30.5	70.3%	24.9	69.8%	24.8	69.8%	24.8	70.3%	24.9	70%	24.9
N	44,517.0	85.6%	30.4	61.9%	22.0	6.6%	2.3	61.6%	21.9	61.9%	22.0	62%	22.0
P-PM	17,892.0	85.0%	30.2	74.3%	26.4	74.3%	26.4	74.3%	26.4	74.3%	26.4	74%	26.4
PN-PZ	75,544.0	85.8%	30.5	74.7%	26.5	72.1%	25.6	72.1%	25.6	74.7%	26.5	75%	26.5
Q-QA10.3, 101-939	8,449.0	83.8%	29.8	44.6%	15.8	43.6%	15.5	43.6%	15.5	43.6%	15.5	45%	15.8
QA75.5-76.95	11,182.5	85.0%	30.2	40.2%	14.3	8.9%	3.2	8.9%	3.2	8.9%	3.2	40%	14.3
QB-QC	9,691.5	84.8%	30.1	65.6%	23.3	65.6%	23.3	65.6%	23.3	65.6%	23.3	66%	23.3
QD	19,134.5	85.3%	30.3	65.2%	23.2	50.2%	17.8	50.2%	17.8	50.2%	17.8	50%	17.8
QE-QR	27,832.0	85.8%	30.5	75.5%	26.8	75.5%	26.8	75.5%	26.8	75.5%	26.8	75%	26.8
R	11,431.0	84.9%	30.1	67.9%	24.1	67.9%	24.1	67.9%	24.1	67.9%	24.1	68%	24.1
S	2,982.0	85.3%	30.3	45.1%	16.0	45.1%	16.0	45.1%	16.0	45.1%	16.0	45%	16.0
T	39,014.5	85.9%	30.5	72.2%	25.6	70.6%	25.1	71.2%	25.3	71.2%	25.3	72%	25.6
U-V	1,242.5	85.2%	30.2	74.0%	26.3	74.0%	26.3	74.0%	26.3	74.0%	26.3	74%	26.3
Z	1,988.0	82.8%	29.4	62.7%	22.3	62.7%	22.3	62.7%	22.3	62.7%	22.3	63%	22.3
TOTAL	402,357.0	85.4%	29.4	62.7%	22.3	62.7%	22.3	62.7%	22.3	62.7%	22.3	63%	22.3

76

Figures 3.10. Calculating Successive Fill Ratios for Merger of the Public Library's Adult Fiction Collections Illustrated in Figure 3.8

| | Current number of items | | | Total current items | Planned total items (from | Linear inches | Linear inches | Shelves used per SF section | Maximum SF working capacity | Maximum working capacity per SF (inches) | SF sections needed |
| | Main Library | Branch A | Branch B | (a + b + c) | Fig. 3.8) | per item | (e x f) | shelving | (percent) | (h x i x 35.5) | (g / j) |
	(a)	(b)	(c)	(d)	(e)	(f)	(g)	(h)	(i)	(j)	(k)
Adult Fiction											
General	15,000	2,000	3,500	20,500	26,000	0.98	25,480.0	7	86%	213.7	119.2
Mysteries	750	300	350	1,400	2,650	0.98	2,597.0	7	86%	213.7	12.2
Science Fiction	200		100	300	600	0.98	588.0	7	86%	213.7	2.8
Westerns	150			150	250	0.98	245.0	7	86%	213.7	1.1
Romance	400	250	300	950	2,000	0.98	1,960.0	7	86%	213.7	9.2
Total	16,500	2,550	4,250	23,300	31,500		30,870				144.4

			Merged Collections							
			- - Eventual - -		- - - Opening Day - - -		Main Library		Main + Branch A	
	Rounded SF sections needed	Inches available	Fill ratio	Inches filled per shelf	Fill ratio:	Inches filled per shelf	Initial fill ratio:	Inches filled per shelf	Initial fill ratio:	Inches filled per shelf
		(l x h x 35.5)	(g /m)	(n x 35.5)	((d x f) / m)	(p x 35.5)	((a x f) / m)	(r x 35.5)	(((a + b) x f) /m)	(t x 35.5)
	(l)	(m)	(n)	(o)	(p)	(q)	(r)	(s)	(t)	
Adult Fiction										
General	120	29,820	85%	30.3	67%	23.9	49%	17.5	56%	19.8
Mysteries	13	3,231	80%	28.5	42%	15.1	23%	8.1	32%	11.3
Science Fiction	3	746	79%	28.0	39%	14.0	26%	9.3	26%	9.3
Westerns	2	497	49%	17.5	30%	10.5	30%	10.5	30%	10.5
Romance	10	2,485	79%	28.0	37%	13.3	16%	5.6	26%	9.1
Total	148	36,778								

Figure 3.11
Merging Periodicals from a Main Library and Two Branches for a Collection Shelved Alphabetically by Title: Listing of Titles for Each Original Location

	Current number of volumes	Total linear inches	Anticipated annual growth (volumes)	Linear inches per volume
Main Library periodicals:				
Title A	30	30.0	1	1.00
Title B	20	50.0	4	2.50
Title C	67	100.5	2	1.50
Title G	0	0.0	2	1.75
TItle H	50	50.0	1	1.00
Title J	66	82.5	3	1.25
Title M	24	36.0	2	1.50
Title N	42	52.5	2	1.25
Branch A periodicals:				
Title C copy 2	67	100.5	2	1.50
Title D	31	31.0	2	1.00
Title E	36	45.0	4	1.25
Title F	40	60.0	0	1.50
Branch B periodicals:				
Title I	28	35.0	2	1.25
Title J copy 2	66	82.5	3	1.25
Title K	32	48.0	2	1.50
Title L	32	24.0	4	0.75

Figure 3.12
Merging Periodicals from a Main Library and Two Branches for a Collection Shelved Alphabetically by Title: Merged List with Notes

	Current number of volumes	Total linear inches	Anticipated annual growth (volumes)	Linear inches per volume	Notes
Title A	30	30.0	1	1.00	
Title B	20	50.0	4	2.50	
Title C	67	100.5	2	1.50	
Title C copy 2	67	100.5	0	1.50	Interfile backfiles; cancel copy 2
Title D	31	31.0	2	1.00	
Title E	36	45.0	4	1.25	
Title F	40	60.0	0 -		Title has ceased publication
Title G	0	0.0	2	1.75	New title; no backfile
TItle H	50	50.0	1	1.00	
Title I	28	35.0	2	1.25	
Title J	66	82.5	3	1.25	
Title J copy 2	66	82.5	0	1.25	Interfile backfiles; cancel copy 2
Title K	32	48.0	2	1.50	
Title L	32	24.0	4	0.75	
Title M	24	36.0	2	1.50	
Title N	42	52.5	2	1.25	

Figure 3.13
Merging Periodicals from a Main Library and Two Branches for a Collection Shelved Alphabetically by Title:
Calculating Inches Required for Each Title

	Current number of volumes	Total linear inches	Annual growth (volumes)	Linear inches per volume	Planning horizon (years)	Total growth (volumes) (c x e)	Total growth (inches) (d x f)	Total inches needed (b + g)
	(a)	(b)	(c)	(d)	(e)	(f)	(g)	
Title A	30	30.0	1	1.00	10	10	10.0	40.0
Title B	20	50.0	4	2.50	10	40	100.0	150.0
Title C	67	100.5	2	1.50	10	20	30.0	231.0
Title C cop	67	100.5	0	1.50	10	0	0.0	
Title D	31	31.0	2	1.00	10	20	20.0	51.0
Title E	36	45.0	4	1.25	10	40	50.0	95.0
Title F	40	60.0	0	1.50	10	0	0.0	60.0
Title G	0	0.0	2	1.75	10	20	35.0	35.0
TItle H	50	50.0	1	1.00	10	10	10.0	60.0
Title I	28	35.0	2	1.25	10	20	25.0	60.0
Title J	66	82.5	3	1.25	10	30	37.5	202.5
Title J cop;	66	82.5	0	1.25	10	0	0.0	
Title K	32	48.0	2	1.50	10	20	30.0	78.0
Title L	32	24.0	4	0.75	10	40	30.0	54.0
Title M	24	36.0	2	1.50	10	20	30.0	66.0
Title N	42	52.5	2	1.25	10	20	25.0	77.5
								1,260.0

Changing to a different collection layout model also poses similar challenges. Integrating all or a larger portion of oversized material means taking into account an increase in shelf spacing and planning linear space for the two previously separate collections in an integrated sequence, as would integrating various AV formats with print materials.

PREPARING THE COLLECTION LAYOUT

The final step in preparing a collection layout plan is to map onto the stack layout the direction in which the collection ribbon will be shelved, the specific locations where significant segments of the collections will start and stop, the fill ratios to be used in each segment, and the locations of any growth joints.

Analyzing Collection Ribbon Options

Before settling on the direction in which the collection ribbon will flow, it may be helpful to consider the advantages and disadvantages of several options. Figures 3.15A through 3.15C (pp. 83–85) show three possibilities for the stack layout shown in Figure 3.1.

Option A provides the user a fairly logical layout. Where the collection ribbon progresses from one stack block to the next, the start of the next installment of the collection ribbon is visible, with one exception. This exception occurs when the collection transitions from Block D, row 16 (refer to Figure 3.1 for block and row labels) to Block H, row 8. This may be somewhat counterintuitive for the user, and would probably require signage.

Option B corrects this problem by starting the collection ribbon at the opposite end of the shelving area. Because of the placement of seating and HVAC ducts relative to the stacks, this layout also has some awkward transitions getting into and out of Block B. Users could also be confused by the proximity of the beginning and end of the ribbon. However, crossing the major aisle is accomplished in a way that will be more obvious to the user.

Both Options A and B assume that the collection ribbon will be arranged to cross the major stack aisle as little as possible. Option C tests the opposite approach and shows why it should be avoided for the stack layout shown. Although this approach works well for the first three ranges, after that the intrusion of seating and the HVAC duct complicate the collection ribbon considerably. Not only would this layout require considerable signage for users to find their way through the stacks, but the traffic patterns of browsers would be awkward and could potentially congest some areas of the stacks. (This may be somewhat overstating what would actually happen; however, consider the potential for awkward collisions between users if this were an area where high-user collections were shelved and users typically browsed the collections, concentrating on the materials rather than on their surroundings. Perhaps not the most likely scenario, but easily avoidable with a smoother layout of the collection ribbon!)

Figure 3.14 A
Merging Periodicals from a Main Library and Two Branches for a Collection Shelved Alphabetically by Title:
Calculating Starting Point for Shelving Each Title

	Total current collection (inches)	Total growth (inches)	Total inches needed (a + b)	Number of shelves (c / q)	Starting point (running shelf number) (note 1)	Ending point (running shelf number) (e + d)	Starting point this title			Ending point this title		
							Section number (note 2)	Shelf number (note 2)	Inches right (note 2)	Section number (note 3)	Shelf number (note 3)	Inches right (note 3)
	(a)	(b)	(c)	(d)	(e)	(f)	(g)	(h)	(i)	(j)	(k)	(l)
Title A	30.0	10.0	40.0	1.3	0.0	1.3	1	0	0	1	2	10
Title B	50.0	100.0	150.0	5.0	1.3	6.3	1	2	10	2	1	10
Title C	100.5	30.0	231.0	7.7	6.3	14.0	2	1	10	3	3	1
Title C copy 2	100.5	0.0										
Title D	31.0	20.0	51.0	1.7	14.0	15.7	3	3	1	3	4	22
Title E	45.0	50.0	95.0	3.2	15.7	18.9	3	4	22	4	0	27
Title F	60.0	0.0	60.0	2.0	18.9	20.9	4	0	27	4	3	27
Title G	0.0	35.0	35.0	1.2	20.9	22.1	4	3	27	4	5	2
Title H	50.0	10.0	60.0	2.0	22.1	24.1	4	5	2	5	1	2
Title I	35.0	25.0	60.0	2.0	24.1	26.1	5	1	2	5	3	2
Title J	82.5	37.5	202.5	6.8	26.1	32.8	5	3	2	6	3	24.5
Title J copy 2	82.5	0.0										
Title K	48.0	30.0	78.0	2.6	32.8	35.4	6	3	24.5	6	6	12.5
Title L	24.0	30.0	54.0	1.8	35.4	37.2	6	6	12.5	7	2	6.5
Title M	36.0	30.0	66.0	2.2	37.2	39.4	7	2	6.5	7	4	12.5
Title N	52.5	25.0	77.5	2.6	39.4	42.0	7	4	12.5	7	7	0
	827.5	432.5	1,260.0									

Figure 3.14 B

Sections of shelving needed:

M   6 shelves/SF section x 35.5"/shelf x 90% maximum wo   191.7 usable inches per SF section

N   1260.0 inches shelf space required / 191.7 usable inche   6.6 SF sections needed

O   7 SF sections, rounded x 6 shelves/SF section x 35.5"/:   1491 total inches of shelving

P   1260.0 inches shelf space required/1491 total inches sh   85% fill ratio at end of year 10

Q   85% fill ratio at end of year 10 x 35.5"/shelf =   30.0 inches used per shelf

Note 1:   For Title A: 0 + D
For subsequent titles: F (previous title)

Note 2:   Assume shelving is set up with 6 shelves/section.
Then, divide E by 6 to obtain the section number.
Round up the remainder to the next whole number to obtain the shelf number.
Subtract the unrounded whole number portion of the remainder from the remainder and multiply by Q
to obtain the inches to the right of the shelf where the run should begin.

Note 3:   Same steps as Note 2, but using F in place of E:
Assume shelving is set up with 6 shelves/section.
Then, divide F by 6 to obtain the section number.
Round up the remainder to the next whole number to obtain the shelf number.
Subtract the unrounded whole number portion of the remainder from the remainder and multiply by Q
to obtain the inches to the right of the shelf where the run should end.

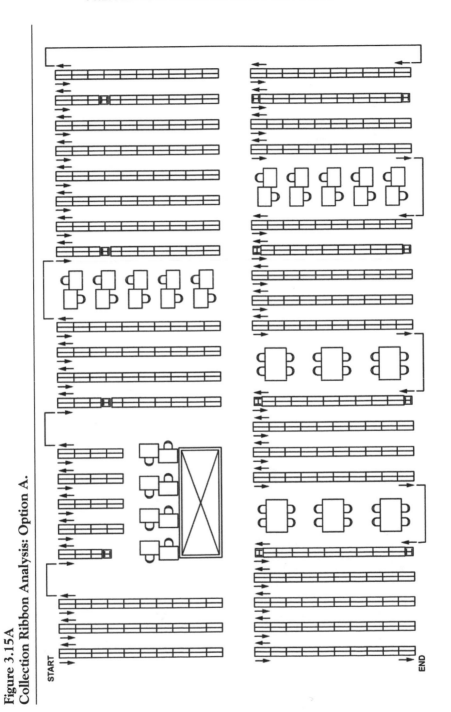

Figure 3.15A
Collection Ribbon Analysis: Option A.

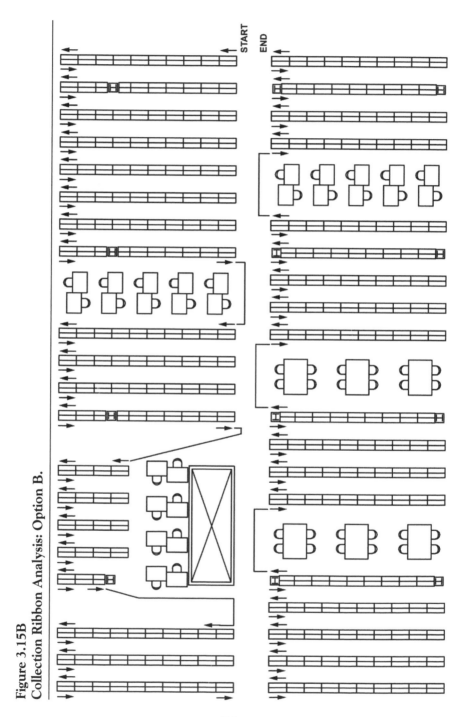

Figure 3.15B
Collection Ribbon Analysis: Option B.

84

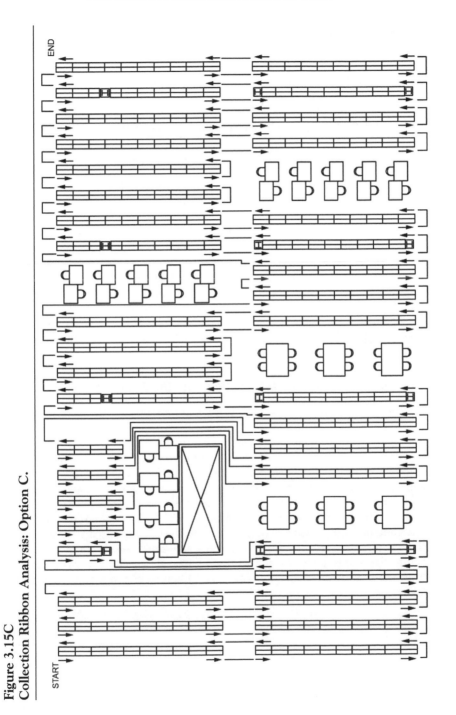

Figure 3.15C
Collection Ribbon Analysis: Option C.

Selection of Option A or Option B might also depend on where users entered the stack area. If the entrance were at the top left of the figures, Option A's placement of the start of the collection ribbon would be within sight of the entrance. Option B might be preferred if the entrance were on the far right of the figure, or if the library placed a premium on the ease of transition across the major stack aisle. For another, very good discussion of factors to consider in planning a collection layout, see Judith Compton Ellis (1988, 285–87).

Calculating Shelving Requirements for Collection Segments

Calculating the stack capacity of each row of a shelving area and the number of sections of shelving required for each significant collection segment can make the process of mapping the collection onto a layout plan faster and easier. The spreadsheet shown in Figure 3.16 illustrates calculation of the SF capacity of each row configuration, and Figure 3.17 (p. 88) illustrates the calculation of growth joints and SF capacity for each significant collection segment of the merging academic collections previously illustrated in Figures 3.7 and 3.9. Note that both the sections allocated to specific collection segments and to growth joints are rounded. Sections allocated to collections are rounded up, on the assumption that the library will not want to compress collections into fewer sections of shelving than calculated by using a higher than calculated fill ratio; sections allocated to growth joints are rounded down.

Mapping Collection Information onto the Stack Plan

With a detailed list of how many sections of shelving each collection segment needs, it is now a relatively straightforward matter to transfer this information onto the stack plan. Figure 3.18 (p. 89) shows a stack plan annotated to show the start and stop points for collection segments and growth joints, and Figure 3.19 (p. 90), which would be attached to Figure 3.18, shows the corresponding notes on type of material, shelving setup, and successive fill ratios.

Note that the allocation of SF sections shown in Figure 3.18 was adjusted slightly from those calculated in Figure 3.17 to accommodate the area's intermittent 24-inch-wide sections, so that each collection segment will begin at the top of a new section of shelving. This adjustment results in more shelving being allocated to collections, with the additional capacity needed being taken from the growth joints. Figure 3.20 (p. 91) compares the planned and actual allocations.

Figure 3.16
Calculating Stack Capacity for Figure 3.1

Block	Number of rows with this configuration (a)	SF per row (b)	Shelves per SF (c)	Nominal width per shelf (d)	Actual width per shelf (e)	Linear inches capacity this block (a x b x c x e) (f)	Equivalent capacity in nominal 36" wide SF sections (f / (7 x 35.5)) (g)	Block's total equivalent capacity (h)	Equivalent capacity this line (b x c x e) / (7 x 35.5) (i)	Equivalent capacity this row configuration (i)
A	6	10	7	36	35.5	14,910	60.0	60.0	10.0	10.0
B	2	2	7	36	35.5	994	4.0		2.0	
	2	1	7	24	23.5	329	1.3	37.3	0.7	2.7
	8	4	7	36	35.5	7,952	32.0		4.0	4.0
C	2	8	7	36	35.5	3,976	16.0		8.0	
	2	2	7	24	23.5	658	2.6	78.6	1.3	9.3
	6	10	7	36	35.5	14,910	60.0		10.0	10.0
D	4	8	7	36	35.5	7,952	32.0		8.0	
	4	2	7	24	23.5	1,316	5.3	157.3	1.3	9.3
	12	10	7	36	35.5	29,820	120.0		10.0	10.0
E	2	1	7	24	23.5	329	1.3		0.7	
	2	8	7	36	35.5	3,976	16.0	97.3	8.0	8.7
	8	10	7	36	35.5	19,880	80.0		10.0	10.0
F	2	1	7	24	23.5	329	1.3		0.7	
	2	8	7	36	35.5	3,976	16.0	77.3	8.0	8.7
	6	10	7	36	35.5	14,910	60.0		10.0	10.0
G	2	1	7	24	23.5	329	1.3		0.7	
	2	8	7	36	35.5	3,976	16.0	97.3	8.0	8.7
	8	10	7	36	35.5	19,880	80.0		10.0	10.0
H	2	1	7	24	23.5	329	1.3		0.7	
	2	8	7	36	35.5	3,976	16.0	77.3	8.0	8.7
	6	10	7	36	35.5	14,910	60.0		10.0	10.0
						169,617	682.6	682.6		

87

Figure 3.17 Calculating Rounded Sections Needed for Collection Segments and Growth Joints for Layout of Q–Z Monographs in Move and Merger of Academic Main Library and Four Branch Libraries

LC class	Current items Main Library (a)	Branch A (b)	Branch B (c)	Branch C (d)	Branch D (e)	Current items (a+b+c +d+e) (f)	Planned total (from Fig. 3.7) (g)	Linear inches per item (h)	Total linear inches (g x h) (i)	Number 36" SF sections needed (from Fig. 3.9) (j)	Rounded 36" SF number sections needed (k)	Cumulative total, SF sections (l)	Growth (inches) ((g - f) x h) (m)	Percent of growth (m / 25,928) (n)	Raw growth joint allocation (36" SF) (n x 147) (o)	Rounded growth joint allocation (36" SF) (p)
Q-QA10.3, 101-939	4,000			100		4,100	7,700	0.92	7,084.0	33.1	34	34	3,312	12.8%	18.8	19.0
QA75.5-76.95	1,000			3,500		4,500	9,500	1.00	9,500.0	44.5	45	79	5,000	19.3%	28.3	28.0
QB-QC	6,000					6,000	7,750	1.06	8,215.0	38.4	39	118	1,855	7.2%	10.5	11.0
QD	10,000				3,000	13,000	17,000	0.96	16,320.0	76.4	77	195	3,840	14.8%	21.8	22.0
QE-QR	20,000					20,000	22,750	1.05	23,887.5	111.8	112	307	2,888	11.1%	16.4	16.0
R	8,000					8,000	10,000	0.97	9,700.0	45.4	46	353	1,940	7.5%	11.0	11.0
S	1,400					1,400	2,650	0.96	2,544.0	11.9	12	365	1,200	4.6%	6.8	7.0
T	27,000	250		350		27,600	32,850	1.02	33,507.0	156.8	157	522	5,355	20.7%	30.4	30.0
U-V	1,000					1,000	1,150	0.92	1,058.0	5.0	5	527	138	0.5%	0.8	1.0
Z	1,400					1,400	1,850	0.89	1,646.5	7.7	8	535	401	1.5%	2.3	2.0
Total	79,800	250	0	3,950	3,000	87,000	113,200		113,462	531	535		25,928	100.0%	147.0	147.0

Total SF sections available for growth joint allocation:

Total capacity of shelving area =	682.6 SF equivalents of 36" nominal sections (from Figure 3.16)
- Total capacity required =	535 SF equivalents of 36" nominal sections (total of column (k), above)
Available for growth joints =	147.6 SF equivalents of 36" nominal sections

Adjusted, 147.6 SF becomes 147 SF sections.

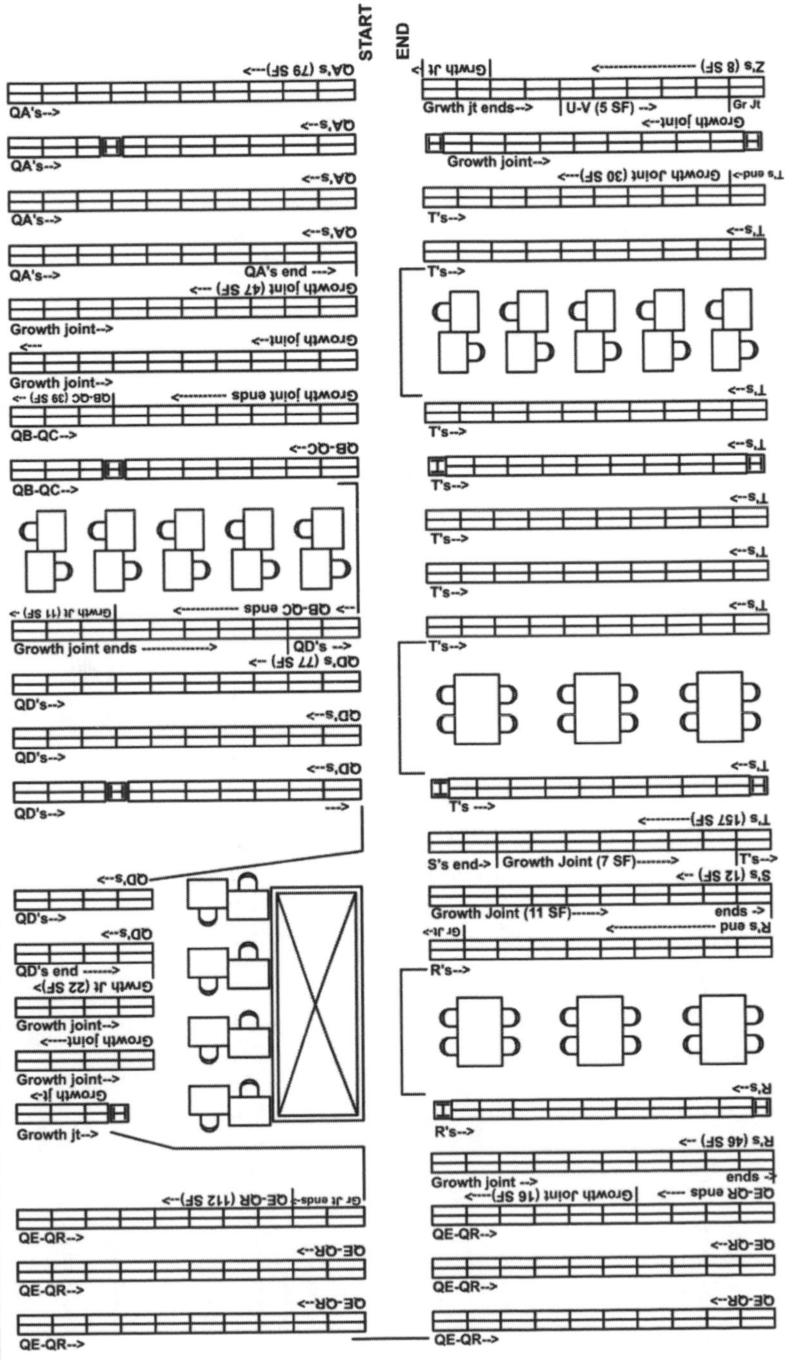

Figure 3.18 Layout of Q–Z Monograph Collection Illustrated in Figures 3.7 and 3.9, Using Collection Ribbon illustrated in Figure 3.15B and Growth Joints Calculated in Figure 3.17

Figure 3.19
Attachment to Collection Layout Plan Shown in Figure 3.18

Collection segment	Type of material	Rounded number of 36" SF (Fig 3.17:k, p)	Set up: use x shelves per section	Inches filled per 36" Shelf: Main Library collections (Fig. 3.9: u)	Inches filled per 36" Shelf: Main Library plus Branch A collections (Fig. 3.9: w)	Inches filled per 36" Shelf: Main Library plus Branch A & B collections (Fig. 3.9: y)	Inches filled per 36" Shelf: Main Library plus Branch A, B & C collections (Fig. 3.9: aa)
Q-QA 10.3, 101-939	monographs	34	7	15.5	15.5	15.5	15.8
QA 75.5-76.95	monographs	45	7	3.2	3.2	3.2	14.3
Growth joint	*monographs*	*47*	*7*	*leave empty*	*leave empty*	*leave empty*	23.3
QB-QC	monographs	39	7	23.3	23.3	23.3	*leave empty*
Growth joint	*monographs*	*11*	*7*	*leave empty*	*leave empty*	*leave empty*	17.8
QD	monographs	77	7	17.8	17.8	17.8	*leave empty*
Growth joint	*monographs*	*22*	*7*	*leave empty*	*leave empty*	*leave empty*	26.8
QE-QR	monographs	112	7	26.8	26.8	26.8	*leave empty*
Growth joint	*monographs*	*16*	*7*	*leave empty*	*leave empty*	*leave empty*	24.1
R	monographs	46	7	24.1	24.1	24.1	*leave empty*
Growth joint	*monographs*	*11*	*7*	*leave empty*	*leave empty*	*leave empty*	16.0
S	monographs	12	7	16.0	16.0	16.0	*leave empty*
Growth joint	*monographs*	*7*	*7*	*leave empty*	*leave empty*	*leave empty*	25.6
T	monographs	157	7	25.1	25.3	25.3	*leave empty*
Growth joint	*monographs*	*30*	*7*	*leave empty*	*leave empty*	*leave empty*	26.3
U-V	monographs	5	7	26.3	26.3	26.3	*leave empty*
Growth joint	*monographs*	*1*	*7*	*leave empty*	*leave empty*	*leave empty*	22.3
Z	monographs	8	7	22.3	22.3	22.3	*leave empty*
Growth joint	*monographs*	*2*	*7*	*leave empty*	*leave empty*	*leave empty*	*leave empty*

Figure 3.20
Comparison of Calculated and Actual SF Allocations for Collections and Growth Joints in Figure 3.18

	Planned SF sections			Actual SF sections		
		Growth			Growth	
LC class	Collections	joint	Total	Collections	joint	Total
QA	79.00	47.00	126.00	78.67	47.00	125.67
QB-QC	39.00	11.00	50.00	38.67	11.00	49.67
QD	77.00	22.00	99.00	76.67	23.33	100.00
QE-QR	112.00	16.00	128.00	112.00	16.00	128.00
R	46.00	11.00	57.00	46.33	11.00	57.33
S	12.00	7.00	19.00	12.00	7.00	19.00
T	157.00	30.00	187.00	156.67	30.33	187.00
U-V	5.00	1.00	6.00	5.00	1.00	6.00
Z	8.00	2.00	10.00	8.00	2.00	10.00
	535.00	147.00	682.00	534.00	148.67	682.66

If the library wished, the layout could have been further modified through the manipulation of growth joint allocations so that some collection segments that strictly ought to begin one or two sections into a row, for instance, the QE–QR and T segments, start instead at the aisle. The advantage of this approach is that the beginning of the collection segment is more immediately visible to the user trying to locate it from a main stack aisle.

In each case, reduction or manipulation of the growth joint allocation will theoretically result in less space being available for growth in a collection segment at some point in the future, requiring additional stack shifts. However, if the planning horizon is fairly long, and funding levels and publishing output uncertain, allocation of growth space may well be at best an uncertain exercise in any case.

Although preparation of the collection layout plan is in theory straightforward, it involves lots of detail and is tedious. It is easy to lose track of your place in either the spreadsheet or the plan. For the move to go smoothly, it's critical that the collection layout plan be accurate. Plan to work with someone else, get someone else to check your work, or at least check it yourself on another day (Chappell 2006, "Paper Shifts").

The completed collection layout plan provides the map that will be used throughout the remainder of the move. If the library plans to use a moving company to carry out the move, the collection layout plan may become part of the Request for Proposal documents, and will at least be used as the shared master plan for work to be accomplished. If the library plans to carry out the move itself, this will be the document move supervisors refer to as the authority for what goes where. It is therefore important that the library reach internal agreement on the layout plan before the move begins, and that once agreement is reached, multiple copies of the plan are made and shared with all concerned parties.

Shelf Spacing Notes

Attach to the collection layout plan a statement of the standard shelf spacing planned (e.g., "unless otherwise stated, all shelving will be set up with seven shelves per section, with 11-inch clear space between shelves, and material will be shelved on all seven shelves") . Identify areas where any other spacing will be used and specify the spacing to be used in those areas. Plan to have the shelves adjusted before the move begins, to avoid adding time to reshelving operations. If the collection plan for a new building is developed far enough in advance, setup of the shelves at required spacing may be specified as part of the shelving installation contract.

Detailed Collection Layout for Periodical Titles

Correctly placing periodical volumes in the new location requires that shelvers know precisely where to start each title and how much space to leave for each title's growth. The challenge is compounded when collections are being merged from several different locations. Figures 3.11 through 3.14 showed how to calculate the amount of space to leave for each title. A modified version of Figure 3.14, shown here as Figure 3.21, should be attached to the collection layout plan to specify where each title's volumes should be shelved. Before the move begins, the library may wish to mark the shelves with sticky notes or index cards and easily removed tape (blue painter's tape, available in the paint departments of hardware stores and large chain stores such as WalMart and Target, is a good option) to indicate the starting and stopping points for each title, allowing reshelving to proceed at more than one point in the collection at one time. The cumulative measurements can serve as checkpoints to monitor the accurate placement of materials as the move progresses. The same principle could be used for shelf space allocation for sets and other serial publications. (For another spreadsheet approach, see Table 4 in Brogan and Lipscomb 1982, 378.)

Reshelving and Preshelving Areas

The collection layout plan must also identify the locations of any reshelving or preshelving areas. If the library provides shelves throughout the collection where patrons are asked to leave materials to be reshelved, identify these on the plan, noting that they are to be left empty. If stack maintenance staff do not have a separate workroom, alcove, or other enclosed area for preshelving on a specific stack floor and will need to have shelving allocated for this purpose, that must also be identified on the collection layout plan, with instructions to leave the shelves empty (Cravey and Cravey 1991, 28).

Figure 3.21
Attachment to Collection Layout Plan: Periodical Shelf Space Allocation

	Shelves needed for this title	Starting point (running shelf number)	Ending point (running shelf number)	Starting point for this title			Ending point for this title		
				Section number	Shelf number	Inches right	Section number	Shelf number	Inches right
Title A	1.3	0.0	1.3	1	0	0	1	2	10
Title B	5.0	1.3	6.3	1	2	10	2	1	10
Title C	7.7	6.3	14.0	2	1	10	3	3	1
Title C copy 2									
Title D	1.7	14.0	15.7	3	3	1	3	4	22
Title E	3.2	15.7	18.9	3	4	22	4	0	27
Title F	2.0	18.9	20.9	4	0	27	4	3	27
Title G	1.2	20.9	22.1	4	3	27	4	5	2
TItle H	2.0	22.1	24.1	4	5	2	5	1	2
Title I	2.0	24.1	26.1	5	1	2	5	3	2
Title J	6.8	26.1	32.8	5	3	2	6	3	24.5
Title J copy 2									
Title K	2.6	32.8	35.4	6	3	24.5	6	6	12.5
Title L	1.8	35.4	37.2	6	6	12.5	7	2	6.5
Title M	2.2	37.2	39.4	7	2	6.5	7	4	12.5
Title N	2.6	39.4	42.0	7	4	12.5	7	7	0

Shelving Setup Note: Use 6 shelves/section of shelving for all titles.

STRUCTURAL CONCERNS

One final note. Find out the live load capacities of your facility and have a structural engineer verify that individual areas are capable of supporting the material planned for them. Various figures are cited in the library literature, ranging from 125 pounds per square foot to 200 pounds per square foot, as adequate to support print material,* with the requirements for compact shelving being approximately double that; this is a matter where the advice of a structural engineer should be sought. When a building originally planned for another use is being repurposed as a library, it's particularly important to have a structural engineer perform an assessment. Office and residential space is typically constructed with less live load capacity than is required for book stacks, for instance.

A structural engineer may also advise on working within live load limitations or on strategies for reinforcing a structure that has inadequate live load capacity. This, in combination with cost estimates for any modifications, may provide the background information needed to assess the cost-benefit trade-offs for working within existing limitations, modifying the structure, or considering the construction of an addition or new facility with the required structural strength.

---

*For instance, Leighton and Weber (1999, 422) state that "150 [pounds per sq foot] . . . is standard for stack rooms, and up to 175. . . may be required for rather dense book-storage areas and map cases . . . 300 pounds per sq foot. . . is recommended for areas where compact movable shelving is anticipated, although some may argue that this is excessive. . . . Today it has become customary . . . to construct all library floors strong enough to carry a live load of up to 150 pounds per sq foot."

II

PLANNING THE COLLECTION MOVE

After completing the collection layout plan, the next question is, who will move the materials? For most libraries that can afford the expense, the answer will be a moving company, but will it be a specialist library mover? If the library itself undertakes the move, will additional individuals be hired for the move, or will volunteers be sought? And there are further variations in the assignment of specific responsibility for planning and carrying out the move.

Whether the library opts to work with a moving company or handle the move itself, several general questions must be considered:

1. Who will be involved in the planning and execution of the move, and what role will each play?

2. How much time can be allowed for the move? What is the window of opportunity? How long will the move realistically take, given the number of labor hours available and physical constraints? Could the duration of the move be shortened with the addition of move labor hours or the removal of specific physical constraints? If labor is limited, is it possible to lengthen the move? What are the advantages and disadvantages of each option in terms of cost, access, staff time commitments, and available labor resources?

3. Will the library maintain patron access to the collection during the move, and, if so, how?

4. How will the library present the move to the public, and what public relations opportunities does the move present?

5. How will preservation concerns about the handling of materials be addressed?

Chapter 4 addresses these and other general considerations. Concerns specific to selecting and working with a moving company are addressed in Part III, and concerns specific to the library that elects to execute a move itself are addressed in Part IV.

4 GENERAL CONSIDERATIONS: WHO, WHEN, AND HOW?

WHO PERFORMS THE MOVE?: OPTIONS

Most libraries completing a major move associated with a building project will know well ahead of time whether they will be able to hire a mover or need to complete the move themselves. This decision will have been discussed as part of the project budget. However, even if you know a mover will do the collection move, or that staff will have to manage and maybe even carry out the move, it's worth reviewing the options and discussing individual roles and responsibilities. This helps prevent problematic assumptions about who is responsible for different elements of the project (for instance, who is responsible for planning the collection layout, for recruiting and hiring move staff, for labeling the stacks and adjusting shelf spacing, etc).

This chapter helps the reader identify options that may not be obvious by reviewing who will be involved in the planning and execution of the actual move and what their roles will be and identifying what will be done during the move, as well as how, when, by whom, and why.

Libraries' contents comprise various types of collections, user and service furniture and equipment, and office contents. Although this book concentrates on moving library collections, this section also takes into consideration how these other elements of library contents may affect options for moving the collection. Some typical options, and their pros and cons, are discussed below.

Plan Using Staff and a Consultant; Move Using a Moving Company

This option places the least strain on staff resources, but is likely to cost the most.

A consultant, experienced in moving library collections and in dealing with moving companies, may help by serving as the library's representative, identifying matters that may have been overlooked or insufficiently considered by the library, anticipating potential problems in relations with a moving company, and resolving those problems before they become major issues. In addition, a consultant may bring a level of analytical expertise and practical problem-solving skill to bear on the problems of a major move. A consultant may not be necessary if there are already on staff individuals with strong analytical, problem-solving, and communication skills, and they can be given sufficient time from their normal responsibilities to plan and oversee the move project.

Consultants may be asked to assist in various ways. A consultant might provide advice on resolving specific problems, detail a set of procedures, review or develop an RFP, assist in liaison with the moving company, oversee a staff-done move, or perform this entire set of responsibilities.

Even if a consultant is used, the library should not expect to turn over entire responsibility for the move to that individual, as the final authority on what will work for a given library must rest with the library and its staff. In addition, there is much planning work that it will not make practical or economic sense for the consultant to perform, for example, measuring the collection or inventorying the shelving (although a special team of well-trained temporary hires could be used for this work). Rather, the consultant becomes a part of the library's planning team, with a key role in educating the staff and serving as their advocate.

Using a moving company, particularly a moving company with experience in the type of move contemplated, will also relieve the library of responsibility for locating appropriate individuals to supervise and carry out the move and for obtaining the necessary equipment and vehicles.

Again, the library should expect a staff person to liaise with a moving company representative throughout the move, monitor move progress and mover performance for conformance with agreed-upon standards, respond to questions that will arise, and communicate information from the moving company to other library staff.

Generalist Moving Companies versus Library Movers

A small number of companies specialize in moving libraries. There are distinct advantages to working with one of these. In general, they are familiar with library and librarian concerns, vocabulary, and classification schemes. Most have carried out many library moves, have the specialized equipment, and know the techniques for planning the move efficiently. If a problem occurs, they have probably seen and resolved it before. In short, they have experience.

Generalist moving companies will also bring to the job a professional attitude, but their experience is more likely to be in moving furniture and office or household equipment. Judging from reports in the literature, generalist moving companies are more likely to need close assistance from library staff.

If a moving company will be used, using a library mover is strongly recommended.

Plan Using Staff Only; Hire a Moving Company

If the library has on staff and can release from normal responsibilities someone with good analytical, planning, practical problem-solving, and communications skills, hiring a consultant may not be necessary. However, it is necessary to recognize the considerable amount of time planning and overseeing the move will consume. Another option, particularly for small public libraries, is to tap the expertise of a board member or a community member. Retired experts may be a good source of planning assistance. Some towns have programs that allow senior citizens to earn tax credits by working for town agencies, and this might be another source of assistance. As with any volunteer "hire," the library will have to assess whether the payback warrants the investment in training.

In the case of a minor stack shift within an existing facility, the stack maintenance supervisor will typically oversee the work; however, it may not be reasonable to expect this individual to oversee the planning and execution of moving and merging the collections of several major facilities. In addition, the responsibility for serving as the library's legally designated representative in executing a contract with a moving company should generally be handled by a senior staff person who has an overall understanding of library operations and resources, experience in contract negotiations, and a sensitivity to the financial and legal ramifications of questions and problems that may arise.

Plan and Move Using Staff

Using staff to execute the move in addition to planning for it puts the greatest strain upon staff resources. Using staff to plan the move is a good idea, particularly if the staff include one or more people who are detail oriented, are quantitative, and have a track record of successful planning. However, libraries planning this type of move should be aware of the significant amount of time required for planning and supervising a move. Staff given lead responsibility should not be expected to maintain their other responsibilities without additional support. Required reading for libraries considering planning and carrying out a move using staff include Bayne (1990) for detailed discussion of planning considerations; Moreland, Robison, and Stephens (1993) for a description of some of the positive effects such a move can have; and Weaver-Myers and Wasowski (1984) for the impact on staff of planning and managing a move without relief from regular responsibilities.

Loading and pushing book trucks, or packing, lifting, and moving heavily loaded boxes for any length of time, requires good cardiovascular conditioning and strength training. Be very cautious about asking staff members to undertake this work. Staff whose regular work assignments are sedentary cannot be assumed to have the fitness to do this type of task for any length of time. Consider injuries and other health problems that may arise. Some staff members who should decline for health reasons may feel compelled to participate to avoid embarrassment or to be seen as a team player. Jerry McCabe, in a personal communication (June 19,1997), suggested that as a rule of thumb, if the average age of a staff is more than say, forty, then the likelihood of a staff injury or health problems is too great, and a mover should be hired. Libraries with unionized staffs should find out how the union views this sort of work. Libraries with small staffs and relatively large collections may not have the in-house labor to execute a move. Nonetheless, where no financial or volunteer resources exist, it may be the only option. If so, prepare to limit the amount of work done each day to a manageable amount.

Plan Using Staff; Move Using Staff and Additional Hires

A more reasonable variation is to have some staff members serve as supervisors or lead crew members, but hire temporary staff for the move. The selection criteria for hiring temporary staff should include the physical ability to perform heavy lifting and pushing for extended periods of time; ability to learn to read call numbers and to alphabetize; willingness and ability to report to work promptly and regularly, and to follow direction; and availability to work on the project until its completion. Student populations (particularly college students) can be a good source of temporary labor for a move, provided the move is done when classes are not in session, and that individuals meet the criteria above. An advantage of hiring members of the library's natural user community is that these individuals may feel they have a stake in making sure the move is done well and therefore may be more likely to take a degree of pride in their work. Despite this, the physical part of a move is hard, tedious work. Provide food and encouragement to help keep morale strong, and be prepared for attrition.

Plan Using Staff; Move Using Staff and Volunteers

Using volunteers can have both benefits and disadvantages. The benefits include free labor and the potential for building a sense of community commitment to the library. People who invest labor in a project frequently develop a sense of ownership in it.

The disadvantage is that volunteers are not paid; the library may have less control over their performance and behavior. For a move to run efficiently, particularly a large and/or complex move, it is critical that all the individuals performing the move regularly report to work on time, take direction, and continue to work on the project for long enough that there is some continuity and predictability. The comments above about the physical demands of moving apply here, too. Offer food and encouragement, but be prepared for attrition.

Nonetheless, it may be possible to use volunteers very advantageously, particularly if the volunteers are adults who are part of a larger organization. Consider contacting scouting and service organizations and local businesses with a track record of encouraging community participation.

To take advantage of the public relations potential of using volunteers, without incurring the problems associated with relying exclusively on them, consider using volunteers to perform an initial, visible, or symbolic portion of the move, then rely on paid temporary staff or a moving company to perform the bulk of the work.

A small public library variation on this option is for the librarian to perform the planning and to use community volunteers (high school students and adult volunteers) to perform the move. If the move is not too complicated (for instance, a straight shelf-to-shelf move), this strategy can work, and in some cases it may be the only viable option.

Use More Than One Moving Company: When and Why to Consider This

In some circumstances it may be appropriate to consider using more than one moving company. For instance:

a. **Hire a Library Moving Company to Move Collections and a General Moving Company to Move Library Furniture and Office Contents.** Movers who specialize in moving libraries typically operate in a national or at least regional market. Because they may be operating at a distance from their home office, there may be operational costs, such as local housing for key employees, that a local company would not incur. It may therefore make economic sense to separate a contract for moving a library and its collections into two parts. This may be done by setting up the RFP so that two distinct portions of the move are identified, and bidders are invited to bid on either or both portions of the project.

This approach does pose the potential problem of coordinating workflow and building access for two operations. For this reason, if two moving companies are used, it will be operationally easier if they complete their work sequentially rather than simultaneously. If this is planned, it is important to detail in the RFP and/or the subsequent contract what happens if the mover that is scheduled to complete work first is unable to do so within the scheduled period of time, and the work of the second mover is therefore delayed. A delayed start date will have adverse economic consequences for the second mover, so there must be a clear understanding of whether the first mover or the library and its parent organization are liable for compensating the second mover for any economic damage.

A variation on this is using an in-house transportation unit, such as a university or municipal transportation department, to move furniture and office contents. In this instance, particularly if use of the in-house unit is mandated (legally or politically), it will be important to assess in advance the unit's competence and the degree of education and oversight library staff will need to exercise. An advantage of using an in-house unit would be avoiding the potential legal complications of using a second generalist company, but a potential downside is that, like volunteers, the in-house unit isn't being paid by the library to do this specific job and may therefore be less responsive to the library's concerns and less inclined to use the library's preferred methods for handling, packing, and moving materials.

b. **Hire a Library Specialist Moving Company to Move the Collections, and a Second, Specialized Moving Company to Move Valuable Artifacts or Rare Materials.** If the library is the owner or repository of artwork, valuable artifacts, or rare materials, and the library specialist company does not have the expertise or equipment to handle these items, it may be appropriate to hire another company that specializes in the handling of these items for this part of the move.

Finally, if library staff, volunteers, or temporarily hired staff are moving the library collections, it may still be appropriate to hire a general moving company to move furniture and equipment.

One final note: If you plan to reuse existing shelving, try to have the same company move the collections and also disassemble, move, and reassemble the shelving, to avoid potential scheduling conflicts (Kozlowski 2005, 23). If your library is in earthquake country, though, be sure that shelving is reassembled by library shelving specialists (Dimenstein 2004, 42).

THE PLANNING TEAM

Purpose

The purpose of the initial planning team is to decide how and when the move will take place, as well as who will be responsible for specific actions and operations. Once it has been decided whether staff, volunteers, or a moving company will carry out the move, the planning team may become responsible for managing the move, monitoring progress, conformance to agreed-upon plans, and answering questions and resolving problems as they arise.

GENERAL CONSIDERATIONS: WHO, WHEN, AND HOW?

Composition and Roles

The planning team should comprise key library staff members plus other stakeholders. These might include specific library department heads and key members of the senior administration or their representatives, a representative from the library's house and grounds or building maintenance staff, someone from the parent organization's (university or municipal) physical plant department, a public safety representative, a health and safety representative, the consultant (if one is being used), construction managers if the move involves a new or renovated facility and work timing requires coordination, plus others whose expertise may be needed. Depending on the number of individuals involved, it may be desirable to designate a smaller core planning team that meets to develop the plan and convene the full group less frequently to review and comment upon the core group's work.

Titles and functional area names differ from organization to organization; however, certain key functions should be represented, as discussed below.

Department Managers

Include those department managers responsible for significant collections. This should include individuals responsible for circulating and noncirculating monographs and bound periodicals, as well as any other large collections. Managers responsible for smaller or more specialized collections—for instance AV materials, microforms, software and CD-ROMs, archival or special collection materials, reserves, and in-process volumes—should be included in at least an initial planning meeting to identify special concerns related to the packing, handling, and transportation of their materials; however, if these concerns can be addressed at the outset, it may not be necessary for these individual to be part of the core planning group.

Department managers should also be involved in planning if staff members and office contents will be moved. Department heads must be kept informed about the intended time frame and ongoing progress of such a move, so that they can plan workflow within their departments accordingly and respond in an informed manner to questions and concerns their staff will raise. Depending on the way communication normally flows within the organization, department heads may also filter and convey back to the move planning group concerns raised by staff, which may range from suggestions for a better way to perform an operation to health and safety concerns.

Staff with Experience Moving Library Collections

The stack maintenance supervisor will probably have experience shifting collections and practical knowledge of the collection that no other staff person can provide. Specific library staff members may have been involved in planning or executing moves at the current institution or elsewhere (Weaver-Meyers and Wasowski 1984, 23).

PLANNING THE COLLECTION MOVE

House and Grounds/Building Maintenance Representative

The individual(s) directly responsible for caring for the facility may also have the most ready knowledge of its specific characteristics, including door widths, floor surfaces likely to be damaged by the rolling motion of carts, maintenance problems with elevators and doors, and other details that will critically affect the move operation. In addition, the department responsible for custodial services may provide cleaning services and items such as carpet runners.

Physical Plant Representative

The department responsible for maintaining the structural integrity of the facility and its surrounding area, and for renovation work, will have to be consulted to determine whether the path proposed for the move, and particularly for any vehicles used to transport materials, is acceptable. In addition, in the case of major, between-building moves, structural modifications to one or another building may be necessary, for example, a window removed and a ramp constructed to create a second path for removing materials from a building. In a setting where there are underground tunnels beneath paved areas adjacent to one or another of the facilities, the department responsible for structural integrity issues should also be able to advise on the maximum vehicle tonnage the area above each tunnel can support.

In any move involving elevators, those responsible for elevator maintenance must be involved. Provision must be made for all elevators in both old and new locations to work as reliably as possible for the duration of the move. This may mean arranging a preventative overhaul before the beginning of the move and making special arrangements for quick-response service should an elevator malfunction during the move. Don't assume that just because a building is new, its elevators are in perfect working order; they will have been used by the construction crew for some time. Having all elevators in reliable working order is critical because if any elevator fails, there is often no other practical alternative to moving materials vertically, and the move will come to a halt.

This is particularly important if you are working with a moving company and have included a clause requiring completion of the move within a specified period of time. If an elevator goes out of service, and the library is contractually responsible for maintaining it in an operational condition, you may lose your right to enforce the completion date clause.

Public Safety Representatives

If any streets must be closed for some or all of a move, the appropriate public safety representatives have to be consulted as early as possible. Alternative arrangements for collection security may be necessary. For instance, if the library normally relies on a theft detection system at the building exit, this may have to be removed to facilitate the rapid exit of materials being moved from the building, although this also presents an opportunity for individuals who wish to steal materials. If the theft detection system remains in place, care must be taken in removing from the building AV materials that may be affected by magnetic fields.

Issues of personal and building security also have to be considered. The different rhythm of operations during a major move can sometimes mean that normal provisions, such as entrance and exit security, are loosened, or the people performing these operations are somewhat disoriented or distracted. If exits are added to the building to facilitate the move of materials, past provisions for exit control may not be adequate. The public safety representative may be able to help identify ways of reducing the potential for harm. Consider, for instance, requiring individuals working on the move who are not members of the regular library staff to wear some sort of identification, whether a badge or a distinctive T-shirt; posting exit control monitors at temporary exits; and formal end-of-day inspection of exits before securing the building at closing time.

Health and Safety Representative

If the move will include any fumigation, involve a health and safety representative from your parent organization to review the specific chemicals proposed for use and the method of application. A health and safety representative may also address staff member concerns about such matters as allergies and changes in climate control (particularly if physical modifications are being made to the building, and heating and air conditioning control may be compromised). In addition, ask either the health and safety representative or the physical plant representative whether the facility has any asbestos that might be disturbed by the move. If so, ask the health and safety representative to recommend appropriate measures to safeguard staff health.

Consultant

A consultant may provide a variety of services, but can probably be most helpful in anticipating and recommending solutions to potential problems, as well as advising on which conditions may be considered normal during a move.

Construction Representative

If you are moving into a new facility, or if the facility you are moving from is scheduled for renovation, representatives of the construction company may have to be involved, particularly if the timing of construction or renovation work must be coordinated closely with the move. Although the ideal situation is to have a new facility complete well before materials are moved into it, this cannot always happen, and punch list (or other more substantial) work may be taking place simultaneously with the start of the move. (Legal advice may be needed if the library is considering taking full or partial occupancy before the contractor has turned over a new building, as a contractor will sometimes argue that occupancy equals acceptance, and this may undermine the library's legal basis for getting punch list work completed.) In this instance, it is important to accurately estimate the duration of each step of the move, so that the construction or renovation project managers have specific and realistic dates to work within.

IDENTIFYING A TARGET TIME FRAME

Scheduling a major move will depend on various factors, including availability of the new space; the use planned for the old space; minimizing disruption of service to users; availability of the moving company or staff who will perform the move; preservation and practical concerns, such as typical weather during a given season; and opportunities for positive publicity, such as anniversary dates or donor availability.

Although in some instances the time frame will be dictated by space utilization issues (the new facility is ready, and old facility is needed right away), generally there is some latitude for scheduling. Some considerations in date selection are discussed below.

Building and Shelving Readiness

Moving into space that is not completed poses a number of problems. Legally, the library may not be able to move until it or its parent organization has accepted the building and taken legal possession. Logistically, until the building is done, there is likely to be competition for use of the loading dock and elevators, which will slow down the move. The construction contractors will not want the movers there. Practically, if construction is still ongoing, there may be health, conservation (dust), safety, or insurance issues with moving in.

For all of these reasons, if you are moving into a new or renovated facility, consider carefully the possibility of slippage in the construction completion date, with particular attention to whether shelving and other collection housing will be completely installed far enough in advance of the planned move start date to allow verification of the shelving layout and marking of collection locations.

Moving Crew Availability

If you plan to use a moving company, be aware that companies specializing in moving libraries are often booked months in advance. This is especially true of popular times such as school vacation periods. If you plan to do the move yourself, consider your primary source of labor (students? volunteers? staff?) and whether they are likely to be available.

Minimizing Disruption of Service

Timing the move so that it will take place during expected periods of light service demands means fewer frustrations for both patrons and staff. Although the library may make alternate provisions for service during the move period, that service is likely to be less than a patron would receive during normal operations and to require more effort by library staff. So, for example, for a college or school library, scheduling a move during a vacation period would normally be preferable to scheduling it during a reading or final examination period.

A secondary benefit of scheduling a move during a period of normally light service demand is that if the library or a moving company plans to hire some of the library's normal client population to perform the move (e.g., students), these individuals are more likely to be available during vacations.

Collection Use

There are pros and cons to scheduling the move to occur when greater or lesser proportions of the collection are in use. Moving when more material is in circulation means less material to move, and therefore a faster and less expensive move. However, these benefits have to be balanced against the need to leave space in the correct locations to shelve the in-circulation material when it is returned. This requires that the collection layout plan take into account material in circulation at the time the plan is prepared and that placement of materials at the time of the move scrupulously follows the collection layout plan.

Some libraries encourage borrowers to take out as many books as they can prior to the move and then return them to the new library. This can be a great public relations mechanism; however, consider that individual borrower preferences will likely mean that more materials will circulate from some segments of the collection than others. Using a single fill ratio across even fairly small segments of the collection will not smooth out these differences, so later stack shifting may be needed.

Another collection use consideration is whether and when to weed and shelf-read. Shelf-reading will probably be necessary after the move, if for no other reason than to assure that moved material was reshelved in the correct order. It also makes sense to shelf-read before moving a collection. Moving a collection poses enough opportunities for materials to go astray even when they start out in the correct location; shelf-reading before the move begins can help minimize these.

If you are working with a moving company and have contractually required them to achieve a certain level of accuracy in the shelving of materials, it is even more important to be able to document that the materials were in good order before the move. If the move includes integration of multiple collections, reducing shelving errors in the primary collection before the move will reduce the time required to interfile materials from secondary collections.

It also makes sense to weed the collection before the move, if time allows, reducing the linear footage of materials that must be moved. Also, removing fragile materials from the general collection for repair, binding, or replacement before a move reduces the likelihood that at-risk and already-damaged material will be further harmed. Moving imposes some physical stress on materials, so removing the most vulnerable items from the collection allows them to be separately handled with greater care. Another argument for weeding before the move is to make the new facility as attractive as possible (Kirby 1995, 26).

Staff

Consider matters of staff morale, fatigue, and the time demands of other responsibilities.

A first step is to identify which operations should be maintained and which staff members should work during the move. If specific work areas will be directly affected, and work in the area will be impossible, can the work area temporarily be relocated elsewhere? Can individuals temporarily be assigned other duties? Work from home? Can staff be requested to schedule their vacation time to coincide with this period? Will the library or its parent organization consider simply giving these individuals time off, in addition to regular vacation leave? Conversely, for staff needed during the move, can they plan their vacation time around the move? Can the library or its parent organization offer any motivating inducements (e.g., overtime pay, compensatory time off) for nonexempt staff who may be asked to work beyond their normal hours?

For instance, one could argue that the ideal time to move collections, in terms of minimizing disruption to users, would be when the library is normally closed, for instance between midnight and 7:00 AM, yet practical concerns of staff morale would normally argue against this plan. A less extreme example is moving during school vacation periods. Although this may minimize disruption to users, it may mean that staff members' family vacations have to be rescheduled. Advance warning and planning can help reduce these types of problems.

Weather

If the move includes pushing loaded book carts outdoors, carefully consider whether it can be scheduled during a period of the year when dry weather and moderate temperatures normally occur, and prepare contingency plans in case you must move in wet weather and/or extreme temperatures. Reflecting on a January 1996 move at the University of Rhode Island (URI) College of Continuing Education, beset by three major snowstorms in two weeks, Joanna M. Burkhardt wrote, "fully loaded book trucks do not move well in snow and ice, nor do they easily roll up and down the loading tailgates of the moving trucks. The wheels of fully loaded three-shelf book trucks buckle under the weight of the books. The book trucks were dented and otherwise damaged by the rigors of moving through the snow and ice on the uneven city streets" (1998, 501–2).

Public Relations Considerations

Does a particular time period offer public relations advantages? Would the schedule coincide with a significant anniversary date in a way that would allow the library to capitalize on positive publicity? Or would it be preferable for the move to occur when there is no other major event competing for publicity (and perhaps a labor pool)? Consider, too, that things can go wrong with even the best-planned move. It's probably wise to leave some time between a move's scheduled completion and a celebration to fix any unforeseen errors. If everything goes well, staff will have time to rest and get used to the new location.

Time Frame Reality Check

Estimating the amount of time a move takes requires some careful calculation, and is discussed in more detail in Chapter 9. (Although Chapter 9 is intended for those planning an in-house move, its analytical tools will also help double-check time estimates provided by a moving company.) In advance of doing a detailed estimate, it is possible to get a very rough idea of the approximate duration of a move by finding out how long a similar move took.

Because so many variables can affect the length of a move, try to find a move of about the same number of volumes, complexity, basic approach, size, and type of workforce. Appendix B provides a convenient summary of moves reported in the English-language library literature.

Although it is possible to get a sense of whether a move may take approximately one day, one week, several weeks, or longer from these generalized reports, it is difficult to use them to make accurate predictions about the exact duration of a specific move. In his survey of thirty moves completed between 1921 and 1952, John Kephart figured that "probably between 20 and 200 books can be moved a minute, if the [move] plan is drawn up carefully in advance" (1952, 2–3). The duration of a move will be determined by a number of interacting factors, including the number of people executing the move, their individual productivity, the length of the working day and week, the packing and transportation methods used, the numbers of elevators and egress points available in each building, the distance between old and new sites, effectiveness of the move planning, effectiveness of project supervision and management, and the complexity of the move.

In contemplating a proposed time frame for a move, consider the following:

1. Does it appear that the move can realistically be completed within the desired time frame? Looking at the literature and talking to colleagues, have moves of similar size and complexity been successfully accomplished with the same types of resources and constraints, within the same time frame?

2. How much latitude does the time frame allow for schedule slippage? Have you allowed yourself recovery time in case an elevator fails, volunteers quit, there's a major storm, or some other unforeseen event occurs?

3. What are the consequences of schedule slippage? Is renovation work scheduled to begin in the old facility the week after you move out, or will the facility remain vacant for a year? Is a celebration ceremony with full press coverage planned for the day the move is scheduled to end, or have you allowed yourself a grace period for pickup and recovery? Do fall semester classes start the week after the move is scheduled to be completed, or not for a month?

As the preceding questions suggest, it is strongly recommended that move planners allow extra time and not commit themselves to an overly ambitious schedule. If the move is completed ahead of or on schedule, the extra time can be used to allow staff to familiarize themselves with the new facility, for cleanup, for making handouts and signage, and for familiarizing users with the new layout. You will not regret allowing *more* time than needed. However, individual move planners must work out time allowances within the context of their move's practical and political constraints.

If it is essential to complete the move within a specified period of time, detailed analysis will be needed, and the move planners must be prepared to commit extra labor and equipment to complete the work if the rate of work falls behind schedule. For an excellent article on planning a constraint-driven move, see Tatterton and Braid (1973). Through careful analysis, the planners were able to successfully meet stringent goals for access (no item inaccessible for more than two hours) and project completion (all items moved in less than ten weeks).

HANDLING, PACKING, AND TRANSPORT METHODS AND PRESERVATION CONCERNS

During a move, every item is packed, transported, and unpacked. The amount of handling, and the proportion of the collection handling may accelerate the normal rate of collection deterioration (Amodeo 1983, 82). The individuals performing move operations may be less motivated than the library's usual staff and patrons to treat materials with care and respect, and the method of handling, packing, and transport selected; attention to training move staff in proper handling procedures; and monitoring move operations for compliance with these procedures all have the potential to affect the long-term physical health of the collection.

There are two approaches to considering the matter of packing and handling methods for moves. One says that the amount and type of handling an item receives during a move is not essentially different than what would normally be expected in a public access collection, and that no individual volume is handled so much, or is likely to be handled so roughly, that significant harm should be expected.

A second approach considers that although no one given volume may be damaged, the cumulative damage a move inflicts will appear in the long term, in higher than anticipated repair rates.

A combination of these philosophies may be the most practical. For valuable, rare, or irreplaceable materials, exercise the best care possible. For the bulk of the library's collections, specify methods that are consistent with good preservation practices but also allow fast and easy handling of individual items.

Climate Control

A common preservation concern for many types of material is some type of climate control. For archival and special collections, this could involve a range of special procedures, perhaps including climate-controlled vehicles and loading areas. For most library materials, the goal should be protecting material from extreme conditions.

One common concern is what to do if it is raining or snowing outside, and materials must pass through an outdoor area (a good reason for scheduling a move when neither is likely to occur). If the planned route is outdoors and the material *cannot* get wet because it is valuable or vulnerable to damage, consider making an allowance for delays in the schedule. On the other hand, it may be satisfactory to shrink-wrap moving carts or to cover a loading dock with a canopy or tarp.

Because the intensity of rain or snow may render any of these measures ineffective, it is particularly important for the move manager to have the power to stop the move if, in his or her judgment, continuing the move operations risks damaging collection material.

Cleaning

Materials should be cleaned before the move, to help keep the new location clean. In addition, dust can hide signs of damage to materials, and moving materials covered by many years' accumulation of dust can aggravate allergies. Cleaning may be done as part of the move or beforehand, as a separate project. Chapter 11 provides detailed information on planning and carrying out a cleaning project.

Pest Control Measures

Another preservation issue is making sure pests do not move into a new facility along with the collections. Fumigation and other pest control measures can have health and safety consequences for humans, so use of pest control measures should be considered carefully.

Protecting Bindings

Bound volumes should be moved in a way that minimizes stress on the binding. Methods that pack the book in its normal orientation, spine vertical, are preferable to those that pack the book fore edge down and spine up. A sample of the advice against fore-edge shelving comes from Ogden: "Books should be held upright on shelves. . . . Books should not be stored on the fore-edge. . . . storing a book spine down rather than spine up will prevent the text from pulling out of the binding due to its weight" (2007) and "books should not be stored on the fore-edge" (1994, Storage Methods, 1); Swartzburg: "When a book is askew on a shelf, stresses are placed on the spine leading to premature cracking or tearing, then covers become loose and corners break. . . . Books that are shelved with the fore-edge placed on the bottom will soon fall out of their cases; *gravity always wins*" (1995, 57); and Harvey: "Books and their binding are best shelved upright, unless they are very tall or wide, in which case they should be housed flat. Leaning books place undue strain on the spines, sewing and edges, and contribute to unnecessarily rapid deterioration; simply keeping books upright is helpful. Books should not be shelved on their fore-edges as this causes the text block to pull away from the covers of the book" (1993, 95). Amodeo (1983, 82–83) provides a number of very useful observations on the preservation impact of collection moves, and initiated a series of letters, listed in the Annotated References. Figure 4.1 illustrates the preferred and not-preferred orientations.

Figure 4.1
Orientation of Bound Material: Preferred and Not Preferred

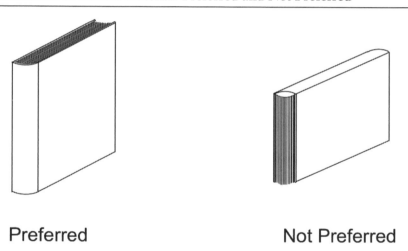

Preferred   Not Preferred

Individuals executing the move should be trained in the proper way to remove a bound volume from the shelf—depress the volumes on either side of the target volume, gently grasp the target volume on either side of its covers with the thumb and fingers, and remove it from the shelf—NOT hooking a finger into the headcap of the volume and pulling on that. The purpose of this method is to avoid failure of the headcap and tearing the spine of the binding (Ogden 2007, 2). Explaining the reason for this may help movers remember and comply with this instruction. Figure 4.2 illustrates the correct and incorrect methods.

Figure 4.2
Right and Wrong Way to Remove Bound Volumes from the Shelf

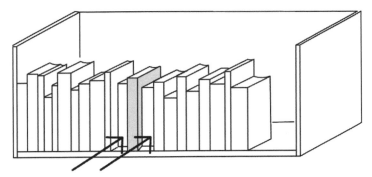

Right: Step One

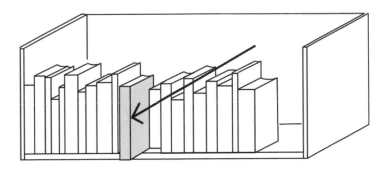

Right: Step Two

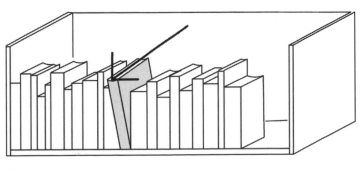

Wrong

Another consideration is to identify packing and transportation methods that minimize the likelihood of material being jostled or dropped, causing abrasion or damage to bindings.

If book trucks are used to transport bound volumes, it is important to instruct move staff to push book trucks at a reasonable speed and not engage in competitive racing, which could lead to book trucks tipping over. The shelves of book trucks used for moving must be deep enough that bound volumes' covers do not extend unsupported and unprotected beyond the edge of the book truck shelf. Bound volumes should be packed firmly enough to prevent volumes from leaning, but not so tight that covers suffer abrasion when they are unloaded. To minimize the chance of material falling off book trucks while in transit, either the book truck shelves should be sloped, or a means of securing the material on the shelves should be devised. Giant rubber bands (placed so they do not compress or distort the bound volumes), shrink-wrap, and other types of covers are all possible ways of achieving this goal (Amodeo 1983, 82–83). Book trucks transported in vans must be secured to prevent their moving around or tipping over in transit (Shercliff 1974, 25).

Comparison of Packing and Move Containers and Methods

There are three major methods of packing and moving bound volumes: on book trucks, in cartons, and by hand. Atkins and Teper's report of ARL libraries' moving practices found that 73 percent of temporary moves utilized book trucks (2005, 69). A fourth method, the trough, is reported rarely in the literature. See Sell (1954, 792, 795) for a description of a giant book trough, six feet long, "designed by a staff brother-in-law." It required two men to move and was moved atop a book truck. Not addressed in the article were securing books from falling out of the trough, its maneuverability, and the trough's capacity in comparison to book trucks or cartons. The author is hard pressed to see any advantages to this method.

Book Trucks

Book trucks offer a considerable number of advantages:

1. Bound volumes may be placed on them upright and be packed to prevent leaning or crowding, consistent with good preservation practice.

2. With the addition of safety straps, giant rubber bands, a cover, or wrapping material, bound volumes may be secured from falling off the book truck while it is in transit. Amodeo (1983, 83) suggests creating giant rubber bands from inner tubes. Mason (1983, 232) suggests wrapping the book truck with corrugated paper.

114

3. Spine labels are visible, making it easier to reshelve and to find material in transit (important if a volume has to be retrieved during the move).

4. Use of book trucks minimizes handling of materials (Kurth and Grim 1966, 149; Chappell 1964, 18). Book trucks comprise both container and wheels, whereas cartons and troughs must be packed with books, then placed on a dolly or cart for movement to the new location. If the move distance is far enough to require use of a motor vehicle, book trucks may be wheeled directly onto the truck, though the truck may have to be modified to prevent book trucks from shifting in transit (Slight 1967, 241).

5. The library will already own some number and design of book trucks.

At the same time, standard library book trucks have several potential disadvantages:

1. Shelves may not be deep enough to protect book spines from scuffing and other damage.

2. Book trucks equipped with four swivel casters may be difficult to steer accurately.

3. Book trucks designed for within-building reshelving may not hold up to heavier or outdoors use in a move (Alley 1983, 182); Haka et al. (1983, 153) suggest loading book trucks from bottom to top to reduce stress on book truck joints. Amodeo, in a response on the same page, agrees, and further notes this procedure would reduce the possibility of a book truck tipping over.

4. Books placed on unmodified standard book trucks are not protected from dust, rain, or snow.

5. Loading book trucks onto a van for transport between buildings requires a ramp.

The first three concerns can be addressed by using custom-constructed book trucks, or by renting book trucks designed for moving from a specialist moving company. The design for a custom-constructed book truck is described in detail in Alley (1979, 33–37). Features of the design include a size calculated to exactly fit into a book lift, thus taking full advantage of its capacity; oversized rubber industrial casters, designed to roll easily and carry the weight of a full load of books; and deeply recessed shelves, intended to protect book spines. The fourth concern can be addressed by covering or wrapping the book truck. For libraries without access to a loading dock, purchasing, renting, or borrowing a temporary ramp for the move can address the last concern.

PLANNING THE COLLECTION MOVE

In sizing book trucks for a move, consider the fit and maneuverability of the cart within the narrowest book stack aisles and in elevators. Get a sample cart well ahead of the move and test its loading and moving characteristics (Hamilton and Hindman 1987, 4). Because elevators often constitute a bottleneck in move operations, consider the number of book trucks that can fit in one elevator, both in terms of floor space and weight, and the effect this will have on the number of volumes that can be moved in one elevator trip.

Cartons

Many libraries and moving companies use cartons or boxes of various sizes and durability to move books. Advantages include the following:

1. They may be available free (e.g., beer cartons or copy paper boxes).

2. They provide protection from dust and precipitation.

3. If sealed, they may provide some assurance of security for materials in transit.

4. They are useful if materials need to be stored before reshelving, and shelving is not available. If bound volumes must be stored in cartons for some time before reshelving, less damage to the volumes' spines may result if the volumes are packed flat (Hofstetter 1993, 14).

However, there are significant disadvantages, which make this, at best, a second choice:

1. There is no perfect way to pack books in a carton. To minimize damage to bindings, they must be packed flat in the carton. Because cartons will be stacked, the books must be packed solidly from top to bottom. However, unless the books are from a very homogenous part of the collection, there will be some variation in their height, and some parts of the pile will not be fully supported (Kelsey and Kendrick in Nitecki and Kendrick 2001, 151). If books are packed spine up so that spine labels can be read (for instance, as suggested by Hoxsey 1995, 28), the bindings will obviously be stressed. If they are packed upright, the spine labels cannot be read, making it more difficult to correctly shelve the box's contents in the new location. In addition, some books will inevitably be taller than others and may be damaged by crushing when other cartons are piled on top of them (Kelsey and Kendrick, 151).

2. Filled cartons are typically piled several high for transport on dollies; they may be piled in taller stacks for transport on vans. Thorne (1955, 842) notes that in the move of the San Diego Public Library in 1954, the movers placed "two flat planks. . . on the rims of the open boxes . . . up to four and five boxes high. There was no weight at any time on the books because all books were packed below the level of the box rims."

GENERAL CONSIDERATIONS: WHO, WHEN, AND HOW?

Unless the box is constructed with enough rigidity to prevent crushing, damage may be done to the binding (and to the box).

3. Cartons are typically reused throughout a move, so a carton that initially is rigid enough to protect its contents may not stay in that condition throughout the move.

4. Cartons are easily misplaced. Adams (1954, 5) lists both this point and the next one.

5. Carton contents cannot always be packed or unpacked in order.

If cartons must be used, consider the following (Spyers-Duran 1965, 27–30 speaks to some of the following points):

1. What size carton will work best? Using the same size carton throughout the move is important, both so that loaded cartons may be stacked and moved in a stable pile ("Prevailing in the Interim, Part II 1990, 4), and for the spacing issues noted below. The literature is full of reports of moves using different sizes of cartons and boxes, usually with detailed rationales for the type of carton or box used in the particular move (see both the Annotated References and Appendix B). For moves in which the contents of one shelf will be replaced directly onto another shelf, consider sizing the box to hold exactly the amount, or exactly half the amount, of material that will be placed on one shelf. This will aid accurate spacing of the material and can be used to allow simultaneous reshelving in multiple areas.

2. How strong should the carton be? Measure the average number of bound volumes the carton is intended to hold, determine a maximum weight per volume (use maximum rather than average to avoid having cartons that will only accommodate the average or lighter than average volumes in the collection), then calculate the maximum weight per carton. Add a safety factor. How many cartons will be stacked on top of each other, and for what period of time? Can crush-resistance be added in?

Consider the experience of the library for Purdue University's Department of Earth & Atmospheric Sciences, reported in Laffoon, Richardson, and Melhorn (1991, 95), "An initial attempt to separately stack the boxes [for temporary storage] in five layers almost ended in collapse, because the loose filling would not support the accumulated weight. The boxes therefore were stacked three high, and covered with 30 sheets of masonite to fully distribute the load of the overlying two layers of boxes."

Will the cartons be provided flat? What tools and supplies will be needed to assemble them? Will the method of assembly affect the cartons' durability and crush-resistance? Discuss your requirements

117

and concerns with a carton manufacturer. Get price estimates based on quantity purchases, including delivery.

3.   How will the cartons be moved, and what is the maximum weight the moving tool can handle? If cartons will be piled on dollies, how much weight can the dolly hold?

4.   Will the packed carton be too heavy for a mover to lift and place on the dolly? Jerry McCabe (personal communication, June 19, 1997) suggests limiting the weight per carton to 35 pounds, to avoid fatigue to the mover. One article mentions using boxes sized to fit two to a shelf for long-term storage, and cautions, "Be prepared for complaints about the weight. They will be upwards of eighty pounds each." (Prevailing in the Interim, Part II 1990, 5). If one can anticipate "complaints about the weight," one can also reasonably anticipate fatigue. Limiting the weight seems like a much more reasonable approach!

5.   How stable will the cartons be when loaded onto the moving dolly? If cartons fall off a moving dolly, the movement of the volumes within the carton could contribute to binding damage. How many cartons will be stacked on one dolly? Taller stacks of cartons loaded on a moving dolly will probably be more prone to fall off.

6.   Using a hard-shell bin with a fitted lid would address many of these concerns. As an added bonus, if the lid fits tightly, the bin is weatherproof and ought to be insect proof, making it a good choice if material must be boxed-up and stored for a period of time (Kelsey and Kendrick, 152).

By Hand

The moving line and the book brigade both have great public relations value. They attract media attention, they involve the community, and they can seem like an easy way to move a lot of material quickly and inexpensively. In the moving line method, each individual carries an armload of books from the old location to the new location, while maintaining his or her place in a line. In the book brigade method, a handful of books is passed from hand to hand along a line of people stretching from the old location to the new location. Both methods have similar advantages and disadvantages (Tucker 1999, 77–84):

The advantages

1.   Good public relations value. Good photo opportunities.

2.   Few special skills and little training required.

3.   Little expense.

The disadvantages

1. Monotonous work; boredom can lead to sloppiness.

2. Books not protected from the elements, unless special precautions are taken.

3. Books possibly dropped, with both damage to bindings and text blocks.

4. Generally dependent on volunteers, with attendant management problems.

5. Easy for materials to become disordered in transit, although various strategies are offered in the literature for reducing this. However, the library using either method should plan on intensive shelf-reading and reshelving after the materials arrive at their destination.

Nonprint Materials and Other Items Requiring Special Considerations

Bound volumes comprise the bulk of most library collections, and techniques developed for moving library collections focus on moving bound volumes. Collection materials that are nonstandard sizes or composition pose special problems and will likely require some modification of whatever techniques have been identified for moving general collection materials.

Archival and Special Collection Materials

Some archival and special collection material may be handled like other general collection material if it is not particularly fragile or rare, or if there are no special safety concerns. For other material, specialized procedures may have to be developed to ensure physical integrity, loss prevention, and confidentiality.

The National Archives and Records Administration has identified the following criteria for collection housings suitable for a move:

1. well-protects and supports the materials,

2. prevents viewing or rifling the contents,

3. allows for proper labeling, and

4. aids in maintaining sequence and order during the move (Pilette 1995).

A good starting point is to inventory the collection and identify any condition issues that will need to be taken into account. There are several good reasons to conduct an inventory. First, it establishes an accurate list of the items you had before the move and should have after the move. Without such a list, you cannot be sure whether an item that's missing after the move was left in the old location, lost in transit, or never there. The inventory may also provide an opportunity to discover misshelved items long considered lost (Cronenwett 1999).

Second, it provides an opportunity for you to identify condition issues. Will items need to be reboxed, and how many? How many different types of housing are now being used, and will this affect shelving plans for the new location? Are the collections dusty? Is there any evidence of insect infestation, mold, or mildew? Does the collection include particularly fragile formats that will require special handling? In reporting on the move of its collections, the American Heritage Center at the University of Wyoming noted that replacing weak and old containers with ones of uniform size prior to a move aided not only in protecting materials to be moved, but also in planning space. To safely move some formats (e.g., glass negatives), they found it necessary to design their own storage containers. Artifacts were wrapped in unbleached cotton and packed in large flat boxes. Sculpture was crated, or wrapped in bubble-wrap. Maps and materials in flat files were moved in their drawers and conveyed on the type of carts (buffaloes) used by glass installers (White and Cook 1994, 16–17).

Edwin Wolf II, in his report on the Library Company of Philadelphia's 1966 move, noted, "I felt that the rare books and the thousands of volumes with broken bindings would be more easily and more safely handled if they were put onto shelves in a moving case rather than down into boxes or cartons" (1966, 173). For this move, custom moving carts were designed and constructed that accommodated three feet of materials on a shelf, could be wheeled, and had a removable front.

Fragile materials may be shrink-wrapped, to give them "greater physical integrity and stability" (Hansen and Honea 1990, 18; see also Kellerman 1993, 117–28). This method has been used successfully for items with "loose covers, rotting leather bindings, detached brittle pages, fragmenting yellow paper" (Kellerman 1993, 119); scrap books, boxes, files, unbound sheet music (Hansen and Honea 1990, 18); and unbound items being stabilized by inserting a piece of acid-free board cut to size. The reports cited advise poking a hole in the shrink-wrap after the item has been enclosed.

Other archives have wrapped material in acid-free paper or a fiber-reinforced plastic said to inhibit ultraviolet light (Morrow 1990, 427). Boxes of material may also be placed on a pallet and the entire pallet shrink-wrapped (Harrington, in Newman and Jones 2002, 9).

Mary Frances Morrow's 1990 survey of ten archives' moves addresses other special problems related to such moves. Archival collections are more likely to be shipped to the library or archives, and maintaining security during shipment is of greater importance. Depending on the sensitivity, rarity, and value of the material, different methods will be needed. At a minimum, an accurate list of the items being shipped is necessary. Consider requiring sign-offs at the sending and receiving ends of each shipment, and whenever the material changes hands; sealing the truck; and having an archives representative travel in the truck. If material must be packed in shipping containers, be certain the containers are strong enough that they will not crush, spell out in detail how the material should be packed, and if possible have someone trained in handling fragile or rare materials actually pack the material (Mattern, in Newman and Jones 2002, 49).

For moves within a building, consider designating staff to walk along with each team of movers or stationing a staff member at each doorway to ensure no materials are removed without authorization.

Many archives opt to pack and sometimes move collections themselves, to ensure collections are handled properly (Morrow 1990, 428–29). If a moving company will be used, request a list of archives they have moved, and talk to their references.

Do a final walk-through of the old facility after the move, checking under and behind shelves, to be absolutely certain nothing has been inadvertently left behind (Backman, 6 and Taylor, 81–82, in Newman and Jones 2002), and do a thorough shelf-reading of the collection in its new location to identify anything inadvertently misshelved (Taylor, 82).

Audiovisual Formats

Consider the following when selecting packing and transport methods:

Records: Protection of the LP record jacket will require extra deep book truck shelves. Older, more fragile disks may need extra padding or bubble-wrap to protect them from fracture if the move is being conducted over bumpy terrain.

DVDs, compact discs, videocassettes, and audiocassettes: Normally stored in plastic cases, which should also protect the recording during a move.

Filmstrips and slide-tapes: If stored in a box (as part of a set), move them in that box to retain protection.

Microforms

Microforms are typically moved in their cabinets. A fully loaded microform cabinet is very heavy, and movers should be alerted ahead of time that this method of moving microforms is planned.

Folios and Other Nonstandard-sized Print Material

Transport these flat, either on specially sized book trucks or specially sized boxes.

Children's Toys, Pop-Up Books

If the shape of these is too irregular to move them easily on book trucks, consider placing them in cardboard boxes and placing those on book trucks. Jerry McCabe, in a personal communication (January 21, 2009), cautions, "pop-up books should never be packed tightly; doing so will destroy the pop-up feature."

COMMUNICATION

The right frequency, tone, and type of communication with library staff and with the public is critical to the move being perceived as a success.

Communicating with the public and with library staff not immediately involved in planning for the move is important for several reasons. It lets both constituencies know what to expect and when, it gives the library planners an opportunity to set realistic expectations about the level of service and the amount of disruption, and it allows the library to set the tone for the upcoming event. Although communication with each constituency is important, the content and means of communication with each may be somewhat different.

Communication with library staff should focus more on the effect the move will have on their work and their operational units, and what will be expected of them. It is critical to let staff know what to expect when, which aspects of the move are controllable, and whom to contact if they have questions or concerns not answered in the information that is being communicated. As Calderhead states, communication with library staff opens the door for "feedback, new perspectives, and the creation of an atmosphere of inclusion and disclosure" (1996, 66).

Soliciting and adapting plans in response to feedback also helps create staff buy-in, which reduces confusion, grumbling, and frustration and may help staff accept and deal more easily with change (Fowles 2004, 52).

Different types of information may have to be communicated in different ways. For example, it may be useful to have an initial briefing on the move for all library staff well in advance of the planned start date, to review the general scope, sequence, and timing, and to give staff an opportunity to ask questions and make suggestions. Done far enough ahead, when the move is still in the conceptual planning stage, this can be an opportunity for the move planner(s) to identify potential problems that may not have already surfaced in discussions with key staff, to benefit from suggestions, or to bring to the surface and address misconceptions before they gain widespread currency.

As the schedule becomes better defined, this type of brief information could be communicated to staff through a memo, as well as through department heads. As the starting date for the move approaches, it might be appropriate to hold another briefing for all interested staff to identify individuals responsible for key issues, including the person or people to contact for specific problems. If a moving company is being hired, this would be a good time to introduce their key people, so that library staff can begin to recognize people they may be seeing with some frequency. Arrangements for any alternate work assignments or locations should be handled on an individual basis through supervisors. A bulletin board, set up where both staff and library users can see it, may provide information on the planned schedule, a list of areas currently affected and a schedule of those that will be affected next, answers to move-related questions, and additional relevant information.

GENERAL CONSIDERATIONS: WHO, WHEN, AND HOW?

Before the start date for the move, distribute detailed instructions for moving to all staff. The list (modeled on Spyers-Duran 1964, 8–13) should include the following:

1. The moving schedule, in as much detail as possible. Focus on when operations and departments will move, to answer the question, "When will I be moving?"

2. The sequence of the move.

3. Assigned duties of specific library staff. Identify the library's move coordinator and move supervisors and who is responsible for resolving specific problems.

4. Duties of other library staff members (e.g., packing office contents). Also, tell library staff what they may *not* do (e.g., give instructions to movers).

5. Packing instructions for office contents and instructions for labeling boxes of office contents.

6. If library staff will participate in collection move operations, detail packing methods and move procedures, schedules, etc.

A major move can be very disruptive and stressful. It will certainly involve a change in routine, extra work, and learning new locations. The overall goal of communicating to staff about the move is to reduce stress by introducing the notion of change slowly and with a level of specificity appropriate to the timeline, to allow staff to become used to the idea and incorporate planning for it into their work lives. Absence of information about a move encourages rumors to flourish, so it is well worth being proactive and providing staff with the information that will make it easier for them to do their jobs well. For an excellent discussion of internal move-related publicity, see Fraley and Anderson (1990, 116–22).

The goal of communication with the public is to inform them about upcoming changes in service, and it has a public relations element. The move is, hopefully, a harbinger of better library service through expanded or improved facilities or better arrangement of the collections, being undertaken on behalf of the library's clientele. The means of communicating with the public will be determined largely by the nature of the library and its user community.

For a university community, a letter might be sent out from the library director to academic and administrative deans and department heads, or the information may be communicated through whatever administrative or academic groups the director is a member of. It might be publicized in the school newspaper(s), on the Library's Web page, and through handouts distributed at the library and in other key locations across campus.

For a public library, representatives from the print and electronic media might be invited to a briefing, and press releases could be distributed. As the move date approaches, press photographers might be alerted of photo opportunities, such as capturing the first cart of books leaving the old building or entering the new building. The director might send letters to school librarians and principals and to leaders of other key user communities. Groups that regularly use a library's meeting rooms or any other resource should be informed well in advance if the resource will be unavailable for a period of time during the move.

For special libraries, in addition to personal contact with key researchers and stakeholders, consider publicity in a house newsletter, announcements, and a celebration sponsored by the library. For a discussion of publicity and the move of a corporate library, read McCaughan (1991, 183–88).

For all libraries, use your facility as an information distribution point; your current users are the people who will be most affected, and they will want to know as early as possible what to expect.

Bear in mind that some people just won't get the message. Karen Mier (2005, 13) notes that for the move of college and hospital libraries, they "put multiple notices on two system-wide electronic communication networks . . . , in printed employee publications, in the student newsletter, and in information that went to physicians. We told people who walked in our door and put a sign on our door for weeks before the move. . . . Even with these efforts, we still had trouble reaching all the floor nurses, department office staff, and part-time students. Weeks after the move, we would still get occasional comments like, "You moved?!""

TEMPORARY MOVES

An increasing number of library moves involve moving to temporary locations. In many instances, a library is being renovated area by area, while services and collection access are maintained, necessitating multiple sequential moves out of unrenovated areas and into renovated areas. In other instances, the entire library (or a selection of material and services) is relocated to a temporary location for the duration of the renovation, then returned once the renovations are complete.

One disadvantage of both approaches is that each item will probably be moved at least twice, and the overall cost of the move will be more than if it were done in a single shift. In addition, these moves are likely to include the reuse of existing book stacks, which must also be moved. Each approach has unique characteristics.

Successfully carrying out sequential moves within a building requires careful planning and sequencing. The stress of planning, managing, and executing a move is extended over a long period of time. Staff throughout the library may have to make do with less-than-ideal work and service areas, and morale may need to be aggressively bolstered. On the other hand, by definition, no one part of a sequential move is as large (or time-consuming) as would be a move of the entire collection. The need to continue move operations over an extended period of time provides an opportunity to hire and train in-house staff and an organizational structure specifically for this purpose. Over the course of the moves, all involved will develop expertise and likely develop pride in their new abilities.

Moving to a temporary location involves finding a facility in an acceptable location, and with an appropriate structure. If the temporary location is small, the collection may have to be split, with some items being stored until the new facility is ready. This obviously requires decisions about which items will be stored, whether they will be accessible while in storage, changing their catalog records, and communicating with library users and neighboring libraries about the new temporary location and any access limitations. These decisions are discussed in greater detail below.

Sequential Moves

If the library is to be renovated while remaining in service, each affected area will at some point need to be emptied of collections, shelving, and furniture, and sealed off while the work is completed. The basic sequence of work requires that some extra shelving (or other means of housing the collection) be available.

Ideally, the goal here is to vacate area A, renovate area A, then move area B's collections into A. When area B is vacant, it may be renovated, and area C's collections may then be moved into it. And so on. The problem is that collection A has to go somewhere first!

If a relatively small amount of material is being moved at one time, it could be placed on numbered book trucks, arranged in call number order in a large open area (such as an emptied classroom, reading room, or meeting room, or perhaps a cafeteria, gymnasium, or storefront). In choosing a place to store book trucks, consider security, environmental controls, and access convenience. (How close is it? How easily can a book truck be moved to it?)

Larger amounts of material could be housed on shelving set up specifically for that purpose. This requires that the area used have sufficient live-load capacity to support loaded book shelving, at least 150 pounds/square foot. Bear in mind that typical office, meeting room, and classroom construction is built with much less live-load capacity and will not support loaded book shelving; seek advice from a qualified structural engineer.

If the shelving will be reused, first determine whether all of the library's shelving is of the same type. Even if all the shelving is of one type, say 90-inch-high, 9-inch nominal depth steel cantilever shelving, many libraries will have shelving from several different—and incompatible—manufacturers. More obviously, case and cantilever, wood and steel, and different widths of shelving will not be interchangeable. Inventory each type, and carefully count the number of each type used when laying out shelving in the renovated areas.

Allow time to clean reused shelving and determine whether it should be repainted. If repainting, check out the proposed method, its durability, whether it can be done on site, whether it needs to cure before material can be reshelved, and the colors available. (For instance, electrostatic painting can be done overnight on site [Jerry McCabe, personal communication, January 21, 2009]). Do a test.

Particularly in earthquake country, have the shelving taken down and set up again by a contractor familiar with library shelving. Check carefully to be sure all bolts and bracing are kept when the shelving is disassembled and are reinstalled per the manufacturer's specifications to be sure the shelving retains its structural stability. If the shelving is to be stored off-site for any length of time, consider holding on to the nuts and bolts in your office until they're needed; there's a strong possibility they will not come back from storage with their shelving. Just be careful to label them clearly and make a note of where you have stored them, so that you can find them when it's time for reassembly.

Using a stack mover is another possibility. Stack movers are specialized equipment designed to move fully loaded steel shelving. Although this method requires a larger team, the time saved may more than make up for the additional labor/hour and cost of renting the stack mover (Tetro and Callahan 2002, 4). Additional considerations include allowing space to maneuver an entire range and stabilizing and preparing the range to be lifted (including checking and securing the ranges' interior tension bracing, removing some books and shelves to provide clearance to engage the stack mover, removing overhead bracing, and clearing the path of travel) (9–10). To ensure safety, plan on keeping anyone not immediately involved (12) out of the move area.

Consider marking the layout of the shelving on the floor with masking tape. This may sound dumb, but it works like a charm. It's easy for you to make sure the shelving will fit as planned before installation begins, it's easy for the contractor to see exactly where you want the shelving to be placed, and it's easy for you to see whether the shelving was put where you wanted it.

Keeping staff and the public up to date on where material is located and which areas are closed is particularly important in sequential moves. Be sure your reference and circulation staff know on a daily basis where collections are located so that they can help library users. Strongly consider having near the entrance a bulletin board with up-to-date maps, handouts, and information, and also put the same information on the library's Web site in an easy-to-find move information tab or page. Communicating clearly and setting the right tone is essential to managing the expectations of users and staff. Try to convey a sense of humor, as well as excitement about the improvements that will (eventually) result. People who know what's going on and why are more likely to feel like they are part of the project. Acknowledging that this is a pain, but infusing it with a sense of humor, helps defuse the inevitable irritation we all feel when inconvenienced.

Moving to a Temporary Location

Temporarily relocating the library and its services during a renovation is very much like a "normal" move, with a couple of additional considerations.

Choosing an appropriate temporary facility is usually the biggest challenge. As mentioned previously, floors in the chosen facility must be able to support fully loaded shelving. Purpose-built office spaces will not have the live-load capacity required. Good possibilities include one-story buildings built with a concrete slab on grade, former parking garages, and heavy manufacturing facilities; however, it's critical to seek the advice of a qualified structural engineer to make sure the places you're considering will not crack or collapse under the weight of loaded steel shelving.

The location of the temporary facility must also be considered. How close is it to the library's permanent location? Is it easy to find and convenient? Is it safe at night as well as during the day? Is it handicapped accessible?

Preservation concerns must also be taken into account. Is the temporary facility clean and free of insect and rodent infestations? How adequate is its climate control system? Is it air-conditioned? Heated? Does it have enough light, and the right type? Is it secure? If the materials to be moved are archival or special collections, these concerns assume much greater importance.

Normally, the temporary facility will not be as large as the permanent library, and decisions will have to be made before the move about what will be included and left out. Logistically, the easiest option is to reduce the number of general user seats. At an average of 25 to 30 square feet per seat, this space mounts up quickly. In addition, excluding collections, or specialized user seats (like those at microcomputers or at AV or microform equipment) means finding another place for the items that have been excluded, which reduces intended space savings! Temporary libraries will also generally reduce service and staff areas to the bare minimum; the decision of what this is will vary depending on the length of time the library expects to be in its temporary location, and other local factors.

If only part of the collection will fit into the temporary facility, a decision will have to be made about which part can be spared, and how it will be stored. For the sake of clarity, and to avoid the additional work of temporarily changing records, it is strongly suggested that the part stored be easy to describe (e.g., "all bound periodicals before 1990" or "the Smith Memorial Collection"). It is tempting to consider identifying higher-use material, but be careful to take into account the additional work required to identify, mark, and selectively remove these items and to update their records, as well as reintegrating the split collections when they return to the permanent library. Resist this impulse if at all possible.

If the collection must be split, then how will the stored part be housed? The usual answer is that it will be boxed, and the boxes will be arranged in piles. If this is being contemplated, reread the warnings on the danger of damage to box contents and proceed with caution. Can platforms be constructed to house pallets of boxes so that no box has another on top of it? Can crush-resistant, hard-shell plastic crates be used (and how much weight is the crate designed to support)?

In addition, number the boxes or crates (label at least two sides) and make a record of each box's contents, as well as its linear measurement and volume count. Seal the boxes securely to avoid vandalism, prevent insect or rodent damage, and exclude dirt. Inventory the boxes on their way out of the library and on arrival at the storage location. Check to make sure all the boxes arrive, and note any condition issues upon arrival. When the time comes to return to the permanent library, reverse the procedure, logging boxes out of the storage location and into the permanent library. If any boxes are missing, compare the inventory of boxes logged into the storage location upon move-in with the inventory upon move-out. To avoid concerns about individual volumes being lost, compare the volume count when each box is opened with the count taken when it was packed. Use the linear measurements to mark where each box should be shelved on the new facilities' shelves.

After move-in, conduct a thorough shelf-reading, liberally thank everyone who has helped in any way, and take a well-deserved vacation.

III

WORKING WITH A MOVING COMPANY

Once a collection layout plan has been developed and an approximate time frame and other resource constraints have been identified, detailed planning of the collection move begins in earnest.

Removing material from its current location, transporting it to the new location, and placing it on new shelves may be done either by a moving company hired to perform this work or by an in-house crew. Some of the advantages and disadvantages of each option were outlined in Chapter 4. The four chapters in Part III focus on the special concerns of selecting and working with a moving company: identifying which responsibilities belong to the mover and to the library, preparing a Request for Proposal (RFP), selecting a mover, and carrying out the move with a mover.

As discussed in Chapter 4, there are generalist moving companies and moving companies that specialize in moving libraries. The comments in Part III assume the moving company is a specialist in moving libraries. Part III also assumes that the library will prepare a Request for Proposal (RFP) as a means of inviting competitive proposals from several moving companies.

Part IV will address operational issues of managing and executing a move in-house, including planning move logistics and carrying out the move.

Even if your library plans to hire a moving company, Part IV may be helpful in understanding the constraints under which a move takes place and some of the problems that may occur. It may also help you assess whether the moving company is packing, transporting, and reshelving the material efficiently.

5 LIBRARY AND MOVER RESPONSIBILITIES

A successful move using a moving company requires a good working partnership. Both library and mover must share a clear, unambiguous understanding of each party's responsibilities. Chapter 5 discusses some of these responsibilities and how they may be assigned, with sections written from a librarian's perspective and a mover's perspective. However, it is important that each library review carefully, for itself and in detail with its selected moving company, precisely who is responsible for what for the specific move they are planning. The objective is to not assume anything—to know at the outset what needs to be done; to assign responsibility for the performance of each action to the moving company, the library, or both; and to not leave any steps unassigned, overlooked, or under the assumed responsibility of the other party.

LIBRARY AND MOVER RESPONSIBILITIES FROM A LIBRARIAN'S PERSPECTIVE

Moving companies are in business to make money. When a mover signs a contract to perform a move, it is agreeing to provide a specified set of services and work under a specific set of conditions for a specific sum of money, all of which are spelled out in the contract. If you ask the mover to provide a service that was not identified in the contract, it is fair for it to request additional payment. The major expense of a move is labor. Therefore, anything that affects the length of the move will cost the mover more money.

Prior to the move, the library's major responsibility is to set out accurately and completely what it expects the moving company to do and the conditions under which the mover will be expected to perform. These will normally be captured in a Request for Proposal (RFP) document. During the move, the

131

library's major responsibilities are to ensure that the conditions under which the moving company is expected to operate are those identified in the RFP, to ensure that the work the moving company is performing is the work the company agreed to perform, and to identify and work with the moving company to identify ways of resolving unforeseen problems.

The moving company's major responsibility prior to the move is to gauge as accurately as possible the extent of the move and its complexity, and to provide to the library as competitive a price as possible given a realistic assessment of the work required. Because price is always a factor in the selection of a moving company (even if it is not the sole or deciding factor), moving companies will make assumptions about the work they will need to perform and construct their bid price accordingly. Once the RFP has been reviewed, any changes negotiated, and a contract signed, the moving company and the library have a legally binding agreement that certain work will be performed in specified ways for a specified price. After this point, changes in the scope of work or conditions will likely carry some change in price. It is therefore critical that the library both know and detail in the RFP the work and conditions expected during the move.

Establishment of a good working relationship between the moving company and the library, and demonstration of appropriate flexibility on the library's part, can foster appropriate flexibility on the part of the moving company. But because the moving company is in business to make money, the library cannot expect it to perform additional, previously unspecified work just to be nice. Additional work means additional labor hours and overhead, and although the company may have included a contingency allowance in its internal estimates for unforeseen conditions, these are more likely intended to cover unforeseen conditions nominally within its control: a truck that breaks down, the need for an additional supervisor, more packing materials being needed than were estimated, and the like.

At the same time, the library has to be businesslike and thorough in administering the contract. The library is paying the mover to accomplish specific tasks detailed in the RFP and any subsequent documents included as part of a signed contract. It is the library's responsibility to monitor the mover's work to ensure that the mover's performance of these tasks is as specified, and to call to the mover's attention any discrepancies so that they can be reviewed and resolved promptly while the problem is hopefully small and easy (and therefore inexpensive) to correct. If the library's move coordinator is not certain whether something is being done as per the contract, it is probably better to bring the matter up and discuss it as soon as possible, to determine whether it is substantive.

What happens if you discover partway through the move that the library apparently overlooked or inadvertently omitted some key element of work from the scope of the contract? First, reread the contract language carefully, to be certain that the work you think was omitted was not, in reality, actually contemplated. Then, there are several options. One is to discuss the matter with the moving company and ask it to prepare an estimate for performing this work in addition to that already contracted for. A second is for library staff, or temporary staff hired by the library, to perform the work, either now or later. A third option, not possible in all instances, may be to let the work remain unperformed.

In general, addressing this sort of problem will draw on several of these approaches. If the work truly is not within the scope of the contract, the library may ask the moving company to provide an estimate to perform the work, determine whether the work could be done by staff, assess whether the work can be put off, and weighing all of these options, make a decision. The important point is to not let these things slide.

There may be some matters that cannot easily be resolved. For instance, the library may have included language that it thought clearly required specific work or use of a specific method, and the moving company read the requirement in a totally different way because its usual practice gives it a different mindset. In each instance, the library must assess whether it is important to insist on exact performance of the task or method or an alternative offered by the moving company is acceptable. To establish a good working relationship, and to set the tone for give and take on the part of the mover, it is important to be flexible where appropriate and possible, and to reserve insistence on precise conformity with the contract for those instances where conformity is necessary. In a less flexible approach to contract administration, it is also possible to keep a running tally of the monetary value of library concessions (that is, deviations from the contract as identified by the library) and to use this as a tool for negotiating the mover's performance of work not explicitly identified in the contract.

Effective administration of the contract between library and moving company requires that each have a representative officially designated to speak and make legally binding commitments. It's worth including a clause in the RFP stating that only the library's designated representative is authorized to give official verbal instructions to the moving company and that the moving company shall not consider instructions received from other members of the staff. Alternatively, the library might wish to require that all official instruction to the moving company be in writing. Instructions to staff concerning the move should also make clear that only the library's official representative is authorized to instruct the movers.

Library staff must be informed that any concerns they have about the move are to be expressed to the library's official representative, not directly to the movers. Some staff members will question why they cannot ask an individual mover ("who's so nice") to carry a box of personal belongings ("just two or three") , or fix a misshelved sequence of journals ("But they're wrong! Shouldn't we make the movers fix them now?") . The library's representative alone will be in the position of understanding the contract, the constraints within which the contract is being administered, and the history of other problems that may have already been addressed. He or she will also be in a position to determine the merit of a staff person's concern, and, if warranted, relay it to the moving company in an appropriate context and with an appropriate level of priority. Failure to filter staff concerns can lead to the moving company receiving conflicting instructions, time wasted on work outside the contract, and work interruptions, all of which will increase the length of the move (and cost the library money).

During the move, the library's move coordinator should inspect the work at least daily and keep a log of problems that arise, when and how they are communicated to (or from) the mover, actions taken to resolve the problems, and whether and when the problems are satisfactorily resolved. Although most problems can be handled through verbal communication, serious or ongoing problems should be communicated to the mover in writing, and the communication should document the history of the problem to date.

At the conclusion of the move, the library should conduct a final inspection of the work to determine whether it has been completed acceptably and whether all problems noted during the move have been resolved to the library's satisfaction. A list of deficiencies remaining to be corrected, called a punch list, should be prepared and reviewed with the moving company. Final acceptance of the mover's work should not be given, and final payment should not be released, until all punch list work is complete.

Withholding final payment until all punch list work has been done gives the library leverage in ensuring that the work is completed to its satisfaction; however, it is important that the RFP and contract include a payment schedule that explicitly withholds a specified percentage of the project cost until final acceptance of the project and specifies that the library (or its parent organization) will be the sole judge of the project's acceptability.

LIBRARY AND MOVER RESPONSIBILITIES FROM A MOVER'S PERSPECTIVE

Michael J. Kent, William B. Meyer, Inc.

Mover's Introduction

A library mover will want to introduce himself and get to know you and your project before the bid process begins. Quite often this is the only chance the mover will have to personally discuss your project and offer solutions without the competition being present. This is an opportunity for the mover to gain insight into specific difficulties that may be part of the move and into the library's concerns. The mover will be interested in this because it will help him more accurately estimate the work involved in the move and the cost to him of performing the move. It can be important for the librarian as well as the mover. It affords the library the opportunity to become familiar with various movers and to hear proposed solutions or methods of handling certain aspects of the project.

LIBRARY AND MOVER RESPONSIBILITIES

Early Planning

It is never too early to begin planning your move. As library movers, we have found that in many instances library staff have not quantified what needs to be moved and have not determined whether changes in the collection layout will be made. Early planning may well start as early as two to three years in advance. Begin by subdividing your collection by classification and subclassifications and measuring it in linear inches. If not already done, develop a database that can be updated as the collection grows. This information will become a vital ingredient in your Request for Proposal (RFP). A library mover will want to know the extent of the material to be moved in linear inches or feet in order to best develop a move plan.

A library mover can become your best friend! Give movers a chance to discuss your project and their qualifications in the early planning stages. You may discover some cost saving methods that can be used in planning and executing your move. You may also find that you wish to prequalify some movers and eliminate others before the bid process begin.

Developing a complete and accurate RFP will result in good competitive bidding and completing the move within budget and on schedule. From a mover's viewpoint, there are several issues worthy of note.

Liability

This is an area often misunderstood. There are several areas of concern where responsibility and the dollar amount required should be clearly identified. Most library movers have had to deal with unstated or implied insurance or liability requirements that were only alluded to in the "fine print" of a contract. It is important to bring your requirements out in the open and to be able to discuss them in simple terms that all parties can understand.

A Certificate of Insurance is a standard form covering automobile liability, general and comprehensive liability, and workers' compensation insurance. Property damage insurance covers any damage caused by the mover to your building, grounds, or vehicles, and describes the mover's liability per limits set forth in the certificate of insurance.

Cargo liability is a term covering all items being moved by your mover, for instance collection materials, furniture, and equipment. In most cases, the standard liability for a mover is $.60 per pound per article, although this may vary from state to state. If the collection contains specific items of unusual value, it is important to identify them. It is not fair to conceal the value of this sort of material, particularly if a claim for damage or loss needs to be made later on. Consult legal and insurance representatives and establish whether you want self-insurance for the move or you want the mover to be fully liable for full replacement value, with or without a deductible. Liability needs to be established in lump sum form or per truck load form, and a certificate of liability or insurance should be submitted. The RFP should clearly state your needs in this regard.

WORKING WITH A MOVING COMPANY

Responsibilities

Responsibilities should be clearly identified. Obvious mover responsibilities are to pack, move, and unpack the books in sequence; move materials, furniture, and equipment as identified in the RFP; and provide packing materials and moving equipment necessary to properly carry out the move. Areas where assignment of responsibility may not be clear are

packing and unpacking

office contents and

common areas such as storage rooms, supply rooms, and technical services shelf contents;

collection measurement and layout;

transfer into new cabinets of materials such as microforms, files, and maps; and

security/safety.

For each area, identify whether the mover, the library, or both will have responsibility.

In addition, it is important to state your expectations of your mover in the following areas:

Before the start of the move:

Preplanning meetings: How many meetings do you expect the mover to attend? How much time will this total?

Once the move has begun, will the library require:

a daily productivity report?

daily meetings?

Each of these requirements takes time, and therefore will cost the mover money, so it's important for the mover to understand up front the library's expectations in these areas.

Qualifications

Library moves can be a simple shelf-to-shelf book move or a more technical integration or segregation of books. Whatever the case, if you want an experienced library mover, then make that part of the RFP. State in the RFP that, as part of the qualifying process, a bidder must have planned and moved three to five libraries similar in scope to your project. Be specific . . . identify the criteria you will use to evaluate movers' minimum qualifications: for instance, state that the mover must have moved 500,000 volumes, segregated bound periodicals, integrated collections from three libraries into one. Make sure your qualifications are realistic and relate to your specific project. You want to be able to use these criteria to identify bidders

136

who have completed projects of similar scope and complexity to the one you're contemplating, but not eliminate all bidders!

If you carefully and completely describe bidder qualifications in the RFP, you have ensured yourself the opportunity to choose the best library mover for your project and allowed yourself the latitude to eliminate low bids from unqualified bidders.

Timing and Walk-Through

The RFP should be sent out to prospective bidders in advance of a "walk-through" by each bidder. This gives bidders the opportunity to read the RFP beforehand and see what questions they need answered during the walk-through.

The walk-through may be done en masse at a mandatory bidder's conference or by appointment. There are pros and cons to both. A bidder's conference is convenient for library staff in that the walk-through questions and answers are done once and all bidders see and hear the same thing. This should provide you with good competitive bids, assuming that your RFP specification is clear and complete. However, don't expect to learn anything from the bidders during a bidder's conference, as they will not share thoughts and ideas with you in front of the competition.

The other option, an individual bidder walk-through by appointment, is time consuming and raises the possibility of misinterpretation of various facts by the bidders. However, this approach does provide the opportunity for the library to interface with individual movers, to get a better feeling for their qualifications, and to possibly learn about some cost and time-saving methods they employ. This may also be achieved by having met potential bidders in the early planning stages or by having the best bidders appear for individual presentations.

Bid Evaluation

Qualified library movers travel all over the country to bid on projects. Bidder conferences are usually attended by the three to five library moving companies best known in the industry *and* some local moving companies that in many cases haven't a clue about the technical aspects of a library move. While developing your RFP you took into consideration qualifications. If you determined that you wanted a qualified library mover and set parameters, then address this in your initial bid evaluation. Eliminate those not qualified, even if they were low bidders. Often, these low bids were such through lack of understanding your project.

Evaluating the remaining bids becomes a process of reviewing each segment of the movers' proposals. Cost should not be the only factor. Review the move plan to ensure that all of your requirements have been met. A low bid may not have included an important aspect of your RFP (i.e., measure and map the collection, accomplish the move in a certain time frame, clean the collection, etc.).

WORKING WITH A MOVING COMPANY

The Move Process

Joint Planning

Joint planning between the selected library mover and the library is the most important ingredient in creating a good move. Joint planning will ensure that all of your requirements and the movers' are understood. It will also establish your relationship with the mover. Experienced library movers recognize the important of joint planning and will be able to assist you in setting agendas and timing for these sessions. The total agenda may take several sessions and should cover

scheduling and priorities;

collection layout and measurements;

furniture layout;

special needs (rare books, photos, special collections, etc.);

communications (phones, two-way radios, daily status reports, etc.);

key contacts;

move methodology;

security;

responsibilities;

staff packing and labeling information;

permits, licenses, insurance certificates, etc.;

transfer of files, microforms, etc., from old cabinets to new;

integration and/or segregation needs;

cleaning of collection;

punch list of building conditions prior to the move; and

project coordination with other contractors.

Joint planning should continue during the move itself, but only as needed to keep the lines of communication open. The mover's project manager and his staff of supervisors will each have areas of responsibility, as discussed in preplanning sessions. Appropriate lines of communication should be established and adhered to.

Should you decide that it is necessary to meet daily with the project manager to review various activities, talk with the mover to find a mutually convenient time and keep it brief. A daily status report from the mover showing productivity and progress within the move plan may be enough to keep the library staff informed.

138

LIBRARY AND MOVER RESPONSIBILITIES

Move Plan

During joint planning, the mover will also develop his move plan. This may consist of simple adjustments to the plan submitted by the mover in the bid proposal, or, if major changes in the requirements of the project have occurred, the mover may prepare a new move plan.

The move plan will consist of a master schedule for the collection move as well as moves of staff office contents, furniture, and other materials to be moved as part of the overall move project. Daily objectives should be part of this plan. In order to support the master schedule, a team schedule is prepared showing manpower allocations and team packing/unpacking schedules for the collection move. The team schedule will include daily productivity standards, such as packing 1,000 linear feet per day per team and what portion of the collection will be packed and moved on a given day.

Appropriate staffing of the move team with movers and supervisors will ensure a smooth, continuous, and efficient move.

Move Start-up

The initial start-up of the move is all in the hands of the mover, assuming premove joint planning sessions have been productive. Particularly if the project is large, the first day or two may be mostly devoted to mobilizing manpower and equipment, and the amount of material actually moved may be low despite considerable work having been performed. Productivity will appear to be low; however, this is as expected. Patience is a virtue at this stage.

Move Operations

The mover's project manager will develop a move plan that will involve daily activity and productivity. A daily status report should be submitted to you and will keep you informed as to progress in comparison to the planned timeline of the project. Even a well-planned and managed move will usually have its interruptions; however, in a well-planned and managed move, these will be handled efficiently through a good line of communications between the mover and the library.

All movers have experienced many unforeseen delays due to factors beyond their control. It is important for the library to understand the effect of unforeseen delays on the mover and work with him to anticipate possible problems, to prevent them whenever possible, and, in those instances when it is impossible to prevent problems, to minimize their effect as much as possible. This is not just a matter of being nice: since time is money, it will also help you avoid cost overruns. Delays such as elevator breakdown, power outage, compact shelving breakdown, unscheduled dock deliveries, and the like can add time to the mover's timetable and cost, which may result in additional cost to you.

Keep in mind that if the mover's staff consists of thirty-five workers, a delay of an hour or so is costly, especially if there are numerous delays over the span of the project. It is best to require documentation of delays on the daily status report. A delay resulting in cost overruns may have been caused by the failure of another contractor to abide by previously agreed-upon contract conditions. With appropriate documentation as backup, these costs may be passed on to the responsible party rather than being absorbed by the library. The daily status report may also be used to document any damage to the building, to collections, or to furniture and equipment that is being moved.

Experience has shown that a good relationship between the mover and library supervisory staff goes a long way in ensuring the success of the move. Be flexible, and remember to smile!

Project Closure

As the project comes to an end, the library should have a good understanding of the accuracy and completeness of service that has been provided by the mover. If the library has developed a punch list to review with the mover's project manager, this should not be left to the last minute, because some items may be more easily and efficiently addressed during the move.

This is the best time to review the project and have a clear understanding of what, if any, changes to the project cost have occurred. Any documentation of damage to inventory or buildings should be reviewed prior to the departure of the mover's project manager.

A well thought out, planned, and executed move will result in congratulations for you, your staff, and your mover.

6 PREPARING A REQUEST FOR PROPOSAL (RFP)

PURPOSE OF THE RFP

A Request for Proposal, or RFP, is a formal document that solicits proposals (bids) from moving companies. It describes the work to be performed, and the legal and operational conditions under which it is to be performed. It is the basis upon which each moving company prepares its proposal, and typically becomes part of the actual contract.

The RFP typically details not only what is to be done, but how and when it is to be done, the conditions under which it is to be done, who is responsible for which actions, who will have the right and responsibility to make which decisions, and any other contextual or legal information relevant to the move.

Because the RFP becomes both the legal and operational basis for work performed by the mover, it is critical that it be accurate and detailed, and that it be reviewed by legal counsel.

ELEMENTS OF THE RFP

Several types of information must be conveyed by the RFP: about the library or organization, the amount of work the library wants the mover to perform, mover qualifications, and legal conditions. Each organization will have its own approach to writing RFPs, and different RFPs may cover specific elements in greater or lesser detail. However, the elements of an RFP will normally include

1. a statement of the document's purpose;

2. background information necessary for the bidder to properly understand the RFP, including terminology and any other specific general concerns that may have a bearing on the proposal the mover is expected to provide;

141

3. a description of the project's scope;

4. a description of required services;

5. a statement of any additional or optional services that may be considered as a part of the mover's proposal;

6. bidder qualifications, required or desired;

7. instructions for submitting the proposal and bid;

8. conditions of the proposal;

9. conditions of any subsequent agreement (contract);

10. detailed information affecting the scope of the move, generally contained in appendices, including, for example,

   a. a description of the collections to be moved and any collection integration to be performed,

   b. a list of any equipment and of any furniture to be moved,

   c. measurements of the collections to be moved,

   d. plans of the facilities and areas involved,

   e. loading dock locations,

   f. elevator load limits and

   g. details on known potential problem areas, such as walkways likely to be damaged by wheeled vehicles or paved areas where there are load limits; and

11. a bid form.

Each of these elements and its contractual purpose from the library perspective is discussed in the following pages. Bear in mind that an RFP and the contract into which it will eventually be incorporated are legal documents. The information presented in the following pages is intended to give a library perspective on the purpose of each element; it is not intended to substitute for legal advice. State and local variations in specific laws and institutional legal experience and practices make it critical that the library have the RFP reviewed by its parent organization's legal counsel before the RFP is sent out.

A BRIEF RFP

In some instances where the planned move is very small, a library or its parent institution may not want to undertake a full-blown RFP. In this situation, what is the least amount of information the RFP should include? Following are suggestions:

1. The linear measurement of the material to be moved

2. Its present location

3. The new location

4. Any restrictions on date and time

5. Anything the library feels is unusual or special about this move

6. Legal material required by the parent institution

The decision about when to use a brief RFP and when to use a full-blown document with all of the clauses described below will depend not only on the size of the move, but also on the personality and experience of the key decision makers and the institution. For moves that will take more than a day or two, though, strongly consider investing in the time and effort to learn more about your proposed partner in the move and give yourself a chance to engage in a dialogue about your mutual assumptions. In general, this approach will save time and trouble and ensure that the move is done accurately, safely, on time, and within budget.

MECHANICS OF RFP PRESENTATION

An RFP is often long and complex. It will become the basis for detailed discussion of what should happen during the move and who is responsible for performing specific actions, so it is important to be able to identify and refer clearly to specific elements of the RFP. For ease of reference, number each section and subsection hierarchically. For example, numbering for a hypothetical Section 3, describing the scope of the move, might begin as follows:

Section 3. Project Scope

    3.1 Description of Move

    3.2 Collections

        3.2.1 Types of Collection Materials

        3.2.2 Extent of Collections, by Location

            3.2.2.1 Location A

            3.2.2.2 Location B

            3.2.2.3 Location C

        3.2.3 Layout Plans for Current Collection Locations

            3.2.3.1 Location A

            3.2.3.2 Location B

            3.2.3.3 Location C

        3.2.4 Layout Plan for New Collection Locations

            3.2.4.1 Location D

            3.2.4.2 Location E

    3.3 Shelving

and so forth.

ELEMENTS OF THE RFP AND THEIR CONTRACTUAL PURPOSE

This section describes elements that might be included in an RFP and their contractual purpose, without suggesting specific wording. The elements are arranged in the approximate order in which they might appear.

1. A statement of the document's purpose: A brief statement summarizing the purpose of the document: that it is intended to define the specifications and requirements for, and solicit quotations or bids from, prospective contractors for the moving and integration of the library's collection materials and selected furnishings and equipment. Typically the RFP, the mover's response, and any mutually agreed upon modifications are later incorporated into the contract between the library and the successful bidder. A statement to this effect should also be included in this section, as notice to the mover that the information provided in its response will be used in this way.

2. Background information or introduction: This section provides the contextual information the mover needs to properly understand what services the library is asking it to bid upon. Content of this section will vary according to the needs of the individual library, but might include the following:

    a. **A listing of the current and future facilities, with their full and abbreviated names** (e.g., "The John and Jane Smith Memorial Library, referred to hereafter as 'New Main' " or "The Chemistry and Chemical Engineering Branch Library, referred to hereafter as 'Chem'").

        This listing helps familiarize the reader with the number of locations involved in the move and identifies the abbreviated names by which they will be identified in the body of the document.

    b. **A statement on the construction status of specific facilities** (e.g., "New Main is currently under construction and completion is expected by [date]," or, "After the Library moves from Old Main, renovation work is planned to begin on [date]").

        Buildings under construction are subject to schedule slippage and the ongoing completion of punch list work. These conditions may mean that the loading dock and elevators the mover needs to efficiently execute the move may have to be shared with other contractors. Moves out of buildings in which subsequent construction is planned are often subject to tighter completion pressures, as the renovation contractor pushes for access to begin its work.

        It is important to identify either condition so that the mover can ask questions about shared access to elevators and loading docks and accurately gauge the impact this might have on its operations and expenses.

c. **A brief description of the type of shelving** (e.g., cantilever or case-type), including whether compact shelving is provided and, if so, whether it is mechanically or electrically operated.

d. **External schedules that may affect the move and a statement of any related concerns.** (For example, "The University offers classes to students throughout the year with only brief vacation periods between quarters. The move will take place during the Summer Quarter, and because use of the library's collections and services is substantial during this period, it will be desirable to minimize the duration of the move and to plan carefully the move paths and sequence of operations") .

e. **A brief description of the types of materials and furnishings to be moved.** The description of materials might include a listing of the collection types (bound materials, AV recordings, DVDs, government documents, pamphlet files, material in process, mending, microformats, archival and special collection materials, realia, toys and games, map files, and any other formats specific to your collection, particularly unusual ones that may require special handling).

The description might further identify how the materials are currently classified and arranged (for example, "Collection materials are currently classified according to Library of Congress (LC), Dewey Decimal (DDC), Superintendent of Documents (SuDocs), and other, local, classification schemes").

Like the listing of buildings, this gives the potential bidder some sense of the complexity and difficulty of the handling and shelving aspects of the move, by identifying the range of types of material.

The brief description of furnishing and equipment provides a summary of types of items. Include in separate appendixes inventories of specific furniture and equipment items to be moved. In this section, consider using the phrase "the furnishings and equipment to be moved shall include, *but not be limited to* . . . ." Although the inventories attached as appendixes should be as complete and accurate as possible, it is likely that a small number of items will have to be added or deleted from the list, and this phrasing alerts the mover of this possibility.

This should not be taken as a license to add large quantities of items to the list provided in the RFP; the intent is to notify the mover that, as of the date the RFP is being written, the list cannot be considered final. If a mover is concerned about this wording, consider committing to a maximum percentage change: for instance, that the number of items will neither increase nor decrease by more than, say, 10 percent.

Movers will also need to know whether the library's shelving is to be moved, and whether they will be expected to move it. This is a good place to provide this information. State clearly who will be responsible for any disassembly and reassembly (the mover? in-house crew? a separate contractor?) and any related timing considerations.

f. **At a minimum, a statement that the library will prepare and make available to the successful contractor a collection layout plan.** It is preferable to include in the RFP at least a preliminary collection layout plan, or a general description of the proposed collection arrangement, so that, in conjunction with the description of the current collections and their arrangement, and its own inspection of the current facilities during the walk-through conducted as part of the bid process (see Chapter 7 for more on this topic), the mover can accurately assess the complexity of the work the library wishes to have performed.

This section should also include a statement that the collection layout plan is the official description of where and how material will be shelved (e.g., "All collection material shall be shelved according to the Collection Layout Plan").

g. **A definition of what the library means by the term "move"** (e.g., "The Contractor shall remove all books, periodicals and newspapers from their present shelves in existing order from left to right, shall place them on book trucks, shall move them to the new designated locations, and shall reshelve them in the same order as directed by the . . . Library Staff at predetermined locations on the shelves as indicated by the . . . Library Staff" [Kurth and Grim 1966, 213]).

This statement may seem obvious to the librarian, but may not be so to all bidders, particularly if the bidding is open to first-time library movers. It could also be modified to note requirements for item-by-item collection integration, separation of specified items, or other specific tasks required in the move being contemplated.

3. A description of the scope of the project: The purpose of this section is to describe the move in some detail, with a focus on the materials to be moved. The text in this section will probably be fairly brief, with the bulk of the information provided in the appendixes. This section and the following one comprise the core description of what the mover is expected to undertake, and therefore should be as accurate, detailed, and complete as possible. Include the following elements:

a. **A narrative description of the scope** of the move, including what is to be moved, where it is to be moved, and parties with whom work must be coordinated. From this section, refer to appendixes that provide additional information on the following:

b. **Collections**

   i. Provide as an appendix a *detailed description of the types of collection materials to be moved.* Include a description of any collection mergers or integration the mover is expected to perform. If you are merging two or more collections and expect the mover to perform item-by-item integration resulting in a single sequence of individual items arranged in call number order, it is important to state this explicitly.

   In at least one instance, a library specialist mover tacitly proposed to provide only shelf-by-shelf integration in response to an RFP calling for simply "collection integration," and tacitly assumed that library staff would perform the final item-by-item interfiling. This would have required the library to provide a considerable amount of labor after the move, so it is important to specify unambiguously exactly what is needed. As with other facets of mover qualifications, on this matter it also pays to check each mover's references.

   Detail, too, any changes in classification or arrangement that will be taking place in conjunction with the move. For a complex move, this description may extend to a number of pages; however, it is critical to provide the mover with a level of detail sufficient to plan the move and its expenses accurately.

   (a) Identify collections that will be moved in cabinets (e.g., microforms, maps, AV materials, CD-ROMs, and diskettes). Describe the number of drawers, dimensions, and, if known, approximate weight of each cabinet. State the mover's' responsibility for moving these collections intact.

   ii. Provide as a separate appendix *an itemization, by current location and type, of the materials to be moved, in linear feet or shelf inches.*

   If there are areas where the extent of the materials may be estimated rather than measured, as might be the case if materials were boxed and stored in piles, it is important to

147

identify the information provided as an estimate and to be honest about the level of accuracy possible.

It is important to neither underestimate nor overestimate the accuracy of the information provided, so that the mover neither over- nor underestimates the difficulty and expense of performing the work required, nor has cause to later think the library intentionally misrepresented the scope of the work in order to elicit a lower bid price (or was careless).

Include and separately itemize collection material that may be in process, being repaired, or awaiting binding at the time of the move.

iii. Provide *collection layout plans* for the current facilities, showing the current locations of materials (as of a specified date), and the detailed collection layout plan for each new facility, showing the location of each significant collection segment, fill ratios for each segment, and identifying the shelf spacing and fill ratios for each segment, where blocks of shelving are to be left empty, and any other relevant detail.

c. **Shelving.** Provide a separate listing of the types of shelving in the current and new facilities. Include in this listing a description of the shelf spacing desired and whether the library or the mover will be responsible for performing the shelf spacing. If the shelving has cross-bracing, has tie bars above the ranges, or is bolted to the floor, specify its careful removal and reinstallation, and consider detailing the installation criteria needed to meet code. In earthquake county, check whether additional tie bars or other stabilization methods should be added.

State here whether the mover will be responsible for dusting or vacuuming the shelves in the new facility before shelving materials; if the mover will be responsible for relocating shelving units, specify that here also.

d. **Furnishings and equipment, office contents, and supplies** Provide separate appendixes listing furnishings and equipment to be moved. Identify responsibility for packing and moving office contents: for example, if staff offices are moving to a new location, and new furniture is being provided, is the mover expected to provide boxes, and how will the contents of staff desks and files be moved?

It is strongly recommended that staff be responsible for packing their own desk and file contents, so that each person knows where his or her working tools are and can maintain control over the confidentiality of materials in the files. It is also recommended that staff be responsible for personally moving any valued personal items that might be lost or damaged in a move, both for their own peace of mind and to avoid the potentially difficult question of who is responsible for compensating a staff member if a personal item is lost or damaged in the move.

Clearly identify any exceptions: for instance, that scanning workstations will be moved separately, or that photocopiers operated within the library by an outside vendor will be moved by that vendor.

Movers may want to be provided with an estimate of the number of boxes of office contents to be moved; however, a listing of the number of staff positions, offices, or workstations to be moved may be helpful as an alternate measure of the scope of this portion of the move.

If card catalog cabinets are to be moved, state whether they are to be moved with their drawers intact or removed. If they are to be moved intact, identify who will be responsible for securing the drawers. If the drawers are to be removed, identify who will remove them and consider identifying how they will be transported (in a specially designed box supplied by the library? Kurth and Grim, 213), and who will be responsible for replacing the drawers or transferring the cards at the destination.

e. **Facilities and their locations** Provide a complete set of plans of each current and new facility, unless these are already part of the collection layout plans. Also provide a street map (or campus map) showing the location of each facility and the distance and streets and pathways between each facility. On the map, identify one-way streets, loading dock locations, any areas where access will be restricted, and the nature of the restrictions (e.g., no vehicles over x tons permitted, or access permitted only between 10:00 PM and 6:00 AM).

4. <u>A description of the services required:</u> This section complements the preceding one, focusing on services to be provided by the mover rather than the materials to be moved. These two related sections could be combined. Service issues to address include the following:

a. **A general statement of responsibility** It is worthwhile to include a general statement that the mover is responsible for all supervision, labor, materials, supplies, and equipment to perform all services contemplated under the RFP in a workmanlike and timely fashion, and that the mover may not use any of the library's equipment or personnel except as specifically provided for in the RFP.

The purpose of this statement is to locate primary responsibility for the move with the mover, by specifying that if there is any perceived ambiguity about who is responsible for what, the mover will be responsible.

It provides the library with recourse in case the mover says, for example, that it assumed the library would perform a specific task (for example, adjusting shelf heights, performing item-by-item integration, or shelf-reading collections after the move; removing trash generated by the move), provide certain supplies (e.g., markers, labels, tape), or provide certain equipment (telephones, trash cans, refrigerator, dumpster). Unless the RFP says the library will do or provide something, this language makes it the mover's responsibility. Similarly, using the phrase "workmanlike and timely" signals that the job will be done in conformance with accepted standards of performance.

Consider including a statement that the library "expects to receive, consider and utilize such time-saving suggestions from the successful Bidder which are his to make because he is an experienced professional mover" (Spyers-Duran 1965, 41).

b. A **time frame**

i. *Start and completion dates.* If there are specific dates on which or by which the move *must* begin or end, identify them here. If there is a maximum duration, or a desire to minimize the duration of the move, say so in this section.

ii. *Sequencing and schedule.* If the library has a preferred or required sequence for the move, detail it. If the library wishes the mover to suggest a sequence for the move, within certain limits, specify those limits (e.g., the main library must be moved first, then the branches; however, the mover may choose to move one or another branch first).

iii. *Any limits on daily hours of operation.* If there are limits on when the mover will be permitted to conduct operations, for instance for reasons of staff liaison, building access, or noise control, specify them here. For example, perhaps the library is located in a quiet residential neighborhood and operations can only take place during weekdays. Jerry McCabe, in a personal communication (January 21, 2009), notes that traffic regulations in congested urban areas may prohibit trucks from parking and prevent work being done during the daytime or rush hour, thus forcing work to be done at night or on weekends. Or perhaps the library wishes to minimize disruption to patrons and wants work to be performed only in the evening and on weekends. In any case, if you do not specify any restrictions, the mover may elect to perform the work at its own convenience.

c. **Collection access during the move.** A major collection move will be disruptive.

Some libraries have the option of simply suspending service for the duration of the move; others do not. For reasons of public safety and efficient workflow, the public will probably have to be excluded from at least the immediate area where work is taking place and from any move traffic paths within and around a facility. If the public is allowed inside the facility while the move is taking place, the areas that are off-limits must be clearly identified.

Because the mover will be hampered by having to work around library staff or patrons, consider carefully the trade-offs between public access and move efficiency. At the same time, the library will probably want to have some way of retrieving material from the collections being moved. The following deal with these issues:

i. *Exclusion of the public from work areas.* Describe whether, or the extent to which, the public will be excluded.

ii. *Daily progress reports and/or meetings.* You will probably want to receive daily progress reports, detailing the starting and ending call numbers of each collection segment moved each day, which can provide not only a measure of progress but an important tool for locating materials. Meetings take time (and therefore cost the mover money), but can be a useful touch point. If you want one or both of these services, say so here.

iii. *Provisions for paging materials.* If the library wishes to be able to retrieve materials from the collection during the move, who will be responsible for this operation, the library or the mover? Must materials be retrievable within a specified period of time, say twenty-four hours? If the library will provide this service, does it contemplate requiring any information from the mover beyond daily progress reports?

d. **Packing and moving methods.**

i. *Materials.* During a move, collection materials are potentially subject to stressful handling conditions. Preservation education can be particularly important if the mover has not previously moved a library collection.

At least two approaches are possible: the library may specify either the packing and moving techniques to be used, or that the technique selected by the mover meet certain preservation criteria, for instance, that the containers and methods used to pack and move collection materials ensure their protection from any immediate or long-term damage.

Although the first approach gives the library more control, it may also require that the mover perform its work in an unfamiliar way or with materials and equipment the moving company does not regularly stock, and this could potentially increase the bid price. The second approach gives the mover more control, but requires that the library verify that the methods the mover represents as causing no immediate or long-term damage actually do not cause damage. In either case, the library will probably wish to require the mover to provide samples of each packing tool for inspection (Spyers-Duran 1965, 35).

Specific packing and moving methods are discussed in more detail in Chapter 4.

ii. *Furnishings and equipment.* Although most movers can be expected to be familiar with the appropriate techniques for moving office furniture and equipment, libraries may own furniture and equipment items that a mover does not commonly handle, for instance large-scale scanners, servers, exit security equipment, microform reader/printers, and card catalog units. The library may wish to ask the mover to describe the methods proposed to move each of these specialized furniture and equipment items.

e. **Marking methods.** Many movers use adhesive tags or labels to identify groups of materials with their points of origin and destination. The library may want to ask the mover to ensure that adhesive materials will not leave a residue or cause permanent damage; state that the mover is responsible for removing any residue or repairing any damage caused by labels or marking materials.

f. **Security.** During the move, collection materials, furnishings, and equipment will be outside the library's normal security controls and under the supervision and control of the moving company. The library will therefore probably want the moving company to detail the methods it proposes to protect its property from loss or damage from theft, vandalism, and weather damage while outside the building.

g. **Continuous and diligent effort.** Some movers commit to completing more than one project simultaneously, under the supervision of the same staff. This can result in less than satisfactory oversight and control of your project, or in work on your project being temporarily halted while staff and equipment are used elsewhere. The library may therefore wish to have the mover make a statement assuring that the staff and equipment assigned to the library's move will not be assigned to any other client or project until the library's move is complete.

h. **Involvement of the library's staff.** If the library has included in its RFP a general statement of responsibility, it will also have to specifically identify the library staff who will be involved in the move, and what their responsibilities will be.

i. *Library move coordinator.* At a minimum, the library should identify a primary contact person, here called the library move coordinator; state that all official communication with the library must flow through this person; and identify specific rights and responsibilities reserved to the library through this person. These might include coordination with public safety officials, deployment of additional library staff, serving as the final authority for resolving problems that may arise involving the move sequence, materials handling procedures, and behavior of the mover's staff that may be objectionable.

In addition, the library move coordinator may be responsible for the ongoing inspection and review of work, performing a final inspection, and noting any deficiencies that must be corrected by the mover prior to final payment.

ii. *Right to halt work.* A situation may arise in which the library needs to require a change in the mover's procedures or staff, or to stop the work entirely. For example, the library may become aware that procedures harmful to materials are being used, that materials are being placed in the wrong location or out of order, that a member of the mover's staff is behaving in an unacceptable manner, or that a difference of opinion exists about whether inclement weather will harm materials in transit.

In each case, the library will want to be certain it has retained for itself the authority to require immediate correction of the problem and the right to halt work if the problem is not resolved to the library's satisfaction. Although this is a right the library should not exercise lightly, it is a necessary tool to compel that work be accomplished in the manner specified. Without it, there is no effective mechanism to enforce conditions specified in the RFP. The library move coordinator is the logical person in whom this authority should be vested.

iii. *Involvement of other library staff.* It is worth stating explicitly the extent to which other library staff are expected to be involved or not involved in the move. For instance, staff may be expected only to pack their own office contents, but not to be involved in any other physical aspects of the move: packing other materials, loading, transporting, or unloading them.

i. **Contractor's staff.** The mover's staff will be the key to the success of the move. The library will therefore want the mover to provide information about its staff who will manage and execute the move.

   i. *Mover's project manager.* The library will want the mover to designate an individual, here referred to as the mover's project manager, to have overall responsibility for the move and for communication with the library through the library's move coordinator. The library may wish the mover to offer an assurance that the mover's project manager will be on site at all times to direct the work, and that another competent supervisor will be appointed (and the library notified in advance) if the designated project manager must leave the site for any period of time.

   Some project managers are better than others. To gauge the experience of this key person, the library may wish to request the moving company identify him or her by name, provide a resume including a list of moves for which the individual has been the project manager, and provide a list of references. Decide ahead of time whether you will accept another project manager if the person identified in the proposal is not available.

   ii. *Contractor's moving staff.* The library will also want the mover to describe the type and numbers of other staff who will participate in the move. A key question is whether the mover will use its own permanent staff to perform the packing and transportation of the materials, or whether these individuals will be hired locally. The quality and motivation of the moving staff make all the difference in how accurately reshelving is done, the rate of attrition, and ultimately how likely it is the move will be completed on time and with minimal cleanup afterward.

   For a national or regional company, it may cost less to hire locally. In either case, the skill level of these individuals is critical. They must not only be capable of demanding physical labor, but also be able to learn to accurately read call numbers. For these reasons, the library may wish the moving company to detail its screening and training procedures for nonsupervisory personnel.

   After working with Prison Industries of Rhode Island, Joanna M. Burkhardt recommends, "Hire literate movers who speak the same language you do. . . . Communication is closely linked to efficiency and accuracy in moving. If you hire movers who cannot understand your instructions or cannot read the labels on the boxes, the move becomes much more complicated" (1998, 501–2) ; her move took twice as long as planned. Jerry McCabe, in a personal communication (December 10, 2008), noted that guards' hours and shifts may limit the hours during which correctional labor is available.

For these reasons, it is suggested that the RFP include a clause stating that prison labor may not be used, or requiring candidates for the moving crew to pass a test of their ability to read call numbers and follow directions in the same language as the library staff. Also, ask about the days and hours during which the moving crew will be available.

iii. *Identification for contractor's staff.* For security reasons, the library will want to have some means of immediately identifying individuals working for the moving company, and may wish to ask the moving company how it proposes to do this. Will mover employees be asked to wear an identifying T-shirt? A visible ID badge?

iv. *Site work rules.* For preservation, health, public relations, and aesthetic reasons, the library may wish to restrict the presence of food, beverages, smoking, profanity and other inappropriate language, and loud music at the move site. Consider whether you want movers to use the staff refrigerator or keep food on site, and where they will be able to take their breaks.

v. *Right to require immediate removal.* As discussed above, the library will want to reserve for itself the right to require the immediate removal of any of the mover's staff if it is the library's judgment that the person's presence is not in the best interest of the library or the project.

j. **Coordination of work with other agents.** If construction work is proceeding in any of the facilities involved in the move, the library will want to require that the mover cooperate in coordinating the move with the work of other entities, such as a construction contractor, shelving installer, the parent organization's physical plant department, building trades people, and so on.

k. **Move route.** If an exact move route has already been identified, the RFP should document it. Otherwise, if the library or its parent organization wishes to review the route a mover proposes, the RFP might say that the move route shall be developed jointly by the mover and the library, taking into account areas of limited access.

l.   **Parking.** If the move requires trucks, the mover will need secure locations to park its vehicle(s) overnight and when not in immediate use during the move. The RFP should state who will be responsible for arranging this parking, and the location, if already known.

m.   **Access to work sites.** The RFP should specify who will control access to work sites during the move, typically a member of the library or parent organization's staff.

n.   **Loading dock access.** The RFP should specify who will control access to loading docks. Because time available at the loading dock can be a critical constraint governing the flow of work, it will be important for the library to try to maximize the mover's access to loading docks in affected facilities.

   If the library knows in advance that the mover will not be able to have essentially exclusive access to loading docks in one or more affected facilities (for instance, because the library shares use of the facility with another occupant, who also requires access), this fact should be stated in the RFP so that the mover can make an appropriate allowance for the decreased access in planning its schedule and labor requirements.

o.   **Elevator access.** Elevators are another potential constraint on the progress of a move, and the library should accordingly take reasonable steps to ensure that all available elevators are in good working order before the move begins and make provision for their prompt repair if they malfunction during the move.

   At the same time, the mover must be responsible for operating elevators within their specified weight limitations, so as to not cause damage. The library might want to consider requiring pre- and post-move inspections of the elevators to assess whether any damage beyond normal wear and tear occurred during the move and whether to require the moving company to be responsible for the repair of any such damage. For example, who will pay for repairs if the mover jams open the elevator doors or dents the elevator cab?

   So that the moving company can accurately gauge the rate at which materials can be removed from a facility through its elevators, the RFP should include the following information for each facility's elevator(s):

   i.   *Physical dimensions.* The inside cab size, in feet and inches.

   ii. *Load limits.* In addition to identifying the load limits, the RFP should identify any other related potential problems, for instance, that placement of loads within specific elevators must be coordinated with the plant maintenance department.

iii. *Need for elevator operators.* If an operator is required for specific elevators, the RFP should so state and specify whether the library or the mover will be responsible for providing this labor.

iv. *Protection.* Will cab protection be the responsibility of the mover or of the library?

p. **Pre-bid conference and tour.** It is to the library's advantage to provide potential bidders with an opportunity to see the facilities and collections that are to be moved and to ask questions both about the contents of the RFP and what they observe on the tour. This gives potential bidders the opportunity (and the responsibility) of gauging for themselves actual site conditions and verifying the information provided by the library in the RFP.

To ensure that all bidders have an equal understanding of site conditions and the opportunity to benefit from the questions asked by competitors, the library will probably wish to require that all bidders attend the pre-bid conference and tour; if so, this must be stated in the RFP, along with its date, time, and location. The timing, agenda, and conduct of a pre-bid conference and tour are discussed in more depth in Chapter 7. This paragraph might alternatively be included in the Conditions of Bid section.

q. **Pre-performance conference.** The library will want to specify that the mover review with the library its detailed plans for the move far enough ahead of the planned start date that any potential problems can be worked out; this is the purpose of the pre-performance conference.

r. **Prior conditions.** During the course of the move, damage may occur to the library's facilities. Although assigning responsibility for the damage may be difficult if more than one entity is working in the facility at one time, the library may wish to require that the mover and the library representative jointly inspect each facility before the move starts and note any damage, and then conduct a similar audit after the move is completed. Responsibility for damage that occurred during the intervening period can then be negotiated, and, where appropriate, compensation for repair of the damage can be sought from the moving company.

At the same time, efficient conduct of the move may require creation of additional, temporary egress points. In this case, the library may wish to specify that minor alterations in the building may be made after consultation with library staff, provided the building is maintained and left in a secure and safe condition, with no danger of damage to the building or its contents from the elements, no risk of unauthorized entry, and no hazard to those working in the building (Spyers-Duran 1965, 39).

s.   **Site cleanliness.** Trash left on a work site is not only unsightly, but can be a fire or tripping hazard, contribute to logistical problems, and attract insects and rodents. Prompt disposal of trash generated by the move and maintenance of cleanliness on the work site are therefore important.

The RFP should specify this and also state whether the mover will be responsible for daily cleanup and final site cleanup at the conclusion of the move, and be permitted to use the library's trash receptacles (e.g,, trash cans and dumpsters). It's recommended that the library not assume responsibility for daily cleanup, both because the move is likely to generate considerable extra workload, and because the mover will probably want to maintain control over areas in which the move is taking place, so that work materials aren't inadvertently discarded.

The library will probably also wish to specify that if the mover does not maintain site cleanliness to the library's satisfaction or perform appropriate cleanup at the conclusion of the move, the library will arrange to have this done and deduct the charges from the amount still owed the mover. The parties may also wish to negotiate a credit from the mover for use of their dumpster, to cover any additional fee charged by the waste hauler.

5.   A statement of any additional or optional services that may be considered as a part of the mover's proposal

The library may not wish to commit itself to contracting for certain portions of the move or certain related services until it can determine the cost for providing the services or the proposed method in which the services would be provided. These conditional elements may be considered as additional, alternative, or optional services. They should be clearly separated from the services that the library definitely intends to contract for, both in the description of the service desired and the bid form.

Examples of additional or optional services might include a major service such as cleaning or fumigating the collection, or work that might be performed by either library staff or the mover's staff, depending on the cost: for example, adjusting shelf spacing or cleaning the shelves at a move destination prior to the materials being reshelved.

The RFP should clearly state whether the library reserves the right to select one bidder to perform the main body of the work and another to perform optional and additional services. If bids are prepared for optional and additional services on the assumption that these elements might be let separate from the main body of work, the mover might legitimately build in start-up costs for each project.

It would be reasonable to expect that actual costs for the main body of work plus any optional additional services performed by the same staff would be less than if they were performed by two separate staffs, with the cost difference being the elimination of duplicate set-up time. Nonetheless, it may still be worth asking that optional additional services be bid as freestanding operations, with the knowledge that if a single moving company is selected to perform both the main body of work and any optional additional elements, the price can be negotiated.

a. **Coordination of work.** If the library does reserve the right to select multiple bidders to perform the main body of the work and any contracted-for optional or additional services, the library will probably wish to require that mover(s) cooperate together with the library's representative to develop a schedule that minimizes delays or other operational problems.

6. Mover qualifications

It is important that the mover have the experience and resources to complete the move on time, within budget, with all materials accounted for, undamaged, and where they are supposed to be. Generally, this means working with a mover who has experience moving libraries. The library may wish to consider bids from only those movers who can demonstrate a certain level of experience. In some institutions, it may be possible to solicit bids from a group of companies who have been determined to have sufficient relevant experience. In other instances, prequalification may not be an option.

In any case, the library will wish to include in its RFP a request for information that will allow comparing the movers' qualifications. Two sources of additional information are references and financial reports.

a. **References.** Requiring that the mover submit references from moves of a similar size and complexity can help judge other libraries' satisfaction with their services. More useful is a list of all moves of similar size and complexity completed within the past two years or so, and of any size and complexity within, say, five years. For each move, the RFP might require that the mover list the number and type of volumes moved, the dates and duration of each move, and any specific services that were performed, such as collection integration or cleaning, with the name and telephone number of a library contact qualified to comment on the performance of the mover.

The library must be prepared to not only review the list of references in detail, but also talk to staff at the client libraries to determine the quality of the work performed. Chapter 7 discusses checking references in more detail.

b. **Financial status.** The library will want to be assured that the mover has the financial and human resources to mobilize appropriate resources for the move and will not experience cash flow problems that might adversely affect the progress of the move. Toward this end, the RFP might require the mover to submit such documents as its latest annual report, several years of statements of income and retained earnings, and most recent balance sheet and income statement, and to identify the number of full-time, permanent employees.

If the library does not have the in-house expertise to evaluate these documents, advice could be sought from within the library's parent organization, through personal contacts, or from an independent agency.

7. Instructions for submitting the proposal and bid

This section describes what information the library wants the mover to include in its proposal, which costs can and cannot be included in the bid, and mechanics related to submitting the proposal and bid. This material can seem bureaucratic, but it ensures that the library has enough information to evaluate the proposals, and that a fair comparison can be made between competing bids. It may include the following types of information:

a. **Proposal.** The library will wish to specify that the mover's proposal

    i. details the approach to the move according to the specifications of the RFP and information provided at the pre-bid conference and tour;

    ii. responds to every requirement contained in the RFP;

    iii. is complete without reference to other documents;

    iv. is signed by an authorized corporate officer of the firm;

    v. is provided as an original document, along with a number of copies sufficient for evaluation by appropriate individuals and offices within the library and its parent organization;

    vi. is properly addressed (provide the address); and

    vii. is received by a clearly identified date and time. It should be clearly stated whether extensions will be granted and, if so, under what circumstances.

b. **Bid.** The library will want to provide a bid form to ensure that the price for the move is presented clearly, so that unambiguous comparison of competitive bids can be made. (Consider making the bid form the last page of the RFP, both to make it easier to locate and to subtly signal that it is intended to cover the entire work detailed in the RFP.) If the RFP contains alternate or optional services, this paragraph must also specify whether bidders are required to bid on these services as well as the main body of work.

The library may want to require the mover to provide a positive statement that the bid is complete for the entire move as described in the RFP, and that all required planning, equipment, and labor will be provided at no additional cost to the library.

c. **Costs of developing proposals.** The library will probably want to state that the mover is responsible for all costs associated with developing proposals, including attendance at the pre-bid conference and tour.

d. **Billing.** The library will want to require that the mover detail its proposed billing schedule.

e. **Taxes.** Assuming the library is a tax-exempt institution, it will want to provide its tax-exemption number, offer to provide evidence of its tax-exempt status upon request, and specify that all prices be quoted without taxes.

f. **Responses to the agreement conditions.** To minimize the occasion for later discussion, the library may wish to require that the mover provide in its response a positive statement that the terms of the agreement detailed in the RFP are understood, and that any subsequent agreement will incorporate the RFP by reference.

g. **Inquiries about the RFP.** The RFP should state that contractors may request clarifications of the RFP until a stated date and time, and should provide the name, address, and telephone number of a designated contact. In the interest of clarity, the library may wish to require that inquiries refer to specific RFP paragraph numbers and sections and to consider whether to require that inquiries be written. This may seem somewhat bureaucratic, but it can reduce the potential for miscommunication. Requiring written inquiries also establishes a paper trail in case a dispute must be resolved later on.

So that all potential bidders have equal access to all potentially relevant information, the library will want to provide all bidders with a summary of all requests for clarification and the library's responses. The RFP should identify the date by which this information will be distributed and how (e.g., by mail, fax). To protect the confidentiality of the bidders, the names of companies asking questions should not be included.

h. **Calendar of events.** Because of the density of information contained in various sections of the RFP concerning mandatory deadlines for specific actions, it is helpful for both the library and potential bidders to summarize the calendar of events in one section. This might list in tabular form the dates (and where relevant the times) for distribution of the RFP, the pre-bid meeting and tour, the receipt of inquiries, the distribution of responses to inquiries, and the receipt of proposals.

8. Conditions of the proposal. This section details the rights reserved by the library or its parent organization and the obligations assumed by all potential bidders as a condition of their submitting a proposal. The library's parent organization will probably have established practice in this area, which will need to be incorporated in the RFP. This section might include the following:

a. **Pre-bid conference and tour.** State whether a pre-bid conference is required and whether all bidders will be required to attend a common pre-bid conference or schedule an individual conference with the library. (First read Michael Kent's comments on individual versus group pre-bid conferences in Chapter 5.) If there is to be a common pre-bid conference, state the date, time, and location.

b. **Contractor's responsibility for assessment of the extent and difficulty of the work.** The library may well wish to include some type of disclaimer concerning the absolute accuracy of the information provided in the RFP. For example, the library might wish to state that the lists of furniture and equipment represent the most accurate current lists, but that these may change by a small amount; that any maps and plans provided are the best available but may not necessarily reflect current conditions, which are in any event subject to change; and that the collection measurements provided are the library's best estimates as of a specific date.

The library may also want to consider including language to the effect that the mover has full responsibility for properly estimating the difficulties and the cost of performing services required by the RFP and will not be excused from that responsibility, nor will the library pay any extra charges associated with the mover's failure to become acquainted with all information concerning the services to be performed.

Spyers-Duran (1965, 35, 38) suggests using language that "warns the bidder that the figures and descriptions of materials to be moved are generalizations and that it is the contractor's responsibility to acquaint himself with the actual conditions." The specific language used in a sample contract he includes reads: "The

Bidder shall acquaint himself with the conditions existing at the present and new locations so that he may furnish such equipment and labor necessary to provide for the orderly, timely and efficient movement of the property. Failure to inspect will not relieve the Contractor of his responsibility to provide all the services required, and will not constitute any basis for relief of claims under the Contract."

The intent of this section is to make clear that if the mover does not understand any part of the specifications, or is not satisfied with the information or the way it is explained, it must ask for clarification, and that failure to inspect, ask questions, or recognize problems prior to making a proposal will not relieve the mover of its responsibility to provide all of the services required, nor constitute any basis for relief under a subsequent agreement.

This may seem harsh, but it is important to establish at the outset that the mover is expected to bring its best professional experience to bear on planning for the move and preparing the estimate. It is also necessary to protect the library from claims for additional compensation resulting from intentional or unintentional misunderstandings.

c. **Receipt and examination of bids.** All bids should be stamped with the date and time upon their receipt, to document compliance with the specified deadline, and this should be stated in the RFP. The RFP should also state whether the bids will be opened publicly.

d. **Withdrawal.** Occasionally, a bidder may wish to withdraw from consideration, and the RFP should specify any conditions for withdrawal and the dates during which this will be permitted to occur.

e. **Performance bond.** Under some circumstances, for instance if the mover's financial status leaves open some question about its ability to complete the work, the library or its parent organization may wish to require a performance bond. If a performance bond will definitely or may possibly be required, that should be stated in the RFP. Performance bonds cost money, and some movers may object, so this isn't something to be required lightly.

f. **Proposal.** The library will probably wish to state that by submitting a proposal and bid, the moving company acknowledges complete understanding of and willingness to comply with all of the specifications and conditions contained in the RFP and its attachments.

g. **Right to reject proposals.** The library may find, upon examining the proposals it receives, that none is acceptable, and may wish to reject all proposals, or to reopen the bid process. It is worth stating, then, that the library reserves the right to reject any or all proposals.

The library may also wish to state that it reserves additional rights, for example, to check the references provided and make other investigations into the qualifications of bidders; to accept the entire bid, the bid for the main body of the work, or the bid(s) for any additional or optional services; and to waive any formalities.

9. Conditions of agreement. This section details the obligations the successful bidder will assume as a condition of completing a contract with the library or its parent organization. The contents of this section should largely be determined by a lawyer. The elements may include:

a. **A subsequent agreement.** An introductory statement that the conditions set forth in this section, together with the response (proposal), shall be the basis for a subsequent agreement between the parties.

b. **Protection of library property.** A statement that the mover shall be responsible for maintaining a reasonable level of care to ensure that the library's premises and property shall be protected from any theft, damage, accident, vandalism, or otherwise, while the mover is using such property or on such premises. This could be expanded to detail minimal expectations, for example:

   i. protecting carpets, floors, walls, and elevator doors;

   ii. not permanently disengaging or dismantling anything perman- ently attached to library property without prior written permission;

   iii. not disconnecting any utilities;

   iv. keeping the wheels of moving equipment free of oil, sediment, or other materials that might damage carpets and other floor coverings;

   v. determining locations of and working around furniture, and if it is necessary to relocate furniture to facilitate the move, being responsible for replacing the furniture at the conclusion of the move; and

   vi. keeping loading dock doors closed when not in use.

c. **Contractor's insurance** The library or its parent organization will want the mover to provide some assurance that the mover has sufficient insurance coverage to protect the library or its parent organization in case accident or injury occurs during the course of the mover's work. The amount and type of insurance will vary depending on the individual institution's requirements; however, some types of coverage to consider are

   i. general liability,

    ii. vehicle liability,

    iii. personal injury,

    iv. property damage,

    v. Workers' Compensation,

    vi. Employer's Liability Insurance, and

    vii. cargo insurance.*

The RFP might also require that similar insurance be provided on behalf of any subcontractors employed by the mover.

d. **Failure to perform.** The library and its parent organization must have a legal means of recourse if the mover fails to perform work contractually agreed to. Thus, failure to perform must be defined and identified as a breach of the contract, and remedies must be specified (e.g., withhold monies due, terminate the agreement).

e. **Limitation of liability.** There are some circumstances under which damage may occur to either the library or the mover through the fault of neither. These should be specified (e.g., acts of God or a public enemy, war, fires, floods, and so on).

f. **Contractor liability.** There are other circumstances under which damage may occur to the library or its parent organization because the mover or its employees acted with neglect. These circumstances and remedies for damage sustained by the library or its parent organization must be detailed.

g. **Liquidated damages.** Serious delay in completing a portion or all of the move may have a substantial negative effect on the library's ability to provide critical services to its user community. Rather than attempting to quantify the precise value of services, liquidated damages may be assessed at a specified value per day. However, if you get to the point of trying to invoke a liquidated damages clause, be prepared to document in detail that the delay was in no way the fault of the library.

---

*Mike Kent, of William B. Meyer, notes that cargo insurance is a term covering all materials, furniture, equipment, etc. being moved. . . In most cases, the standard liability for a mover is up to $.60 per pound per article. For example, [if] a book weighing one pound is lost during the move, [although it may be worth $500.00], the mover is liable for only $.60. [This is] not good enough! [You must] set a value, [although] this may be difficult. Consult legal and insurance representatives and [determine whether] you want [to] self [insure] for the move or [whether] you want the mover to be fully liable for full replacement value, with or without a deductible.

    . . . some RFPs basically, in a round about way, state that the mover is fully liable for damaged or lost items handled in the move, with no stated value given. . . . Is that fair to the mover when, unknown to him, [he moves] a book . . . worth one million dollars?

    Liability needs to be established in lump sum form or per truck load form and a certificate of liability or insurance . . . submitted. (Personal communication from Mike Kent, May 16, 1997)

h. **Indemnification.** The library or its parent organization may wish the mover to state that it will not hold the library or parent organization responsible for any claims, suits, demands, liabilities, and so on, caused by the mover's omissions or neglect and arising directly or indirectly from the contract or work performed under the contract.

i. **Accident reports.** The library or its parent organization may wish the mover to provide it with copies of any accident reports related to performance of the move.

j. **Independent contractor.** The library or its parent organization may wish to make clear that the mover and its employees are not to be considered employees of the library or parent organization.

k. **Affirmative action.** The RFP should include the library or parent organization's standard statements concerning compliance with affirmative action.

l. **Compliance with labor laws.** The library or its parent organization may want to enumerate specific labor laws with which it expects the mover to comply and require that the mover acknowledge it is familiar with them, will comply with them, and will be responsible for any damages arising from failure to do so. Included in this section might be a statement concerning the use of unionized labor and the payment of union wages if non-union labor is used.

m. **Labor agreements.** The library or its parent organization may want the mover to be responsible for negotiating all labor agreements relating to the move.

n. **Compliance with applicable government rules and regulations.** The library or its parent organization may want to specify that the mover keep itself informed of and comply with all relevant laws and ordinances, and be responsible for any damages arising from failure to do so.

o. **Nonassignability.** The library or its parent organization may want to assert that the mover may only enter into subcontracts with its prior written permission, and that the existence of any subcontracts shall not release or reduce the mover's liability for any breach of contract.

p. **Severability.** The library or its parent organization will probably want to assert that if any term or condition of the contract is found to be legally invalid, that finding will not affect enforcement of the remainder of the contract upon which the invalid portion has no effect.

g. **Waiver.** The library or its parent organization may want to make clear that if it waives the breach of a specific term or condition of the contract, that does not mean it necessarily waives any other breaches. It may also want to specify that breaches of the contract may only be waived in writing.

r. **Notices.** The means by which formal written notices are to be conveyed should be specified (e.g., by certified mail, return receipt requested).

s. **Fees, permits, licenses.** The library should specify whether it or the mover will be responsible for obtaining any required permits, licenses, or inspections, and for payment of any associated fees (Spyers-Duran 1965, 40).

t. **Governing law.** The mover may be headquartered in a different state than the library. The library or its parent organization may want to specify that the contract shall be governed by the laws and statutes of the state in which the library is located. The library may also wish to specify that disputes are to be resolved by binding arbitration held in a designated city convenient to the library.

u. **Entire agreement.** The library may wish to state that the agreement and incorporated documents (including the RFP, the proposal, and any subsequent attachments) comprise the entire understanding between the library and the mover, and that this understanding can only be changed in a document signed by both parties. In case a dispute later has to be negotiated, this establishes written documentation as the sole basis for documenting what was agreed between mover and library. It prevents claims that verbal communications amended the contract.

10. <u>Bid form.</u> The RFP should include a formal bid form, including the following:

    a. **Title**, e.g., "Bid Form for the moving of library materials at Memorial University"

    b. **Brief instructions on what to submit**, e.g., "Complete the Bid Form and return one (1) signed original and four (4) copies with your Proposal and cover letter."

    c. **Bidder's statement** that the undersigned bidder offers to perform the services specified in the RFP for the prices listed.

d. **Itemization of required and optional services to be bid** and corresponding blank spaces for the bidder to fill in with its bid price, e.g.:

"Specified Moving Services $ _____

Option 1. Cleaning $ _____

Option 2 (identified) $ _____

e. **Signature and identification of the bidder.** Provide spaces for the corporate name of the bidder, signature of a corporate officer, the officer's title, and the date of the bid.

f. **Brief instructions on when and where the bid is due**, e.g., "Proposals and bids must be in a sealed package plainly marked as follows and received by (date) and (time)":

Memorial University Library

123 Main Street

Anytown, MA 01000

Attn: Library Move Coordinator

7 SELECTING A MOVER

Selecting a mover via the RFP process starts with identifying possible bidders. The library may choose to prequalify bidders, that is, to restrict bidding on the project to only those moving companies that meet specific criteria, such as successful experience, staffing levels, and financial resources, or it may allow any moving company to bid.

Once the RFP has been sent out, the library will generally hold a pre-bid conference and tour, also known as a walk-though or site visit. The purpose of the pre-bid conference is to give bidders an opportunity to request clarification of elements of the RFP. The tour provides an opportunity to inspect the collections and site conditions. It also gives the library an opportunity to evaluate the types of concerns raised by specific company representatives, and can serve as a first indication of the company's care in reading the RFP and understanding its implications.

Receipt of the formal proposals begins a period of intensive evaluation, involving careful reading, analysis, comparison of the written proposal, and reference checking, and concludes with the identification and rank ordering of proposals. The following pages discuss each step in more detail.

THE PRE-BID CONFERENCE AND TOUR

Purpose

Moving a library or its collections involves the physical transportation of material from one location to another. The ease or difficulty with which this can be accomplished will depend partly on the library's preparation; the orderliness of the collections; the degree of complexity inherent in the work required (e.g., is the move a straight forward shelf-to-shelf move, or will collections be merged or separated?); the facilities themselves; and, for between-building moves, the condition of the surrounding grounds, streets, and walkways.

Although the library should attempt to comprehensively include in the RFP as much information as needed to give potential bidders an accurate and complete view of the physical environment in which the move will take place, a written document cannot provide the level of detailed information gained by direct, personal observation by a knowledgeable professional. The walk-through lets potential bidders make these direct observations.

If the library has included in its RFP a paragraph that places responsibility on the mover for assessing the extent and difficulty of the work, the walk-through also serves as the mover's primary opportunity to make this assessment and to verify that the information provided by the library in the RFP is accurate and complete; also, movers attending the bid conference may wish to have additional time to inspect facilities and collections.

In conjunction with inspection of the facilities and the collections, the pre-bid conference provides an opportunity for potential bidders to request clarification of specific portions of the RFP and for the library to provide bidders with additional, updated, or corrected information. If attendance is required as a condition of bidding, the number of firms represented and the quality of the questions asked will provide an early indication of whether there will be a competitive pool of capable bidders.

The library should plan to have at the pre-bid conference and tour members of its own staff and the parent institution's staff who may be needed to respond to questions. These might include the library or parent organization's lawyer, a representative from the physical plant department, the library director, the move coordinator, the stack maintenance supervisor, and so on. These individuals may want to meet together prior to the pre-bid conference and tour to identify potential questions and appropriate responses or to work out a procedure for responding to questions that may require further internal discussion prior to giving a formal response on behalf of the library or organization as a whole. Arrangements may be made for additional library staff to be available during the tour of specific facilities, for instance, the managers of branch libraries or specialized collections.

An alternative to the group pre-bid conference and tour is to schedule individual walk-throughs with potential bidders. The advantage of this approach is that if their competitors are not present, individual bidders will feel more comfortable discussing their qualifications and possible approaches to handling specific aspects of the move faster and less expensively.

There are significant disadvantages, however: substantially more time is required (which may preclude the attendance of all relevant library and parent organization staff at each walk-through), and there is a likelihood that different information will be conveyed to each bidder or be construed differently by different bidders. Requesting that the best bidders make individual presentations may be one way to get the benefit of their expertise in a setting where they are not revealing proprietary techniques to competitors. Mike Kent, in a personal communication

(May 16, 1997), raised these points and also noted that the library should not "expect to learn anything from the bidders during a [group] bidders' conference . . . they will not share thoughts and ideas with you in front of the competition."

Timing

Schedule the pre-bid conference and tour long enough after RFP distribution that all potential bidders will have received the RFP, thoroughly reviewed its contents, and assessed its implications. The conference should also be scheduled far enough in advance of the due date for proposals that the library will have enough time to prepare and distribute to all attendees a summary of the questions asked and answers given, and that the bidders will have sufficient time to incorporate the information provided into their proposals.

Format

The date, time, and location of the pre-bid conference and tour should have been provided in the RFP. If attendance is required as a condition of bidding, the library should document who attends, perhaps via a sign-in sheet (see Figure 7.1, p. 172, for a sample). If the attendance sheet will be the official record of attendance at a mandatory conference, be sure to announce this at the beginning and end of the conference to ensure that no attendee leaves without signing in. An alternative means of documenting attendance is to require potential bidders to confirm planned attendance in advance, prepare a list if those who plan to attend, and have attendees sign in next to their names and company affiliations (see Figure 7.2 p. 173, for an example).

Providing a written agenda will help move the proceedings along in an orderly manner. A sample agenda is shown in Figure 7.3 (p. 174).

A few items on the sample may benefit from clarification.

Ground Rules

To facilitate preparing a summary of the questions asked and answers provided, the library may wish to record the entire pre-bid conference and tour. This also protects against later claims that inaccurate or misleading information was provided. However, if you plan to record the proceedings, announce this at the outset. Also, plan to use a portable recorder that can easily be carried on the tour of facilities, as questions will likely be asked as the tour proceeds, and have spare batteries or a backup recorder on hand.

To accurately document who asks each question and familiarize the library with potential bidders, ask each speaker to identify himself or herself. To minimize ambiguity about the intent and content of questions, ask that requests for clarification of the RFP refer to specific sections and paragraphs by number. Reserve the right to respond to questions later, so that you are not bound to provide an immediate response to a question for which you may not have all the necessary facts or on which you may need to seek additional advice.

Figure 7.1
Sample Attendance Sheet for Pre-Bid Conference and Tour

Memorial University
Move from Old Main to New Library
Pre-bid Conference and Tour
March 30, 2008

Attendance

Please note: Attendance at this Pre-bid Conference and Tour is required for companies that wish to submit a proposal and bid. This attendance sheet shall be the official record of attendance.

Name	Company

Figure 7.2
Another Type of Attendance Sheet for Pre-Bid Conference and Tour

Memorial University
Move from Old Main to New Library
Pre-bid Conference and Tour
March 30, 2008

Attendance

Please note: Attendance at this Pre-bid Conference and Tour is required
for companies that wish to submit a proposal and bid. This attendance sheet
shall be the official record of attendance.

Company	Representative(s)	Signature
Able Movers	Andrew Able	
Best Library Movers	Bob Best	
	Bill Best	
Caring Carriers	Carla Caruso	
Determined Deliveries	Doug Doe	
	David Dwiggins	

Figure 7.3
Sample Agenda for Pre-Bid Conference and Tour

Memorial University

Move from Old Main to New Library

Pre-Bid Conference and Tour

March 30, 2008

AGENDA

1. Welcome, introduction, review of agenda

2. Ground rules

3. Announcements and distribution of any additional material

4. Questions about the RFP

5. Tour of facilities

6. Follow-up questions

7. Next steps

Announcements and Distribution of Any Additional Material

Any changes in the content of the RFP and any additional material should be distributed in writing to all bidders. You may wish to have a separate checklist for recipients to initial to acknowledge formal receipt of these items. These could be as simple as replacement pages for the RFP that contained typographical errors or substantive additional information (e.g., the deadline for bidding on an optional service will be extended; however the deadline for bidding on the remainder of the package will remain unchanged).

Additional material should be labeled in a way that distinguishes it from the original RFP. For instance, pages correcting typographical errors or amending information originally provided should be numbered to distinguish them from the original page (e.g., "p. 16R for a revision of p. 16 and labeled with a heading "revised [date]"). Addenda should be so labeled, and dated.

Tour of Facilities

The tour should take the movers through each entire facility, focusing on the locations of elevators, loading docks, and other building features that could affect the flow of materials through the building, such as core stack areas with floor levels that do not coincide with floors served by elevators, narrow stack aisles, and other nonstandard and potentially problematic physical features of the facilities. Be sure to let the movers walk through at least each major stack area and give them the opportunity to look in more detail at areas of particular interest to them.

Alert them to potential problems of which you are aware and be honest but fair about the limits of the information you can provide. You may be tempted to hide or gloss over embarrassing stack conditions, but if you expect a mover to deal with it later on, you must show what it will be dealing with or risk a later claim for additional money to cover hidden conditions.

Follow-up Questions

Plan to return to a conference room after completing the tour, to provide an opportunity for follow-up questions. The library may also wish to allow follow-up questions to be submitted for a period of time following the pre-bid conference and tour, to give bidders a chance to thoughtfully consider the implications of the information provided.

Next Steps

The pre-bid conference and tour should close with a review of remaining action steps and deadlines. For example, the deadline for submitting any written follow up questions, the timetable and method (e.g., e-mail, fax) for distributing a summary of the proceedings, and a reminder of the date and time by which proposals and bids must be submitted.

Typical Questions

In addition to requests to clarify specific technical information provided in the RFP, for instance about the extent and nature of the material to be moved (e.g., "Who performed the measurement of material in facility X, and how reliable is that measurement? It seems low.") and the work to be performed (e.g., "Does the library intend to shelve the inactive DDC collection at a high fill ratio, leaving very little growth space?"), questions that may be asked at a pre-bid conference include the following:

Will movers be permitted to make a presentation?

What criteria will be used to select the successful bidder?

Will price be the only criterion?

How reliable are the elevators? What type are they? What are their weight limits?

Can the mover have exclusive access to loading docks?

(for a new or renovated building) Will there be contractors in the building at the time of the move? Will they be union members? Do you foresee any related coordination issues?

Under what circumstance would the optional performance bond be required?

Summary of Proceedings

After the pre-bid conference and tour, the proceedings should be transcribed verbatim and a summary prepared from the verbatim transcript. A summary allows related or repeated questions to be grouped together and responses to be rephrased, streamlining the document and making it easier to read, without omitting or distorting the information as it was presented in the actual transcript. The summary may also include answers that could not be immediately provided during the conference for lack of necessary information or because further internal review was required. The verbatim transcript may be used for reference if a potential bidder questions the accuracy of the summary. The summary should be distributed to all attendees with a brief cover letter and a list of firms represented.

The summary may omit names or company affiliations of movers asking specific questions to protect the competitive confidentiality of those asking the questions. Although the library will have this information on tape and in the verbatim transcript, omitting it from the distributed summary means that who asked what will not be subject to analysis by competing firms for evidence of specific approaches or weaknesses.

EVALUATING RFP RESPONSES

The RFP responses should be evaluated for completeness of understanding of the work required; the method, schedule, and techniques of work proposed; the qualifications of the mover to perform the work; compliance with the required conditions of the proposal; and the price to perform the work.

Evaluation Methods

Because RFP's are complex and lengthy documents, it is usually worth creating a checklist of RFP conditions against which each proposal can be evaluated. This mechanism assures the library that it has not overlooked any important points. The library may also want to devise a numerical method of evaluating responses, assigning specific numbers of points to each section or paragraph of the response. If this is done, points may be assigned to specific sections in proportion to the library's assessment of their importance to the success of the move. Figure 7.4 shows a hypothetical section of an RFP; Figure 7.5 (p. 178) shows the related portion of two hypothetical responses; Figure 7.6 (p. 179) is a checklist showing the non-numerical evaluation of the responses, and Figure 7.7 (p. 180) is a numerically weighted evaluation of the two hypothetical responses.

Figure 7.4
Sections of an RFP

4.2 **Start and Completion Dates for Move.** The move will begin no earlier than July 15, 2008, and must be completed no later than September 1, 2008, however, it is desirable to minimize both the duration of the move and the number of working days to minimize disruption to library users.

4.3 The contractor <u>must</u> specifically address and submit descriptions in writing of the following procedures, within the stated parameters:

A. *Sequence and Schedule.* A detailed sequence and schedule for moving collections and office contents, including the days of the week and hours of work proposed.

B. *Collection Access During Move.* A tracking system that provides the location of collection materials at all times.

C. *Collection Packing and Moving Methods.* The containers and methods proposed to pack and move bound volumes and other collection materials (as described in section 2.3) to assure maintenance of their order and their protection from immediate or long-term damage.

D. *Continuous and Diligent Effort.* A statement of assurance that the services, equipment, and staff assigned to this project will be dedicated solely to it and will not be assigned to any other client of project of the Contractor during the time of this move. etc.

Evaluating the proposals requires close, detailed reading, with attention to what is *not* said as well as to what is said. It is important to be alert for nuances in intent, vague language, the level of detail provided, unstated assumptions, and language that does not directly answer a required question, as well as for information that is simply not provided.

The evaluator must also realize that terminology used by the library may not always be used or understood the same way by a moving company. Get verification of what's really meant by an answer that doesn't "feel right," when the provided answer doesn't seem consistent with the quoted price or with the context. This can be difficult, but it is extremely important. Sometimes the answer can be worked out by close re-reading of the proposal or by checking past performance; the best approach is to do both of these steps, and then ask the company for further clarification.

Using precise, unambiguous language is critical. For example, consider the difference between collection integration and item-by-item integration, which the librarian might assume to mean the same thing. A moving company could conceivably interpret collection integration as placing two previously separate facilities' collections in the same room, in two separate sequences, or placing materials with the same call numbers on adjacent shelves. Use of the phrase "item-by-item integration in a single continuous arrangement" should leave less doubt about what is required. Nonetheless, it is important to check references.

Figure 7.5
Sections of Two Proposals

Able Movers

4.2 Start and Completion Dates for Move. Understood.

4.3 A. Sequence and Schedule.

1. *Daily Hours of Operation.* Able movers proposes to perform move operations on a Monday-Friday schedule between the hours of 8:00 A.M. and 5:00 P.M., for ease of liaison with library and other personnel, and to minimize disruption to the surrounding community.

2. *Schedule and Sequence.* If this daily schedule of operations is acceptable to the library, the proposed move will take between 15-20 days using the staffing levels detailed in response to section x.y. Able proposes to begin the move on July 15, 20--, with completion scheduled for between August x and August y, assuming work proceeds uninterrupted. Able proposes the following move sequence:

3.

July 15	Move microforms
July 16	Move AV collections
July 17 - July 27	Move general collections
	July 17 - July 19 Second Floor collections
	July 20 - July 24 Third Floor collections
	July 25- July 27 Basement collections
July 28	Move current periodicals
July 29-31	Move government document collections
August 1-2	Move reference collection
August 3	Move reserve collection
August 4-6	Completion of any remaining work, shelfreading, inspection of work and problem correction

B. Collection Access During Move. For reasons of public safety and collection security, Able's proposal assumes that only library and mover staff will have access to the collections for the duration of the move. Able will track and report daily to the library's move coordinator the call numbers of materials that have been moved and that are scheduled to be moved on each day of move operations. Able's shift supervisor will assist a designated library staff member in locating any materials in transit that may be needed.

C. Collection Packing and Moving Methods. Able uses custom-built, one-sided wood booktrucks (see photograph on next page of this proposal) to move bound materials between locations. Bound volumes are placed on booktruck shelves in the same orientation as on the library's shelves. Oversize and folio materials are moved flat on specially designed, deep booktrucks... (description of moving methods for microform, AV, electronic, special collection materials). Materials are held in place on each shelf using padded bungee cords, and each booktruck is shrink-wrapped on the loading dock prior to being loaded into the mover's truck for transportation outside the building. This method assures maintenance of the materials' order, provides security against unauthorized removal of materials in transit, and also protects materials from any inclement weather. No materials shall be left on the loading dock or in trucks overnight.

D. Continuous and Diligent Effort. Able Movers will dedicate a team exclusively to this project for its entire duration. Staff assigned to this project will not work on other projects at the same time.

B. Best Library Movers

4.3 A. The proposed move will take no more than 25 working days.

Our hours of work are Monday through Friday, 7:00 A.M. to 3:00 P.M.

We will move the collections in the sequence directed by the library.

B. We will track the locations of materials during the move.

C. Packing methods used by Best Library Movers maintain materials in order and do not damage them.

Figure 7.6
Qualitative Evaluation; Checklist for RFP and Responses Illustrated in Figures 7.4 and 7.5

Able Movers

RFP section	Response Required?	Response provided?	Comments/questions
4.2 Start and Completion Dates for Move	no	yes	ok
4.3 A Sequence and Schedule			
Hours of operation	yes	yes	looks ok; looks like they could be flexible
Move Sequence	yes	yes	generally ok; to discuss: move reference first?
Proposed Schedule	yes	yes	AV collections might take 2 days, not 1; like built-in recovery time at end
4.3 B Collection Access During Move	yes	yes	looks workable; acceptable level of detail
4.3 C Collection Packing and Moving Methods	yes	yes	ok overall; get more detail on method for moving LP recordings
4.3 D Continuous and Diligent Effort	yes	yes	ok

Best Library Movers

RFP section	Response Required?	Response provided?	Comments/questions
4.2 Start and Completion Dates for Move	no	no	no response required
4.3 A Sequence and Schedule			
Hours of operation	yes	yes	no flexibility in hours indicated
Move Sequence	yes	no	Library wanted mover to propose sequence
Proposed Schedule	yes	yes but limited	minimal response; no detail
4.3 B Collection Access During Move	yes	yes but limited	no detail
4.3 C Collection Packing and Moving Methods	yes	no	assurance only; no detail provided
4.3 D Continuous and Diligent Effort	yes	no	this section required an affirmative response

Ambiguous answers are the stuff of which misunderstandings, claims of misrepresentation, and potentially, legal action are made. For this reason, it's extremely important to be alert for apparent inconsistencies, usage of terminology that doesn't appear quite standard, sequences of reasoning that don't seem logical, conclusions that aren't supported by other statements, and the like.

It is also useful to compare proposals. If one proposal is substantially less expensive or faster than the others, it is important to figure out why: Is it because the mover is more efficient, or has identified a better way of performing an aspect of the work, or has the mover misunderstood, overlooked, or in some other way omitted from consideration an element of work that is required? Based on references, does this company have a track record of successful moves, or have past clients had to pay additional amounts to have the move successfully completed?

Figure 7.7
Weighted Evaluation; Checklist for RFP and Responses Shown in Figures 7.4 and 7.5

Able Movers

RFP Section	Response required?	Weight	Response provided?	Score	Possible score	Mover's weighted score	Total possible weighted score	Comments/questions
4.2 Start and Completion Dates for Move	no	0	yes	3	3	0	0	ok
4.3 A Sequence and Schedule								
Hours of Operation	yes	2	yes	3	3	6	6	looks ok; looks like they could be flexible
Move Sequence	yes	2	yes	2.5	3	5	6	generally ok; to discuss: move reference first?
Proposed Schedule	yes	3	yes	3	3	9	9	AV collections might take 2 days, not 1; like built-in recovery time at end
4.3 B Collection Access During Move	yes	3	yes	3	3	9	9	looks workable; acceptable level of detail
4.3 C Collection Packing and Moving Methods	yes	3	yes	2	3	6	9	ok overall; get more detail on method for moving LP recordings
4.3 D Continuous and Diligent Effort	yes	2	yes	3	3	6	6	ok
						41	45	Weighted score: 91.1% of possible 100%

Best Library Movers

RFP Section	Response required?	Weight	Response provided?	Score	Possible score	Mover's weighted score	Total possible weighted score	Comments/questions
4.2 Start and Completion Dates for Move	no	0	no	0	3	0	0	no response required
4.3 A Sequence and Schedule								
Hours of Operation	yes	2	yes	3	3	6	6	no flexibility in hours indicated
Move Sequence	yes	2	no	0	3	0	6	Library wanted mover to propose sequence
Proposed Schedule	yes	3	yes but limited	1.5	3	4.5	9	minimal response; no detail
4.3 B Collection Access During Move	yes	3	yes but limited	1.5	3	4.5	9	no detail
4.3 C Collection Packing and Moving Methods	yes	3	no	0	3	0	9	assurance only; no detail provided
4.3 D Continuous and Diligent Effort	yes	2	no	0	3	0	6	this section required an affirmative response
						15	45	Weighted score: 33.3% of possible 100%

Scoring:

3 = response provided; content fully acceptable
2 = response provided; content partially acceptable
1 = response provided; content not acceptable
0 = no response provided

Weighting:

3 = section requiring a response; important factor
2 = section requiring a response; moderately important factor
1 = section requiring a response; of minor importance
0 = section not requiring a response

Proposal Evaluation Committee

Forming a committee to evaluate the proposals is helpful because it can bring various individuals' readings of the proposals to bear on problems of interpretation. Members of such a committee might include the move coordinator; the stack maintenance supervisor; staff with previous practical experience moving collections, preservation experience, or move-related concerns; staff with contract negotiation experience; and staff concerned with public service aspects of the move.

Depending on the organizational context, it may be desirable to have a proposal evaluation committee formed of library staff members and a second group or committee including key stakeholders in the parent organization, who receive and review a report from the in-library committee. These key stakeholders might include the parent organization's lawyer(s), business officer(s), physical plant representative(s), and possibly representatives of the user community.

Specific Items to Consider

Although every element of the RFP is presumably important (or else it would not have been included), there are specific elements the library should examine in greater detail: schedule, handling and transportation methods, understanding of the work required, references, and, in relation to these factors, the cost. Some specific questions to consider are discussed below.

Schedule

1. Does the proposed schedule comply with any restrictions identified in the RFP for starting and ending dates, sequence, duration, or hours of operation?

2. Does the schedule respond to any concerns expressed in the RFP (e.g., for minimizing the duration of the move or completing it by a certain date)?

3. Is the schedule realistic? Generally, there will be some similarity in the amount of time required to accomplish the same amount of work by moving companies with roughly equivalent workforces. If one proposed schedule appears to be unusually time consuming or unusually speedy, is it because the mover plans to use larger or more crews? If the mover plans to use more crews, can the proposed number operate effectively within the physical constraints of the facilities? The operations management techniques described in Chapter 9 for planning your own move will also help in evaluating this question.

   Writing in the British context, McDonald states, "A good removals contractor will normally be able to move 600–700 metres a day. . . . Merging collections will normally take much longer. . . . Special collections require particular care and attention and hence rather longer periods for moving. . . . Moves will also take longer where the stock is housed in compact (mobile) shelving" (1994, 6).

Handling, Packing, and Transportation Methods

1. If the library has specified particular handling and packing methods, has the mover asserted that those methods will be used?

2. If the library has required that the handling and packing methods selected by the mover meet specific preservation criteria, does the proposed method meet those criteria fully? partially?

3. What provisions has the mover identified for maintaining the security of the collections and other materials during their transport between facilities, including their protection from inclement weather insufficiently severe to halt the move?

4. What provisions has the mover identified to maintain the collection's order during the move?

5. What marking methods are proposed, and do they meet any library requirements for reversibility, or not leaving adhesive residue?

Understanding of the Work Required

1. Does the proposal respond positively to each and every paragraph of the RFP that requires a response?

2. Do the language used, the level of detail provided, and the content of the responses seem appropriate? If less detail than expected is provided, does the proposal contain enough information for a thorough evaluation? If more detail than expected is provided, does it contribute to a clearer understanding of the matter under discussion, or is the mover trying to obscure a potential deficiency? Does the mover use terminology in a manner consistent with the library's understanding, or are there differences that require further explanation or investigation?

Staff and Staffing Levels

1. How many staff members at each levels (e.g., shift supervisor, team leader, team members) are proposed to carry out the move? Do the numbers of each type of staff seem realistic in the context of other proposals and the library's own assessment of the number of individuals required?

2. What are the qualifications and experience of the mover's proposed project manager? Has he or she had experience with other moves of similar size and complexity? How does his or her experience compare to that of project managers proposed by other bidders?

3. What are the qualifications and experience of any other workers provided by the mover, for instance crew leaders or shift supervisors?

4. Does the mover propose to hire locally or to bring in the individuals who will actually move the materials? What screening and training programs are proposed to ensure that these individuals will be able to not only handle the physical exertion of the move, but also read call numbers and handle library materials in a manner consistent with good preservation practices?

5. If included in the RFP, has the mover acknowledged the library's right to require removal of individuals whose behavior may be deemed by the library to be not in the best interest of the project or the library?

References

1. Has the mover provided references with the required level of detail?

2. How many moves of similar size and complexity has the mover successfully completed, and how recently were they performed?

3. Has the mover completed moves of the entire range of types of collection material that are included in this move?

4. Is the duration of listed moves of similar size and complexity in line with the duration proposed for this move? If not, are the reasons apparent?

5. Who was the project manager for recent moves most like the one under consideration? Has the mover proposed the same individual for this move?

6. Has the mover successfully completed moves in the same city or state? If not, are there any idiosyncratic practical, legal, climatic, or other difficulties with which the mover might not be familiar, and does the proposal appear to take these into account?

7. After checking references:

    a. Did the mover accurately present the facts related to the moves listed as references?

    b. Did the mover complete the move within the contracted period of time? If not, what factors contributed to the delay? Were they within the control of the mover? The library? Neither?

    c. Was the work completed within the proposed bid price? Did the mover attempt to charge the library additional fees? If so, for what services (overtime, supplies, specific services)? Were they successful? Did the library feel additional fees were justified? If not, why? Are any of the conditions for which additional fees were charged likely to arise in the move being contemplated?

d. Did the library need to change the scope of work after signing the original contract? Why? Was work contemplated by the library not clearly articulated in the RFP or not fully understood by the mover, or did the library decide to include in the contract additional services not originally contemplated in the RFP? How was this handled? How flexible was the mover in interpreting work contemplated under the RFP?

e. Was all work completed to the library's satisfaction? Would the library hire the mover again? Were there any complications that either the library or the mover did not foresee? In the library's assessment, should these, in fact, have been foreseeable?

f. Did the library experience any problems working with the mover? If so, what sorts of problems, and were they resolved to the library's satisfaction (and how)?

g. Did the library make any claims for damage? If so, what type(s) of damage? How were the claims handled, and how quickly were they settled? (Ladley 1987, 8)

h. For moves managed by the same project manager proposed for your move (i) Did the project manager oversee the move in a professional and competent manner? (ii) Did the library consider the project manager reasonable and fair? Easy to work with?

i. Were there any concerns about the staff hired or provided by the mover to perform the actual packing, transportation, and reshelving of materials? How were these individuals selected and trained? Was there serious attrition over the course of the move? If local individuals were hired, was the library aware of any complaints about the mover from this pool of workers, and did the complaints seem justified in the library's estimation?

j. Is there any additional information the references consider relevant that might bear on the mover's ability to successfully complete the move?

Cost

1. Within the group of bidders whose proposals respond fully and satisfactorily to required conditions of the RFP, appear to fully understand the work to be accomplished, and appear to have the necessary experience, how does the cost for this proposal compare?

2. What is the range of bid prices proposed, and where do individual bidders fall within that range? Are all bids tightly clustered, with little deviation, or is there a cluster of bid prices with one or two outlying figures?

3. In the library's assessment, is the quality of the various proposals roughly proportional to the bid prices? Are there specific bids that appear to offer a good value, that is, an acceptable level of performance at a relatively low price? Are there specific bids that do not offer an acceptable level of performance, and in addition are above the average bid price (and can probably be removed from further consideration)?

4. If the proposal is for a required service and optional or additional services, how does the total cost compare for all elements the library will elect to purchase?

In evaluating the cost, particularly in the case of a bid that is significantly less than the average or falls outside a mid-range cluster of bid prices, the library may wish to consider whether there may be additional costs the mover has not anticipated and factor these into the assessment of the likely cost to use that firm.

For example, has the moving company assumed, rightly or wrongly, that library staff will do all pre-move planning? Adjust shelf spacing? Position bookends? Mark the start and end points for shelving collection segments? Mark fill ratios? Provide supervision? Perform item-by-item collection integration? Do all shelf-reading at the end of the move?

Documenting the Evaluation

The end product of the evaluation process should be a list of acceptable proposals and unacceptable proposals, both arranged in priority order. The formality required for presentation will depend on the organizational context. It is likely, though, that a document will need to be prepared identifying the preferred mover, backup choices, and the rationale for selecting them. This document may also describe the evaluation criteria and methods used. Within the group of acceptable proposals, the reasons to prefer the first choice should be described, and then the reasons for ranking other selections.

The reasons why specific proposals are not considered acceptable should also be described. Examples include insufficient information being provided to evaluate the proposal, the proposal not complying with required elements of the move, the mover not being able to accomplish the work within the specified time frame, and the bid price being significantly more than other acceptable bids. Be particularly careful to document fully why any unacceptable low bidders should not be considered.

For instance, A .E. Lumb notes, "Frequently the cheaper tenderers will employ fewer men and vehicles, and the lower cost may be paid for in the longer period required to accomplish the move. A removal firm inexperienced in moving libraries may easily underestimate a job and thus obtain a contract, subsequently failing to carry out the move efficiently or running into difficulties in fulfilling the contract in the specified time" (1972, 258).

CONTRACT NEGOTIATION

After evaluating the proposals and identifying a preferred and backup contractor, the actual contract must be negotiated and signed. The degree to which the library is involved in this will depend on the organizational context. It is likely, though, that after evaluating the proposals, there will be some matters that still require clarification, for example, whether the library or the mover will be responsible for performing a specific task. These must be finalized before a contract is signed, and if they affect the conduct of the move, the library should be involved in this round of discussions.

If the RFP included optional or additional services that were priced to be provided by a vendor other than the vendor selected for the main move, and the vendor selected for the main move has also been selected to provide optional services, then it may be worth investigating whether a price reduction can be negotiated on the understanding that the mover's mobilization costs are already included in the price bid for the main move.

If the library prefers a vendor because its proposal offers to provide superior services and it has a superior track record in similar moves, but the vendor's price is on the high side of average, it may be worth seeing whether the vendor is willing to compromise on price, or whether there are concessions the library or its parent organization can offer at relatively low cost to itself that would be of value to the mover (for example, free housing at a university dorm or paying for trash removal if that was to be the mover's responsibility).

If the library expects the mover to compromise, it should also be prepared to offer concessions. However, before beginning negotiations, it is important to identify your own bottom line, the value to you of the services offered by the movers, and the value of any concessions you may be prepared to make. It may be helpful to prepare an outline ahead of time identifying your goals, supporting points, countering points the mover may make, and counter-counter points you could make in response. In addition, it may help to write down, for your own reference, your bottom line and a supporting rationale.

If you need substantial concessions from your first choice in order to work within an established budget, be prepared to walk away from the first choice and work cooperatively with the second choice. The confidence of knowing you can work successfully with a second, or even a third, choice will also give you an edge in price negotiations.

BIDDER NOTIFICATION AND CONTRACT SIGNING

Upon successful conclusion of negotiations with a bidder, that firm is formally notified in writing, and arrangements are made to formally sign the contract.

186

Notification of Unsuccessful Bidders

Notification of unsuccessful bidders should wait until a contract has been formally signed with one bidder, in case the front runner backs out at the last minute or some other difficulty develops that prevents a contract from being concluded.

8 CARRYING OUT THE MOVE WITH A MOVER

INTRODUCTION

Hiring a mover means that the library does not have to provide labor and materials to execute the move. Although it may be tempting to think so, this does not mean the library can walk away and expect the movers to complete the move completely on their own. During the course of any move, questions and problems will come up. For instance, unaccounted for material may be found, stack range dimensions may be slightly different than planned, the dock leveler may malfunction, and so forth. Prompt identification and resolution of problems will be critical to the movers' ability to complete the work on schedule.

Establishing an effective working relationship with a mover begins long before the move itself actually begins. An RFP that clearly defines the services the mover is expected to provide; a pre-bid conference and site inspection tour that clarifies any questions left by the RFP; and a well-written, unambiguous RFP response go a long way toward establishing a clear understanding of each party's roles and responsibilities. By the time the move contract is signed, the quality of the working relationship with the selected mover will have already been established.

Signing the contract marks a transition in the relationship between library and mover. The mover is no longer one of several bidders competing to be accepted by the library, but rather the chosen service provider. This may mean a shift from competitive negotiating to a more collaborative working relationship. However, the library must not lose sight of the fact that the mover's bottom line objective is to make money on the move, nor that the library's financial objective is to have the move completed as contemplated for the contracted price.

189

In practical terms, in calculating its bid price, the mover will have made specific assumptions about the amount and type of work needed, how it will be accomplished, and therefore how much the move will cost to execute. This amount will be less than the agreed price, to allow the company to make a profit. Once the contract has been signed, the mover will quite reasonably not want to make changes in either the scope or methods of the move that will add to its expenses and reduce the amount of profit. If unforeseen work needs to be added to the contract, it is reasonable for the mover to request that the library pay for it.

However, the library also needs to be alert for attempts by the mover to diminish the value of the work to be provided or to have the library assume responsibility for work that is defined in the RFP and subsequent contract as the mover's responsibility, particularly if performing these responsibilities will oblige the library itself to incur expense.

Careful administration of the contract will therefore require monitoring and oversight of the work to ensure that the mover provides the agreed-upon services. Particularly if problems develop during the course of the move, the library will be prudent to document the ongoing course of the move and communicate in writing significant information that may bear on the move's progress. This is especially true if the move contract is of some size or complexity.

PRE-MOVE CONFERENCE

The formal start of planning for execution of the move is the pre-move conference. This meeting should be held far enough in advance of the planned start of the move that any problems can be corrected without affecting the move schedule, but close enough to the planned start date that the likelihood of significant facility or collection changes that might affect the move is minimized. It should be held at the library, to allow inspection of the facilities as needed.

The purpose of the pre-move conference is to review the move plan in detail, identify areas of planning that may need further development, review staffing arrangements and roles, and identify and begin to address practical matters such as the mover's work space requirements.

Collection Layout Plan

The pre-move conference should include a detailed review of the collection layout plan, to verify that the mover shares the library's understanding. This is particularly important when the move is not a simple shelf-to-shelf move, but instead involves the merging, integration, or other rearrangement of collections. Go over the fill ratios that the library has calculated and point out where shelves are to be left empty and where you plan to have major collection segments start and stop. If you anticipate specific challenges, apprise the mover of them now and discuss various strategies the library and the mover might use to address them.

CARRYING OUT THE MOVE WITH A MOVER

Schedule

If the start date or schedule would benefit from refinement, now is the time to talk about this. The mover will have other jobs scheduled that require the use of its labor force and equipment, so at this point, it may not be possible to make substantive changes to the planned start and completion dates; however, minor changes may be possible, as may changes in internal sequencing.

Because the library will have to publicize the dates when services will be affected in units being moved, it will want the mover to be as specific as possible about the amount of time the move will take. However, site conditions will affect move progress, and, particularly in a move of some size and involving more than one facility, some schedule slippage may well occur. Asking the mover to provide a range of estimates for the duration of each portion of a multi-part move can be helpful in identifying the earliest and latest dates specific areas or units may be sequentially affected.

Move Routes

The mover will probably have at least a general idea of the routes over which materials may be moved between buildings, but will need to develop a more detailed plan before the start of the move. This may require coordination with physical plant staff and with local public safety officials, particularly if the mover wants the closing of any public streets.

This is also a good time to begin reviewing in detail move routes within buildings and egress routes. If the library shares occupancy of a building with other tenants, will shared space be affected, and, if so, who must be consulted? If specific areas within a building are scheduled to be moved in a particular sequence or by specific dates, will planned move routes in the building require that adjacent collection or service areas be closed to the public or access to them be limited?

It may be helpful for a library representative to walk through each proposed move route with a representative of the mover, with each looking carefully at physical characteristics that may affect the move, and at adjacent service areas that might be affected by the activity of the move.

The mover may wish to evaluate the adequacy of the doors through which materials may be removed from the library: Are they numerous and wide enough to achieve the rate of removal required by the schedule? Is the library or its parent organization amenable to widening a narrow door or creating a new exit for the purpose of the move? For instance, if existing facilities aren't adequate, a window might be removed, its opening widened, or a temporary loading dock built. If any of this is done, who will pay?

The mover will probably want to review the size, location, and capacity of elevators in each facility and discuss with the appropriate library or parent organization representative any preventative maintenance planned prior to the start of the move, any special restrictions or limitations on the use of individual elevators, and procedures and response time for having the elevators serviced if problems develop during the execution of the move.

Packing, Transportation, and Shelving Techniques

The library will want to review in detail the precise methods to be used for packing, transporting, and shelving collection materials, and the training planned for individuals who will actually do the packing and moving. How will the training be conducted? Will a formal class be held, or will training be conducted on the fly? Will the people who are to perform the packing and moving be tested on their knowledge as a condition of their being hired to work on the move? Who will conduct the training, and what is the state of their knowledge? Is the mover receptive to a library staff person conducting a portion of this training if the library so wishes?

Likewise, the library will want to review training and/or testing procedures that ensure the move workers know how to read and accurately arrange all the types of call numbers used in the collections to be moved. The library may wish to offer assistance with this if it has already developed a training program for its own stack maintenance staff, and particularly for any collections involving a classification scheme for government documents (such as SuDocs in the United States) and any local classification schemes. Attention to training in reading call numbers is especially important if the move involves any rearrangement of the collection, or if the mover is to provide item-by-item collection integration. The library will also want to monitor the accuracy of shelving as the move progresses, to make sure that newly trained workers are remembering and correctly using their new knowledge.

Collection Access

This is also the time to discuss in more practical detail how access to the collection will be provided during the move. For instance, what level of detail does the library need in the mover's daily progress reports of call numbers that have been moved? Does it need to know only that part of the QAs (or the 790s) or materials through call number QA76.9 A3 1994 (or 796.96 A3) have been moved? Which library staff person should receive this information? Will library staff have free access to all of the collections throughout the move to search for materials that may have been requested by patrons? If the library intends to circulate material throughout the move, how will reshelving be coordinated with the mover?

Security Measures

In its proposal the mover will have described some provisions for security. These should be reviewed in detail at the pre-move conference, preferably with the local authorities responsible for security of the library's facilities, for instance local police, campus police, contract guards, or the library's own security staff. In addition to obtaining sample mover identification badges, or a detailed description of other means, such as a company T-shirt, by which the moving personnel will be identified, the library will want to review who is responsible for building security, particularly after staff have moved out.

If the mover and library have agreed to create new building exits for the move, how will these be secured? Who will be responsible for securing each facility at the end of the workday? Will the local police authority provide additional patrols in the area or check that the building is locked on a regular schedule? What measures are normally instituted for unoccupied buildings by the local police authority? What security measures do they recommend in addition to those proposed by the library and the mover? Who is liable if there is a breach in security?

Work Space

The mover will need space in advance of the move start date in which to do on-site planning, interview individuals who will be hired to perform the packing and loading operations, and store supplies such as boxes and carts. The library should find out how much and what type of space will be needed, taking into consideration the need for power outlets, telephone service, access, security, office furnishings, and the like. Discuss whether the library or mover will pay for any telephone lines, long distance calls, and fax access.

As the move progresses, the location of the mover's office and staging space will likely need to change, and in moves of some duration involving more than one building, the library should be prepared to provide this type of space in more than one location.

Should space for the movers' staff to take lunch and rest breaks be designated, and should it be separate from that used by library staff? Will the movers be asked to use specific restrooms or those generally used by the public or by library staff?

Now is also the time to start discussing overnight parking requirements for moving vans that may be used to transport materials between buildings. Issues to consider include the maximum number of trucks that will be on site at any one time, their size, security requirements, and whether there are any other special considerations. Detail whether the trucks may leave their motors running while being loaded at a loading dock. Building air intakes frequently seem to be located near loading docks, allowing truck exhaust to get into a building's HVAC system and cause health problems for the occupants. If you don't know where your building(s) air intakes are located, ask your physical plant, building services, or engineering department.

If the mover is not local, arrangements for housing the mover's on-site staff might also be discussed. Learn whether the library or its parent organization has a negotiated discount rate available at a local hotel or motel. Access to this rate is a point that could be negotiated. If a library or its parent organization can provide this service without significant cost (for example, a university might have dorm space or a guest apartment available), it could offer this as a way of building goodwill with the mover at little actual cost to itself. Alternatively, the mover might be expected to absorb this as a normal cost of doing business.

Preexisting Conditions

If the mover will be responsible for leaving the library facilities in the same conditions as before the move or paying for their return to pre-move conditions, it is important to document any preexisting building deficiencies that might later be attributed to the mover's actions. The library should arrange for the conduct of a joint pre-move inspection of the library's facilities to document these. Consider photographing or videotaping building conditions prior to the move (Mareachen 1988, 20).

Building deficiencies include damaged plaster on columns, broken or missing door closers, elevator cabs that don't properly level, chipped paint on book stack end panels, and so forth. At the conclusion of the move, this list will be compared to a similar listing of physical damage and may be used by the library to request compensation from the mover for repair of damage incurred during the move. For this reason, it is important that the list be comprehensive, and that both the library and mover formally review and agree to it.

Roles and Responsibilities

During the pre-move conference, it is also important to review which responsibilities the library and the mover will perform and to establish deadlines for the performance of actions that affect the conduct and progress of the move. For example, if the library will shelf-read the collection prior to the move, the library and mover have to agree upon the last date by which this must be completed without having a negative impact on the move. The colloquial term for deadlines for completing these critical tasks, drop-dead dates, conveys the importance of completing them on time. Because meeting these deadlines is critical to having the project progress on schedule, it is helpful to list the tasks, their deadlines, and who is responsible for completing each one in a dated, written document to which both the library and mover agree and can later refer.

Above all, ask the mover to describe in detail what it plans to do, listen carefully, and ask questions.

BETWEEN THE PRE-MOVE CONFERENCE AND THE START OF WORK

Between the pre-move conference and the start of the move, both the mover and the library work to resolve issues identified at the conference and should expect to communicate with increasing frequency as the start of the move approaches. Pay close attention to completing mutually agreed tasks by their drop-dead dates, documenting work completed, adding issues, and identifying appropriate deadlines for added items as necessary.

START OF WORK

The start of work will be to some extent a trial run. Although both the library and the mover will have carefully planned what they expect to happen, the actual start of work will sometimes uncover something that needs to be fine-tuned. During the start-up period, the library's move coordinator should expect to be on site, monitoring techniques and progress, responding to questions from the movers, and receiving requests to change previously agreed upon matters.

The library may wish to publicize the start of work through appropriate press outlets; however, coordinate the time and place with the mover so that press representatives don't get in the way of move operations.

DAILY OPERATIONS

As the move progresses, the library's move coordinator will want to have regular contact with the mover's project manager. Normally, the mover will have been asked to provide a daily progress report. In some cases, the library will have requested a daily meeting. At such a meeting, the project manager reviews the work performed the previous day, discusses any problems encountered, and reviews the work to be performed that day and any issues that he or she sees coming up. The library's move coordinator can likewise present any problems noted by the library and discuss with the project manager how they may be resolved.

If regular daily meetings are not planned, the library move coordinator and the mover's project coordinator must know how to reach each other quickly in case problems come up. However communication takes place, the library's move coordinator should keep a log of work completed, problems reported to the mover, and how the problems are resolved. Because so much activity takes place quickly during a move, written notes (even very brief ones) are important to understanding later on what, why, when, and by whom decisions were made.

The library's move coordinator will want to augment formal contact with impromptu site visits to spot-check the work in progress. This monitoring activity must be done with care to avoid getting in the way of move operations.

Less formal contact is important, too. The library's move coordinator will want to maintain continuous communication with contacts throughout the library and others who may be involved in the move to ensure that any perceived and actual problems are identified and addressed promptly. Although for the duration of the move the library's move coordinator is the library's official eyes and ears, he or she cannot be everywhere and see everything. The library staff can become an effective distant early warning system, alerting the library move coordinator to developing problems.

For substantial moves, or moves that will last some time, it is worth scheduling weekly status meetings with the mover's project manager and key others (e.g., security and physical plant representatives) to receive progress reports and discuss matters that may arise.

If a large number of departments or constituencies have to be coordinated, it is much easier to schedule a regular weekly meeting and later find that it needs to be only very brief or can be canceled some weeks altogether, than to try to get everyone together on short notice. Also, by regularizing the meeting, if significant problems do arise, the constituencies already have some knowledge of each other and each other's concerns and may be able to work together to resolve the problem more efficiently and effectively.

During this period, the library's move coordinator should be sensitive to the library staff and public's need for knowledge about the progress of the move. As discussed in Chapter 4, various means of communicating with the staff and public can be found, ranging from Web sites, to informal contacts, to bulletin boards, to staff briefings, to all-staff e-mails.

Documenting the Work

Communication between the library and the mover and work performed by the mover should be documented. The purpose of the documentation is to ensure that both the library and the mover share the same understanding of who agreed to what and when, so that if a question related to administration of the contract, the mover's performance, adherence to schedule, or the mover charging extra expenses to the library arises later, it can be answered objectively without need to rely on memory and interpretation.

The documentation must capture important facts, but be brief enough that it gets done in a timely manner. It may be helpful to keep a log of communication with the mover, noting the date and time of pertinent communications, with an outline of topics discussed and any related actions (matters decided, delegated, postponed for later discussion, to be resolved by date x). Although the library should not necessarily assume that the mover will try to take advantage of the library, protecting the library's financial interests requires that the library be prepared to respond to requests the mover may make for additional payments.

Problem Resolution

It is reasonable to expect that various sorts of problems may arise during a move. The problem at hand may be a minor practical one that the mover and the library can resolve on the spot (the mover needs to make signs and would like to use the library's photocopier), it may be one with major implications (the mover believes it is following the collection layout plan exactly, and the collections in a particular segment appear to be more extensive than the library's measurements indicate), or it may have cost implications (despite detailed discussion, the mover and the library find they have each assumed the other would remove government documents coming from storage from the pamphlet file boxes in which they are now shelved so that they can be interfiled with the main, unboxed collection). Each type of problem calls for a different approach in its resolution.

Minor Practical Problems

These are by definition the easiest to deal with, and the library should do its best to resolve them as quickly as possible. What is considered minor may depend on the organizational context and the individual library; however, these are the sorts of problems for which there is a ready solution, the impact on the move schedule is small, and there is little or no cost involved. Resolving these problems promptly and in the mover's favor can help the library build up goodwill and a reputation for helpfulness, both worthwhile to stockpile against later negotiations on more important problems.

Problems with Collection Layout Issues

These generally require rapid response: the move is progressing, and material is on carts waiting to be put on shelves. If the move is allowed to go forward while a solution is found, it may mean that already-shelved material will have to be shifted, at a cost of time and money, and that the arrangement of materials later in the collection sequence will also be affected. If the move is halted while the layout plan is reworked, the mover will be paying for labor it is not using, incurring an extra expense.

The library's move coordinator and the mover's project manager must be able to sit down quickly and identify alternatives: change the fill ratio, place materials on shelves that were to be left empty, reduce the size of a growth joint, or shelve the material in transit and temporarily shift move crews to work in a different area of the collection that will not be affected by the resolution of the present problem. Thorough familiarity with the collection layout plan and the factors it incorporates, as well as having a good spreadsheet model and a computer on hand can aid this process greatly. What may be more difficult is addressing and promptly resolving the political or organizational issues involved if the collection layout plan represents a consensus of competing interests and it must be altered.

For this reason, it will be helpful if the library move coordinator is fully cognizant of the political or organizational issues related to the development of the collection layout plan and has been vested with the authority of all concerned to make changes in the plan when necessary to ensure the progress of the move.

Security Problems

Depending on the specific problem, the library may not want to rely on the mover alone to resolve security problems. If a specific member of the mover's team is not wearing required identification, the mover's supervisor should be expected to take corrective action. If a building or area is found unlocked at the conclusion of the workday, and the mover was to be responsible for locking up, the library will want to address the matter formally, and also assign a library staff member to perform this task or double-check that the building is secure at the end of the workday. If library staff suspect a member of the mover's team is removing personal items from their offices, staff may be cautioned to lock these items away for the duration of the move as a preventative measure, and the issue may be addressed more formally.

Personnel Problems

Personnel problems involving the mover's staff may be tougher to deal with. Even if the library has retained the right to require the immediate removal of a member of the mover's staff whose behavior is not acceptable, who decides what constitutes unacceptable behavior? If a mover makes a comment to a staff person at which the staff person takes offense, should the mover be educated? Reprimanded, but allowed to continue? Immediately dismissed? What if this happens more than once or if the comments appear to be acceptable to the mover's project manager? If a mover is using the wrong packing or handling techniques, what then? Or if, because of a learning disability, a mover is found incapable of shelving materials in call number order? As with other personnel problems, these are matters that call for individual evaluation.

Bear in mind, though, that if the mover has invested time in training local hires, it may be reluctant to fire an individual unless the library can make a strong case.

Contract Interpretation Problems

Contract interpretation problems are the most difficult to resolve and the most likely to result in requests from the mover for additional compensation. For these reasons, considerable time and care should have been invested before signing the contract in reading the mover's proposal, seeking clarification of any ambiguities, and identifying the mover's responsibilities in detail.

In some instances, it may be clear that the library (perhaps inadvertently) omitted some element of work that it needs the mover to perform, or that the mover overlooked a provision of the RFP. In these instances, where one party or the other acknowledges the error, the matter can sometimes be quickly resolved by the library agreeing to extra compensation for additional work or the mover agreeing to perform the work required at no additional charge.

In other instances, when both the library and the mover are convinced their positions are correct and supported by the contract, when the library has decided on budgetary grounds that it cannot pay extra expenses, or when the mover has decided it cannot absorb any additional work without additional pay, extensive negotiation may be required. Resolution of these questions may hinge upon the precise language of the RFP and contract or upon the interpretation of discussions between the library's move coordinator and the mover's project manager.

In preparation for this type of negotiation, it is helpful to prepare a summary of sections of the RFP and any subsequent attachments that may bear on the matter, along with a chronological summary of relevant communications between the library and the mover. Sometimes review of this summarized information clarifies the point in question. If not, the summary may be the basis for further discussion with the library's and mover's appropriate business and legal officers. (If the point in question is purely legal, it may be turned over to the appropriate lawyers. However, it's more likely the point will involve interpretation of operational aspects of the move.) Resolution of serious problems, requiring this level of attention, may be deferred until the move is complete and become part of the discussions about acceptance of the work.

In resolving problems that arise, it is important to focus on the overall goal of the project—successfully completing the move on time and within budget—and to know before entering into negotiations to resolve contract interpretations which of the following is most important in the institutional context: successful completion of the original scope of work, on-time completion of the move, or completion of the move within budget.

ACCEPTANCE OF THE WORK

Upon the completion of the move, the library will want to compile a list of outstanding issues that it feels still need to be resolved. This list of deficiencies, known as the punch list, might include such items as shelf-reading specific segments of the collection where material appears to have been reshelved out of order, evening out the fill ratio in other segments of the collection, repair of columns damaged by the mover's carts, removal of trash from the loading dock, and the like.

In preparing the punch list, the library should carefully inspect the newly moved collection for conformance to the collection layout plan (as modified by mutual agreement of the library and mover during the course of the move) to ensure that materials have been shelved in the proper locations, in an orderly condition, and appear to have been handled appropriately. It should also inspect its facilities for evidence of damage caused by the mover during the move. The list of physical damage should be checked against the list of preexisting conditions that the library and mover made during their joint inspection of the facilities before the start of the move.

After the punch list is created, it should be presented to the mover for response. The mover may accept responsibility for some items, reject responsibility for others, and want to discuss yet others. As part of this process, the library may wish to identify for itself punch list items that it is able and willing to deal with, and which it cannot address easily or at all.

Release of Final Payment

Payment of the mover should have been structured to withhold a portion of payment pending successful completion of the work. Release of this final sum should be contingent on the satisfactory resolution of the punch list and any remaining contract interpretation issues. If the library built into the RFP and the contract the right to deduct appropriate sums for the correction of specified deficiencies, the cost to correct remaining deficiencies should be calculated and formally presented to the mover.

Once any remaining issues have been resolved to the library's satisfaction, the library may wish to document that fact in writing before authorizing the release of the final payment.

IV

DOING THE MOVE YOURSELF

There are a number of reasons why libraries may want to undertake a move themselves. The amount of material to be moved may be small, money may not be available to hire professional movers, or past moves may have been successfully undertaken without using a mover. Whatever the reason, successfully carrying out the move yourself requires considerable. detailed planning and management of people, equipment, space, time, and money. Part IV describes effective and efficient methods to do this.

Part IV assumes that the collection layout plan has already been developed; that the existing collections have been measured, planning has been done for growth, decisions have been made about where and how the collections will be arranged, and a detailed plan has been prepared showing exactly where different segments of the collection will be placed and the fill ratio used for each part of the collection. These planning steps are covered in Part I.

It also assumes the move planner has started to gather a team, identified a target time frame, chosen packing and moving methods, and begun to communicate information about the move to staff. These issues were addressed in Part II, although Part IV provides additional detail about areas of particular concern if you are executing the move yourself.

A successful move starts with a thorough understanding of the work, people, equipment, time, and funding required. For a small, simple move, less detail will be required than for a larger, more complex move, but developing a Work Breakdown Schedule (WBS) will help the planner think through the move thoroughly enough to avoid surprises during the actual move and is a good place to start regardless of the move's size. Using the WBS, the planner can identify the number of people and skill levels, equipment, space, and time required to execute the move, as well as points during the move at which something could go wrong.

For complex moves, mapping the WBS onto a PERT network diagram can help visualize dependent steps and identify a critical path and slack time. Using a Gantt chart may help the planner identify potential problems with the allocation of work teams or critical resources like an elevator or loading dock. Chapter 9 covers these topics in planning move logistics and offers practical advice on resolving common move problems.

Chapter 10 addresses management of move operations: recruiting workers, daily operations, problem resolution, maintaining morale during the move, and completing the move.

9 PLANNING MOVE LOGISTICS

> *Ninety Ninety Rule of Project Schedules: the first 90 percent of the task takes 90 percent of the time, the last 10 percent takes the other 90 percent.*
>
> —Chase and Aquilano (1985, 295)
>
> *Habich's Corollary: Panic early and productively.*

A 2005 study of moves at large academic libraries reported that "29 percent of respondents experienced at least one major problem or setback . . . and many faced multiple difficulties. . . . The most common problem experienced by institutions was insufficient project planning" (Atkins and Teper 2005, 75).

Successful execution of a move first requires a well-thought-through plan. Using a structured planning process helps break the project down into manageable steps, understand dependencies, analyze time and resource requirements, and develop a work plan. Testing the move plan on paper and making refinements until it flows smoothly can make a significant difference in the success of the actual move.

Once the work has been broken down into manageable steps, the planner can determine how long the move will take, the number of people and the equipment needed to execute it, and how much the move will cost. The key is to start planning early.

PROJECT PLANNING STEPS

The level of detail required to plan a move will depend on the move's size and complexity, but the following project planning steps work well for all moves*:

* The project planning steps come from Lewis (2006, Chapter 3).

1. Define the scope of work: Answer the who, what, where, when, why and how questions. How much material has to be moved? How far? What methods may be used? What restrictions will there be on time (duration and hours of operation), budget, staffing, etc.? What are the criteria for success? What will be done, and what will not be done? Will the work be limited to moving, or will it include identifying items that need binding? Conducting an inventory? Cleaning?

2. Identify the major elements of the move and then break them down into smaller activities (i.e., create a work breakdown structure or WBS).

3. Identify risks and impacts (What could go wrong? What impact would that have?) and develop possible solutions.

4. For each activity, estimate the duration, resource requirements, and costs.

5. Prepare the move's master schedule and budget.

6. Document the plan (in a project notebook).

7. Get sign-off by stakeholders, modifying steps 1–6 as needed.

Clearly, planning a simple stack shift, which may be completed as time permits, requires less formal planning than integration of 800,000 volumes from five locations, which must be completed between July 15 and August 15. So, how does this work?

PLANNING A SMALL MOVE

Three ranges of shelving will be added on the second floor, which is overcrowded, and materials will be shifted to fill the new shelving. Service will not be seriously affected, and therefore the work may be completed as time and the availability of staff allow. For this small move, the library needs to figure out the new fill ratios to be used, perhaps identify which call numbers should end up at the start of each new range, and assign staff to shift as time allows.

1. Define the problem and scope.

    a. What/where: shift all the collections on the second floor. No other tasks (i.e., dusting, pulling damaged volumes) will be done at the same time.

    b. Who: existing staff.

    c. When: as time allows, during regular hours of operation.

    d. How: using existing book trucks.

    e. Why: make it easier to shelve books and reduce possible damage, by reducing overcrowding.

2. Create a WBS.
    a. Determine the fill ratio.
        i.   Determine the linear measurement of materials to be moved.
        ii. Calculate the linear measurement of the shelving available after the new ranges are added.
        iii. Calculate the fill ratio.
    b. Train the shelvers.
        i.   Identify a quick and easy way for shelvers to determine when a shelf is at the new fill ratio.
        ii. Write (brief) instructions.
    c. Move the materials.
        i.   Remove materials from the old location.
        ii. Place them on a book truck.
        iii. Move to the new location.
        iv. Place materials on the new shelf at the appropriate fill ratio.
        v.   Return the empty book truck to the old location.
        vi. Repeat i.–v. until all books are in the new location at the correct fill ratio.
    d. Shelf-read to ensure that materials are shelved in order and at the correct fill ratio.

3. Identify the risks: What could go wrong? What impact would it have? What are possible solutions?
    a. Risk: Shelvers could leave too much empty space on each shelf (using the wrong fill ratio).
    b. Impact: Available shelving would be used up before the collections were fully shifted; to make space, the collections would have to be back shifted, taking extra labor-hours, costing more money, and delaying completion of the work.
    c. Possible solutions:
        i.   Give each shelving team a measuring stick the exact length of the shelf space to be filled.
        ii. Mark each shelf with the spot to which it should be filled.
        iii. Check completed work at the end of the day to catch mistakes early and minimize the time required to correct any problems.

4. For each activity, estimate the duration, resource requirements (people, equipment, space), and costs.

   Example (for step c. above):

   c. Move the materials.

       i. Resources:

           (a) people: one trained person

           (b) equipment: one book truck

           (c) space: none needed

           (d) cost: no new costs

       ii. Duration:

           (a) Steps 2. c.i.–v. must be repeated until all books are in the new location at the correct fill ratio.

           (b) Ask two or three shelvers to conduct test trips; time each trip (in seconds).

           (c) Calculate the number of trips required to complete the shift:

               i) Determine the linear measurement of material moved in each trip.

               ii) Divide the linear measurement of existing collections by this number.

           (d) To estimate the total time required to complete the entire move, multiply the number of trips needed by the average time per trip.

5. Prepare the master schedule and budget. Add up the durations estimated for planning, training, moving, and shelf-reading. Since there are no new costs, no budget is needed.

6. Document the plan. For this project, if the library already has a description of proper book-handling techniques, the "notebook" might be as simple as an e-mail documenting the goals, steps, resources needed, and estimated duration.

7. Get sign-off by stakeholders. Is the duration acceptable to the department head and senior managers? If not, can more shelvers be hired temporarily, or can more staff assist?

**But it's only a small move!
Why do I have to go through this whole process?**

For a small move, it may seem like going through this planning process would take longer than the move itself. However, most of the steps above, except for the measurements and calculations, could be done in one or two conversations. And consider the following risks of not planning:

1. The project scope might be misunderstood. (*Oh, you wanted us to pull damaged items at the same time?*)

2. The parameters might be misunderstood (*I thought it was OK to hire extra shelvers! How else are we going to get all this done before classes start?*)

3. The next time a similar project needs to be done, the same problems might occur again. (*Oh, right, I guess we did run into that problem when we shifted the third floor three years ago. Hmm, how did we fix it?*)

James P. Lewis (2006, ch. 3, sec. 1) argues that planning and executing a given project will always involve the same amount of pain. The pain can be experienced either in the planning stage or in the execution of the project if refinement of a project plan (e.g., cleanup) takes place after the (initial) work has taken place.

The literature is full of corroborating evidence in the form of stories about moves in which everything "went well" and the library "only" spent several months after the move cleaning up shelving errors. More recently, as detailed planning has become more widely used for library moves done by library staff, stories have appeared with a happier type of corroboration, like Brinkman and Whiteside's note on a move at the University of Louisville:

> The 1989 move illustrates how time spent in planning results in optimum use of space, and the 2001 planning process demonstrates the benefit of using a spreadsheet such as Excel. Taking exact measurements and making title specific calculations is very time-consuming. . . . But the long-term benefits are well worth the effort! . . . Once the planning was completed, the actual move went very smoothly. . . . The planning was so accurate that, although the growth allocation was for only eight years, the library was able to go for 10 years without any significant shifting or installation of additional shelving. (2002, 15–17)

PLANNING A LARGER MOVE

For a larger or more complex move, the planning needed is more formal and more detailed. What constitutes a larger scale move? To some extent the answer is subjective and depends on the individual library's resources and experience. Clearly the example above is a small-scale move, whereas moving 800,000 volumes from five locations qualifies as a major move. Most moves will fall somewhere in between. However, if the move must be completed within a tight time frame, if there will be a major impact on service, or if significant funding must be obtained to hire additional workers and rent or purchase equipment and supplies for the move, more detailed planning is needed.

Perhaps the most critical diagnostic questions are, "What are the risks of this move not being executed in a satisfactory manner, and what is the impact if that happens? If materials end up in the wrong place? If the move takes longer than it should? If we find out partway through the move that we don't have enough people, book trucks, or vans to do the work?" Regardless of the number of items to be moved, if there's a significant risk of serious impact, the move planner will want the assurance of success that comes with investing time in more detailed planning.

Appoint a Library Move Manager

Because of the amount of work involved in planning and managing a major move done by the library, the library should appoint an individual to be move manager and arrange his or her assignments to allow that person to concentrate on the move. The move manager must be someone who can handle detail; has good analytical, interpersonal, and leadership skills; and has broad knowledge of the library, its staff, its operations, and its facilities. Ideally, this person should have good working relations with units that may be called on for assistance during the move, such as security, transportation, carpentry, and purchasing.

Develop a Planning Calendar

To avoid the Ninety Ninety Rule of Project Schedules becoming a reality, start planning early. The amount of planning time required will depend on the size and complexity of the project. Bayne notes that planning the large, complex move at University of Tennessee, Knoxville, took more than eighteen months (1990, 66), whereas Kurth and Grim followed a twelve-month planning process with the following major steps (1966, 171–87):

Month 1: Preliminary meetings, discussions of general considerations

      Appoint move director and move director's staff

      Consider formation of move committee

Month 2: Inspect building conditions

      Identify furniture and equipment to be moved, need for new furniture

      Identify and inspect collections to be moved; determine whether any collections will be merged; determine need for pest treatment

      Identify offices and agencies with which the move planner must work; make initial contacts

PLANNING MOVE LOGISTICS

Month 3: Identify need for special handling of specific collections (e.g., rare books, maps)

Review collection arrangement issues in more detail

Begin move committee meetings

Designate and equip a move planning room

Month 4: Prepare a detailed plan of book stack areas

Inventory book stacks

Review labor considerations: who will perform the moving?

Review methods of moving: book carts vs. cartons

Make a preliminary determination of the numbers of book carts or cartons that will be needed

Hold all-staff briefing meeting; develop method of regularly briefing staff

Month 5: Begin to measure collections

Begin to study growth of collections and make projections

Month 6: Complete measurement of collections

Complete study and projection of collection growth

Month 7: Survey and tag condition of furniture and equipment to be moved; prepare inventory; plan disposition of surplus items

Decide nature and extent of staff involvement in move

Month 8: Inventory book trucks to be used for move and assess their condition

Dispose of duplicate and exchange material to the extent possible

Review pest control requirements

Prepare provisional collection layout plan for new facility

Hold all-staff briefing meeting

Month 9: Arrange staff visits to new facility

Finalize collection layout plan

Identify and articulate goals of move operation (dates and constraints)

Month 10: Conduct full-day test run of move operations; conduct time studies

Houseclean existing facilities: discard unnecessary supplies, records, and miscellaneous material

209

Recheck accuracy of all figures and data, including collection size, growth projections, and collection layout plan

Reinspect facilities

Month 11: Assure availability of telephone communications in all facilities

Review security considerations for all facilities and materials

Review readiness of collection materials for moving (e.g., planning for mergers, physical condition of fragile materials)

Establish sequence of move operations

Review physical readiness of move labor pool, condition and adequacy of equipment (book trucks, vans, marking supplies)

Formulate move master plan, detailing order of operations and schedule for specific operations

Month 12: Hold all-staff briefing meeting

Elaborate and refine move master plan

Provide staff with cartons for packing office contents

Make arrangements with contractors for moving specialized equipment

Perform any necessary pest control measures

Clean collections

Making your own planning calendar is a good place to start, incorporating your own assessment of the planning steps needed and the time each step will take.

Don't underestimate the work required or the number of people involved in planning and carrying out a large move! Bayne (1990, 59–60) notes that approximately 450 people were involved in the University of Tennessee, Knoxville, move, with 200 FTE alone working on the move of collection material, requiring its own new organizational structure. When comparing the cost of planning and carrying out a move using existing staff and resources to the cost of contracting with a moving company, it is important to identify and make explicit the cost of both the planning and operational labor that will be needed.

Of course, the labor cost of planning will probably be the same, or essentially the same whether the move is carried out with existing labor resources or using a professional mover. However, organizations tend to overlook or ignore the cost of existing staff labor because these individuals' salaries would be paid in any case. What is overlooked is the lost service or production that these individuals would otherwise have performed had their labor not been diverted to the project. If there's no funding available for outside help, this consideration becomes moot; however, it's worth making explicit, if for no other reason than as a public relations statement on the value of library staff and the services they regularly perform.

STEP 1: DEFINE THE PROBLEM AND SCOPE OF WORK

At the start of formal planning, most libraries will have a broad definition of the problem they wish to solve, for example, a certain linear measurement of books and journals need to be moved from point A to point B, arranged in a certain order, spaced to allow a certain amount of growth; the work can start no earlier than date X and must be finished no later than date Y; and the work must be completed for the least amount of money possible. Usually, libraries will still have to decide whether related activities such as cleaning, pulling damaged volumes, and possibly inventorying or installing security tags will also be done at the same time.

Many managers realize that because every volume in the move will be touched, there's an unusual opportunity to make use of that human contact to do additional work at the same time. Whether or not this makes sense depends on several factors.

First, how important is the additional work to the library's overall goals? Are the books so dirty that moving them into a clean, new space is unacceptable? Is there a long-standing need to remove items needing repair? Or is this work optional?

Second, how much extra time does each additional operation take, and how much total time will this add to the move? Can the library pay for the additional hours of labor, and is it acceptable to extend the duration of the move by that amount?

Third, is the library prepared to deal with the by-products of this additional work? If items that need mending are removed, does the library have space to store them? Can it afford to have them repaired or replaced within a reasonable time frame? If they are relocated to a storage area, will their location records have to be changed? How much time and labor cost will that require?

Using the SMART acronym to define project objectives may help decide how much to include. Project objectives should be

Specific,

Measurable,

Achievable,

Relevant, and

Timely or Time-framed or Time-delimited

STEP 2: CREATE A WORK BREAKDOWN STRUCTURE (WBS)

Creating a thorough work breakdown structure (WBS) for a large move is more important than for a small move: it is difficult to accurately estimate the time or cost of something we don't do on a regular basis, exact comparisons aren't available, and the consequences of inaccuracy may be substantial.

As the above example of a small move demonstrates, the idea behind a WBS is simple: to break down the work into small tasks for which reliable time estimates, resource needs, risks, and dependencies can be identified. From the resource requirements identified for the each task, the move planner can then assemble a reliable estimate of the time and other resources required for the move as a whole. For large moves, a graphic representation of the WBS on a PERT network diagram or Gantt chart can help make the project more understandable, identify critical path issues, and provide a tool for diagnosing the urgency of resolving specific problems during the actual move.

The process of creating a WBS is iterative. Starting with the major elements of the move, the move planner gradually breaks down the elements into specific tasks that comprise them. Think of this as starting with the "view from 60,000 feet" and then moving closer and closer to the ground until you can see roads, intersections, and individual houses.

Developing a WBS and translating it into a PERT network diagram may also help show the project in ways that are appropriate for different audiences. For very senior management, trustees, or the public, all that may be wanted is an overview of the major steps ("We plan to start on July 15. The building will be closed July 20–27, and we expect to have everything done by August 15."); student staff hired for the move may need to know in great detail about their specific role in the move. ("Remove books from shelf A, grasping the spine of the book firmly to remove it from the shelf. Place it upright on the book truck, and push the truck to the elevator. Do not run! We do not want you to get hurt, and we don't want the book truck to tip over.")

Identify Major Elements of the Move

Start by identifying the major elements of the move. This is the view from 60,000 feet. The major elements will vary for each move and will depend, for instance, on the type of material to be moved (Are they monographs, periodicals, children's picture books, recordings?), the agreed-upon scope of the project (Will the collections be cleaned as part of the move?), and the facility (Are there specific physical limitations that need to be taken into account? Are there elevators, and if so, how many?).

For a move between buildings (Move A), the major elements might include the following:

1. Vacuum collections.

2. Remove damaged volumes.

3. Move collections from Building A to Building B.

4. Shelf-read the moved collection.

Break Major Elements into Small Tasks

The next step is to break down each major element of the move into smaller tasks. For Move A, Activity 3, for instance:

3. Move collection from Building A to Building B.

    a. Move volumes from Building A to van.

        i.   Remove volumes from shelf; place on book truck.
        ii. Log book truck's ID number and the starting and ending call number of books on the book truck.
        iii. Move book truck from stack location to elevator.
        iv. Load book truck onto elevator.
        v.   Move elevator from stack floor to basement.
        vi. Unload book truck from elevator.
        vii. Move book truck from elevator to loading dock.
        viii. Log book truck number and contents at loading dock.
        ix. Return elevator to stack floor.
        x.   Check and secure contents of book truck.
        xi. Load book truck onto van.

    b. Move volumes from Building A to Building B.

        i.   Check the list of book trucks loaded onto van.
        ii. Verify total number of book trucks on van.
        iii. Secure book trucks in van to prevent shifting.
        iv. Drive van from Building A to Building B.

    c. Reshelve materials in Building B, integrating them with collections already on the shelf.

        i.   Unload book trucks from van.
        ii.   Log out book trucks removed from van.
        iii. Verify contents are intact and in order.
        iv.   Move book trucks from loading dock of Building B to elevator.
        v.   Load elevator.
        vi.   Move elevator from basement to stack floor.
        vii. Unload elevator.
        viii. Return elevator to basement.
        ix.   Move book truck from elevator to stack location.
        x.   Log book truck number and contents.
        xi.   Remove volumes from book truck; interfile.

The process of breaking down the move into smaller activities or tasks will be iterative. As the move planner thinks through the steps comprising a complex move, additional steps that have been assumed or implied will become apparent. To check the completeness of the list, have someone unfamiliar with the planning process walk through the motions of the move as listed, observe, and add to or modify the list as needed.

Tasks do not have to be of equal size, but they do have to be a size that can be easily timed and for which resources can be identified.

Evaluate the Move Route

Because the exact path over which materials are moved will affect the duration and sometimes the equipment and personnel needed, at this point the planner should evaluate possible paths for moving materials within and (if necessary) between buildings.

Begin by inspecting the facility or facilities in detail. Obtain detailed plans of each facility and walk through each possible move route. Pay particular attention to elevators, loading docks, other building egress points, and interior door and aisle widths. Note elevators' cab sizes and weight capacity and the date of their last inspection and service. Look critically at stairwells and consider how they might be used if elevators break down. List each route's advantages and disadvantages, noting specifics on the plans (Kurth and Grim 1966, 30–34). Develop time estimates for activities that depend on the route taken. Based on review of these factors, identify preferred and alternate move routes within and between facilities.

Represent the WBS Graphically: PERT Network Diagrams

Representing the work breakdown structure graphically helps you visualize and analyze the relationship between elements of a move. PERT, Program Evaluation and Review Technique, is a relatively accessible member of a large family of analytical methods developed specifically for project management. PERT network diagrams are a specialized form of flow chart. In addition to helping the move planner visualize and analyze the relationship between move elements, they can be used to identify a critical path (the activities that must be completed on time so that the move as a whole will be completed on time) and where there is slack time, allowing the manager to fine tune a move.** Most of the mechanics of PERT network diagrams can be handled by project management software, such as Microsoft Project, but you need to understand the underlying concepts to use the software effectively.

PERT uses a graphic vocabulary of nodes and arrows to illustrate the relationship between work elements, or activities. It places activities on arrows and events on nodes. Events define the start or completion of activities; for each

---

** CPM, critical path method, is another project management technique that provides critical path scheduling information; however, it does not provide the same degree of detail in addressing the probability of a project being completed in an estimated amount of time. Because time estimates are critical to move planning, the author has elected to focus on PERT. The discussion of PERT techniques draws on Chase and Aquilano (1985, 295–337), Chapter 9, "Project Management," especially Section 9.4, Critical Path Scheduling, and Section 9.5, Time-Oriented Techniques.

activity there are two events. An arrow is drawn from an activity that must be completed first to the activity that cannot start until the first activity has been completed. The PERT method may be used to describe both the major elements of a move and detailed steps, though a given PERT network is limited to events and activities of a single scale (e.g., major events or minor events, but not both at the same time). Examples of events and activities are

Start vacuuming collections (event)

Vacuum collections (activity)

Finish vacuuming collections (event)

Start shelf-reading collections (event)

Shelf-read collections (activity)

Collection shelf-reading is complete (event)

Truck departs Building A (event)

Truck travels from Building A to Building B (activity)

Truck arrives at Building B (event)

Identify Dependent Activities and Lag Times

Before developing a PERT network diagram and time estimate for the project, it's important to be aware of the order in which activities can be completed. Often, we know this intuitively: a book truck will not be loaded onto a moving truck until it has been filled and moved to the loading dock. Sometimes, though, the dependency is not so obvious: starting a move doesn't have to wait until the whole collection has been vacuumed; the vacuuming crew just has to stay ahead of the movers.

Awareness of the various types of dependencies and the concept of lag time can help identify these opportunities for simultaneous work.*** In a move, we will typically see the following:

Finish-to-start dependencies, in which the successor activity cannot start until the predecessor activity has been completed. Examples: Collections cannot be moved into temporary location area A until the previous tenants have moved out. Demolition cannot begin in area B until all collections, equipment, and staff have moved out.

***This discussion draws on the very clear explanation provided in Chapter 4 of Baca (2007).

Start-to-start dependencies, in which the successor activity cannot start until the predecessor activity has started. Example: Collections cannot be shelved in area A until shelving setup has begun (assuming that the shelving assemblers can move fast enough to stay ahead of the movers). Disassembly of shelving in area B cannot begin until the collection move begins (the rate of shelving disassembly can be no faster than the move).

There are also finish-to-finish dependencies and finish-to-start dependencies, but these are less common in moves.

Lag time is another important factor in estimating how long a project will take. Lag time is a mandatory time gap between two activities. The classic example involves painting: you cannot apply a finish coat of paint until the primer has dried, so estimating the duration of a paint job involves applying the primer, lag time for the primer to dry, and applying the finish coat. Lag time might be a factor in a move if shelving is to be washed or repainted as part of the project.

Prepare a PERT Network Diagram

With the WBS and dependency information in hand, we are now ready to represent the move activities graphically in a PERT network diagram. Figures 9.1 through 9.3 illustrate three levels of PERT network diagrams for Move A. Figure 9.1 shows the move's major activities; Figure 9.2 shows an expansion of activity 3, and Figure 9.3 shows a further expansion of activity 3A.

Figure 9.1
PERT Network for Major Activities of Move A

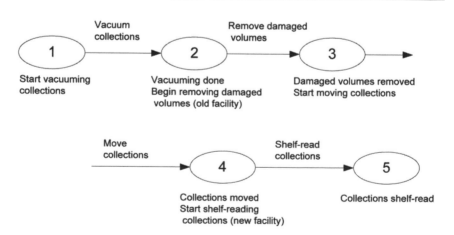

Figure 9.2
PERT Network for Move A, Activity 3

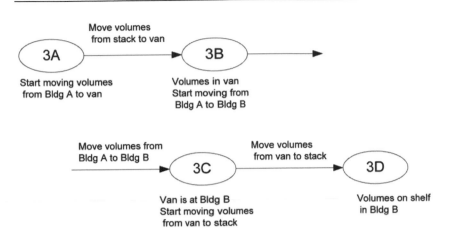

Figure 9.3
PERT Network for Move A, Activity 3A (1 Team)

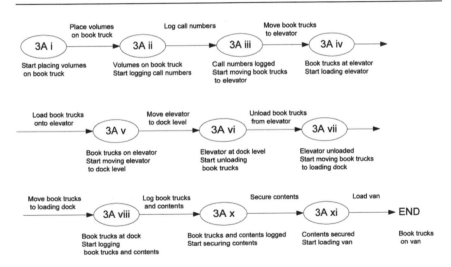

Note the progression in level of detail. Each network represents a different scale of planning, from macro (Figure 9.1) to micro (Figure 9.3).

STEP 3: IDENTIFY RISKS, IMPACTS, AND POSSIBLE SOLUTIONS

Once the WBS is complete, it will often be relatively easy to identify risks, impacts, and possible solutions. Doing this before the move begins will help you decide whether to modify the move plan to minimize the impact of specific risks. It will also minimize downtime during the move if a problem does arise, because you will not have to spend time working out a solution. *Note:* The practical advice offered at the end of this chapter, and in Chapter 10, will provide possible solutions to many common problems!

For instance, if a building has one elevator, what will happen if that elevator fails? Has provision been made for emergency service? If so, what is the promised response time? For instance, if response and repair takes six hours, will the move be suspended for that period of time? Will workers hired for the move be paid and sent home or given alternate assignments?

For moves between buildings, have the book trucks you plan to use been tested for durability under move conditions? If book trucks fall apart as the move progresses, are backups available? How rapidly can replacements be obtained or the originals be repaired?

If workers quit, how will the completion date of the move be affected? Did labor hour planning take into account attrition? Is there a source of additional workers?

The overriding question the move planner needs to keep in mind is, how critical is the completion date for the move? If the move must absolutely be completed by a certain date and time, aim for the greatest possible accuracy in all estimates and planning assumptions. Failing this (perhaps impossible) goal, then the planner should both err on the conservative side in estimating times required to complete tasks and build into the schedule a buffer to allow any delayed work to be completed at the end of the project.

For step 3A of Move A, above, possible risks for selected steps might include the following:

3. Move collection from Building A to Building B.

    a. Move volumes from Building A to van.

        i.   Remove volumes from shelf; place on book truck.
        ii. Log book truck's number and the starting and ending call numbers of books on the book truck.
        iii. Move book truck from stack location to elevator.
        iv. Load book truck onto elevator.
        v.   Move elevator from stack floor to basement.

             Risk: elevator breaks down.

             Impact: move cannot proceed until it is repaired.

Possible solutions:

> Have elevator inspected before move begins.
>
> Have elevator repair company on call with guaranteed two-hour response.
>
> Uuse another elevator via a less efficient route.

   vi.   Unload book truck from elevator.

  vii.   Move book truck from elevator to loading dock.

 viii.   Log book truck number, contents at loading dock.

> **Risk:** book truck logged on stack floor is missing at loading dock.
>
> **Impact:** books are missing or out of order.
>
> **Possible solutions:**
>
> > Wait and see if book truck appears by end of day.
> >
> > Reserve space for missing books in Building B.

  ix.   Return elevator to stack floor.

   x.   Check and secure contents of book truck.

> **Risk:** books fall out of book truck while in transit.
>
> **Impact:** books damaged and out of order.
>
> **Possible solutions:**
>
> > Shrink-wrap each book truck before loading on van.
> >
> > Secure books with bungee cords before loading on van.

  xi.   Load book truck onto van.

> **Risk:** dock leveler breaks during move.
>
> **Impact:** can't roll book trucks onto van.
>
> **Possible solutions:**
>
> > Inspect leveler before move.
> >
> > Have a portable ramp available.

STEP 4A: ESTIMATE EACH ACTIVITY'S DURATION

For a small move, developing a time estimate may be as simple as doing a simple time study to calculate the time required for each key task, multiplying by the number of times each task is repeated, and adding up the results. For larger moves, the same basic steps are done, but in more detail to ensure greater reliability. In this step, we focus on estimating how long each activity will take.

DOING THE MOVE YOURSELF

Time Studies of Move Activities

Once the planner has identified activities comprising a move and the sequence and dependency relationships among them, the amount of time required for each step can be estimated. This is done by developing time estimates for the most detailed activities and adding these together to make time estimates for major activities. In the examples illustrated, this would mean first developing estimates for the activities shown in Figure 9.3, then using these estimates as a basis for the activities shown in Figure 9.2, then building on those to develop estimates for the activities shown in Figure 9.1, converting to appropriate units of time measurement.

To estimate the amount of time required for each step at the most detailed level, use a stopwatch, or at least a watch that displays seconds. The objective is to determine the amount of time, on average, that it will take a move worker to complete each step of the move. It is important to neither overestimate nor underestimate the speed with which the work can be performed, taking into account both variations in individual abilities and the learning curve. For instance, if novice shelvers will do the shelving, time the rate at which both a novice shelver and an experienced shelver work.

Simplified Time Study Method

A simplified time study works well for small, simple moves. Use this approach:

1. Identify the smallest reasonable element to time.

2. Time four to five repetitions of the task.

   a. Time more than one person.

   b. Time people whose skill level represents the people who will actually execute the move (i.e., don't time yourself, and don't time stack maintenance staff unless you and they will actually execute the move).

   c. Use the average of all repetitions.

A time study can answer the following types of questions:

1. How long does it take to vacuum one section of shelving?

2. How long does it take to shelf-read a section of shelving?

3. How long does it take to remove books from the shelf, place them on one book truck, log the book truck number and contents, and move the book truck to the elevator?

4. How long does it take to load the book truck onto the elevator, move the elevator to the loading dock, unload the elevator, move the book truck to the loading dock, log the book truck number, and check and secure the book truck contents?

5. How long does it take to load the book truck onto the van?

This approach also gives you an excellent opportunity to see whether the steps you've identified fully describe the move process. Give your description of the steps to the person you will be timing and ask him or her to follow them exactly as written, then report whether there is any ambiguity or confusion.

Classic Time Study Method

For more complex moves, in which you want to know what steps must be completed on time and to identify where there is "give" in the project, you will want to calculate the critical path and lag times. The first step is to conduct a classic time study. The basic steps are summarized below;**** for further detail, consult a textbook on operations management or project planning.*****

Step 1: Break down the task into its smallest measurable elements.

Step 2: Identify the number of repetitions of the task that must be timed, based on

    a.   the estimated cycle time and

    b.   the estimated number of cycles per year.

Step 3: Time the appropriate number of repetitions of the task.

Step 4: Assess the expertise of the operator timed and normalize the timing.

Step 5: Adjust the normalized time for allow for personal needs, delays, and fatigue.

Step 1 has already been discussed, in the context of developing a WBS and a PERT network.

The classic approach to Step 2 requires consulting a table.****** For most move operations, timing three to five repetitions will probably be adequate. For those readers interested in a more detail, the following list is provided:

For cycle times of more than .200 hours (12 minutes), and where fewer than 1,000 cycles per year are anticipated, the number of cycles to be observed is five.

For cycle times of more than .300 hours (18 minutes), observe four cycles.

For cycles of more than .500 hours (30 minutes), observe three cycles.

For cycles of .800 hours (48 minutes), observe two cycles.

****The section on time studies is based on the presentation in Chase and Aquilano (1985, 269–74). Consult this or another operations management or project management textbook for a fuller introduction to time studies.

*****Chapters 6 and 7 of Lewis (2006) are both detailed and accessible. Chapter 6 covers Scheduling Project Work; Chapter 7, Producing a Workable Schedule. For comic relief and some perspective, see also Chapter 12, Project Management for Everyone: My Head Hurts.

******Such as Exhibit 8.14, Guide to Number of Cycles to Be Observed in a Time Study, in Chase and Aquilano (1985, 273), reprinted from Benjamin W. Niebel, *Motion and Time Study*, 7th ed. (Homewood, IL: Richard D. Irwin, 1982, 337), which is the source of the values cited.

When between 1,000 and 10,000 cycles per year are anticipated, the number of cycles to observe increases by one to two for the cycle times noted.

For very short cycle times (less than 3 minutes) and when the anticipated number of cycles per year is more than 10,000 per year, the number of cycles to be observed increases substantially.

Step 3 can most easily be done by performing a "continuous method" timing, in which a stopwatch is started when the operation begins, and the time is noted as each element of the task is completed. The time to complete each task is then calculated after the timings are complete.

Step 4 requires making a subjective assessment of the observed operator's expertise. This is critical to making a realistic estimate of the standardized or expected time for an operation. If experienced library staff members are timed, but volunteers or new temporary hires will be used for the move, the estimate of time required will probably be less than what can initially be achieved. The observed time may be normalized to account for skill level, as follows:

Normal time = Observed performance time per unit x Performance rating

If the observed time per unit is 4.5 minutes, and your assessment is that the operator observed is performing the work 20 percent faster than a member of the planned labor pool, then the normal time would be calculated thus:

Normal time = 4.5 minutes observed time x 120% performance rating = 5.4 minutes

The accuracy of this calculation obviously hinges on an accurate assessment of the operator's relative skill, which may be difficult for the novice. Another approach is to time an operator with the skill level anticipated for the labor pool planned for the move. Take care, though, to avoid timing someone with no experience, or the resulting time estimate will overstate the total time required. This is of course due to the learning curve. There are statistical methods to adjust for the learning curve; however, it's probably easier and more direct to time someone at the correct skill level.

Step 5 adjusts the normal time to take into account personal needs (breaks), delays (equipment downtime), and fatigue, creating the standard time for the task. The formula most frequently used is:

Standard time = Normal time + (Allowances x Normal time), or ST = NT (1+ Allowances)

Although there are specialized tables listing fatigue allowances for specific industries and activities (for example, see Table 5, Fatigue Allowances (in percent) in Spyers-Duran [1965, 23], which suggests fatigue allowances of 15–30 percent for activities requiring carrying or pushing heavy loads), the most practical approach may be to estimate the length of breaks required during a work day, based on a one-day trial run of move operations.

Learning Curve

The learning curve is both a behavioral and a mathematical concept. Learning curve theory says that workers will become more productive as they gain experience, due to individual learning, improved techniques, and so on (Chase and Aquilano 1985, 355–57). If one can measure the amount of time a novice worker requires to perform a work element on the first try and after x repetitions, it is possible to calculate the improvement ratio, and from that use an improvement curve chart to calculate the cumulative effect (for instance, the charts in Chase and Aquilano, 353–54). Alternatively, if the move planner has experience with prior moves, one can estimate the different rates at which novice and experienced individuals will work. (Again, timing a worker or workers at the anticipated skill level may be the easiest way to avoid over- or underestimating the time required; however, there will be an initial learning period during which new hires will not perform as rapidly as the skilled work who was timed.)

The simplified time study method above addresses the learning curve by timing individuals whose skill is representative of those who will execute the move.

STEP 4B: IDENTIFY EACH ACTIVITY'S RESOURCE REQUIREMENTS

The move planner needs to know ahead of time how many people, book trucks, and vans are ideally needed to most efficiently perform the move, and how much of various supply items should be on hand to complete the move. These calculations are also necessary to estimate the move budget.

The first step is to identify the resources ideally required for each work element. For instance, for Move A, activity 3 might require the following resources:

3. Move volumes from Building A to van.

   A.i. Remove volumes from shelf; place on book truck.

      2 people
      1 book truck
      3 feet of book stack aisle space

   A.ii. Record book truck's number and starting and ending call numbers of volumes on book truck.

      1 person
      clipboard, log sheet, pen

A.iii. Move book truck from stack location to elevator.

> 1 person
> 1 loaded book truck
> approximately 10 assignable square feet (ASF) queuing space in elevator lobby

A.iv. Load book truck onto elevator.

> 2 people
> 1 loaded book truck
> approximately 10 ASF elevator cab space

A.v. Move elevator from stack floor to basement.

> 1 person
> 1 loaded book truck
> approximately 10 ASF elevator cab space
> *Note:* elevator can accommodate 4 book trucks and requires 1 person to operate

A.vi. Unload elevator.

> 2 people
> 1 loaded book truck
> approximately 10 ASF queuing space in elevator lobby

A.vii. Move book truck from basement elevator to loading dock.

> 2 people
> 1 loaded book truck

A.viii. Record book truck number and contents.

> 1 person
> clipboard, log sheet, pen

A.ix. Return elevator to stack floor.

> 1 person
> empty elevator

A.x. Secure book truck to prevent volumes from becoming dislodged in transit.

> 2 people
> shrink-wrap (approximately 10 linear feet per book truck)
> 3 10-foot security straps per book truck
> 1 loaded book truck

A.xi. Load book truck onto truck from loading dock.

2 people

1 loaded, secured book truck

approximately 6 ASF empty space in truck

Looking at the whole of activity 3, the move planner will note that some of the activities require one person, whereas others require two to move a book truck through the entire cycle. With the resource requirements identified for each activity, the move planner can now decide that Team One must comprise two people; Team Two, one person; Team Three, two people; and, Team Four, two people. By performing the same type of analysis for each activity being performed simultaneously, the move planner can develop an assessment of the staffing requirements for the move.

What if you have fewer people available than needed? Then the move will take longer, and the sequence of work may have to be adjusted to accommodate available staffing. For instance, a team may stay with a group of book trucks all the way from their original location to their new location, or the people loading materials at one site may move with the materials to the new site and unload there.

Similar analyses may be performed to identify the number of book trucks and vans that are ideally needed and the quantities of supply items, like shrink-wrap, to stockpile in advance of the move. For instance, if twenty-five book trucks comprise one van load, and at any one time one van is being loaded, one is in transit from Building A to Building B, a third is being unloaded at Building B, and a fourth is in transit from Building B to Building A, then a minimum of 100 book trucks (25 book trucks/van x 4 simultaneous van loads) will be needed. Allowing for delays and for breakdown of book trucks during the move will add to the total the move planner should have on hand at the start of the move.

With these calculations in hand, the planner can adjust the calculations of labor and equipment requirements and prepare a budget.

STEP 5A: PREPARE THE MASTER SCHEDULE

As stated previously, estimating how long a small move will take may be as simple as estimating the time needed for one repetition of each task, multiplying the time/repetition by the number of repetitions, and adding up the results.

For more complex moves, the move planner may wish to do a more detailed analysis, using the PERT network and Gantt charts. To begin, estimate the time required for each activity and integrate these time estimates into the PERT network.

Integrating Time Estimates into the PERT Network Diagram

First, use the time studies completed in Step 4 for each work element in the PERT analysis to identify

a = optimistic time to complete each work element,

M = the most likely amount of time to complete each work element, and

b = pessimistic time required to complete each work element.

Then calculate the expected time (ET) for each work element, as follows:

ET = (a + 4M + b)/6

Next, calculate the variance ($\acute{o}^2$ or sigma squared) for each work element's expected time of completion:

$\acute{o}^2 = ((b\text{-}a)/6\ )^2$

Figure 9.4 shows hypothetical timings for each event shown in Figure 9.3 and calculates the ET and variance for each work element.

These figures calculate the time required for individual iterations of activities. Before completing the PERT network and calculating the critical path and time required for the project, it is necessary to calculate the aggregate time required for the major activities.

Cyclic Activities

On the list of activities for Move A above, note that steps 1, 2, 3, and 4 are broad activities, each comprising multiple smaller activities. Activities 3A, 3B, and 3C are themselves each comprised of multiple activities, and the activities within these steps form cycles that are repeated several times.

For example, if the move planner wanted to spell out in complete detail the work to be performed in step 3A, the list of activities might look like this, assuming a special moving book truck that holds 12 feet or 144 inches of bound volumes, an elevator that holds four of these book trucks, and a moving van that holds twenty-five book trucks:

3.A.i. (1) Remove first 12 ft. of volumes beginning with call number x (or beginning at stack location y) to book truck 1.

3.A.ii. (1) Record book truck number and contents.

3.A.iii. (1) Move book truck 1 to elevator.

Figure 9.4
Calculation of Expected Times for Move A, Activity 3, PERT Network

Activity	Time to Complete (in seconds) Optimistic (a)	Most likely (m)	Pessimistic (b)	Expected time (ET)	Variance	Comments
3.A. Move volumes from Building A to van						
for each book truck:						
3.A.i. Remove volumes from shelf to book truck	120	180	240	180.0	400.0	Fatigue factor
3.A.ii. Log book truck number, contents	30	35	40	35.0	2.8	
3.A.iii. Move book truck to elevator	60	135	180	130.0	400.0	From various stack locations
for group of 4 book trucks:						
3.A.iv. Load book trucks on elevator	80	120	160	120.0	177.8	
3.A.v. Move elevator from stack floor to Basement	40	55	70	55.0	25.0	
3.A.vi. Unload book trucks from elevator	80	120	160	120.0	177.8	
3.A.vii. Move book trucks from elevator to dock	120	180	480	220.0	3,600.0	
3.A.viii. Log numbers, contents of book trucks	120	140	160	140.0	44.4	
3.A.ix. Return elevator to stack floor	40	55	70	55.0	25.0	
3.A.x. Check and secure contents of book trucks	240	360	480	360.0	1,600.0	
3.A.xi. Load book trucks onto van	180	240	300	240.0	400.0	
3.B. Move volumes from Building A to Building B						
for group of 25 book trucks:						
3.B.i. Check log of book trucks loaded on van	240	300	360	300.0	400.0	
3.B.ii. Verify total number of book trucks	60	75	120	80.0	100.0	
3.B.iii. Secure book trucks to prevent shifting	600	900	1200	900.0	10,000.0	
3.B.iv. Drive van from Building A to Building B	1200	1500	1800	1,500.0	10,000.0	
3.C. Move volumes from van and reshelve in Building B						
for each book truck:						
3.C.i. Unload book truck from van	35	45	50	44.2	6.3	
3.C.ii. Log book truck	30	35	40	35.0	2.8	
3.C.iii. Verify book truck contents intact and secure	15	20	30	20.8	6.3	
3.C.iv. Move book truck from dock to elevator	60	65	70	65.0	2.8	
for group of 4 book trucks:						
3.C.v. Load elevator	20	30	40	30.0	11.1	
3.C.vi. Move elevator from basement to stack floor	30	45	120	55.0	225.0	
3.C.vii. Unload elevator	20	30	40	30.0	11.1	
3.C.viii. Return elevator to basement	30	45	120	55.0	225.0	
for each book truck:						
3.C.ix. Move book truck from elevator to stack location	45	120	180	117.5	506.3	
3.C.x. Log book truck number, contents	30	35	40	35.0	2.8	
3.C.xi. Remove volumes from book truck; interfile	180	240	300	240.0	400.0	

3.A. i. (2) Remove second 12 ft. of volumes from shelf to book truck 2.

3.A. ii. (2) Record book truck number and contents.

3.A.iii. (2) Move book truck 2 to elevator.

3.A. i. (3) Remove third 12 ft. of volumes from shelf to book truck 3.

3.A.ii. (3) Record book truck number and contents.

3.A.iii. (3) Move book truck 3 to elevator.

3.A.i. (4) Remove fourth 12 ft. of volumes from shelf to book truck 4.

3.A.ii. (4) Record book truck number and contents.

3.A.iii. (4) Move book truck 4 to elevator.

3.A.iv (1-4) Load book trucks 1-4 onto elevator.

3.A.v. Move elevator from stack floor to basement.

3.A.vi. (1-4) Unload book trucks 1-4 from elevator.

3.A.vii. (1-4) Move book trucks from 1-4 elevator to loading dock.

3.A.viii. (1-4) Record numbers and contents of book trucks 1-4.

3.A.ix. Return elevator to stack floor.

3.A.x. (1-4) Check and secure contents of book trucks 1-4.

3.A.xi. (1-4) Load book trucks 1-4 onto moving van.

Repeat activities 3.A.i. through 3.A.xi until book truck 25 arrives at the loading dock, as part of the four-book truck group comprising book trucks 25–28.

3.A. xi. (25) Load book truck 25 onto van.

Note that for each van load of 25 book trucks, 25 book trucks must be loaded and a total of seven elevator trips must be made, calculated as follows:

(25 book trucks/van)/(4 book trucks/elevator trip) = 6.25 elevator trips

so when one van has been filled, there would be three book trucks left over to be placed on the next van.

Simultaneous Activities

A further complication in estimating total time required for the work to be completed is that several activities may take place simultaneously. Preparing a Gantt chart can help clarify this, by working through when specific physical resources, such as an elevator or a loading dock, will be required, and when specific work teams are expected to perform specific activities. The graphic presentation of this information is quite powerful because it can be easily read and interpreted. Figure 9.5 (pp. 230–31) shows a Gantt chart for activities 3.A.i.–3.A.viii.

On the other hand, preparing a detailed Gantt chart can be tedious. Using a spreadsheet to perform the calculations may help reduce the preparation time and improve accuracy. Such a spreadsheet may also be used to calculate the total time required for a cycle of activities, for instance the time required to load a van with book trucks, although it will not readily show when specific physical resources are in use. Figure 9.6 (p. 232) shows the spreadsheet used to prepare Figure 9.5.

Expansion of a PERT network can also illustrate the order in which resource-dependent steps must take place. Figure 9.7 (p. 233) shows the same activities described in Figures 9.5 and 9.6. Note that activity 3.A.ii. (2) (recording the contents of book truck 2) cannot take place until BOTH activity 3A.i. (2) (loading book truck 2) AND activity 3.A.iii.(1) (moving book truck 1 to the elevator) have been completed. It's obvious why the book truck contents can't be logged until they have been loaded; however, activity 3.A.iii.(1) must precede 3.A.ii. (2) because both activities are to be performed by Team 2. Similarly, activity 3.A.iv.(1–4) (loading the elevator) cannot begin until the elevator is available on that floor (activity 3.A.ix.).

Estimating Overall Move Duration

Using either the Gantt chart or the spreadsheet, the planner can determine that moving twenty-five carts of books from their present stack location onto a van will take a total expected time of 6,190 seconds, or 1 hour, 43 minutes. Assuming each move book cart holds 12 feet of materials, then this amount of time will be required to move each 300 feet of materials from their present location to the van. By building up similar time estimates for each component of the move, the planner can develop an estimate of the time required to complete an entire move cycle, from removing a book and placing it on a book truck, to moving the book truck to the new facility, to reshelving the book, to returning the book truck to the old facility.

Figure 9.5
Gantt Chart for Move A, Activities 3.A.i–3.A.viii

elapsed seconds	0	60	120	180	240	300	360	420	480	540	600	660	720	780	840	900	960	1020	1080	1140	1200	1260	1320	1380	1440
elapsed minutes	0	1	2	3	4	5	6	7	8	9	10	11	12	13	14	15	16	17	18	19	20	21	22	23	24
TEAM ONE	-- Load TR 1 ---->			-- Load TR 2 ---->			-- Load TR 3 ---->			-- Load TR 4 ---->			-- Load TR 5 ---->			-- Load TR 6 ---->			-- Load TR 7 ---->			-- Load TR 8 ---->		
TEAM TWO		TR 1 ---->				TR 2 ---->			TR 3 ---->			TR 4 ---->			TR 5 ---->			TR 6 ---->			TR 7 ---->		
TEAM THREE				----- TR 1 - 4 -----																				
Elevator In Use											---->													
TEAM FOUR																								

elapsed seconds	1500	1560	1620	1680	1740	1800	1860	1920	1980	2040	2100	2160	2220	2280	2340	2400	2460	2520	2580	2640	2700	2760	2820	2880
elapsed minutes	25	26	27	28	29	30	31	32	33	34	35	36	37	38	39	40	41	42	43	44	45	46	47	48
TEAM ONE	-- Load TR 9 ---->			-- Load TR 10 ---->			-- Load TR 11 ---->			-- Load TR 12 ---->			-- Load TR 13 ---->			-- Load TR 14 ---->			-- Load TR 15 ---->			-- Load TR 16 ---->		
TEAM TWO	TR 8 ---->			TR 9 ---->			TR 10 ---->			TR 11 ---->			TR 12 ---->			TR 13 ---->			TR 14 ---->			TR 15 ---->		
TEAM THREE	---->	TR 4 - 8 -----							---->				TR 9 - 12 -----											
Elevator In Use	---->															---->								
TEAM FOUR	TR 1 - 4 -----												TR 5 - 8 -----											

elapsed seconds	2940	3000	3060	3120	3180	3240	3300	3360	3420	3480	3540	3600	3660	3720	3780	3840	3900	3960	4020	4080	4140	4200	4260	4320
elapsed minutes	49	50	51	52	53	54	55	56	57	58	59	60	61	62	63	64	65	66	67	68	69	70	71	72
TEAM ONE	-- Load TR 17 ---->			-- Load TR 18 ---->			-- Load TR 19 ---->			-- Load TR 20 ---->			-- Load TR 21 ---->			-- Load TR 22 ---->			-- Load TR 23 ---->			-- Load TR 24 ---->		
TEAM TWO	TR 16 ---->			TR 17 ---->			TR 18 ---->			TR 19 ---->			TR 20 ---->			TR 21 ---->			TR 22 ---->			TR 23 ---->		
TEAM THREE	---->	TR 13 - 16 -----											TR 17 - 20 -----											
Elevator In Use	---->																							
TEAM FOUR	TR 9 - 12 -----												TR 13 - 16 -----											

Figure 9.5 (Cont.)

elapsed seconds	4380	4440	4500	4560	4620	4680	4740	4800	4860	4920	4980	5040	5100	5160	5220	5280	5340	5400	5460	5520	5580	5640	5700
elapsed minutes	73	74	75	76	77	78	79	80	81	82	83	84	85	86	87	88	89	90	91	92	93	94	95
TEAM ONE	-- Load TR 25 --->			-- Load TR 26 --->			-- Load TR 27 --->			-- Load TR 28 --->													
TEAM TWO	TR 24 --->		TR 25 --->			TR 26 --->				TR 27 --->			TR 28 --->										
TEAM THREE			TR 21 - 24												TR 25 - 28								
Elevator In Use																							
TEAM FOUR			TR 17 - 20										TR 21 - 24										

elapsed seconds	5760	5820	5880	5940	6000	6060	6120	6180	6240	6300	6360	6420
elapsed minutes	96	97	98	99	100	101	102	103	104	105	106	107
TEAM ONE												
TEAM TWO												
TEAM THREE												
Elevator In Use												
TEAM FOUR	TR 25 - 28											

231

Figure 9.6
Time Required to Load 25 Book Trucks onto Van

	Team One	Team Two		Team Three				Team Three (cont'd)		Team Four	
Seconds/activity:	3.A.i. Load Book truck 180	3.A.ii. Log Book truck 35	3.A.iii. Move to Elevator 130	3.A.iv. Load onto Elevator 30	3.A.v. Move Elevator 55	3.A.v. Unload Elevator 30	3.A.vi. Move to Dock 55	3.A.viii. Log Book truck 35	3.A.ix. Return Elevator 55	3.A.x. Secure Book truck 90	3.A.xi. Load onto Van 60
Dependent upon:	none	3.A.i.	3.A.ii.	3.A.iii., 3.A.iv.	3.A.iv. x 4	3.A.v.	3.A.vi.	3.A.vii.	3.A.vi.	3.A.viii.	3.A.x.

Elapsed Time (in seconds):

Book truck number	Load begin	Load end	Log begin	Log end	MovetoElev begin	MovetoElev end	LoadElev begin	LoadElev end	MoveElev begin	MoveElev end	Unload begin	Unload end	Dock begin	Dock end	Log2 begin	Log2 end	Return begin	Return end	Secure begin	Secure end	Van begin	Van end
1	0	180	180	215	215	345	345	375			970	1000	1090	1145	1310	1345			1450	1540	1810	1870
2	180	360	360	395	395	525	525	555			1000	1030	1145	1200	1345	1380			1540	1630	1870	1930
3	360	540	540	575	575	705	705	735			1030	1060	1200	1255	1380	1415			1630	1720	1930	1990
4	540	720	720	755	755	885	885	915	915	970	1060	1090	1255	1310	1415	1450	1450	1505	1720	1810	1990	2050
5	720	900	900	935	935	1065	1505	1535			1690	1720	1810	1865	2030	2065			2170	2260	2530	2590
6	900	1080	1080	1115	1115	1245	1535	1565			1720	1750	1865	1920	2065	2100			2260	2350	2590	2650
7	1080	1260	1260	1295	1295	1425	1565	1595			1750	1780	1920	1975	2100	2135			2350	2440	2650	2710
8	1260	1440	1440	1475	1475	1605	1605	1635	1635	1690	1780	1810	1975	2030	2135	2170	2170	2225	2440	2530	2710	2770
9	1440	1620	1620	1655	1655	1785	2225	2255			2410	2440	2530	2585	2750	2785			2890	2980	3250	3310
10	1620	1800	1800	1835	1835	1965	2255	2285			2440	2470	2585	2640	2785	2820			2980	3070	3310	3370
11	1800	1980	1980	2015	2015	2145	2285	2315			2470	2500	2640	2695	2820	2855			3070	3160	3370	3430
12	1980	2160	2160	2195	2195	2325	2325	2355	2355	2410	2500	2530	2695	2750	2855	2890	2890	2945	3160	3250	3430	3490
13	2160	2340	2340	2375	2375	2505	2945	2975			3130	3160	3250	3305	3470	3505			3610	3700	3970	4030
14	2340	2520	2520	2555	2555	2685	2975	3005			3160	3190	3305	3360	3505	3540			3700	3790	4030	4090
15	2520	2700	2700	2735	2735	2865	3005	3035			3190	3220	3360	3415	3540	3575			3790	3880	4090	4150
16	2700	2880	2880	2915	2915	3045	3045	3075	3075	3130	3220	3250	3415	3470	3575	3610	3610	3665	3880	3970	4150	4210
17	2880	3060	3060	3095	3095	3225	3665	3695			3850	3880	3970	4025	4190	4225			4330	4420	4690	4750
18	3060	3240	3240	3275	3275	3405	3695	3725			3880	3910	4025	4080	4225	4260			4420	4510	4750	4810
19	3240	3420	3420	3455	3455	3585	3725	3755			3910	3940	4080	4135	4260	4295			4510	4600	4810	4870
20	3420	3600	3600	3635	3635	3765	3765	3795	3795	3850	3940	3970	4135	4190	4295	4330	4330	4385	4600	4690	4870	4930
21	3600	3780	3780	3815	3815	3945	4385	4415			4570	4600	4690	4745	4910	4945			5050	5140	5410	5470
22	3780	3960	3960	3995	3995	4125	4415	4445			4600	4630	4745	4800	4945	4980			5140	5230	5470	5530
23	3960	4140	4140	4175	4175	4305	4445	4475			4630	4660	4800	4855	4980	5015			5230	5320	5530	5590
24	4140	4320	4320	4355	4355	4485	4485	4515	4515	4570	4660	4690	4855	4910	5015	5050	5050	5105	5320	5410	5590	5650
25	4320	4500	4500	4535	4535	4665	5105	5135			5290	5320	5410	5465	5630	5665			5770	5860	6130	**6190**
26	4500	4680	4680	4715	4715	4845	5135	5165			5320	5350	5465	5520	5665	5700			5860	5950	6190	6250
27	4680	4860	4860	4895	4895	5025	5165	5195			5350	5380	5520	5575	5700	5735			5950	6040	6250	6310
28	4860	5040	5040	5075	5075	5205	5205	5235	5235	5290	5380	5410	5575	5630	5735	5770	5770	5825	6040	6130	6310	6370

total time required to load and move 25 book trucks onto van = 6190 seconds = 1 hour and 43.2 minutes

232

Figure 9.7
PERT Network for Move A, Activity 3A (4 Teams and 4 Book Trucks)

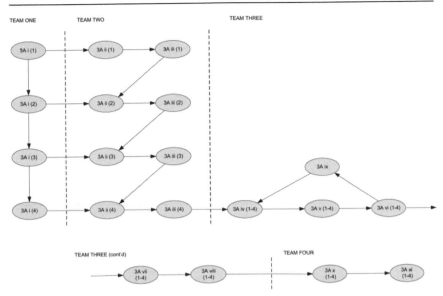

The cycle time may then be used to estimate the overall duration of the move. For instance, assuming the cycle time to move twenty-five book trucks, each with 12 feet of material, from the original location to the new location and return book trucks to the original location totaled four hours, or 240 minutes, then the average time required per linear foot of material would be

240 minutes/(12 linear ft. of material per book truck x 25 book trucks) = 240 minutes/300 linear ft. of material = .8 minute/linear ft.

Thus, moving each 10,000 linear feet of material would take

10,000 linear ft. of material x .8 minute/linear ft. = 8,000 minutes or 133 hours

Note that this is elapsed moving time for the entire moving team, not hours of individual labor. Given an eight-hour workday, moving 10,000 linear feet of material would therefore take 16.6 workdays.

This calculation may also be used to establish checkpoints for evaluating the move's progress, based on the size of various sections of the collection (Ellis 1988, 284). Figure 9.8 (p. 234) illustrates these calculations.

Figure 9.8
Calculating Time Required to Move Segments of a Collection

LC class	Linear feet to be moved	Minutes to move, at .8 min./lin. ft. a x .8	Hours to move, at .8 min./lin. ft. b / 60	Elapsed hours	Elapsed 8-hour days d / 8
	(a)	(b)	(c)	(d)	
A	408	327	5.4	5.4	0.7
B	601	481	8.0	13.5	1.7
C-G	850	680	11.3	24.8	3.1
H-HJ	485	388	6.5	31.3	3.9
HM-HX	1,213	970	16.2	47.4	5.9
J	545	436	7.3	54.7	6.8
K	138	110	1.8	56.5	7.1
L	1,264	1,011	16.9	73.4	9.2
M	1,397	1,117	18.6	92.0	11.5
N	2,295	1,836	30.6	122.6	15.3

Balancing Work Team Assignments

The amount of work assigned each team must be balanced so that each team's work cycle takes about the same amount of time. (See Figure 9.9.) It's important to recognize that each activity may not be performed the same number of times within each team's work cycle. For instance, it may be more efficient to wait to move book trucks from the stack floor to the loading dock until enough trucks to fill an elevator are ready; similarly, one would probably wait to fill a van with book trucks before moving it from one building to another. Figure 9.10 shows a method for calculating work cycle times for four teams performing Move A.

Figure 9.9
Team Cycle Time Calculations

	Activity:		Done in units of:	Estimated Time (ET) per repetition	Repetitions per cycle	ET per activity cycle	Total ET per team cycle	Notes:
Team One	3.A.i.	Load (4) book trucks	1 book truck	180	4	720	720	180 seconds per book truck
Team Two	3.A.ii.	Log (4) book trucks	1 book truck	35	4	140		
	3.A.iii.	Move (4) book trucks to elevator	1 book truck	130	4	520	660	165 seconds per book truck
Team Three	3.A.iv.	Load (4) book trucks on elevator	1 book truck	30	4	120		
	3.A.v.	Move elevator from stack floor to Basement	4 book trucks	55	1	55		wait until four book trucks accumulate at elevator
	3.A.vi.	Unload elevator	1 book truck	30	4	120		
	3.A.vii.	Move book trucks from elevator to loading dock	1 book truck	55	4	220		
	3.A.viii.	Log book truck	1 book truck	35	4	140		
	3.A.ix.	Return elevator to stack floor	1 trip	55	1	55	710	
Team Four	3.A.x.	Check and secure book truck contents	1 book truck	90	4	360		
	3.A.xi.	Load book trucks onto van	1 book truck	60	4	240	600	wait to move van until 25 book trucks are loaded

Figure 9.10
PERT Network for Move A, Activity 3, with Data Used to Calculate Critical Path

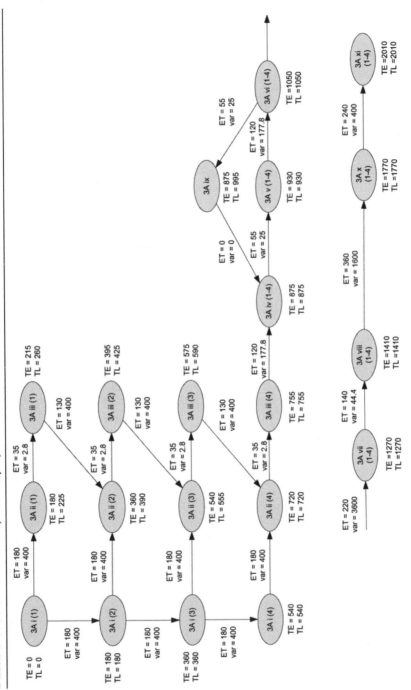

The Critical Path

The critical path is the series of dependent activities that must be completed on time for the move to be completed on time. If any activity on the critical path is delayed, completion of the move will be delayed. These are the activities the move manager will want to focus on while the move is in progress. You'll also want to know which tasks are *not* on the critical path, and how much time (slack time) may be lost on each, before it, too, affects the completion of the move.

Identifying the Critical Path

The formal definition of a critical path is "the longest sequence of connected activities through the [PERT] network and is defined as the path with zero slack time. Slack time . . . is . . . the difference between the earliest expected completion time and the latest expected completion time for an event" (Chase and Aquilano 1985, 308–10). Identifying the critical path involves several steps.

First, the expected times and variances for each activity are calculated as described previously, then these values are added to the PERT chart's graphic representation of sequence and precedence, as shown in Figure 9.10.

Next, the earliest (T_E) and latest (T_L) expected completion times for each activity are calculated and recorded on the PERT chart. Calculation of the earliest expected time of completion (T_E) for each activity is done by setting $T_E = 0$ for the first activity in the network, then working forward through the network, adding the expected times (ETs) of completion for each subsequent activity.

The latest expected time of completion (T_L) for each activity is calculated by setting T_L for the last activity in the network equal to its T_E, then working backward through the network, subtracting from it the ETs for each preceding activity. Slack time is the difference between T_L and T_E. Activities on the critical path are those in which T_E equals T_L, those with zero slack time.

Data for calculating the critical path for Move A, activity 3 are calculated in Figure 9.10. Calculation of slack time (and identification of the critical path) is shown in Figure 9.11, and the activities on the critical path are highlighted in Figure 9.12 (p. 238).

Note that only activities 3.A.ii (1)–3.A.ii (3), 3.A.iii.(1)–3.A.iii.(3), and 3.A.ix are not on the critical path. Inspection of the slack time calculations shown in Figure 9.11 shows that for most of these activities, however, the slack time is more nominal than real, and amounts to less than one minute per activity.

The conclusion drawn from this analysis is that for the move to be completed on schedule, each activity must take place on schedule!

Figure 9.11
Calculating Slack (and Critical Path) for Activities of Move A, Activity 3

Event	Description	TE	TL	Slack (TL-TE)	On critical path?
3.A.i. (1)	Load book truck 1	0	0	0	yes
(2)	Load book truck 2	180	180	0	yes
(3)	Load book truck 3	360	360	0	yes
(4)	Load book truck 4	540	540	0	yes
3.A.ii.(1)	Record contents, book truck 1	180	225	45	no
(2)	Record contents, book truck 2	360	390	30	no
(3)	Record contents, book truck 3	540	555	15	no
(4)	Record contents, book truck 4	720	720	0	yes
3.A.iii. (1)	Move book truck 1 to elevator	215	260	45	no
(2)	Move book truck 2 to elevator	395	425	30	no
(3)	Move book truck 3 to elevator	575	590	15	no
(4)	Move book truck 4 to elevator	755	755	0	yes
3.A.iv. (1-4)	Load book trucks 1-4 on elevator	875	875	0	yes
3.A.v.	Move elevator from stack floor to Basement	930	930	0	yes
3.A.vi. (1-4)	Unload elevators 1-4 from elevator	1,050	1,050	0	yes
3.A.vii. (1-4)	Move book trucks 1-4 to loading dock	1,270	1,270	0	yes
3.A.viii. (1-4)	Record contents of book trucks 1-4	1,410	1,410	0	yes
3.A.ix.	Return elevator to stack floor	875	995	120	no
3.A.x (1-4)	Check contents, secure book trucks 1-4	1,770	1,770	0	yes
3.A.xi. (1-4)	Load book trucks 1-4 onto van	2,010	2,010	0	yes

Figure 9.12
Critical Path for Move A, Activity 3

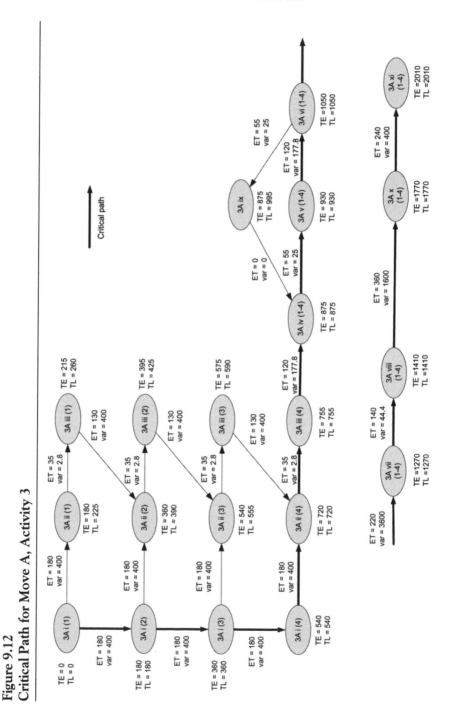

STEP 5B. PREPARE THE BUDGET

Because each move will have some unique characteristics, and each library will identify procedures that work best in its specific situation, the following list of factors to consider in planning a move budget will probably not be comprehensive. However, consider at least these:

Labor

Moving crews: Based on the analysis of crew size and move duration, and anticipated wage rate, calculate:

Days to complete move x (hours/day) x (crews/hour) x (people/crew) x (hourly wage rate/person)

Supervision: Will this be provided by library staff? Will the cost be made an explicit part of the project budget?

Other: Who will drive the vans? What is their pay rate? Will elevator operators or technicians be on call, and will there be an additional cost? Will carpenters be needed to make modifications to the building? Electricians, to install additional outlets or disconnect security systems? Will the cost of relocating OCLC workstations be part of the project cost? Of relocating networked workstations? Will any portion of the move require specialist moving assistance (e.g., to move rare or fragile materials, artwork, or contract equipment such as photocopiers)?

Equipment

Vans: Are vans already owned by the library or its parent organization? Will they be rented? Leased?

Book trucks or cartons: Does the library have on hand a sufficient quantity of these, or will additional stocks be purchased? Borrowed?

Supplies

The project will mostly likely require quantities of small items such as

Tape measures
Clipboards
Dust masks
Self-adhesive notes
Index cards
Pens and pencils
Colored markers

Color-coded labels

Package sealing tape

Publicity

Announcements

Signage for both old and new facilities

Bulletin board for move-related news

Handouts

Move newsletter

Advertising in local newspapers

Revisions of standard library guides

Other

Any additional insurance needed to cover move workers or vehicles

Identification (badges? T-shirts?) and refreshments for move workers

Additional security for the duration of the move

Additional, temporary telephone lines (Fraley and Anderson 1990, 102–9)

Additional, temporary electrical service

Preparation and duplication of plans

Temporary building modifications

Building repair

Furniture and equipment repair or replacement

Surveys

Additional heating and air conditioning expense

Again, this list is not intended to be exhaustive!

STEP 6: DOCUMENT THE PLAN

The project notebook should contain all the information that the move manager may need to resolve problems during execution of the move, all in one easy-to-find location. You will probably want to have it available electronically (on a project Web site or wiki) and in a loose-leaf notebook. It should include at least the following:

1. A statement of the move goals (useful as a context for making decisions later on).

2. Measurements of the existing collections.

3. Assumptions about growth and calculations of the allowance for growth.

4. The collection layout plan and underlying calculations (useful, with items 2 and 3, in resolving layout problems during move execution).

5. A description of move methods, including write-ups that can be copied and distributed to people who will be actually doing the move, providing an appropriate level of detail.

6. A description of the WBS, risks, impacts, and possible solutions.

7. The planned schedule, its calculation, and the critical path (useful in resolving scheduling issues during move execution).

8. The project budget and its elements (useful if questions come up later about whether something was to be covered under the move budget).

STEP 7: GET SIGN-OFF BY STAKEHOLDERS

Asking stakeholders for their approval of the plan makes sure that everyone involved is in agreement on the key elements of the move plan.

1. It provides an opportunity for everyone involved to make sure the scope of the move project should remain as originally envisioned:

2. It provides an opportunity for stakeholders to look at the project from their unique perspectives and offer suggestions to make it better.

3. It gives the move planner formal authority to proceed.

PRACTICAL ADVICE ON PLANNING MOVE LOGISTICS

The library literature contains many reports of moves. Although there are more news accounts than analytical reports, and the reader will want to critically assess some of the methods reported, many news accounts contain nuggets of useful information. Reports of moves that were planned in great detail tend to conclude with remarks that the work was completed as planned. Reports of moves that feature enthusiasm but not much planning tend to blithely conclude with remarks to the effect that the cleanup only took a couple of months.

Appendix B lists moves reported in the English-language literature since 1940 in reverse chronological order, sorted by type of library. The Annotated References provide a guide to the English-language literature on moves and moving from 1940 onward. Following is a sample of practical advice on planning move logistics.

DOING THE MOVE YOURSELF

General

1. Use a small move done well in advance of the main move to pilot test procedures and make time estimates (Chappell 1964, 18–19).

2. Before the move, weed the collection. Before their move, the Centennial Park Public Library in Colorado weeded 30,000 "outdated and underused items" from a collection of 110,000 items (Baumann 2006, 13).

3. If you must leave part of the old library before the new one is ready, consider renting an on-site storage container to house books (Baumann 2006, 15).

4. If in doubt about how much space to allow for part of a collection, use your high-end estimate. It is more difficult and time consuming to find additional space during a move than the reverse (Calderhead 1996, 76).

5. For a large move, "moving collections linearly from start to finish could take weeks, if not months! Providing multiple starting points and accurate fill ratios is critical to . . . success" (Pikul 2006, 214).

Detecting and Limiting Cumulative Measurement and Planning Errors

1. Identify checkpoints within the collection layout plan and require that any slippage in the reshelving of material relative to the plan be resolved within those checkpoints. At the University of Tennessee, Knoxville, a determination was made that problems had to be made within a maximum of 40 single-faced sections (Bayne 1990, 57).

Diagnosing Differences Between Predicted and Actual Cycle Time

1. Variance between predicted and actual cycle times may be due to

    a. time estimates based on atypical labor (skilled labor when unskilled labor will be used or vice versa);
    b. unexpected contention for elevators (and loading docks);
    c. more people needed to push a fully loaded book cart than predicted; and
    d. labor force attrition, leading to reduced team size. (Adams 1954, 7)

Reducing Cycle Time

1. If cycle time is being constrained by lack of elevators, and if using cartons to transport materials, consider installation of chutes or

conveyer belts in stairwells or from outside windows (Leary 1982, 310).

Integrating Collections

1. When integration of smaller collections into a larger collection is planned, move the larger collection first, then the progressively smaller collections.

2. Reserve space for large sets coming from other locations by creating a dummy for each title, noting the source library, call number, and linear measurement of space to be reserved. This minimizes the need for later shifting. (Bayne 1990, 57)

Sequencing

1. Schedule the easiest moves of the largest amounts of material first to minimize the impact of unexpected delays on later stages (Bayne 1990, 58–59).

2. If the old facility is crowded, has slow or no elevators, or has few exit points, consider carefully the maximum number of teams that can efficiently operate in it simultaneously. If the new facility has more elevators, entrance/exit points, and more space, it may be possible to schedule more teams working in the new building than in the old (so, for instance, teams might be simultaneously moving into the new building from several old locations).

3. Move materials into two or more floors of the new facility while restricting move activities to no more than two floors of the old facility. This advice assumes the old facility is crowded and may have fewer elevators or egress points than the new facility.

4. For moves that involve collection integration, separately measure the time for reshelving operations that include interfiling and those that are simple reshelving, and take this into account in scheduling sending and receiving teams. For instance, Bayne (1990, 60) notes that in the collection integration phase of the University of Tennessee, Knoxville's, move, they provided three receiving (reshelving) teams and three sending teams per shift.

Team Composition

1. Organize members of the move operation into teams.

2. Include in each team an experienced library staff member.

3. Recruit team members, rather than reassigning them.

243

4. Consider for team leadership roles staff from units with experience shelving (e.g., circulation, reserve, current periodicals, interlibrary loan).

5. In making an in-house shift in a large academic library, one planner found that moving one double-faced section of material took 1.25 team hours (2.5 person hours), including shelf-reading, travel time, loading, unloading, and making end cards (Chappell 2006, "Moving Library Collections: Knight Library, Shift," 1).

6. In planning a law library move, one planner found that "one packer/ unpacker can handle 2,000 volumes per day (half that number if you are using boxes)" (Benamati 1988d, 7).

7. The optimum number of teams will depend on the number of move routes, egress points, elevators, vans, etc. (Bayne 1990, 59–60).

8. Emergencies occur; choose at least two of the most reliable staff members to serve as backup move managers (Bryant 2004, 5).

9. At each end of the move, have a library staff person who is knowledgeable about the overall situation and able to resolve problems that will arise (Kephart 1952,4).

10. Consider the following labor allocation guidelines from a large move (modified from Kurth and Grim 1966, 151–52):

    At old location:
    a. Pull books from shelf—1 worker
    b. Place books on book truck—1 worker
    c. Push book truck to elevator—1 worker
    d. Operate elevator—1 worker
    e. Push book truck from elevator to loading dock—1 worker
    f. Push book truck from loading dock into van—1 worker
    g. Supervisor—1 worker

    At new location:
    a. Supervisor—1 worker
    b. Push book trucks from van to loading dock and elevator— 1 worker
    c. Operate elevator—1 worker
    d. Push book trucks from elevator to stack area—1 worker
    e. Reshelve books—2 workers

And from a smaller move (Hoxsey 1995, 28):

At old and new locations (each):

a. Load books into crates/unload books - 4 workers
b. Operate hand truck—2 workers
c. Supervise loading/unloading of books—2 staff members
d. "Floaters" to assist as needed—2 staff members
e. Supervise driver - 1 person

Team Allocation

1. If collection integration is required at the new facility, the reshelving teams will be slower than the teams removing materials from the shelf at the old facility and more reshelving teams will be needed (Bayne 1990, 58).

2. The maximum number of shifts and number of teams should be governed by the number of competent supervisors available (Spyers-Duran 1965, 7; Roberts 1966, 108).

3. The rate at which the move can progress will likely be governed by the rate at which material can be reshelved (Kurth and Grim 1966, 163).

4. Teams performing different types of work may develop expertise at different rates, and this may necessitate a different allocation of teams as the work progresses (Roberts 1966, 108).

Current Periodicals

1. Create a database of current periodical titles, call numbers, current and planned locations (by sequence number), and space required. Use the database to create two sets of labels. Affix one set of labels to new locations to indicate shelving sequence and to reserve space for specific titles. Package current periodical issues in boxes and fix the other set of labels to the boxes to identify the contents (Bayne 1990, 61).

Number of Book Carts Required

1. The number of book carts will be determined by the maximum number of teams working at one time and the number of carts needed per team. For instance, one team may need four sets of book carts: one being loaded, one being unloaded, one in transit to the new site, and one being returned to the old site (Bayne 1990, 63).

2.	Commenting on the 1999 move of 2.1 million volumes at the University of Kentucky, commercial mover Bill Overton said, "The ideal during the move is at any one time to have 200 of our 600 carts in the old building, 200 in transition, and 200 in the new building" (Bruns 1999, 49).

Book Cart Dimensions

1.	Make sure the book carts you plan to use can fit comfortably in all stack aisles. In narrow aisles, consider using single-sided book carts (Bryant 2004, 5).

By preparing a detailed plan, the move planner has made it much more likely that the move itself will go smoothly, and that when problems come up, they can be resolved quickly and easily.

REFERENCES

Note: References found in the annotated bibliography are not repeated here.

Baca, Claudia M. (2007). *Project Management for Mere Mortals: The Tools, Techniques, Teaming, and Politics of Project Management.* Addison Wesley Professional, Available at proquest.safaribooksonline. com/ 9780321423450/ch04lev1sec2 (accessed December 12, 2007).

Chase, Richard B., and Nicholas J. Aquilano, (1985). *Production and Operations Management: A Life Cycle Approach.* 4th ed. Homewood, IL: Irwin.

Lewis, James P. (2006). *Fundamentals of Project Management.* 3rd ed. Amacom, available via SafariBooks at proquest.safaribooksonline.com/978081 4408797/ (accessed December 12, 2007).

10 EXECUTING THE MOVE YOURSELF

When a library plans and executes a move itself, it takes on a range of responsibilities that a moving company might otherwise handle. Among these are recruiting, training, and supervising the individuals who will actually perform the move; identifying, purchasing, renting, leasing, or constructing appropriate equipment; dealing with facilities issues; overseeing the daily operations of the move on a detailed level; identifying and resolving problems as they arise; and addressing potential health and injury issues.

Not every move will involve all of these issues. For a relatively small, internal stack shift, these issues may likewise be small and easy to manage; however, as the size and complexity of the move increases, so, too, will the scope and complexity of the operational issues involved.

RECRUITING WORKERS

Staff

For a small, internal stack shift, the move workers may be the normal stack maintenance staff. Because these individuals' capabilities are already known, they are already trained in handling methods and in reading call numbers, and they presumably have a stake in ensuring that the work is done correctly, they will probably be the move planner's first choice for move workers. If, as in many libraries, the stack maintenance staff work part-time, perhaps their weekly assignments can be increased for the duration of the move, or, if individuals have assignments in multiple departments, perhaps they can be assigned exclusively to the move for its duration.

Other library staff might be reassigned, or volunteers solicited from within the staff. However, think carefully before asking staff to perform the physical work of moving. A fully loaded book truck may weigh up to a thousand pounds (Wells and Young 1997, 43). Loading and moving book trucks and packing and moving boxes is hard physical work. Doing it for any length of time without injury or fatigue requires training in proper ergonomics as well as physical conditioning.

Consider staff members' physical limitations and the amount of time any one staff member can afford to contribute, in terms of both maintaining regular work assignments and endurance. In his report on the staff-only move of the Dowagiac Public Library, Mark Ames noted that after a move of only a few days' duration, "Somewhat disorganized and filled with aches and pains, our first day of reopening was a busy one" (1973, 9). For example, asking staff to schedule themselves for three two-hour shifts may be more successful than assigning staff to work one six-hour stint.

If soliciting volunteers from within the staff, screen for people with allergies and respiratory or orthopedic health problems that might be exacerbated by the dust and physical labor inherent in move operations. Carol Hole's (partially) humorous comments on the physical labor involved in library work note that "the average book weighs maybe a pound" (1988, 2).

When determining the average number of volumes that book brigade members will be expected to handle, consider the cumulative weight handled and possible repetitive stress injuries from repeatedly grasping and passing batches of several pound weights. Consult with the library or parent organization's insurance carrier to ensure coverage for injuries to staff that might occur while performing work that is outside the normal work assignment.

There are at least two monetary advantages of using staff to perform a move. First, staff members may be more efficient than other workers, because they are already trained and have a vested interest in seeing that the work is done right. Second, if the move work can be performed within already-budgeted hours, there may be no additional direct cost. Indirectly, there may be a cost associated with work deferred in order to reassign individuals to the move; however, this may be of less concern to the library.

When the library faces a move too large to be handled by the available staff, it will have to recruit additional people, either paid temporary hires or unpaid volunteers. There are advantages and disadvantages to using each, although the choice may depend more on cost issues than any other factors.

Volunteers

For the library with a very tight budget, using volunteers to execute a move may be the only viable option. Using volunteers can also be a positive public-relations move, giving members of the library's user community a chance to show their commitment to and support of their library. A well-executed volunteer-based move can build community support and provide the opportunity for good public relations stories and photos.

Volunteers can come from many sources. Service organizations looking for community service projects are an excellent source of volunteers, partly because they often come with their own team leaders who take charge of ensuring group attendance. For longer-duration moves, the library could schedule various groups of volunteers for specific work shifts based on the groups' availability: for instance, scout troops might be available after school during the work week (or all day, if the move is scheduled for a school vacation period); adult members of a church or community group might be available only on weekends.

Volunteers from the community at large might be recruited through notices posted at the library and at area businesses, advertisements placed in the local newspaper, notices on community access cable TV, and announcements to community groups. The announcements should specify the date(s) and time(s) volunteers are needed, qualifications (must be able to lift boxes weighing x pounds), and the name and telephone number of the library contact person or where to pick up an application/volunteer form.

Like paid staff, volunteers should be screened to ensure that individuals with health conditions that might be aggravated by the move are not exposed to risk. Consider identifying jobs with minimal lifting or minimal dust exposure for those who want to participate but can't or shouldn't perform the main task of moving materials; for instance, perhaps there is a need for someone to keep a log of materials leaving point A or arriving at point B, or to provide refreshments to the volunteers at break times, or to help make signs. The library should also consult with its insurance carrier and any organizations supplying volunteers about liability and coverage for any injuries that might occur during the move. Lynn Kirby notes that one public library turned down offers of volunteer assistance because of potential liability problems (1995, 27).

The downside of using volunteers is that for moves of longer duration; motivation and fatigue may negatively affect productivity and attendance. It is relatively easy to maintain enthusiasm for a one- or two-day move; however, relying exclusively on the same volunteers for moves of longer duration may mean accepting a high rate of attrition, as muscles become tired and other commitments must be attended to. Consider also the maximum number of volunteers library staff can effectively supervise. The Vineland Public Library used community volunteers and the National Guard to move a collection of 60,000 volumes in 1976. Library planners figured they could effectively supervise twenty to thirty volunteers at one time and noted, "the one night that we had more [volunteers] was the only time that we had mistakes that took time to rectify" (Snyder 1976, 3).

Other significant disadvantages to using volunteers are the following:

1. Coordinating volunteers' schedules is likely to be time consuming. Volunteers "come when they can and stay for varying periods of time" (Spyers-Duran 1965, 6). Consider sending each volunteer a letter confirming his or her work schedule, describing where to report, and a description of the work to be performed. Also consider a two-tier reward system, with different gifts for volunteers who work different

amounts of time. Hamilton and Hindman, for instance, gave each volunteer a "We Made the Move" pen; volunteers who completed six hours of service received a mug decorated with a picture of the new library (1987, 6) .

2. Because volunteers typically cannot work for long periods of time, training must be kept brief. This suggests that move methods used with volunteers must be kept simple, and moves of any complexity cannot be considered (Spyers-Duran 1965, 6).

3. The quality of work and the level of interest brought to a move by volunteers will vary and cannot be determined ahead of time, so there is an element of risk in relying on this source of labor. Some volunteers may be enthusiastic about the idea of volunteering, but bring more energy than care to their work (Tucker 1987, 98–99).

4. The price of using insufficiently trained workers may be weeks of after-move shelf-reading and collection shifting (Spyers-Duran 1965, 6).

5. Supervision and termination of volunteers is difficult, because of public relations issues. Volunteers cannot be told to perform tasks; they may only be asked (Spyers-Duran 1965, 6). In addition, in the case of unacceptable behavior, it is difficult to terminate a worker who has not first been hired. Consider setting a minimum age for volunteers. Establish guidelines for behavior, and "if there are volunteers who cannot abide by them, thank them and send them home" (Hamilton and Hindman 1987, 6).

6. Additional insurance coverage may be needed. Each volunteer should be asked to sign in and out each time he or she works, and a record should be kept of each volunteer's name, address, Social Security number, age, and hours worked, for liability purposes (Hamilton and Hindman 1987, 6). As mentioned above, Lynn Kirby reports that one public librarian turned down offers of volunteer help because of potential liability problems (1995, 27). Tucker also notes, "[T]he responsibility in case of accident may lie fully on the shoulders of the library. . . . [Determine] the extent of that responsibility and the amount of insurance coverage [that may be needed]. . . . One of the best ways of reducing the library's liability is to take affirmative steps towards safety and prevention" (1987, 17).

Paid Temporary Hires

The library may also have to temporarily hire individuals to perform the move. Sources of temporary additional hires could be the library's usual labor pool or temporary agencies.

As with members of the permanent staff or volunteers, the job descriptions for any temporary hires should explicitly describe the physical working conditions and require the ability to repeatedly lift groups of volumes, push loaded book trucks, and work in conditions that may include dust and dirt, so that the library can be sure these hires will be capable of working under typical move conditions. Consider testing applicants on their knowledge of the library's classification scheme or their ability to learn classification schemes (Caywood 1992, 35).

An advantage of using paid temporary employees rather than volunteers is that, particularly for moves of longer duration, the motivation to work is provided by pay rather than goodwill, and attrition may be lower. In addition, should the need arise, it is easier to fire a paid temporary employee than a volunteer; there is less loss of goodwill to the library. On the other hand, paid temporary employees may be less interested in the library than volunteers, less knowledgeable about it, and perhaps less interested in the goals of the project.

Some temporary workers will quit partway through the move as they find the physical work is too tiring or too boring, or because of unexpected outside circumstances. Consider either hiring more temporary workers than you think are needed or establishing a list of alternates (Kurkul 1983, 233). Leary (1982, 313) suggests hiring 15 percent more workers than are needed and planning to retain some workers for post-move cleanup operations.

TRAINING AND SUPERVISING WORKERS

All workers will have to be trained and supervised. Training will fall into at least four categories: reading call numbers, methods for handling materials, project goals and workflow, and work standards and expectations.

Reading Call Numbers

All move workers, except perhaps truck drivers, should be able to read call numbers in the classification system used for the library's general collections. If the library uses specialized classifications for other collections, for instance a classification scheme for government documents (such as SuDocs in the United States), or a local classification system for its AV material, it may be necessary to train only those individuals or teams who will be working with those collections; however, the library will have much greater flexibility in assigning workers if all workers can read and use all the library's classification systems. This training is critical, because the accuracy of book placement and the amount of shelf-reading and cleanup required after the move will depend on how well the workers can read and use call numbers.

Presumably any library staff members participating in the project will not need to be trained to use the classification system used for its general collections, but consider that some staff may need to be oriented to any specialized classifications they don't regularly work with. For volunteers and temporary paid hires, consider making participation in the project contingent upon achieving a satisfactory score in a test of call number reading skills. The library might also want to offer individuals the option of taking a pretest to identify those who may be exempted from call number training. Another approach is to train all workers to use each classification system, test to ensure mastery of the knowledge, and then assign individuals who test best in specialized classifications to the teams handling those collections.

Handling Methods

All move workers should be familiar with the correct handling and packing methods for each type of material that is being moved. This training might cover topics such as how to remove a bound volume from the shelf, how to place it on the book truck, dusting or cleaning procedures, replacing the material on the shelf, how tight to pack together material being reshelved, and the consequences of exposing collection material to rain or snow.

Have sample materials and equipment on hand to demonstrate (Kurkul 1983, 231). To reinforce the reason for taking this care, the training might also include information on the cost to repair or replace damaged collection items and on the fragility of acid paper.

Project Goals and Workflow

Everyone participating in the move, including permanent library staff, will need to be oriented to the goals of the project and its workflow. Daily work goals may be provided in a daily morning briefing, but before the move begins, hold a meeting to describe the major steps of the move, where material will be moved from, the order in which various areas of the collection will be moved, the physical paths workers will take, any anticipated common problems and their solutions, reporting relationships, and who has the authority to stop work and resolve problems.

Work Expectations

Be sure to tell move workers what is expected of them: that they report to work on time; the number of unexcused absences allowed; any behavior the library considers unacceptable and its consequences; dress standards; wearing identification badges or T-shirts; the daily work schedule (including when breaks are scheduled); where food and beverages are permitted; whether smoking is permitted, and, if so, where; whether portable stereos (boomboxes) or iPods are permitted; and what to do in case of personal injury, in case of damage to materials, and in case of fire or other emergency. The library may want to put work expectations in writing. Check with your parent organization to see whether it wants workers or volunteers to sign an insurance release.

Maintaining Morale

Maintaining morale is important. Moving is difficult, dirty work, and keeping people motivated will make the work go faster and more agreeably. This is particularly true if the library is depending on volunteer labor to complete a move. Orienting move workers to the goals of the project, keeping them apprised of progress, providing constructive feedback on performance, and praising good work can all help. Tangible tokens of appreciation may also make a difference. Have good free food available at breaks and consider providing free meals to volunteers and awarding T-shirts to volunteers who complete their scheduled shifts (e.g., "I helped move the Hometown Public Library, June 21–22, 20__!" with the library's logo). All serve as motivational tools and thanks for a job well done.

Graphic representations of the work completed and left to do can help explain progress more directly than words; consider using a simple thermometer-type graphic to represent the percent of the move completed or floor plans of stack areas colored to show where volumes have been already moved out or reshelved. Use a macro-level PERT diagram or a move schedule to show progress by coloring in or crossing out the work that has been completed.

If multiple teams are working on the move, consider posting daily productivity statistics for each team. However, be aware that there may be a downside to this. If several teams' work has to be synchronized, competition may encourage individual teams to work at rates that lead to one team working at a rate that others cannot match. Another approach might be to post the overall productivity results for the entire move effort on a daily basis, for example, "Today we moved x volumes, 10 percent more than our previous daily best!"

Physical Safety

Move workers should be instructed in correct lifting techniques and safe weight limits, safe operation of a book truck (how many workers it takes to push a loaded truck up a ramp, avoiding behavior that might cause a book truck to tip over), symptoms of heat exhaustion (for hot-weather moves), and reporting workplace injuries and how to get them treated. Also include instruction in personal safety, including end-of-day shutdown procedures and a caution against returning alone to an empty facility.

EQUIPMENT

For a stack shift within an existing library, the only equipment needed may be measuring tapes or rulers and the existing stock of book trucks. For larger moves, additional means of conveying books from one location to another will be needed, and the library may wish to consider having custom book carts made specifically for the move. For moves that require the relocation of stacks as well as materials, the library may wish to consider stack movers. Chapter 4 contains a discussion of the relative merits of using book trucks and crates to move materials.

Book Trucks

The planning process described in Chapter 9 may be used to determine the number of book trucks needed for the move. Book trucks vary in size and capacity, so determining the number of book trucks needed starts with measuring the linear inches of material that one book truck can hold. The more linear inches of material that can be moved at one time, the faster the move should proceed. This is because the amount of time required to load the incremental amount of materials onto a cart is small in relation to the amount of time required to then move the entire cart of material from origin to destination; thus the per-volume move time decreases with increased cart capacity.

Custom-constructed book carts may provide more capacity than commercially available carts and may be less expensive. (See, e.g., Alley 1979, 33–37). These may be particularly cost-effective if the library can have custom carts constructed in-house for the cost of materials. Heavy-duty, specialized book trucks can sometimes be rented from moving companies. If you plan to use standard book trucks and need more, and your library is part of a system, consider asking the other libraries in your system to each lend one or two (Minter 2007, 45).

Cartons, Boxes, and Crates

Some libraries may wish to pack books into plastic storage crates or cardboard cartons. Cardboard cartons may be available free or very cheaply from community sources, and thus be an attractive alternative for the move planner with a small or nonexistent budget. Before committing to using any of these options, though, read Chapter 4 and consider the preservation and operations impact of their use. Following are some questions to consider:

1. Can volumes be packed flat, or in an upright position, so that their bindings are not stressed?

2. Are the containers of equal size and stackable? If so, can they be stacked without pressure and weight bearing on the books inside?

3. How will the containers be moved? Will they be loaded onto dollies? Bookcarts?

4. Will move workers be expected to carry the containers? How much will a loaded container weigh, and how long will a typical move worker be able to continually carry them? The critical question affecting operational efficiency is probably what size maximizes the linear footage of material that one worker can move. For a discussion of crate size, see Jesse (1941, 331–32). Bendix (2005, 13) notes, "Crates are generally very heavy and should not be moved by those unused to lifting weights all day."

5. Can the library ensure a supply of clean boxes or crates (either brand new or thoroughly clean), or will they have to be cleaned before the move? How are they constructed?

6. Will they withstand repeated use, or will they have to be replaced after two or three uses? This is the number of uses reported by Armstrong (2005, 4).

7. If using cardboard boxes or cartons, will they have to be sealed? How long? Masking tape dries out; a better choice is strong packing tape (Anderson 2007, 31–33).

Consider providing box packers with a sample of a properly packed and labeled box (Anderson 2007, 31–33). To determine the number of boxes needed for a move,

1. Measure the linear inches of material that can be packed in one box (that is, the number of inches the material would occupy if shelved on a shelf).

2. Divide the total linear inches of material to be moved by the linear inches that can be packed in one box. This yields the number of boxes needed to house the entire collection; if the collection is to be boxed up and stored, you now have the number of boxes you will need:

(Linear inches of material to be moved)/(Linear inches of material/box) = Number of boxes

If material will be boxed, taken to the new location, and reshelved immediately, you will have to determine the number of boxes that will be in motion during one complete round trip and then how many times each box can be reused. This takes a couple more steps:

1. Measure the linear inches of material that can be packed in one box, as above.

2. Determine the number of boxes that can be transported at one time to the new location.

3. Estimate how long it will take to move the load of boxes to the new location and how many additional boxes can be be packed and moved to the new location while the first load is being unloaded and its boxes moved from the new location back to the old location. *Making a Gantt chart will help work out steps 1–3.*

4. After determining the number of boxes that will be in use during one complete round trip, determine the number of times each box can be reused. If you are purchasing the boxes, ask the supplier for help with this. Be cautious; overestimating the number of times the box can be reused could leave you short of boxes as the move progresses. Ask your supplier how quickly you can get more boxes, or whether you can return unneeded boxes at no charge.

William W. Armstrong (2005, 4), in his report on the closing of the LSU Chemistry Library, noted "the optimal number of boxes to have in circulation at any given time was 300–400. . . . By the time the library move had been completed, a total of 4,382 boxes had been packed, shipped, unpacked, and reshelved. . . . There was an average turnaround time of two to three days from the time the materials were picked up and delivered to the time they were available to patrons on their new . . . shelves."

Stack Movers

Special dollies exist that can move fully loaded book stacks. The advantage of this approach is that it eliminates the need to empty a book stack, disassemble it, reassemble it in a new location, and replace the books on it. There is a considerable time saving if the objective is to simply move book stacks into a new location without rearranging the collections. Stack movers are particularly useful when an area needs to be carpeted. Alley (1982), Segesta (1986), Meinke (1988), and Fitt (1989) describe various designs of stack movers and their use.

BOOK BRIGADES AND MOVING LINES

An equipment-less (or virtually equipment-less) method for moving library materials, the book brigade is a line of people stretching from one stack location to another, which works by passing individual volumes from one person to the next. Book brigades rely on having enough people in line that no one person absorbs too great a portion of the work, and so that the work continues to flow smoothly without interruption.

A moving line consists of a line of people who each in turn pick up an armload of books and walk from one location to another while maintaining their relative place in line.

Book brigades and moving lines are best suited to moves of limited scope and duration, where there is a plentiful supply of enthusiastic volunteer labor, and where public relations can benefit. For larger, more complex moves, consider using a book brigade or moving line for the move's ceremonial kickoff, to showcase community involvement and support. A notable disadvantage of both techniques is that materials are handled a lot. If they are handled roughly or dropped, significant damage may be done.

Reverend I. J. Herscher (1938, 329) noted semihumorously about the 1938 move into St. Bonaventure College's new library:

> Pitching and catching [books] seemed to be the order of the day, although there was at times more pitching than catching. Some movers used basketball tactics in their work, and more than one was caught dribbling.
>
> Many of the books . . . did not stand the shock of being moving very well. Some of them suffered excruciatingly, others had nervous

prostration and went all to pieces. Most of the boys [performing the move] knew that the new Library was well equipped with a good work room for repairing and rebinding books.

Book Brigades

The following method for estimating the number of individuals and time required to move materials using a book brigade draws on an account by Barbara Cliff and Randa Strom (1995, 7–8) of moving a high school library:

1. Measure the distance between shelves in the old and new locations.

2. Determine the average distance between individuals, based on a trial run. Consider the longest distance or number of steps each individual will be asked to take.

3. Calculate the number of individuals required per work shift by dividing total distance (no. 1) by the distance between individuals (no. 2).

4. Measure the linear footage of material to be moved.

5. Determine the average linear footage one person can grasp.

6. Calculate the number of handfuls of books that must be moved (no. 4 divided by no. 5).

7. Determine the time required for one pass: conduct a trial run to determine the amount of time required (in minutes) to pass one handful of books from the old to the new locations.

8. Determine the total number of hours required: multiply the time required for no. 7 by the number of handfuls that must be passed (no. 6); divide by 60 to convert minutes required to hours required .

9. Calculate the number of work shifts required: determine the length of time each group of individuals will participate in the human chain and divide the total time required (no. 8) by this number.

10. Add to the total number of work shifts the amount of time necessary before the work shift starts to check in individuals and brief or train them, and the amount of time necessary for breaks and to debrief them at the end of the work shift.

11. Calculate the number of individuals required by multiplying the number of work shifts required (no. 9) by the number of individuals required per work shift (no. 3).

12. Calculate the total time required by multiplying the total number of work shifts required (no. 9) by the total time per work shift (no. 10).

Moving Lines

In the moving line method, each individual picks up an armload of books and walks in line from the old location to the new location. Once the armload of books is placed on the shelf in the new location, the line circles back to the old location, with each person still maintaining his or her position in the line. Following are some pointers on operating a moving line:

1. Consider how large an armload of books one person can hold for the distance to be traveled. Stickney and Meinhold (1955, 253) and Kulp (1952, 457) suggest respectively that one foot of material or ten books are a good amount, but this seems too much to me.

2. Watch out for overly eager individuals who may want to pick up more weight than they can carry the entire distance required (Long and Meyer 1954, 795).

3. Have a trained staff person load each volunteer, so that the books are placed in the mover's arms in order (Stickney and Meinhold 1955, 254). Similarly, have trained staff unload volunteers and reshelve the material.

4. Consider securing the bundle of books in order, so that they will not get out of order while in transit.

5. Provide volunteers with a sequential number, indicating the relative placement of their load of books. One library provided each volunteer with a pin-on placard, onto which a sequential label was pasted. On each trip, a new label was pasted on. This assured reshelvers at the receiving location that no materials had gotten lost in transit and let the reshelvers focus on reshelving rather than inspecting call numbers (Stickney and Meinhold 1955, 254). Another library inserted destination slips in each armload of books (Kulp 1952, 457).

MOVING ITEMS OF EQUIPMENT

Specially sized carts with appropriate weight-bearing capacity will be needed to move items such as atlas cases and microform cabinets. Because of the weight involved and the potential for damage to the items and injury to staff if moved improperly or carelessly, these should be moved by staff who have experience and expertise in this area, for instance, the institution's transportation, maintenance, physical plant, or buildings and grounds staff.

Contractual, lease, or warranty terms for other equipment, such as photocopiers, scanners, and microform reader/printers, may require that only an authorized agent move them. Check contract, lease, and warranty terms in advance and determine the lead time required by the specified agent to schedule any work that must be performed.

PRE-MOVE SETUP

Before the move begins, plan to complete the following steps:

1. Adjust the *spacing of the shelving* according to the collection layout plan. This saves time during the actual reshelving of materials (Kurkul 1983, 232).

2. *Dust the shelving* in the new location a short time before the move begins (Kephart 1952, 3).

3. Mark the shelving with the *starting and ending locations of major components* of the collection.

4. Consider *color-coding* major stack blocks, areas, or floors. This allows use of corresponding color-coding on book truck or carton labels, an easy means of quickly identifying destinations (Kephart 1952, 2).

5. Mark the *fill direction* on each range (Ellis 1988, 287).

6. Indicate the *fill ratio* to be used within each component of the collection. Consider marking the fill ratio on individual shelves.

7. Reserve *space for large sets* coming from other locations by preparing and inserting into the primary collection dummies noting the title and linear space required. The same approach could be used for individual periodical titles where these are to be integrated into previously separate monograph collections. This minimizes the need for later shifting (Bayne 1990, 57).

8. Mark shelves and/or sections that are to be left entirely *empty*.

9. Place a *bookend* on each shelf where one will be needed (Ellis 1988, 287).

10. For areas where *periodicals* will be shelved, mark the starting point and space needed for each title. For each periodical title, create two identical sets of labels with the call number, title, measurement, and a unique identifier. Place one label at the old shelf location and the second at the new shelf location. Mark the exact spot on the shelf where the run should start with the left edge of the label. Mark the exact spot where the volumes being moved should end with a colored flag. Consider marking growth space to be left empty with a different color flag (Hitchcock, Sager, and Schneider 2005, 6).

11. Identify and mark the locations of *placement benchmarks* to restrict the impact of planning and measurement errors (Bayne 1990, 57).

12. Produce sequentially numbered *labels* to identify each book truck load (or carton contents) moved.

13. Prepare two sets of *log sheets* to record the sequence numbers and contents of each book truck as it exits the old facility and enters the new facility.

14. Check with the shelving manufacturer or installer to determine whether the *book stacks* may be *loaded unevenly* without any hazard of the range tipping or becoming unstable; that is, whether one side of a range may be loaded completely while the other side is empty. It may be helpful to ask whether possible scenarios could make the shelving unstable, for instance loading one side of a shelving unit with oversized volumes printed on heavy clay-coated paper. Installing tie bars or bolting shelving to a concrete slab may help reduce the possibility of tipping. If tie-bars are to be reused, check their integrity (Kathman 1983, 153). Also, determine whether ranges that abut a wall or column need to be attached to it to provide stability.

15. Distribute *kick-step stools* throughout the stacks so that one will always be immediately accessible when needed (Ducas 1985, 78).

16. If needed, produce and tape in place placards directing members of the move crew to specific work locations (Bryant 2004, 6).

Additional comments about specific steps:

Item 3. Mark the exact shelf locations where each classification or major subclass will start and end, so that material can be simultaneously reshelved in several locations. These markers also serve as placement benchmarks and assist the move supervisor in determining whether material is being reshelved at the anticipated fill ratio.

Marking should be done with a labeling material that can be completely removed after the move, without leaving a residue on the stacks, but that will stay in place for the duration of the move.

Item 6. There are a number of practical ways to get the fill ratio right:

   a. Mark it on each shelf. Use a piece of masking tape, an adhesive dot, or some other stable indicator that will not leave adhesive residue. For collection integration, either use different color indicators (e.g., a red dot for the main collection's fill ratio, a blue dot for the second collection's fill ratio, and a yellow dot for the third collection's fill ratio) or mark the fill ratios sequentially after each collection has been moved, so that only a single marker is placed on a shelf at any one time. The latter approach has the advantage of perhaps being less confusing, but it is more time consuming, as it requires multiple passes through the stacks.

b. Issue each reshelver a spacing device, such as a wood block, which can be placed on the right side of each shelf and the books shelved up to it (Hammer 1960, 394). For integration of multiple collections and for areas of the collection where different fill ratios are required, each spacer could be marked appropriately. For simple moves, this straightforward device should work well; however, for complex moves with many different fill ratios, the many different-sized spacers that would be required could require careful labeling and the creation of a substantial inventory.

c. Issue each reshelver a ruler. Label the end of each range (or each section) with the fill ratio to be used when reshelving materials in it that day. This approach has the advantage of requiring less time to mark, but it places more responsibility on individual reshelvers for the correct measurement of this critical element. It's not recommended for the following reasons:

   If a large number of individuals are involved in reshelving operations, there's greater likelihood of variation in the actual fill rate, which increases the likelihood corrective shifting will be needed later.

   Also, measuring takes longer than using a spacing device or referring to a marker on each shelf. Because the shelving rate tends to be the limiting factor in move operations, it may slow down the entire move.

Item 7. Dummies, or cardboard placards, should be large and sturdy enough to survive the move. On each dummy list the title, call number, source library, and shelf space required. Shelve, and then move the dummy with the main collection. When reshelving in the new location, mark the shelf with the starting and ending point for the set, and leave the dummy on the shelf to identify the set for which the space has been reserved (Bayne 1990, 57).

   The same approach could be used for bound periodical back files. In this case, the dummy should include the linear measurement of the existing back file; the space to be reserved for growth; any variant titles; whether there are duplicate copies coming from separate locations and if so, whether they are to be interfiled, or each sequence maintained separately; and whether the title is active, ceased, or on order (Roberts 1966, 106).

Item 11. The spacing of benchmark locations will depend on how much material you are willing to shift when a shelving problem is discovered. If a benchmark is placed at the end of each range, then correction of mistakes and miscalculations may be confined to a relatively manageable area and amount of time and labor.

Item 12. Labels for this purpose should be large enough to allow quick recording of the starting and ending call numbers of material shelved on a book truck or placed in a carton. Using preproduced labels will save time and eliminate the possibility of duplicate numbering.

Another approach is to use sequentially numbered, two-part labels. Both parts are filled in with the starting and ending call numbers of the content. One part is adhered to a carton of books as it is packed, indicating its contents, while the other part is placed on the shelf at the destination to indicate the location where that carton is to be reshelved. This approach seems to be most useful when materials are to be placed in storage for a period of time, for instance while a building undergoes renovation. In this case, a third duplicate label, attached to the sending log and kept as a finding aid, could be helpful.

If the contents information could be easily copied onto multiple labels, four labels could be produced for each book truck or carton: one for the book truck or carton itself, one for the sending log, one for the receiving log, and one to be placed on the shelf at the destination.

Item 13. The purpose of the log sheets is to track the progress of the move (How many book trucks were moved today?), help locate specific items needed by patrons during the move, and document that no materials are unaccounted for at the end of the day (all the book trucks that left the old building arrived at their new locations).

The log sheet can be a simple page, with columns for book truck number, starting call number, and ending call number of each book truck's contents.

FACILITIES ISSUES

Many of the facilities issues faced by the library executing its own move are similar to those faced by the library contracting with an outside moving company.

Elevators

Elevators are a critical resource for any move that involves more than one floor of a building. Usually when an elevator fails, the alternative—moving materials between floors via stairwells—requires different, additional equipment, and is considerably slower than moving materials between floors on book trucks via an elevator. Thus, elevator failure can either slow or stop a move. In buildings with a single working elevator, it is especially critical to ensure its continued operation during the move.

Elevators should be inspected and preventative maintenance performed in advance of the move's start date. Arrangements should be made for prompt service if the elevator(s) fail during the move. Protect elevator cabs from damage by installing protective padding (De Jager and Malan 1989, 117). Vacuum the elevator tracks frequently during the move, to prevent jams (Leary 1982, 312). Find out in advance whether a special operator must operate the elevator, and consider whether there may be a time saving in assigning one person to control access to the elevator. Some older, special-purpose elevators may require a special operator. Owen Slight (1967, 243) suggests assigning a lift controller to reduce contention over elevator use. If possible, obtain an elevator key (Bryant 2004, 6). Determine whether elevators can be set so that they operate only by key from within the cab, to reduce contention (Leary 1982, 312).

Ideally, move operations should have the exclusive right to elevator access. In buildings where the library shares an elevator or elevators with other tenants, enhanced elevator access may need to be negotiated for the duration of the move. For shared-occupancy buildings with multiple elevators, perhaps exclusive use of one elevator could be ensured. For single-elevator buildings, consider whether exclusive access can be negotiated for certain hours of the day; move operations requiring an elevator could be conducted only during those hours. If elevator access must be shared, the move planner should estimate the additional time this will add to each elevator trip and factor it into the move schedule.

Buildings Without Elevators

Libraries located on other than the entry floor of buildings without elevators will have to identify an alternate way to move materials vertically. Temporary external elevators, ramps, scissor lifts, chutes, and conveyor belts have all been used for this purpose.

A temporary external elevator may be built by a construction firm and rented to the library. Consider the capacity that might be needed, where it would be located, the egress points (Would windows have to be removed and openings in the building expanded to accommodate egress?), safety, liability, and insurance issues (Tucker 1987, 22–23).

Temporary ramps may be helpful in moving materials from a floor that is not quite level with the ground level outside (e.g., offset half a story above or below ground).

A scissor lift might be useful for moving material from a mezzanine stack to a main floor (Hamilton and Hindman 1987, 4). Allen (1950, 724–26) notes use of a modified forklift outdoors to move materials from a building without an elevator.

Chutes constructed in stairwells are particularly useful for moving boxed material.

Conveyer belts are likewise suited to moving boxed material. They may be used in several locations over the life of a move. These may be available from rental agencies or as loans from agricultural coops (Tucker 1987, 22; Thorne 1955, 841).

Loading Docks

Like elevator access, access to loading docks can be another bottleneck. Buildings typically have only one loading dock, so competition for access to it may be keener than for access to elevators. Deliveries of mail and maintenance supplies and removal of trash may all need to be carried out while the move proceeds, even in a building where the library is the sole occupant. Talking with the providers of these services before the move may secure their cooperation in waiting a few minutes for loading dock access while the move is underway or in scheduling their deliveries and pickups to take place outside the hours of move operations.

Any loading dock equipment, such as dock levelers and dock doors, should be inspected prior to the move, and preventative maintenance and any necessary repairs should be performed.

For a large move, it may be desirable to create additional locations where material can be removed from the building and loaded onto trucks. The costs of modifying an existing door or window and the construction of a temporary loading dock may be more than offset by the labor time saved by being able to maintain two simultaneous streams of material exiting the building. In some instances, creation of a temporary loading dock may be necessary because an existing dock may not be large enough to accommodate the trucks being used for the move, or it is situated far from appropriate or usable elevators.

Accessible Pathways Outside the Building

If the move will use trucks or vans to move materials between buildings, it is important to determine whether roadways to the loading area(s) can support the loaded weight of a truck and whether paving material either will not be damaged or can be repaired. For instance, are there utility tunnels of any sort beneath the path proposed to access the building? Is the paving material brick or cobblestone? Concrete? How sound is the paving material, and who is responsible for its maintenance? If the truck damages paving material or a tunnel in the course of executing the move, who will be liable for its repair? The library? If access to the building will require that trucks park in a public street, consult the appropriate public safety authority.

Traffic Control and Parking Management

If the move is to take place on public streets, consider whether they might be temporarily closed to traffic. Can parking meters be hooded in the immediate area of move operations to give move staff more working space (Hamilton and Hindman 1987, 7)?

264

Book Truck–Accessible Pathways Within the Building

Within the building, walk the move route. Look for possible obstructions that can be moved out of the way in advance of the move. Is there furniture in an area that is to be used as a staging area for either empty or full carts? Are there loose floor tiles or carpet that should either be secured or removed in advance of the move? Are there internal doors not required for compliance with fire safety codes that could be removed?

Protecting the Building

Before move operations begin, the move planner will want to ensure that reasonable precautions are taken to protect the interiors of any buildings where move operations will be taking place. These precautions may include installing protective padding/mats inside elevator cabs, laying plywood on mats in move paths, wrapping columns adjacent to major move paths with cardboard to protect them against damage caused by book cart collisions, and the like. The time and effort expended in preventative precautions will be paid back later by faster cleanup and lower repair costs.

Lighting and Electrical Service Controls

Know where light switches and breaker boxes are located, how to use them (and whether breaker box access is permitted), or whom to call to operate them (Grey 1992, 331). Know whom to call and the expected response time in case of an emergency.

DAILY OPERATIONS

Each move will develop its own rhythm. However, this section offers some suggestions on conducting the daily operations of a move.

Move Manager

Identify one person as being in charge of move operations. The move project manager should be able to give full-time attention to move operations. This is the person who will have the authority to start and stop move operations, identify daily move goals, monitor progress and the methods used by workers, and resolve problems as they arise. The move project manager must have a clear understanding of the goals and flow of the move and of problems that may arise and be able to develop solutions quickly and accurately.

DOING THE MOVE YOURSELF

Daily Start-up

Daily start-up of move operations might include taking attendance or asking the move workers to sign in, making sure the required equipment is in the appropriate locations, checking carts with loaded books to ensure those in place at the end of the preceding day are all accounted for, doing a quick walk-through of the move area to ensure the area is free of obstructions, and then briefing the move workers. The briefing might include answering any questions the work crew may have, providing feedback on work performed the preceding day, reviewing goals for the coming day, giving a status report on the move, and detailing the day's work assignments.

Breaks

Moving is hard physical work, and breaks are important. However, because the smooth flow of the move depends on each move team completing its work just before the next team needs it, it's important to schedule breaks to not disrupt the steady flow of materials. This can be done by either having team leaders schedule breaks during a team's slack periods or having the entire move operation stop at specified times. Breaks scheduled during a team's slack period will probably interfere less with overall progress, but scheduling them requires some judgment.

If the library has a hard and fast policy excluding food and beverages from the building, identify a separate location where move workers can relax and eat during their breaks. It's helpful for move workers to have access to a refrigerator in which to store lunches and beverages and to find a break area where food and beverage vending machines are available.

Move Procedures

For large moves, involving an entire library, a description of move procedures should be prepared and distributed to each member of the staff. This should detail packing and labeling instructions for collections, and for staff furniture, equipment, and office contents, floor plans for the old and new buildings, schedules, and a list of supervisory personnel and their responsibilities (Bayne 1990, 61).

Communications

Cell phones or walkie-talkies are recommended for the move planner and supervisors. Telephones may not yet be connected in the new facility, and telephone service in the old facility may have been switched off. Further, move supervision takes place in the stacks, on loading docks, and along the move route, where there won't be phones.

266

MONITORING PROGRESS AND WORK COMPLETED

One of the project manager's primary responsibilities is to monitor the progress of the move and the quality of the work completed. Perhaps the most important issues are whether materials are being placed in the correct location and order and whether the work is being completed at the rate anticipated.

Placement of Collections

Identify placement checkpoints or benchmarks at intervals throughout the collection. If placement of material is either ahead of or behind planned placement as identified on the collection layout plan, correct it before proceeding beyond the checkpoint. By identifying checkpoints at regular, relatively small intervals, any corrective back shifting or spacing out of collections that has to be done will be reasonably limited in scope.

If a placement problem develops, it is important to determine as quickly as possible the reason for it and to correct it. Is the correct fill ratio being used? Were the planning measurements accurate? Is unplanned-for material being integrated into the area? Are the materials being shelved in the area the correct ones, or are materials being shelved out of sequence, from another part of the collection?

Schedule

Pre-move planning should have included determining how long it should take to move various parts of the collection and the dates by which each part should be done. Monitoring the amount of work completed each day and comparing it to the projected rate will let the move manager determine whether the work is going as fast as expected and how this will affect the overall completion date (Ellis 1988, 284).

As a motivating device, consider placing a brightly colored placard at the stack location where you expect a crew to complete work for the day (Ellis 1988, 287).

Compliance with Procedures

Plan to spot check work quality. Are books being shelved in the correct call number order? If interfiling is required, is the right amount of space being left for materials that will arrive at a later stage of the move? If cleaning is required, are the correct procedures being used, and is the result acceptable? Are materials being handled and packed correctly? Are materials being logged out of and into buildings? Are there any behavioral problems?

267

End of Day Routines

At the end of each day, the move manager might want to hold a short meeting to debrief workers on problems encountered that day or anticipated for the next day; ascertain the status of each team's work; praise good work; correct problems that have come up; and formally sign workers out, verifying completion of the day's work.

The move manager might also want to get a count of full book trucks awaiting shelving and the call numbers of material on them, calculate the number of volumes moved that day, and compare the work completed with planned progress to date. The manager will probably also want to walk through the move site to ensure that it is secure, there are no fire hazards, and the area is ready for the start-up of operations the next day.

At the end of the day, and at lunch and break times, leave book trucks and dollies fully loaded, in place and ready to go when operations resume. "The entire activity is much like starting and stopping a production line; work needs to be at the stations at the first bell in the morning and after the breaks" (Fraley and Anderson 1990, 170).

Trash Disposal

Provide trash receptacles at each end of the move and dispose of trash as it is generated (Fraley and Anderson 1990, 169). Trash can be a fire hazard, and the more discarded cartons, used labels, and the like are left lying around, the greater the opportunity for a carton of packed material to be become mislaid. It's much easier to gauge the progress of the move and see whether things are out of order if move areas are kept neat and clean.

PROBLEM RESOLUTION

Despite good planning, it's impossible to foresee everything, and some sort of problem will come up (though with good planning, we hope that the problems will be small and manageable). Some common problems and their solutions are addressed below.

Collection Layout Problems

A common problem is that the collections are not ending up on the shelves exactly where you thought they would—they are taking up either more or less space than shown on your plans.

Build checkpoints into the move. These are predetermined stack locations at regular intervals, where the progress of placement of collections onto shelves is checked against the preset plan and corrections can be made if necessary. Brogan and Lipscomb (1982, 379) recommend one checkpoint per range. The closer together the checkpoints, the less corrective work will be required if a discrepancy is found.

Possible causes include inaccurate implementation of the fill ratio by move workers, inaccurate estimation or measurement of the collections to be moved, and inaccurate measurement of the shelving upon which they are being placed.

The fill ratio is the percentage of each shelf upon which materials are shelved. In practical terms, it is the number of inches of each shelf that is filled with materials (see Chapter 2 for a detailed discussion). At the outset of the move, workers should be instructed how many inches of each shelf to fill; it may be helpful to mark the stopping point with masking tape on each shelf, or on enough shelves that move workers do not have to constantly measure the fill ratio. Although slippage of an inch or two on the fill ratio may not seem important, it accumulates.

Consider slippage of 2 inches per shelf. Over one single-faced section of shelving, with seven shelves, it accumulates to 14 inches; over a range of ten sections of shelving, it accumulates to 140 inches or 11 feet, 8 inches, the equivalent of a little more than half a section of shelving (or probably more, assuming each shelf would not be completely filled). Over two sides of a ten-section range, the layout would be off by at least a section, and so on.

The ideal solution is to go back and reshelve, correcting the fill ratio; however, if this is not practical, an alternative solution is to adjust the fill ratio for the next segment of the collection to be shelved. (The problem with the alternative solution is that it will throw off the allocation of growth space and eventually require that back shifting be done. However, it may still be a viable, or the only, option if time is of the essence.) Because correction of this problem is time consuming, it is important to monitor carefully the fill ratio move workers are using.

Collection size may be either under- or overestimated. Material in circulation, at the bindery, or in-house awaiting repair may have been neglected in estimating the extent of the current collections. For runs of bound periodicals, a consistent number of shelf-inches per year may have been assumed, and new titles, changed titles, or inactive subscriptions may have been omitted from the calculations. On the other hand, estimates of collection size done well before the move may have assumed a growth rate that was not supported by funding or may have not taken into account a last-minute weeding of the collection.

Underestimating collection size means the move planner will have to either quickly increase the fill ratio and acknowledge that there will be less growth space available later, or identify additional shelf space in which to shelve the excess, usually not a viable option. Overestimates of collection size may pose fewer practical problems for the move, but the appearance of nearly empty shelves could pose a public relations problem. Collections may be spread out by leaving top and/or bottom shelves empty or by leaving whole sections of shelving empty between segments of the collection.

Shelving might be incorrectly measured in several ways: The available inches on each shelf may have been incorrectly measured, the shelving may not be of uniform width throughout a facility (especially in older buildings where shelving has been added over the years, and in stack rows that engross columns), and the number of shelves per section of shelving may not be consistent. Measurements based on plans may be inaccurate if the plans are not complete and current; plans of shelving layouts for new buildings may reflect the architects' intention rather than what was actually installed by the shelving contractor (i.e., the plans may be "as-designed" rather than "as-built"). Although the causes of the space shortfall or surplus vary, the remedies are the same as those outlined above.

Personnel Problems

Attrition

Moving is difficult, repetitive physical work, and over the course of a long move, workers may decide to quit. Loss of a significant percentage of the workforce will affect the rate at which the move can progress. Being prepared to address the attrition problem may take several forms: over-hiring at the outset, having additional individuals on call, adjusting the work teams, and adjusting the schedule.

Hiring more individuals than initially needed to meet a schedule may seem wasteful; however, it has some advantages. All the workers may be trained together before the move begins, eliminating the necessity for later training as new workers are hired. The entire group, working together from the outset, may become a cohesive unit; there should be less loss of productivity from the addition of new hires that need to become familiarized with move procedures. Finally, if attrition is less than anticipated, the move may be completed early.

A list of individuals qualified to perform the move work might be maintained, and these people could be hired and trained only as the need arises. The library might choose to ask, or pay, these people to attend training sessions held for the rest of the move workers, to reduce the need to conduct ongoing training as they are hired and plugged into gaps caused by attrition.

Adjusting the work teams, for instance, consolidating two teams decimated by attrition, will keep the move going, but will not keep it on schedule. Rotating work assignments may be useful, though, as the move progresses, to make the work more interesting or less fatiguing to individual move workers. It may also be necessary as the mix of work required to execute the move changes.

Adjusting the schedule and accepting a later completion date may the only viable option if there is significant attrition and additional workers are not available.

Disciplinary Problems

Disciplinary problems include tardiness or irregular attendance, lack of adherence to prescribed materials handling practices, and inappropriate behavior.

Regular, on-time attendance is particularly important to move operations because move workers must usually work in teams. If one member of the team isn't on time, the whole team's effectiveness suffers. The move manager will want move workers to sign in each day, to take attendance, and to consider dismissing any worker who is late to work (or returning from a break) more than a specified, limited number of times.

Preventing damage to books relies on move workers handling and packing materials appropriately. Even though you will have trained move workers in proper book handling techniques, monitor and gently correct them as the move progresses.

Behavioral issues may be tougher to resolve. In addition to behaviors that would be unacceptable in any workplace, move-specific problems might include using loud or inappropriate language in public areas and eating, drinking, or smoking inside the library building. Explain the rules carefully during training, monitoring behavior as the move progresses, and provide consistent feedback, but also be clear about what the library can and cannot tolerate.

SECURITY ISSUES

During a move, the library's usual security provisions will have to be adjusted. Matters of personal security and security of the collections both need to be considered, and the library's location and the likelihood of security problems will influence the extent of precautions the library may want to take.

Entrance and Exit Control

The nature of move operations may expose move workers to personal security risks that would not be present during normal library operations. If the library building is closed to the public during the move, move operations may be taking place in relatively isolated portions of a building.

Additional exits and entrances may have been created to provide a reasonable flow of materials out of or into the building. Unless provision is made for monitoring security at both old and new building entrances and exits, this combination of circumstances could invite unauthorized individuals to enter the building, with the possibility of either threats to the personal security of move workers or the theft of library materials.

If move operations are taking place at a building entrance, move workers may be able to double as building security monitors, and a team leader may be assigned responsibility for ensuring the entrance is secure whenever move workers are not immediately in that location. Alternatively, the library may wish to designate an individual or individuals to be responsible for monitoring the security of each entrance.

Robles (1996, 429) provides a detailed description of entrance and exit control procedures implemented during the move into the new Stiern Library at California State University, Bakersfield. She notes that anyone in the library building was required to wear a badge and that "In simplest terms, the procedure was "no badge, no access, no exceptions." CSUB's badges were numbered and color-coded to separately indicate staff and others; Robles notes that personalized badges (names, or ideally, photos) would have made badge swapping more difficult.

Keys

The move manager should have at least one set of keys to everything, from file cabinets to elevators, and buildings (Grey 1992, 330). In a large institution, keys to certain areas of the building (e.g., areas controlled by physical plant, house and grounds, campus computing) may not normally be issued to library staff. Planning meetings conducted well before the move should discuss how access to these areas will be handled and how quickly access can be provided in an emergency if the move manager cannot be issued keys.

Identification

Issues of personal security require that everyone authorized to be inside an otherwise empty building have some type of visible identification, whether a move T-shirt or an ID badge, and that issuance of identification be carefully controlled. The move manager should know who everyone is and each person's role in the project (Grey 1992, 330).

In-Transit Materials

The storage of books in transit from one building to another also should be monitored. At the end of each day, there will be loaded carts of books at each staging point of the move. The security of staging points should be assessed. Although staging points within a building's secure zone (whether secured by an alarm system or by locks) should be safe from theft overnight, consider carefully the security of loading dock areas, which may not be within an alarmed area, and of any trucks that may be left loaded with materials overnight.

The library may also want to consider the security of materials during daily move operations. Do move operations require that carts of material be left unattended in areas where the public could gain access, particularly where there is also ready access to a building exit? If so, the library may wish to revisit and revise that portion of the move plan.

Daily Site Shut-Down

The library will probably also want to make one person responsible for walking through the move site at the end of each day of move operations to ensure that no fire hazards exist and that all entrances and exits have been locked.

HEALTH AND SAFETY ISSUES

Moving library materials is hard physical labor, distinct and different from most libraries' daily operations. Both the nature of the work and the conditions it creates raise specific health and safety issues.

Book Stack Stability

Check the stability of the stacks in both the old and new locations to determine whether additional cross-bracing or tie bars are needed. If the shelving has been in place for some time, particularly in earthquake country, determine whether changes in code require more or different bracing. For new shelving, check with the manufacturer to find out whether they may be loaded unevenly; that is, whether one side of a range may be fully loaded while the other side is empty. Ask whether the shelving must have tie bracing installed or be bolted to a concrete slab to ensure it will not tip over. For shelving that dead-ends against a column or a wall, determine whether it must or should be attached to ensure stability. If bracing is being reused, have its integrity checked to determine whether it still provides the intended stabilization (Kathman 1983, 153).

Floor Loading

Confirm that the floors in the new location have sufficient live-load capacity to support fully loaded book stacks at the planned spacing. Confirm that storage areas where packed cartons or book trucks may be stored or staged are strong enough to support them (Wiegandt-Sakoun and Gunet 1990, 104). This might be of particular concern to libraries located within office buildings, where live-load capacities in nonlibrary areas, such as hallways and nominal office spaces, were probably constructed with less weight-bearing capacity than required for libraries.

Move Route

Walk through the move route pushing a loaded book truck and look for potential safety hazards, for instance:

1. *Stairways:* Are stairs in good condition, or (particularly outdoor stairs) are pieces missing? Are there smooth areas conducive to slipping? Are the treads loose or partially missing? Are handrails present and secure? Is there adequate lighting? (Tucker 1987, 17–18)

2. *Floor surfaces:* Is carpet intact and secure, or are there worn spots, holes, and loose seams that might be tripping hazards? Is tile flooring smooth, or are the edges of tile cupped and individual tiles missing? Are wood floors smooth, or are individual boards loose or uneven? Are any of these conditions rough enough that they might cause a book truck or a dolly to overturn?

273

3. *Outdoor move routes:* Are there potholes in paved surfaces? Loose bricks in brick walks?

4. *Elevators:* Do elevator cabs stop level with the floor reliably and on all levels of each facility? What is the maximum load each elevator can carry?

5. *Ramps:* How steep are ramps that will be used for the move? How many people will be needed to safely push a loaded book truck or dolly up the ramp? How many are needed to safely control a book truck descending the ramp?

This list is not intended to be exhaustive, but to suggest the type of questions the move planner should keep in mind while inspecting the move route. Keep in mind also the times of day during which the move will be conducted and the type of weather that might occur during the move. Where may additional lighting be needed? Are there locations where an outdoor canopy should be erected for the duration of the move to protect materials from the elements or to protect steep or already slick surfaces from becoming dangerously slippery?

Insurance Issues

The library should consult its insurance carrier to determine whether additional coverage is needed for any injuries that might be incurred during the move by members of the library's permanent staff who are performing work outside their regular assignments, any temporarily hired staff, and any volunteers.

Dust and Allergies

Moving collections that have not been cleaned in some time will probably raise dust. If the move is taking place in an occupied building, dust raised by the move may get into the building's air handling system and be distributed to occupied areas, and some staff or members of the public may have allergic reactions. Be prepared to find alternate work locations for staff for whom this is a health issue, and consider posting notices alerting the public. Offer dust masks to move workers.

If removal or demolition of any part of the building must be done in conjunction with the move, ask a health and safety official to inspect the area for asbestos well before the start of the move so that appropriate abatement measures can be taken if necessary.

Public Access During Move Operations

Although the public will probably be interested in move operations, and although libraries may not want to restrict access to collections, the public should be excluded from a move site for safety, operational efficiency, and public relations reasons:

1. *Public safety:* Moves assume a pace of their own, and there is the potential, though it may be slight, for a move worker to inadvertently run into a patron with a book cart or for a patron to trip over moving supplies.

2. *Operational efficiency:* If move workers must be on the lookout for patrons or must stop their work to explain move operations to patrons, that will diminish the rate at which the work of the move itself can proceed. If the stacks have been shelf-read immediately prior to a planned move, allowing the public in might also risk undoing that work.

3. *Public relations:* The stacks will not look their best during a move, and materials may not be easy to find.

Of course, most of these arguments could be reversed. Move workers could be trained to respond appropriately to requests for information from the public on the progress of the move (and allowance made for the amount of time this might take), and the public could be allowed into the stacks if provision is made for a level of caution by book truck movers and for ensuring there are no tripping hazards.

COMPLETING THE MOVE

Once all the collection materials are on the shelf at their new locations, the major part of the work is over, and the move manager may be tempted to collapse in exhaustion and declare the work complete. Checking the completed work against the original plan, cleaning up, redoing stack signage, and creating a punch list of corrective and other cleanup tasks will make completion of the move work more finite and help track completion of the remaining work.

Punch List Creation

The punch list is a detailed listing of work that needs to be corrected. It inventories problems of all types and may be arranged by location or by type of problem; for instance,

1. Collection problems

1.1 QA76–QA101: some volumes out of order; needs minor shelf-reading

1.2 TA 1 (periodicals): titles intermixed, major shelf-reading/shifting needed

1.3 G–HV7965: 30 percent fill ratio used instead of 50 percent

1.4 HV7966–J: 80 percent fill ratio used instead of 50 percent

1.5 BFs: still need to be cleaned

or,

1.1 Adult fiction: some volumes out of order; needs minor shelf-reading

1.2 YA nonfiction: 80 percent fill ratio used instead of 50 percent

1.3 300s: still need to be cleaned

1.4 Adult periodicals: growth space left after several ceased titles; no space left for new titles; needs to be respaced

1.5 780–790: 30 percent fill ratio used instead of 50 percent, etc.

2. Facility problems

2.1 Elevator 2 makes a scraping noise between first and second floor

2.2 Touch up painting needed on columns adjacent to second floor main stack aisle

2.3 Carpeting in lobby is stained and needs to be cleaned

2.4 Replace door to room 299, removed to facilitate move, etc.

3. Furniture problems

3.1 Desk from 320A is missing

3.2 Three carrels from third floor need carpentry repairs

3.3 Upholstery torn on five reading chairs from level two, etc.

The punch list is developed by the move manager and others based on a detailed inspection of the collections and the facility once the move is considered complete.

Checking Completed Work

Once all the collection materials have been moved to their new locations, verify that everything has been shelved as planned. Using the original collection layout plan (modified to reflect changes agreed upon during the move), the move manager may check the stacks to verify that the starting and ending call numbers for each row of shelving and the fill ratios used are those that the plan called for. Note discrepancies and then assess their impact and import.

If fill ratios had to be altered during the course of the move, was the intent at the time to back shift later to spread out the available growth space more evenly? If the actual layout achieved during the move differs from the collection layout plan, by how much does it differ, and what effect will the difference have on either library operations or patrons' ability to use the collections? Has signage already been prepared based on the planned collection layout? How easily can it be altered? Does the actual layout of the collection result in awkward relationships between collection segments and the physical configuration of the stacks? More important, have materials been shelved in the correct call number order? If collections from different locations were to be interfiled, has that been done on an item-by-item basis, or are materials from each location grouped on the shelves? Are shelves that were intended to remain empty in fact empty? Are materials unboxed that were to be unboxed? Are materials that were to be cleaned in fact clean? Do the shelves look reasonably neat and orderly? Does everything look right?

In addition to checking the collections, the move manager and others should check the building and its furniture. What damage has been done to the building, and what work is needed to repair the damage? It is likely that at least some touch-up painting will be needed, and after the hard work of the move, plan to have the elevators serviced.

Cleanup

Once the move is done, protective coverings may be removed from the floors, walls, and elevator cabs. Move supplies may be removed from the stacks. The entire area should be vacuumed thoroughly to remove dust and debris resulting from the move, and carpets and floors should be washed as necessary. New stack and directional signage may be made. Any of these tasks that remain to be done should be added to the punch list.

Punch List Resolution

Once a complete and detailed punch list has been compiled, the actions necessary to resolve each item may be identified and responsibility for these actions assigned. To track completion of the work, it may be helpful to compile the punch list in a sortable format, to make it easy to identify work to be done by a specific individual or group, in a specific area, or by a specific deadline. Figure 10.1 (p. 278) shows a simplified spreadsheet model, which could be sorted several ways.

When Is the Move Really Done?

Although the library may reopen its stacks once the relocation of materials and the immediate cleanup are done, completion of all items on the punch list heralds the final completion of the move. Resolution of punch list work may continue for several months, depending on the nature and extent of corrective work that needs to be undertaken, but in many cases it can take place out without disrupting the public.

MAINTAINING SERVICE DURING THE MOVE

Well in advance of the move, the library should decide the extent to which it can maintain services during the move. The size, complexity, and duration of the move will obviously have a bearing on this. For a minor stack shift, services will probably be unaffected. For a major move from one facility to another, extraordinary measures may be needed. Most libraries will probably want to

Figure 10.1
Sample Punch List

Item number	Room number	Date noted	Description	Action needed	To be done by	Date completed
1.1	350	7/7/2007	QA76-QA101: some volumes out of order	shelfreading (minor)	stack maintenance	8/15/2007
1.2	420	7/20/2007	TA 1 (periodicals):titles out of order	shelfreading/shifting (major)	stack maintenance	
1.3	320	7/2/2007	G-HV7965: 30% fill ratio used instead of 50%	shifting (major)	stack maintenance	
1.4	300	7/6/2007	HV7966 - J: 80% fill ratio used instead of 50%	shifting (major)	stack maintenance	
1.5	220	8/1/2007	BFs still need to be cleaned	clean BFs	stack maintenance	8/16/2007
2.1		8/1/2007	Elevator 2 makes a scraping noise between 1st & 2nd floor	inspection/repair	elevator contractor	8/5/2007
2.2	220	8/1/2007	Columns adjacent to main stack aisle gouged	plastering, painting	painting contractor	
2.3	100	8/1/2007	Main Lobby carpeting stained	shampoo	cleaning contractor	8/5/2007
2.4	299	8/1/2007	Door removed for duration of move still missing	reinstall	carpentry contractor	
3.1	320A	7/16/2007	Desk missing	locate	transportation dept.	8/1/2007
3.2	300	7/20/2007	Three carrels damaged in move	repair	carpentry contractor	
3.3	220	7/15/2007	Torn upholstery on five reading chairs	reupholster	upholstery contractor	9/1/2007

maintain some level of service, and the question will be what is reasonable given the user community's needs and the disruption expected during the move. For multi-branch libraries, the answer to the service question may be relatively simple: to redirect users to branches unaffected by the move. Services the library might want to maintain fall into several broad categories: providing access to collections, providing study facilities, and providing reference and other staff assistance.

Collection Access

Concerns about operational efficiency and patron safety may dictate closing the stacks to the public for the duration of the move; however, a retrieval service operated by library staff could still provide access to collections either on demand (time consuming for staff) or at specified times of the day. An advance notice request system could be set up allowing users to make requests online, by phone, by fax, for later pick-up.

To provide access, the library must know where materials are at all times. Keep track and communicate this information daily. Consider posting this on a move Web site, for easy access by both staff and the public.

If materials are being reclassified or moved to a new status (e.g., print journals being moved to closed storage or being assigned new call numbers), include in the project plan the time required to relabel and to change the location or status information in the online catalog.

The library will also want to alert neighboring libraries of the upcoming move and may want to make arrangements to direct its users to these alternate locations for the duration of the move.

Access to nonprint collections poses special challenges. Access to electronic, AV, and microform collection materials require users have equipment , and library policy may not allow circulation of materials in these formats. Setting up a reduced-scale nonprint collection reading room within the building is one solution to this problem. This area could be equipped with one or two of each type of equipment needed to use nonprint collection materials. During the 1990 move at Northeastern University, such a room was set up and promptly dubbed "Noah's Ark" by staff because it had two of each type of item.

Although this may mean users have to wait to use material, it does allow the library to provide some access. Alternatively, libraries that do not normally circulate these materials might change that policy for the duration of the move.

Study Space

Setting up a reduced-scale reading room could also meet the most urgent need for in-library study space for the duration of the move. Alternatively, as the move progresses, stack and reading areas where move operations have concluded or where they have not yet begun could be used by the public, if access to them can be provided without affecting move operations or compromising user safety.

Services

The widespread availability of Web-based library operations and services offers options for maintaining some services. A means of checking out materials and handling returns should be provided for the duration of the move, and a temporary circulation desk may be set up contiguous to a building entrance. Reference service could be provided by e-mail, phone, or text messaging. If interlibrary loan requests are not being handled online, this is a good time to think about starting to do so. Current periodicals and back issues of print journals could be paged.

COMMUNICATING WITH THE PUBLIC

Every library's public will be affected by the move. They will be interested in the move's duration and want to know what changes are being made, and to some extent, how the move will be conducted. The move presents the library with a challenge and an opportunity. The challenge is how to overcome a potentially disruptive event in the relationship between the library's user community, and the opportunity is to show that library staff know what services their users want and have figured out how to minimize users' inconvenience. It's also an opportunity to showcase improvements that will be available after the move.

Before the Move

Well before the move begins, communicate to the public what to expect, including the level of service available during the move; how long the move will last; what, if anything, the library would like its users to do before, during, or after the move; and the benefits that users will enjoy as a result of the move. If the move is being undertaken out of necessity, for instance because the library has run out of space and funding isn't available to expand or replace the building, that can also be stated in a politic manner.

The media chosen by the library to communicate these messages will depend on its public and its size and will range from informal conversations with key stakeholders to Web site announcements and e-mail alerts, to library newsletters, to articles in the user community's print publications, to community access TV and other, larger, more formal media outlets.

During the Move

During the move the library may wish to capitalize on the potential for good publicity and provide photo opportunities and press releases for local media outlets. If the library remains open during the move, prominently displayed posters or graphics can chart the progress of the move; post copies of press releases, photos, and status reports. The library might also want to provide a forum for the public to ask questions about the move and have library staff respond.

After the Move

Completion of a major move, particularly one that relocates services from one building to another, calls for some sort of celebration, to provide closure to what may have been a disruptive and difficult experience, recognize the hard work expended by the entire move team, and mark the beginning of a new period in the life of the library. To separate the closure function from the celebration function, the library may wish to have separate internal and external events marking the conclusion of the move; the internal event could be less formal but should include everyone affected by the move. It should be an opportunity to relax, socialize, and recognize the effort everyone has contributed.

The public celebration could be an opportunity for officials of the library's parent organization to celebrate the role of the library in its community and for the library to publicize the changes made as a result of the move. Tours could be given of the newly arranged areas, and wayfinding handouts could be distributed along with more general brochures describing the library's services. The idea here is that the move has been a big enough event to capture the public attention, and the library should leverage that attention to build positive publicity for its services.

V

SPECIAL TOPICS

Some moves pose special problems. The collections may be dusty or dirty. Poor environmental conditions may have allowed infestations of insects or outbreaks of mold. Inadequate space or staffing over a long period of time may have led to disorganized conditions, with material "shelved" on the floor, or in somewhat less extreme conditions, shelved wherever space was available rather than in sequence by call number. These are the sorts of conditions that make the move planner wish for another assignment!

The two chapters that follow provide practical advice on dealing with these difficult conditions. Chapter 11 addresses cleaning collections and detecting insect and mold infestations. Chapter 12 provides practical strategies for dealing with several types of disorganized conditions and offers a case study relating how these strategies were used to address a real-life, worst-case scenario.

11 CLEANING COLLECTIONS

Joyce Frank Watson

Is there a librarian anywhere who is satisfied that the collections are kept sufficiently clean? Dusting the collection has gone the way of handwritten catalog cards. If your library is typical, it has been years since the books were last vacuumed—or perhaps they've never been vacuumed.

In this chapter we are speaking of the cleaning of whole collections of non-rare materials—usually monographs and bound periodicals—which involves dusting the volumes, using either a vacuum cleaner or a treated cloth, and cleaning (vacuuming or wiping) the shelves.

In a recent informal survey of librarians who were asked if their library had a regular cleaning program for the book collection, the most common responses were "no," and some variation of "you've got to be kidding." Alas, among those who had tackled a cleaning project, one mentioned using a feather duster to dust the tops of the books (an exercise in redistributing the dust), and several reported dusting the canopy tops and the empty part of each shelf, but not the books! At a recently opened large public library, custodians on the staff dusted the empty half of the shelves with treated cloths, but were instructed not to touch the books!

Let's be clear about cleaning the book stacks. The BOOKS should be dusted, and then the SHELVES should be dusted, in that order. Dust is unsightly on the shelves, but it does the most damage to the books. A dusty film on books encourages mechanical damage and acid deterioration. Dust also holds moisture and food particles, creating an ideal setting for book beetles and mold spores. Next to maintaining appropriate and stable temperature and relative humidity, effective housekeeping is the most important preventive preservation method.

When a collection is to be moved, libraries often consider vacuuming the books as part of the move. After all, every book is going to be handled anyway. If the library has no regular cleaning program, a move may be the only opportunity to have the books dusted.

It makes sense to consider dusting book collections in conjunction with a move, but be realistic about the amount of work involved, and ramifications for the move schedule. Will the schedule allow enough time? Will the budget cover the additional costs?

IS CLEANING REALLY NEEDED?

Evaluate the overall physical condition of the collection. How dusty are the books? Do your hands need washing after handling just a few? How long has it been since the books were last dusted? And how long is it likely to be before they are dusted again? How valuable are they? Does it matter if they're left dusty? How much at risk are they? Is the relative humidity high enough that doing nothing may be courting mold? Or so low that a coating of dust puts already dry books further at risk?

What is the nature of the collection being moved? If you are moving a collection with a very high circulation rate, some of the books will show signs of heavy use and may be in need of repair, but they won't be very dusty, and a collection cleaning project may not be needed. Less-used materials that have not circulated for years will have accumulated a lot of dust on their top edges, but is the cost and effort of cleaning justified? A new collection won't need vacuuming. On the other hand, books that have been shelved uncovered, through a dusty, dirty building renovation, must be vacuumed thoroughly to remove layers of fine construction dust lodged on every exposed surface.

Assuming the collection to be moved does not include rare materials and is in reasonably good condition, the most cost-efficient cleaning job you should consider—and the happy medium that this chapter addresses—is to vacuum the top edges of the books. This is where most dust settles, and the approach allows removal of most of the dust with a reasonable amount of work.

If the project is worth doing and appears realistic in terms of time and money, how does one proceed?

WHAT EQUIPMENT SHOULD BE USED?

The goal of cleaning the collections is to remove the dust, not redistribute it. An old-fashioned feather duster should not be used. Applied to the tops of books, it will dislodge the existing layer of dust, but much of that dust will settle right back on the books. A treated cloth to which dust adheres is a considerable improvement and can be used anywhere by any number of people.

Vacuum cleaners are better yet, but require more planning to use, as well as more equipment money. Some types are more effective than others. Ordinary vacuum cleaners do remove dust from the books (and the shelves), but much of that dust, albeit in finer particles, comes back into the surroundings through the exhaust. Vacuum cleaners that have a water filter (like the Rainbow brand) are effective, as fine dust particles and mold spores are trapped in the water. HEPA vacuum cleaners use filters fine enough to trap mold spores and are ideal, and Filter Queen vacuums have a filtration rate comparable to HEPAs.

If you plan to vacuum books while they are on the shelves, the hose has to be extra long. A 14-foot hose will reach the top shelf of a 90-inch stack range and its canopy while still furnishing strong suction. Typical vacuum attachments include a crevice nozzle and a round dusting brush—often a synthetic model that is short-lived, with the bristles quickly becoming stubby and useless. Slightly more expensive horsehair dusting brush replacements are well worth the cost, as they are more flexible and less abrasive to books, and they last longer.

Especially in the case of more valuable books, experts recommend wrapping the end of the vacuum attachment (usually the crevice nozzle) with cheesecloth to lessen the danger of small pieces of the book tearing loose and being sucked into the vacuum cleaner. That is also good practice when vacuuming the inside pages of any book. However, when only the outsides of books are being vacuumed, the round dusting brush used without cheesecloth is faster and more effective. Stress to your workers that the books must be kept tightly shut during the vacuuming process to avoid pushing the dust into the pages or having pieces of the pages tear loose.

Don't Overlook the Simplest Alternative

If vacuuming cannot be done because of its cost or the complications it would add to a tight schedule, consider using treated dust cloths. They are effective and convenient. If kept on hand they can be used when and where they are most needed by any number of people, with no planning necessary. To be sure your treated cloths leave no residue on the books, conduct a quick test by weighting the cloth with a heavy object against a clean white piece of paper for a day or two, then sprinkle the paper lightly with pencil sharpening dust or colored chalk to see if there is any residue on the paper. Test several brands if you can, then choose one that leaves no residue.

As in the vacuuming process, books must be kept tightly closed when dust cloths are used to wipe the edge of the text block.

WHEN SHOULD CLEANING BE DONE?

Books may be vacuumed before they are moved, while they are being transported to their new location, or after they've arrived. They may be vacuumed while shelved or on book trucks.

If books can be vacuumed either before they are moved (with sufficient time given to the task) or after they're in the new location, the move schedule will not be compromised. Of these two possibilities, if the books are especially dusty it is preferable to vacuum them before they are reshelved in their new location to avoid bringing dust into the new area.

Cleaning books during a big move introduces complications. There may be workers at both ends, with a third team shuttling book trucks back and forth. The insertion of a vacuuming procedure into the middle of this chain can play havoc with a move schedule. Any slowdown, for example hitting a patch of books needing to be bundled for repair or having a vacuum cleaner break down, may throw the whole schedule off. Factors like the differing speeds of workers and the need to take breaks must be scheduled into the process.

To minimize these problems a cleaning station may be set up, a sort of way station where filled book trucks go in at one side to be vacuumed and come out the other after the cleaning. In the move process plenty of dust gets shaken loose as the books are set down on the book trucks, making this a good spot to do the vacuuming. If there are enough book trucks available, the cleaning station team may be kept well supplied with full book trucks, enabling team members to keep ahead of the flow needed to keep other team members on the move.

Having each worker take a book truckload of books through the moving and the cleaning stages isn't recommended. Because the book trucks will probably have to be kept in order, such a plan essentially slows down the overall progress to the work speed of the slowest worker.

THE CLEANING PROCEDURE

Before you move books to a new location, wash the bookshelves onto which the collection is being moved and let them dry thoroughly. This should be done whether the shelves are old or brand new.

Vacuuming the tops of books without moving them from the shelves is possible if there is sufficient air space above the books so the round dusting brush will fit. Or a long, skinny brush attachment specially designed to fit into narrow spaces (like window louvers) may be used. Figure 11.1 illustrates these attachments. It is important for workers to be able to see what they are doing and to keep the attachment horizontal. Taller workers may manage using a standard library kick stool, but most will require higher, rolling ladders. This procedure works best when books are all of a similar height.

If book height varies greatly, or if there is minimal air space at the tops of the books, the books must be tipped out for vacuuming or actually removed from the shelf. They may be vacuumed while being held, one or two books at a time, or placed on a book truck top shelf for vacuuming and then returned to the shelf.

If books are cleaned while they're on the shelves, be sure workers start at the top of each section and vacuum down to the bottom. Once finished on both sides of an aisle, vacuum the aisle floor before going on to the next range. With the proper floor attachment, it will take just a minute or two and will remove just that much more dust before its gets redistributed back onto books in the area.

Figure 11.1. Vacuum Cleaner Attachments Used for Cleaning Collections. Photo by Joyce Frank Watson.

Anticipate More Than Just Dusty Books

Especially if books are handled individually, workers will inevitably come across books that seriously need repair. It will be wise to resist the temptation to remove them unless they have detached boards or loose contents—an eventuality that may actually occur during the cleaning and moving process. Work out a procedure beforehand for handling these materials and let workers know what they're to do. An increasingly popular way to stabilize such books (and defer treatment until the book is actually used) is to shrink-wrap them on the spot, leaving a small printed label under the wrap explaining to potential users that they may indeed borrow the book.

Except in warm, humid climates, insect infestation is likely to be found, if at all, in individual scattered volumes. Be sure your movers and vacuumers know what to look for. Frass (beetle droppings) will fall out of a book that is (or has been) infested. It looks like fine sand and is usually in shades of gray or brown. If the problem is severe, frass actually collects on the shelves in a pattern where it falls out of each book at the spine (see Figure 11.2, p. 290). Any books that, when moved, reveal frass on the shelf, should be removed immediately and sent for either fumigation or freezing. Books located nearby—directly across the aisle, on the adjoining shelves, and on the shelf behind—should be carefully checked for infestation.

Figure 11.2. Frass on the Shelf at the Base of a Binding: Sign of a Severe Beetle Problem. Photo by Joyce Frank Watson.

Mold growth on books is yet another potential problem. Typically the mold has been caused by past water damage or the premature shelving of books that were returned wet to the library. In warmer, more humid climates, library stacks may have pockets of high humidity or unstable relative humidity that bounces between high and low readings. Ask your workers to watch for the fuzzy grey/white growth, especially on older bindings, that is characteristic of mold (see Figure 11.3).

Where widespread mold outbreaks are found, vacuumers should wear protective masks and gloves. Long-sleeved shirts, washed frequently to remove mold spores, keep the spores from accumulating on workers' clothing. Workers who have allergies should not be working with moldy books. Mold spore counts taken in the aisles of affected collections are usually not particularly high; when the moldy books are handled, however, the spore counts increase dramatically.

Where mold is severe, vacuumed books and shelves should be wiped down with an ethyl alcohol solution and allowed to dry.

WHO SHOULD DO THE WORK?

A relatively simple vacuuming procedure can be done by either library staff or an outside contractor, but there are several advantages to doing the cleaning in-house, with library staff and/or custodians. This allows you to work out details as you go along and change procedures as needed. Your custodians know their way around the building, have building keys, and can cope with problems like tripped circuits. They may appreciate the opportunity for overtime work. If the job is done while the books are on the move, library staff will be better able to guarantee that books don't get out of order.

If you use student helpers, don't assume they are experienced users of a vacuum cleaner. For example, most will need to be reminded that sucking up rubber bands, paper clips, gum wrappers, etc., cuts a vacuum cleaner's suction power down to naught.

Figure 11.3. Mold on Bindings. Photo by Joyce Frank Watson.

PLANNING AHEAD

Don't underestimate the time you'll need for set-up. Each day of a moving/cleaning project requires that equipment be assembled and checked—vacuum cleaners and/or treated cloths, kick stools, rolling ladders, book trucks, extension cords, power bars. Supplies include vacuum filters and extra attachments. Check electrical outlets to be certain they're functional, and know where the circuit breakers are located for each electrical outlet. Schedule regular filter changes on the vacuum cleaners—daily if the vacuums are being used several hours each day.

ESTIMATING TIME AND COSTS

If you vacuum either before or after the books are moved, estimating the cleaning time is straightforward. Work out your plan and do a test run of several one- or two-hour vacuuming stints (using different workers), then extrapolate from your results. (Don't expect all workers to be willing to vacuum books all day long. Though some may do so without complaint, for others it is a b-o-r-i-n-g job, and you'll get better service from these workers with shorter shifts.) Besides finding out how long the vacuuming really takes, you'll discover glitches in the procedure that can be eliminated before the move begins.

If cleaning is done during the move, estimating time required is more difficult. Estimate the time it takes for a truck of books to be vacuumed and amount of time required to move the trucks to and from the cleaning station. This will add to the length of an average move cycle and will decrease the number of trucks that can be moved in one day. Adding any steps to the move cycle also increases the likelihood that something will go wrong—-and you must build in a cushion for that possibility.

AND DON'T FORGET. . .

Besides taking a hand at vacuuming yourself, visit the workstations frequently to see what new efficiencies the workers have learned, and make sure they're shared with the others. Team members will welcome whatever morale boosters you can devise. Free sodas or coffee and donut breaks should take place well away from the book stacks, and workers must wash their hands before returning to work. Photo displays of the work in progress may be shared with library staff.

12 MOVING FROM DISORGANIZED CONDITIONS

In most instances, the collections a library plans to move are arranged in some sort of order and with some degree of neatness on shelves and are moved to shelves in another location. Now and then, however, a library will need to move materials from disorganized conditions. The degree and type of disorganization may vary, from materials placed on shelves but in no particular order, to piles of materials allowed to accumulate without any obvious logic and with no inventory or bibliographic control over the contents. This chapter offers guidance on dealing with several types of disorganized conditions, and a case study.

TYPES OF DISORGANIZED CONDITIONS

The move planner may be confronted with several types of disorganized conditions:

1. Collections may be shelved in multiple locations and sequences within a single building. Rather than shift entire collections to make space for growth, a library may have shelved a series or a specific collection in an area where some additional shelving could be installed. A major gift of material may have been received, or collections consolidated, and the expedient short-term solution may have been to shelve these materials separately.

2. Collection materials may be "shelved" on the floor or placed horizontally on top of normally shelved materials, as the library ran out of shelving space to hold them.

3. Collections may be stored in extremely dirty conditions.

4. Items may be stored in boxes, either labeled or unlabeled.

5. Material may have been simply heaped in piles, to be dealt with later by someone else.

The full range of disorganized conditions is probably as varied as the institutional circumstances that allow them to develop, so it's likely this list is not comprehensive. However, these types of conditions are representative, and the means of dealing with them provide an approach that may be built upon.

Multiple Locations and Sequences

Integrating materials shelved in multiple locations and sequences within a single building into a single sequence can be done in the same manner as integrating holdings from multiple different buildings, as discussed in Part I. The important step is to identify the smallest relevant collection segment and to measure the amount of material in each segment in each location.

For instance, if the bound journal collection has been split by date and shelved in two (or more) locations, and the current plan is to reunite these runs, then the smallest relevant collection segment will be the individual journal title. If a major collection of material in a specific subject area has been shelved separately while it was being evaluated and now is ready to be interfiled, then the smallest relevant segment might be the classification range into which the material will be integrated.

Once the material in each location has been measured, the measurements may be integrated into a spreadsheet such those shown in Figures 3.7 and 3.8 (pp. 73 and 74) for monographic materials and Figures 3.11 through 3.14 (pp. 78–82) for periodical titles.

Move operations will have to take into account that material is coming from several different locations; this can be done by calculating and shelving according to successive fill ratios (see Figures 3.9 and 3.10, pp. 75–76 and 77); by reserving space for large sets with dummy cards, as described in previous chapters; or by moving simultaneously from all locations where same-class material is shelved.

Items "Shelved" on the Floor, or Horizontally on Top of Shelved Material

This is a common problem that develops when collections grow faster than shelving capacity. To plan the integration of material that's not on the shelf, the key is to collect or estimate its linear measurement as accurately as possible. If the material is in order, in neat piles on the floor, it may be relatively easy to measure how many inches it would take up if it were on the shelf. If not, count the number of volumes and convert this number to a linear measurement using one of the average inches per volume figures suggested either in Appendix A or one of the sources noted in Chapter 1.

When material is removed from the shelf and packed for relocation, packers should be instructed to include loose material that falls within the call number range of the material removed from the shelf. If the material is being loaded onto a book truck, it may be possible to immediately integrate the material from the floor in sequence with material removed from the shelf. One caveat: this will add some time to the packing operation and requires that the individuals packing the materials be conversant with the classification scheme.

An alternative is to have loose material moved separately into proximity with the main sequence of material; however, this requires a second collection integration step be performed at the destination location. It's probably more efficient to handle each item only once, though conducting a time study on a sample set of materials would provide empirical evidence on this point.

Collections Stored in Extremely Dirty Conditions

As Joyce Watson noted in Chapter 11, there is probably no librarian anywhere who is satisfied that the library's collections are sufficiently clean. Chapter 11 describes cleaning procedures for effectively dealing with conditions of normally expected dust and dirt. There are some situations, however, which go beyond normal expectations. Materials may have been sent to a storage facility where normal janitorial services were not provided, or where the library was not able to control access to the storage area. Perhaps windows in the facility were broken, allowing access by birds, or there was a water leak.

Before moving material stored in these conditions, the library will obviously wish to clean them. However, before following the cleaning procedures described in Chapter 11, it may be necessary to perform a preliminary housecleaning. This might include removing or sweeping up large pieces of debris, then vacuuming the floors, so that collection cleaning work may proceed in sanitary conditions. Workers should be provided with dust masks and gloves to avoid allergic reactions. If birds or small animals may have had access to the collection material, consult a health professional about the risk of infections from droppings and take appropriate precautions, both in handling the materials and performing any preliminary cleaning.

Material Stored in Boxes

Moving material stored in boxes back onto shelves poses at least three problems: identifying the material in each box, determining its linear extent, and integrating it into an already existing shelving sequence. To integrate boxed material into an existing sequence requires determining the linear extent of materials in each relevant collection segment. Unless the contents were measured before boxing and labeled, each box will probably have to be opened, its contents measured, and the items inspected to determine the call number range. Alternatively, the number of items in each box could be counted and an estimate made of their linear extent by using one of the average width/item figures from

Appendix A or one of the sources cited in Chapter 1. This box-by-box information could then be recorded and integrated into a planning spreadsheet.

If the move planner is pressed for time, and the boxes are of uniform size and packed at a uniform fill rate, it may be possible to estimate the average number of shelf inches of material per box and use this as a gross planning figure. If using this approach, though, there will be some discrepancy between the estimated and actual inches per box. The amount of the discrepancy will become apparent when the material is shelved. A prudent approach would be to allow some extra shelf space.

Once the linear extent of the boxed material has been determined for the smallest relevant collection segment, planning may proceed as described in Part I, treating the boxed material as though it were the contents of a separate facility.

Material Heaped into Piles

In a worst-case scenario, material may have been simply heaped into a pile, to be dealt with later by someone else. If the move planner is lucky, there will be some degree of organization to the heaps.

The first task in this situation is to establish order. If there is absolutely no rhyme or reason to the heaps, consider first setting up tables onto which material may be sorted in rough order (e.g., by type, or by rough classification order). Although sorting could be done on the floor if it is clean enough, this causes more strain on the sorters' backs. From this point, the material could be sorted into finer classification segments, and items measured, or counted, and their linear extent estimated as already discussed.

If temporary shelving can be set up or shelf space temporarily made available, the material could be shelved in classification order and its linear extent then measured. If temporary shelving isn't available, consider boxing material after it has been sorted and measured, being careful to label the boxes and to keep a detailed list of the material in each box.

A CASE STUDY

Background

In the late 1980s, when the Northeastern University Libraries planned its central Snell Library, one objective was to integrate into it collections then stored in a remote warehouse under conditions that were far from ideal. Stacks in Dodge Library, the old main library, had long since reached their maximum capacity, and collections had for some time been boxed and sent to storage to make space for newer acquisitions.

The storage facility comprised three large rooms on two floors in a warehouse building owned by the university. Initially, for a variety of reasons, boxes of materials being sent to storage were left in large piles. Eventually warehouse-style shelving was erected in each room, and materials were, mostly, unboxed and arranged in order on these shelves.

At the time of the move, the majority of these materials, totaling approximately 14,000 linear feet, had been shelved; however, piles of boxed material occupied approximately one-third of the largest room. Although the shelved material could be measured in a straightforward manner, dealing with the piles of boxes posed some interesting problems.

Assessing the Extent of the Collections

The first problem was determining the type and amount of material in the boxes. The piles of boxes were quite large—approximately six feet tall by six to eight feet wide—and they extended in rows perhaps 20 feet in length. The situation was complicated by the fact that the library shared use of this particular storage room with other university units, and materials belonging to these other units were mixed in with the library's. There was no map identifying the location of each unit's materials. Furthermore, the same type of boxes were used to ship library materials and those from other units, so there was no easy way to distinguish ownership without inspecting the individual contents of each box. The ideal solution would have been to unbox, sort, and shelve all the material prior to the move, but this could not be done because of lack of time, space, and money.

It was decided that the best approach was to first inspect as many boxes as possible to determine the location of material belonging to the library, then develop an estimate of the extent of those materials based on crude sampling techniques.

The first step was to make a reduced-scale layout of the room, showing the locations of columns, existing book stacks, and the various rows of piles. An outline plan of the room from the university's space inventory provided a starting point for this step.

Next, a detailed survey of the visible boxes (those on the outside of the rows of piles) was undertaken. Each visible box was opened and its contents inspected. A determination of ownership was made and the type of material identified; both were then noted in abbreviated form in a visible location on the outside of the box, using a marker and large print, easily legible from a distance.

From this survey, it was possible to determine that the library-owned materials in the rows of piles comprised at least government documents, bound periodicals, gift material, the contents of a disbanded special collection, and some archival material. Happily, there also appeared to be some coherence in the arrangement: boxes of a given type of material clustered together. This made it possible to map the approximate locations of the clusters onto the previously prepared plan and to estimate the approximate percentage of each row comprising each type of material.

The next step was to estimate the number of boxes of each type of material. This required assuming that boxes hidden in the core of the rows of piles were approximately the same dimensions as those that were visible, and that their contents were consistent with visible adjacent boxes. The author thinks, only somewhat tongue in cheek, that her undergraduate geology courses were good preparation for this exercise. Assessing the likelihood of the interior boxes' contents being the same the exterior boxes' contents could be done by considering the layers of boxes as strata. Looking at the exterior boxes as rock outcroppings and considering how the strata of boxes might have been laid down in sequential deposits to form these outcroppings provided clues to the density and length of the invisible internal strata of boxes. A tolerance for dirt was also an asset.

The process worked as follows. First, an estimate was made of the number of boxes in each row of piles. Each row was measured, and an estimate of the number of boxes in a cross-section of each row was made, based on the number of boxes visible at the end of each row. The approximate number of boxes in each row was then estimated, based on the length of the row.

Next, an estimate of the number of boxes of each type of material was made, by multiplying the approximate number of boxes in a given row by the estimated percentage of that row comprising a specific type of material.

Last, an estimate of the approximate linear footage of materials in an average box was made. By multiplying that figure by the estimated number of boxes, an estimate of the linear footage of each type of material was developed.

It will be obvious from this description that only a very approximate estimate was possible using these techniques. Nonetheless, the process yielded considerably more information than the library had at the outset of the process: we knew, more or less, what material was in the rows of piles, where it was, and how much of it there was. The next challenge was how to move it from storage and integrate it into the library's other collections.

Preparing to Move the Materials

Preliminary inspection of the boxed material in storage had revealed gifts awaiting review, bound periodical volumes that appeared to be duplicates, superseded volumes of reference material, and a range of other material. Before the material was moved, a determination had to be made whether the material should be retained or discarded, and, for the material that was to be retained, whether it should be shelved with the library's general collections or placed in the compact shelving area of the new building reserved for less-used material.

This assessment required a second, and more detailed, review of the material in boxes, by collection development staff. Several categories of disposition were identified (e.g., discard, move to the planned compact shelving area, or move to the general collections shelving).

To facilitate easy identification of each category of material by the movers, signs for each category were photocopied onto a different color paper. As collection development staff determined the disposition of each box, an appropriately colored sign was taped to that box, so that, for instance, each box to be discarded had a pink "DISCARD" sign taped to it.

The color-coding and preprinted signs made it possible to quickly pull together all materials with a shared disposition status and reduced the possibility of a handwritten note being misread; it also relieved the collection development staff of the work of writing their disposition decision on each box.

Because of the size of the rows of piles, the collection development assessment work had to proceed in phases, and because of the weight of the boxes, the assistance of stack maintenance staff was sought and obtained. The outer layer of one row was reviewed and marked by collection development staff, then stack maintenance workers removed that layer of material from the row, separating for disposal those boxes whose contents were to be discarded and piling together those that were destined for other specified locations.

Lack of floor space for these review and sorting operations was a significant constraint, particularly at the beginning of the project. The timing of the work was such that work was taking place as the rest of the move proceeded, and floor space was freed up as the movers began to transport boxes of material to the new building. This allowed stack maintenance staff to remove more boxes from the rows of piles at one time, in turn allowing the collection development staff to review more boxes of material at one time.

Cleaning the Collections

The warehouse room in which boxed material was stored had a number of broken windows through which birds entered and exited. The warehouse itself was located on an urban street with significant traffic, and although this storage room was on the second floor, a certain amount of dust and grime had settled on the boxes, and in instances where boxes were not securely closed, on the contents inside.

A professional moving company was being used, and the RFP called for collections to be cleaned as a part of the move; the execution of this requirement was particularly important for the collections being moved from the storage facility. The library was concerned that dust and grime from these materials might soil carpeting or furniture in the new building, or that the dust might infiltrate the building's air handling system. It therefore required that cleaning of materials from storage be done in the storage facility. Cleaning procedures followed recommendations from the New England Document Conservation Center to use lint-free cloths sprayed with Endust and then left overnight to evaporate.

Moving the Collections

Moving the collections required that materials be unboxed, arranged in approximate call number order, moved to the correct new location, and placed on the shelf. The difficulty inherent in this process was that the library did not know before each box was opened exactly what would be in it. This meant we could not accurately allow for space within the general collections into which materials from storage could be integrated.

Had we been able to unbox and arrange the materials prior to the move, we could have accurately measured the collections in detail and left shelf space in the general collection for material that should have been shelved there. However, this was not the case. The pragmatic solution was to use spare shelving capacity in the compact shelving area as the destination for materials that otherwise might have been integrated into the general collections.

Lessons Learned for Moving from Disorganized Conditions

The first and most obvious suggestion concerning disorganized conditions such as the one described in this case study is to not let them develop. Work saved at the time disorganized conditions were allowed to develop had to be spent later. In this case, not only was the material unavailable to users, but the library was unsure what it owned.

Further, the conditions of storage were poor from a preservation perspective, and the effort required to review the disposition of the material was hampered by the physical labor required to examine individual volumes and by the dust and grime.

At the time we wrote the RFP soliciting bids for the move, we were only able to provide movers with a rough estimate of the number of boxes that would need to be moved. Although we were careful to share with the movers the limitations of our information and to show them the conditions in the storage facility, moving materials from this area was probably the most difficult challenge of a large, complex move, for both the library and the movers.

The second, and equally obvious, suggestion is to start as early as possible, particularly when faced with conditions that involve multiple challenges. We ended up working under some time pressure to complete assessment of the collection while the move was underway. In our case, lack of floor space effectively prevented us from doing a significant amount of this work before the move. Had additional shelving and the staff to unbox and shelve the material been available, we could have avoided this situation.

Third, develop fallback options. Just because you can't do what you know should be done (e.g., unbox the materials and organize them before the move) doesn't mean there aren't alternatives, and just because the task may seem overwhelming (How *do* you estimate the amount of material in a messy pile of boxes 20 feet long and 6 feet high?) doesn't mean it can't be done.

Breaking the problem down into smaller questions and tasks helps make manageable tasks that at first appear impossible. However, it is equally important to be aware of, and acknowledge, the assumptions and limitations attendant upon a second- or third-best solution so that these can be taken into account when decisions are based on less than ideally derived information. Finally, and most important, keep your sense of humor and a sense of perspective. Moving from disorganized conditions is a character-building experience, but it can be done!

APPENDIX A:
AVERAGE WIDTHS OF MATERIALS

ACADEMIC LIBRARY COLLECTIONS

Figures A-1 through A-4 (pp. 304–6) present the average widths of materials in the collection of Snell Library, Northeastern University's main library (and excluding collections in its Law Library). For bound materials, the contents of every twentieth shelf were measured to the nearest ¼ inch, and items on the shelf were counted. The raw measurements and item counts were then summed for each classification range, and the total measurement for each classification range was divided by its total item count to arrive at an average item width. For nonprint materials, the same procedure was followed, except that the contents of every fifth shelf were measured and counted. These measurements were done in 1997.

As noted in Chapter 1, a number of factors may influence the average width of materials. Figure A-5 (p. 307) illustrates this variation by comparing the average widths of monographs by LC class calculated for this work with those calculated from data presented in two other sources (the two listed below that break out volume widths by LC class).

PUBLIC LIBRARY COLLECTIONS

Figures A-6 through A-8 (pp. 308–10) present the average widths of adult, juvenile, and nonprint materials in the Flint Memorial Library, the public library for North Reading, Massachusetts, from measurements taken in 2008 using the basic procedures detailed above. To obtain a reasonable sample size, every fifth shelf was measured and counted, except in the homogenous adult fiction collection, where every tenth shelf was measured and counted. Figure A-9 (p. 311) compares these measurements with others reported in the literature.

The following works contain additional tables listing average widths of materials:

Brawner, Lee B., and Donald K. Beck Jr. (1996). *Determining your public library's future size: A needs assessment and planning model.* Chicago: ALA. Table A.1 (p. 123) lists number of items per linear foot and per square foot for adult general hardback books (on 90-inch-, 66-inch- and 42-inch-high shelving), paperbacks (on 90-inch- and 66-inch-high shelving), current periodicals (displayed), back periodicals (boxed/bound, on 90-inch-high shelving), government documents, audiotapes, videocassettes, compact discs, children's hardback books (on 42-inch- and 66-inch- high shelving) and children's easy/picture books (on 42-inch-high shelving).

Conversion factors derived from a count of the National Library [of Canada]'s monograph collection. (1981). *National Library News, 13.* Table 2 (p. 14) lists volumes per foot for standard and folio volumes by LC class.

Ellsworth, Ralph E. (1973). *Planning manual for academic library buildings.* Metuchen, NJ: Scarecrow Press. Summarizes planning standards then in use by the University of California and WICHE, including square footage allowances and items per 3-foot double-faced section for books, government documents, microfilm reels, microcards, newspapers, periodicals, phono records, reference books, map cases, pamphlet files, and slide cabinets. Also summarizes Canadian standards (volumes per linear foot, undifferentiated by type or classification).

Klasing, Jane P. (1991). *Designing and renovating school library media centers.* Chicago: ALA. Appendix E (p. 98, section E) lists the number of "average size," picture, and reference books per shelf.

Kurth, William H., and Ray W. Grim. (1966). *Moving a Library* (New York: Scarecrow Press, 1966). Table 23, p. 198, lists number of books per foot by LC class, and for all classes.

APPENDIX A: AVERAGE WIDTHS OF MATERIALS

Metcalf, Keyes D. 1999. *Planning academic and research library buildings*. 3rd ed. by Philip D. Leighton and David C. Weber. Chicago: ALA. Table B.12 (p. 730) lists volumes per standard shelf and volumes per single-faced section for circulating nonfiction, fiction, economics, general literature, history, reference, art, technical and scientific, medical, public documents, bound periodicals, and law volumes.

Roberts, Justine. (1984). "Stack capacity in medical and science libraries. *College and Research Libraries*, 45 (July): 306–14. Table 3 presents the average inches per volume and the range of volumes per foot for serials and monographs. Table 4 presents the range and mean volume widths for combined monograph and serial collections by type of library (all, health sciences, and science). Table 5 summarizes a range of width per item found for monographs and serials in seven studies of science and health science libraries.

Spyers-Duran, Peter. (1965) *Moving library materials*. rev. ed. Chicago: ALA. Table 1 (p. 3) lists volumes per foot, and per single- and double-faced section of shelving for bound periodicals, fiction, general literature, law, medicine, and technical and reference material.

Wittenborg, Karen, and John F. Camp. (1977). *Shelf Space Projection Survey*. n.p.: SUNY Council of Head Librarians; ERIC Document ED 156 140. Table III (p. 14) lists average volumes per foot at forty SUNY libraries (excluding community colleges).

APPENDIX A: AVERAGE WIDTHS OF MATERIALS

Figure A-1
Average Width of Monographs and Bound Periodical Volumes in a University Library Collection

	Monographs				Bound periodicals		
	Volumes measured	Total inches	Inches per volume		Volumes measured	Total inches	Inches per volume
A	102	99.75	0.98	A	229	451.75	1.97
B	314	322.00	1.03	B	55	97.50	1.77
BF	494	456.00	0.92	BF	151	252.00	1.67
BL-BX	322	329.00	1.02	BL	26	41.50	1.60
C	78	99.50	1.28	C-F	308	548.50	1.78
D	1,002	1,119.75	1.12				
E	562	622.75	1.11				
F	267	285.75	1.07				
G	86	97.50	1.13	G	38	77.75	2.05
GN	132	121.25	0.92	GN	73	12.75	0.17
GV	175	122.75	0.70	GV	56	93.50	1.67
H-HA	65	71.00	1.09	H-HA	77	137.25	1.78
				HB-HJ	712	1,309.00	1.84
HB-HJ	619	600.25	0.97				
HM-HQ	552	537.25	0.97	HM-HV	163	284.25	1.74
HT	91	86.25	0.95				
HV	124	118.00	0.95				
HV6000	198	192.75	0.97	HV6000	49	77.75	1.59
J	552	544.75	0.99	J	182	294.75	1.62
K	225	248.25	1.10	K	35	69.75	1.99
L	567	465.25	0.82	L	227	358.75	1.58
M	163	180.50	1.11	M	31	68.50	2.21
N	436	427.75	0.98	N	79	150.75	1.91
P-PL	553	525.00	0.95	P	351	535.75	1.53
PN	470	462.25	0.98				
PQ	448	443.00	0.99				
PR	1,012	1,011.00	1.00				
PS	937	900.25	0.96				
PT	137	150.75	1.10				
Q	195	194.50	1.00	Q	165	256.00	1.55
QA 1-74	242	154.75	0.64	QA	438	708.00	1.62
QA75-	848	845.75	1.00				
QB	89	91.25	1.03				
QC	456	486.50	1.07	QC	566	1,134.50	2.00
QD	356	342.00	0.96	QD	504	993.00	1.97
QE	92	96.75	1.05	QE	59	134.50	2.28
QH	232	222.75	0.96	QH	770	1,402.75	1.82
QK	114	110.75	0.97				
QL	130	142.75	1.10				
QP	329	371.00	1.13				
QR	83	84.00	1.01				
R	1,135	1,102.50	0.97	R	830	1,393.25	1.68
S	105	100.75	0.96	S	27	52.00	1.93
T	100	122.75	1.23	T	1,003	1,799.50	1.79
TA	369	347.00	0.94	TA	22	35.25	1.60
TC-TH	171	179.75	1.05				
TJ	100	102.75	1.03				
TK	249	288.75	1.16				
TL	39	56.00	1.44	TL	14	31.50	2.25
TN	15	15.25	1.02	TN	20	21.50	1.08
TP	96	98.25	1.02				
TR	36	23.50	0.65				
TS	98	95.25	0.97				
TX	43	27.50	0.64	TX	15	33.25	2.22
U	94	85.75	0.91	U	7	12.75	1.82
V	27	25.50	0.94	V	10	20.50	2.05
Z	137	121.50	0.89	Z	96	175.25	1.83
Total	16,663	16,576	0.99	Total	7,388	13,065	1.77

Figure A-2
Average Width of Reference Monographs and Reference Abstracts and Indexes in a University Library Collection

	Reference Monographs				Reference Abstracts & Indexes		
	Volumes Measured	Total Inches	Inches Per Volume		Volumes Measured	Total Inches	Inches Per Volume
A	20	34.50		A	134	235.25	
BF	20	29.75					
BL-BX	16	35.75					
C-F	38	102.75					
E	45	70.75					
F	16	34.25					
GV	26	35.50					
				H-HA	38	67.74	
HB-HJ	106	218.25		HB-HJ	37	59.00	
HM-HQ	21	23.25					
J	43	56.00					
K	162	300.25					
				L	10	35.25	
M	19	24.00		M	7	10.25	
N	24	48.00					
				P	29	35.00	
P-PL	37	48.00					
PN	39	84.75		PN	21	35.50	
PR	13	20.50					
PS	19	29.00					
Q	15	27.00					
QA75	24	31.50					
QC	20	33.50		QC	30	71.00	
QD	33	54.25		QD	181	334.00	
				QH	38	70.25	
QL	24	33.50					
QR	21	29.75					
R	27	37.25		R	19	34.50	
S	21	25.00		S	12	25.25	
				T	24	70.00	
TA	38	61.25					
TK	16	26.50					
TN	23	35.50					
U	22	26.75					
Z	383	529.50					
Total	1,331	2,146.50	1.61		580	1,082.99	1.87

Note: The average inches per volume is only presented for all reference monographs and for all reference abstracts and indexes because the sample size for individual classifications is not large enough to develop an accurate average figure. The count of volumes measured and total inches in each classification is given as background information only.

Figure A-3
Average Width of Government Publications in a University Library Collection

SuDocs classification	Pieces measured	Total inches	Inches per piece
AE	68	35.25	0.52
C, CS	1,606	277.75	0.17
D	102	56.75	0.56
E	68	27.75	0.41
ED	107	36.00	0.34
EP	202	70.50	0.35
FA	83	27.00	0.33
HE	605	196.75	0.33
I	888	233.75	0.26
IC	16	35.25	2.20
J	258	59.25	0.23
L	533	51.75	0.10
LC	98	48.25	0.49
NAS	150	51.50	0.34
PR, PrEx	62	51.75	0.83
S	68	110.00	1.62
T	92	25.75	0.28
TD	170	48.25	0.28
X/A (bound)	27	64.25	2.38
X/A (unbound)	95	34.25	0.36
House Journal	11	32.50	2.95
Rpt. of Clerk of the House	15	28.75	1.92
Senate MS Rpt of Priv Bills	15	28.75	1.92
Y	2,096	821.00	0.39
Document Abstracts & Indexes	178	261.75	1.47
Total	7,613	2,714.50	0.36

Figure A-4
Average Width of Audio and Video Formats in a University Library Collection

	Items measured	Total inches	Inches per item
CD's in jewel cases (excluding sets)	343	137.25	0.40
CD sets in jewel cases	28	33.25	1.19
3/4" video tapes in plastic cases	60	97.00	1.62
VHS tapes in plastic cases	254	317.50	1.25
audio cassettes in jewel boxes	91	62.25	0.68
audio cassettes - cassette only	69	30.50	0.44

Figure A-5
Comparison of Average Widths of Monographs by LC Class

	Monographs				
	Volumes Measured	Total Inches	Inches Per Volume	Kurth&Grim *Moving A Library**	"Conversion Factors..."**
A	102	99.75	0.98	1.40	1.00
B	1,130	1,107.00	0.98	1.04	0.92
C	78	99.50	1.28	1.21	1.00
D	1002	1,119.75	1.12	1.21	1.20
E	562	622.75	1.11	1.25	1.20
F	267	285.75	1.07	1.28	0.92
G	393	341.50	0.87	1.09	0.92
H	1,649	1,605.50	0.97	1.11	1.00
J	552	544.75	0.99	1.16	1.09
K	225	248.25	1.10	1.62	1.20
L	567	465.25	0.82	0.99	0.86
M	163	180.50	1.11	0.95 n/a	
N	436	427.75	0.98	1.10	0.75
P	3,557	3,492.25	0.98	0.98	0.92
Q	3,166	3,142.75	0.99	1.10	0.86
R	1,135	1,102.50	0.97	1.02	0.86
S	105	100.75	0.96	1.19	0.71
T	1,316	1,356.75	1.03	1.24	0.80
U	94	85.75	0.91	1.29	1.00
V	27	25.50	0.94	1.11 n/a	
Z	137	121.50	0.89	0.86	0.75
Total	16,663	16,575.75	0.99	1.11 n/a	

* Inches per volume calculated by dividing volumes per foot into 12. Volumes per foot are listed in Table 23, page 198 of Kurth, William H., and Ray W. Grim, Moving a Library (New York: Scarecrow Press, 1966).

** Inches per volume calculated by dividing volumes per foot into 12. Volumes per foot are those listed for standard (not folio) volumes in Table 2 on p. 14 of "Conversion Factors Derived From a Count of the National Library [of Canada]'s Monograph Collection," National Library News 13 (1981). No figure is listed in this source for overall volume width.

Figure A-6
Average Width of Adult Fiction and Nonfiction in a Public Library Collection

Adult fiction (hardcovers)	Items measured	Total inches	Inches per item
A	110	125.00	1.14
B	169	197.50	1.17
C	90	102.00	1.13
D	75	95.75	1.28
E	53	65.50	1.24
F	48	62.25	1.30
G	76	91.75	1.21
H	133	164.00	1.23
J	33	34.25	1.04
K	59	65.75	1.11
L	83	97.00	1.17
M	132	165.50	1.25
N	26	33.00	1.27
P	80	99.25	1.24
Q	27	32.50	1.20
R	57	60.00	1.05
S	110	137.25	1.25
T	35	42.25	1.21
U	25	30.50	1.22
W	67	82.25	1.23
Total	**1,488**	**1,783.25**	**1.20**

Adult fiction (paperbacks)	Items measured	Total inches	Inches per item
Romance	85	95.50	1.12
General	105	115.25	1.10

Adult non-fiction	Items measured	Total inches	Inches per item
0	94	96.25	1.02
100	116	115.25	0.99
200	127	126.50	1.00
300	1,004	698.75	0.70
400	77	74.00	0.96
500	246	232.99	0.95
600	701	662.50	0.95
700	492	404.00	0.82
800	352	353.00	1.00
900	749	815.25	1.09
Biography	279	352.50	1.26
Total	**4,237**	**3,930.99**	**0.93**

Adult large print	Items measured	Total inches	Inches per item	Notes
Fiction	227	256.00	1.13	
Non-fiction	74	84.00	1.14	Includes Biographies

Adult reference	Items measured	Total inches	Inches per item	Notes
Classified reference	435	663.15	1.52	Excludes BIP, Readers' Guide, Facts on File
Encyclopedias	77	112.50	1.46	Americana, Britannica, World Book

Figure A-7
Average Width of Juvenile and Young Adult Fiction and Nonfiction in a Public Library Collection

	Items measured	Total inches	Inches per item
JJ Hardcovers	307	121.75	0.40
Advanced picture books	42	18.50	0.44
Easy Reader hardcovers	119	59.50	0.50
Easy Reader paperbacks	73	13.75	0.19
Middle Reader hardcovers	80	40.75	0.51
Middle Reader paperbacks	182	54.25	0.30
Juvenile nonfiction	1,339	600.75	0.45
Juvenile biography	163	83.50	0.51
Juvenile paperbacks	99	50.00	0.51
Juvenile fiction	359	309.50	0.86
Young adult (YA)			
Fiction	186	188.25	1.01
Graphic novels	104	58.75	0.56
Paperbacks	100	75.25	0.75

Figure A-8
Average Width of Audio and Video Materials in a Public Library Collection

	Items measured	Total inches	Inches per item
Adult audio books			
on CD			
fiction	64.00	55	1.16
non-fiction	40.00	35	1.14
on cassette			
fiction	133.50	83	1.61
non-fiction	88.75	77	1.15
DVD's			
fiction	104.00	173	0.60
nonfiction	69.50	115	0.60
Video cassettes	166.50	128	1.30
CD's			
Folk	15.75	23	0.68
Opera	13.75	18	0.76
Blues	5.00	8	0.63
New Age	7.75	13	0.60
Keyboard	12.00	15	0.80
Choral	16.00	21	0.76
Jazz	33.00	51	0.65
Chamber music	15.00	21	0.71
Vocal	14.50	22	0.66
Orchestral	32.50	51	0.64
World	15.75	24	0.66
Holiday	18.25	29	0.63
Country	13.25	22	0.60
Pop/rock	90.75	144	0.63
Sound tracks	29.00	45	0.64
CD - average	**332.25**	**507.00**	**0.66**

Figure A.9
Comparison of Average Widths of Public and School Materials

	Public Libraries Holt (1989)		School Library Media Centers Baule (1999)		Bugher (2007)		Impact (2005)	
Type of Collection	items per linear foot	inches per item	items per linear foot	inches per item	items per linear foot	inches per item	items per linear foot	inches per item
Adult								
Trade books	8	1.50						
Art books (6-7/lin ft.)	6	2.00						
	7	1.71						
Reference books & bound periodicals								
(5-7/lin. ft.)	5	2.40						
	7	1.71						
Juvenile/School								
Reference books					6	2.00	6	2.00
							7	1.71
Secondary reference books			8	1.50				
Periodicals- journal thickness			50	0.24				
Periodicals - magazine thickness			100	0.12				
Periodicals							11	1.09
Easy books/primers	24	0.50						
General fiction & nonfiction	16	0.75			20	0.60	13	0.92
Picture/thin					10	1.20	10	1.20
Standard size			20	0.60				
Elementary school books			12	1.00				
Middle school books			10	1.20				
High school			10	1.20				
Videos							8	1.50
Videocassettes			24	0.50			3	4.00
Cd's and cd-roms							8	1.50

APPENDIX B: TWO HUNDRED MOVES REPORTED IN THE LITERATURE, 1929–2006

HOW TO USE THIS APPENDIX

When planning a move, it's useful to see how other libraries have handled similar challenges. Most of us think our type of library has special constraints, so I have grouped the moves by type of library and then in reverse chronological order.

However, don't limit yourself to browsing only within your type of library! There are more similarities than differences between us, and the intrinsic problems of moving library collections are the same today as they were in 1929, even if we now have spreadsheets, databases, and drafting software to make the work go (mostly) faster.

The tables area arranged in this order:

Public libraries (32 moves)

Special libraries

    Medical and health sciences libraries (11 moves)

    Law libraries (13 moves)

    Government, state, and national libraries (16 moves)

    Miscellaneous special libraries (5 moves)

School libraries (7 moves)

Archives and special collections (27 moves)

Universities and colleges (89 moves)

APPENDIX B: TWO HUNDRED MOVES REPORTED IN THE LITERATURE

Public Libraries (moves 1-20)

Location	Reason	Collection size	Moved by whom	Approx. date	Approx. duration
1. Farr Branch, Weld Library District (Colorado)	new branch library	110,000 items	movers	August 2002	5 days
2. Fort Smith Public Library	new building	160,000 titles	library staff	Dec. 8, 2000 to Feb. 23, 2001	3 months
3. Medicine Hat (Alberta, Canada) Public Library	100-year flood	80,000 books; five years of 269 periodical titles	library staff plus almost 100 volunteers	Jun 7-8, 1995	15 hours
4. Portland, OR	move to temporary facil	875 tons of material	patrons	1995	3 weeks
5. Estes Park, CO	new facility	29,300 books	staff, 100+ volunteers	June 12-13, 1991 (book move)	2 days
6. Mexico, Missouri	move building	n/a	prof. movers	December 1990	3 days
7. Hobbs, NM	renovation	81,000 books	library staff: packing prof. movers: transport	1990?	packing: 8 days move: 3 days
8. Cedar Rapids, IA	new facility	150,000 books, magazines	staff; 320+ volunteers, prof. movers	January (1987?)	6 days
9. Western Springs, IL (youth services)	reorganization	20,000 books	prof. movers	August 1984	2 days
10. Reading, MA	new facility	78,000 items	300 volunteers	(1984?)	n/a
11. Albany County (WY)	new facility	100,000 volumes	700+ volunteers, staff	July (1980?)	1 week
12. Chugiak-Eagle River (Alaska) (branch)	expansion	12,000 volumes	staff and volunteers	July-Oct. (1977?)	
13. Bettendorf, IA	new facility	65,000-70,000	20,000 by patron check-out remainder n/a	Summer 1976	n/a
14. Vineland, NJ	new facility	60,000 volumes	200 volunteers, staff 50 National Guard	1976	2 days
15. Dowagiac, MI	expansion; move to temporary facility	n/a	staff: packing; transport: Dept. of Public Services	April (1973?)	4 days
16. Johannesburg, South Africa	expansion	150,000 bound serials 6,071 bound newspapers 100,000 storebooks	staff and prof. movers	12/69 - 6/70 July 1968 June 1970	1 day n/a
17. San Antonio, TX	new facility	600,000 books	prof. movers	Jan. 1968	3 days
18. Middlesex County Library Ontario, Canada	new facility	15,000 books	n/a	1967	1 day
19. Library Company of Philadelphia	new facility	235,000 books	prof. movers	Feb. 1966	n/a
20. Pratt, KS	new facility	40,000 volumes	500+ volunteers	April (1966?)	5 1/2 hours for 38,000 volumes

Public Libraries (moves 1-20, continued)

Location	Type of container	Transport method	Special problems	Citation
1. Farr Branch, Weld Library District (Colorado)	boxes	n/a	temporary shutdown of second branch for renovation; organizational changes; new shelving not as expected	Baumann (2006)
2. Fort Smith Public Library	book trucks	rented van	staff only; inaccurate measurements; muddy parking lot; unfinished loading dock	Cash (2001)
3. Medicine Hat (Alberta, Canada) Public Library	book trucks; wooden shelving units	n/a	emergency conditions; move ran 2- 9:30 pm, and 8:30 am – 4:30 pm on two successive days; public mobilized by broadcast media; move back took five days	Evans (1996)
4. Portland, OR	none	modified book brigade	n/a	"Multnomah..." (1995)
5. Estes Park, CO	80 plastic milk crates	fork lift truck		Hoxsey (1995)
6. Mexico, Missouri	n/a	n/a	relocation of an historic Carnegie building	Lamb (1991)
7. Hobbs, NM	2,100 boxes	trucks		Adams (1990)
8. Cedar Rapids, IA	100 rented bookcarts	trucks	no elevator access to 3 levels management of volunteers	Hamilton & Hindman (1987)
9. Western Springs, IL (youth services)	boxes on wheels	within building		Kurtz (1988)
10. Reading, MA	n/a	n/a		"Library Move ..." (1984)
11. Albany County (WY)	n/a	human chain, trucks	management of volunteers staff/volunteer assembly of shelving	Kinney (1981)
12. Chugiak-Eagle River (Alaska) (branch)	n/a	within building	shelving	Kallenberg (1977)
13. Bettendorf, IA	n/a	n/a		"Don't Return..." (1976)
14. Vineland, NJ	1,500 30" x 10"x 8" boxes	book brigade	National Guard schedule	Snyder (1976)
15. Dowagiac, MI	250 cartons for OS books, records storage boxes	boxes, trucks	selection of materials for small, temporary facility	Ames (1973)
16. Johannesburg, South Africa	cardboard boxes	within building		Clifton (1971)
17. San Antonio, TX	beer cartons	trucks	rain	Sexton (1968)
18. Middlesex County Library Ontario, Canada	50 bookcarts	2 liftload trucks		"Middlesex County..." (1967)
19. Library Company of Philadelphia	custom book cases tote boxes on wheels; newspapers, OS	trucks	no elevator rare and fragile material irregular shelf layout	Wolf (1966)
20. Pratt, KS	n/a	book brigade		"500 Pratt Volunteers" (1966)

Public Libraries (moves 21-32)

Location	Reason	Collection size	Moved by whom	Approx. date	Approx. duration
21. Glencoe, Ontario, Canada	collection exchange	4,000 books	staff	May 1966	four days
22. Racine, WI	new facility	60,000 books 3,000 recordings	Jaycees and 1,600 volunteers: books and recordings moving co.: magazines, etc.	(1957?)	8 hours 3+ days
23. Midland County, TX	new facility	50,000 volumes	30 Jaycees, staff	July 18-19, 195(7?)	21 hours
24. Lorain, OH	new facility	58,000 books 48,653 unbound magazines 29,907 newspapers	16 library staff;packing 423 hours' labor: Jaycees	November 1957	5 1/2 days: move 2 weeks: remaining reshelving
25. Toledo, OH branch	new facility	12,000 + books	library, janitorial staff	April 11, 195(7?)	1 day
26. Brooklyn (NY)	expansion	550,000 volumes	12 high school boys	(1955?)	3 months
27. Westfield, NJ	new facility	45,000 volumes	10,000 vols: public 35,000 vols: prof. movers	October 1954	n/a
28. Long Beach, CA (branch)	new facility	19,000 volumes	2 librarians, 2 pages, 2 movers	(1953)	1 1/2 days
29. San Diego	new facility	14,863 boxes of materials	phase one: staff phase two: staff plus prof. movers	1952, 1954	n/a
30. Newark, NY	renovations	2,000 books	2 staff, 2 town workers, 3 trustees, plus a group of boys	1950?	6 hours
31. Toledo, OH	new facility	347,000+ volumes vertical files, pictures, trade catalogs, maps, etc.	prof. movers	(1940?)	48 hours
32. Baltimore	new facility	400,000+ volumes	prof. movers	Winter 1933	10 days

Public Libraries (moves 21-32, continued)

Location	Type of container	Transport method	Special problems	Citation
21. Glencoe, Ontario, Canada	100 cartons	bookmobile	complete replacement of collection	Whiteway (1966)
22. Racine, WI	n/a	book brigade		Paulson, Hoyt, and King (1958)
23. Midland County, TX	80+ boxes	n/a		Kinzer (1958)
24. Lorain, OH	n/a	moving van	night schedule	1. King (1959) 2. Paulson, Hoyt, and King (1958) 3. "Moving Day" (1958)
25. Toledo, OH branch	cartons	moving van		Wells (1957)
26. Brooklyn (NY)	bookcarts	within building		Allen (1955) Hardkopf (1955)
27. Westfield, NJ	Ply-fibre bundles in bins on casters	trucks		Wright (1955)
28. Long Beach, CA (branch)	8 giant book troughs	trucks		Sell (1954)
29. San Diego	cardboard boxes	pallets on trucks and forklift	window conveyor belt no bids on phase one	Thorne (1955)
30. Newark, NY	n/a	within building	short notice	Messinger (1951)
31. Toledo, OH	boxes	trucks	collection integration, reorganization fumigation	Schunk (1941)
32. Baltimore	1,400 boxes, 36" x 18" x 12"	van	collection mergers	Josselyn (1933)

Special Libraries

Medical & Health Sciences Libraries

Location	Reason	Collection size	Moved by whom	Approx. date	Approx. duration
1. Howard University (DC); Louis Stokes Health Sciences Library	new building	169,200 book volumes; 4,000 serial titles with 1,149 active subscriptions; over 2,000 nonprint titles	move contractor	June 11-June 26, 2001	15 days
2. University of Arkansas for Medical Sciences Library	remote storage to relieve overcrowding	45,000 linear inches	University's contracted movers	July 21-25, 1996	5 days
3. University of South Carolina Medical Library	growth space reallocation	89,000 bd. per. vols.	15 library staff	1986	47 hours
4. Witwatersrand Medical Library (South Africa)	new facility	100,000 volumes	movers	December 1982-February 1983	n/a
5. Royal Victoria, Montreal	reorganization	n/a	library staff	1981	3 days
6. Chapel Hill, NC university health sciences library	collection relocation	177,000 volumes	2 teams of 4 persons; 3 hired from temporary agency	1980	15.5 days
7. University of Cincinnati health sciences library	respacing collection	120,000 per. vols. 2,389 titles	students	summer (1980?)	1 week
8. U. Southern California medical library	new facility	27,000 serial volumes	University Operations and Maintenance staff	(1968?)	approx. 1 week
9. National Institute of Health	new facility	n/a	transportation, library staff	(1967?)	n/a
10. National Institute of Health	new facility	70,000 volumes	library staff, contract labor	November (1953?)	7 8-hour days
11. Danville, PA medical library	relocation to temporary location then to new facility	30,000 bk.and journal vols. 600 audiovisuals	prof. movers	n/a	4 14-hour days for each move

Medical & Health
Sciences Libraries (continued)

Location	Approx. duration	Type of container	Transport method	Special problems	Citation
1. Howard University (DC); Louis Stokes Health Sciences Library	15 days	book carts	vans	pre-move weeding; delay in completing construction; narrow aisles didn't accommodate planned book carts; problem with allowance for growth space; too many visitors.	Bryant (2004)
2. University of Arkansas for Medical Sciences Library	5 days	industrial book carts	vans	marking older journals to be moved; book carts shrink-wrapped	Theilig (1997)
3. University of South Carolina Medical Library	47 hours	booktrucks	within building	sign removal by custodial staff	Carlson (1987)
4. Witwatersrand Medical Library (South Africa)	n/a	boxes	two-wheelers; trolleys; lifts; trucks	weeding; reclassing from LC to NLM; cleaning all books; inadequate materials; poor coordination of operations by movers; bad weather	Robertson (1983)
5. Royal Victoria, Montreal	3 days	booktrucks	within building		Ducas (1985)
6. Chapel Hill, NC university health sciences library	15.5 days	booktrucks	within building	journal space allocation	Brogan & Lipscomb (1982)
7. University of Cincinnati health sciences library	1 week	booktrucks	within building		Broaddus & Hurlebaus (1981)
8. U. Southern California medical library	approx. 1 week	20 booktrucks	panel truck	collection integration boxed material in storage	Uzelac (1969)
9. National Institute of Health	n/a	booktrucks	n/a		Martin (1968)
10. National Institute of Health	7 8-hour days	36 booktrucks with safety straps	automobile truck	elevator contention attrition	Adams (1943)
11. Danville, PA medical library	4 14-hour days for each move	heavy duty cardboard moving boxes	boxes on moving dolleys	moving company without library moving experience	Roth (1985)

Law Libraries

Location	Reason	Collection size	Moved by whom	Approx. date	Approx. duration
1. Sidley Austin Brown & Wood (London)	new offices	n/a	professional movers	May 7-10, 2004	weekend
2. Clifford Chance (London)	new offices	25,000 items	moving company	August/September 2003	4 days
3. University of Washington Law Library	new facility	350,000 volumes	professional movers	Summer 2003	6 weeks
4. Supreme Court of Ohio Law Library	new facility	n/a	professional movers	February 2003	weekend
5. Lovell's (London)	new offices	n/a	external movers	July 2002	weekend
6. Holme Roberts & Owen (Denver)	new offices	13,000 volumes	movers	(1989?)	3 days
7. Powell, Goldstein, Frazier & Murphy	new offices	n/a	professional movers	(1988?)	weekend
8. Crowell & Moring (DC)	new offices	n/a	office movers	January 1987	one weekend
9. University of Michigan Law Library	addition	300,000 volumes	library staff, temporary employees	(1981?)	4½ days
10. U. of Illinois Law Library	reclassification	320,000 volumes	570 hours of student help, library staff	1978	3 weeks
11. U. Southern California law school library	stack reorganization	100,000 volumes	100 students	1979 November 1966?	2 weeks+ 10½ hours
12. Harvard Law School Library	reorganization & relocation	300,000 volumes	high school students	1960?	5 months
13. Social Law Library (Boston)	new facility	40,000 vols., furniture 55,000 volumes	prof. movers janitors	Dec. 1939 Jan. 1940	8½ 8-hour days 29 days, 2.5 hours/day

Law Libraries (continued)

Location	Type of container	Transport method	Special problems	Citation
1. Sidley Austin Brown & Wood (London)	n/a	n/a	merging two libraries; moving to compact shelving	Monk (2005)
2. Clifford Chance (London)	crates provided by moving company	n/a	paper reduction and archiving	Berry (2004)
3. University of Washington Law Library	book carts	n/a	22" wide aisles in old library; start delayed by construction delays	Hazelton & Franklin (2004)
4. Supreme Court of Ohio Law Library	n/a	n/a	moving shelving and books; evaluating 7,000 boxes of material in a warehouse; moving company disregarded library shelving locations; library eventually told movers to leave and spent rest of year sorting out collections; dissention between shelving and book movers	Kozlowski (2005)
5. Lovell's (London)	n/a	n/a	weeding prior to move	Rawlinson (2005)
6. Holme Roberts & Owen (Denver)	n/a	n/a	planning based on 35.5" shelves; actual shelves only 30" wide	Estes (1989)
7. Powell, Goldstein, Frazier & Murphy	n/a	n/a	librarian not present during move; movers placed materials in wrong order; inaccurate blueprint for new location; shelves in new library mislabeled	McCarrier (1988)
8. Crowell & Moring (DC)	n/a	n/a	many delays	Callinan (1988)
9. University of Michigan Law Library	cartons: 1,000: 11" x 13" x 24"; 500: 11" x 13" x 18"	hand trucks		Leary (1982)
10. U. of Illinois Law Library	booktrucks	within building	collection reclassification	Johnson (1980)
11. U. Southern California law school library	booktrucks	within building	collection reclassification	Wilkins (1967)
12. Harvard Law School Library	n/a	book brigade		"Harvard..." (1960)
13. Social Law Library (Boston)	boxes; boxes, 41 1/2" x 11 1/2" x 9"			Stebbins (1941)

Governmental, State, and National Libraries

Location	Reason	Collection size	Moved by whom	Approx. date	Approx. duration
1. Idaho State Library	reorganization	n/a	[Idaho] Correctional Industries	Spring 2002	n/a
2. British Library (London)	new facility	8 million volumes	contractor	1990's	2 years
3. U.S. Geological Survey Library (Reston, VA)	return material from offsite warehouse	200,000 volumes; 350,00 maps; 650 map cases	moving company	Dec. (1992?) to May (1993?)	n/a
4. Natural Resources Institute (Great Britain)	merger, relocation	n/a	prof. movers	phased: 1988-1990	various
5. CABI, IIE England	merger, relocation	CABI: 35,000 volumes 100,000+ reprints	prof. movers	September 1988	6 days
6. New Zealand Ministry of Agriculture and Fisheries' Central Library	relocation	1,000 periodical titles	Ministry of Works and Development staff	July 1983	6 days
7. Wolfner Library, Missouri	new facility	140,000 volumes (braille), phono disc, cassette, etc. 1,000+ record and cassette machines	library staff, pre-release prisoners	April (1982?)	move: 1 week
8. BLL, Boston Spa, England	expansion	n/a	113 staff; 12 teams of 8 members	1980	1,252 man-weeks, including 64 man-weeks of supervision
9. (UK) National Lending Library	new facility	50,000 serial titles 150,000 monographs	7,000 hours student labor 850 hours of supervision	July - Sept. 1972	8 weeks; 7,000 man-hours student labor; 850 hours supervision
10. Library of Congress	stack cleaning	9 million volumes	Collections Maintenance staff	1971 start	estimate: 3 years
11. (UK) India Office Records	new facility	600,000 volumes	prof. movers and staff	9/67 - 1/68	4 months
12. Great Britain national library	new facility	250,000+ volumes	staff, prof. movers	1965?	20 working days
13. National Diet Library (Japan)	new facility	2 million+ volumes	n/a	Aug. 2-25, 1961	21 working days
14. Technical Library, US Naval Proving Ground Dahlgren, VA	new shelving	11,000 documents	library staff, station maintenance crew	(1958?)	21 hours of work
15. Louisiana State Library	unsafe building conditions	90,000 books+	30 library staff, plus others 40 prof. movers	(1957?)	3 days
16. Pennsylvania State Library	new facility	360,000 volumes	prof. movers, staff	1931 (?)	n/a

Governmental, State, and National Libraries (continued)

Location	Approx. duration	Type of container	Transport method	Special problems	Citation
1. Idaho State Library	n/a	n/a	within building	weeding & reorganizing collections; not enough communication with staff	Fowles (2004)
2. British Library (London)	2 years	crates	n/a	unknown number of books; moving from multiple locations; integrating long-separated collections; multiple shelving configurations	Greenwood & Shawyer (1993)
3. U.S. Geological Survey Library (Reston, VA)	n/a	carts ; maps moved in their cases & moved on specially constructed wheeled pallets	covered trucks	moving map collections & books; moving to compact shelving; plan was for a linear move but contractor bid on a shelf-to-shelf move; warehouse mezzanine without elevator; collapse of 56 shelves due to poor coordination at warehouse	Keck (1993)
4. Natural Resources Institute (Great Britain)	various	crates	n/a	interim off-site storage	Lumley et al (1991)
5. CABI, IIE England	6 days	crates	n/a	fragmented journal runs liftless Victorian building company underestimated project scope	Hamilton (1991)
6. New Zealand Ministry of Agriculture and Fisheries' Central Library	6 days	cardboard cartons holding 18" of publications	n/a	carpet damage schedule	Stoddart & Hughes (1984)
7. Wolfner Library, Missouri	move: 1 week	hampers	moving trucks	shelving also moved	Miller (1982)
8. BLL, Boston Spa, England	1,252 man-weeks, including 64 man-weeks of supervision	n/a	within building		Leadley et al (1981)
9. (UK) National Lending Library	8 weeks; 7,000 man-hours student labor; 850 hours supervision	hods on trollies	trucks	integration of transferred serials	Tatterton & Braid (1973)
10. Library of Congress	estimate: 3 years	n/a	n/a	disorganized conditions fragile bindings	"LC Begins ..." (1972)
11. (UK) India Office Records	4 months	book trollies	vans	integration of series	Lancaster (1969)
12. Great Britain national library	20 working days	wire baskets, 2' x 3' stacked in tiers of 3 on bogies	vanloads of 15 tiers of 3 b	collection integration	Allardyce (1966)
13. National Diet Library (Japan)	21 working days	collapsible flight metal containers	5-ton trucks and 2-ton trailers		Suzuki (1963)
14. Technical Library, US Naval Proving Ground Dahlgren, VA	21 hours of work	booktrucks	within building	move from file cabinets to shelving	Waldron (1958)
15. Louisiana State Library	3 days	5,000+ boxes	large vans	building safety issues no preparation time	James (1957)
16. Pennsylvania State Library	n/a	packing boxes, 24" x 15" x 12"	trucks		Sheetz (1932)

Miscellaneous Special Libraries

Location	Reason	Collection size	Moved by whom	Approx. date	Approx. duration
1. Hereford Catherdral (UK)	new building	n/a	n/a	November 1995 - April 1996	n/a
2. INIST; France	new location, building; consolidation	20,000 periodical titles thousands of dissertations, research reports, proceedings, and other monographs	prof. movers	1989	about 8 weeks
3. Ayerst Laboratories Research, Princeton, NJ	relocation, new facility	n/a	prof. movers	1984	approx. 6 weeks
4. Atlas Powder Co. Wilmington, DE	new facility	387 boxes of material	prof. movers	Feb. 195(5?)	one weekend
5. St. Paul, MN seminary	new facility	40,000 volumes	260 students	January (1950?)	3 hours

Location	Type of container	Transport method	Special problems	Citation
1. Hereford Catherdral (UK)	n/a	n/a	moving the Chained Library, rare books with chains, accessible on by a narrow spiral staircase	Williams (1998)
2. INIST; France	crates	semi-trailers	move between cities consolidation of three facilities safety concerns for shelving, flooring at one old facility	Wiegandt-Sakoun & Gunet (1990)
3. Ayerst Laboratories Research, Princeton, NJ	900+ cartons	3 moving vans	move between Canada & US temporary facility; disordered cartons	Boyajian (1986)
4. Atlas Powder Co. Wilmington, DE	boxes	n/a		Little (1955)
5. St. Paul, MN seminary	custom-built book trays book brigade			Shanahan (1950)

APPENDIX B: TWO HUNDRED MOVES REPORTED IN THE LITERATURE

School Libraries

Location	Reason	Collection size	Moved by whom	Approx. date	Approx. duration
1. Gay Memorial Junior High School (Harlinger TX)	new facility	n/a	200 students in physical education classes	1996?	one day
2. Austin, MN HS	remodeled facility	26,000 books	120 students per period & staff	1993/94	24 periods; 12 hours
3. Natick, MA private school	renovation	10,000 volumes thousands of periodicals, phonograph records, AV materials	librarian plus school staff and students	1989	packing: 2 days unpacking and move in: 2 months
4. Monrovia, IN Jr/Sr HS	renovation	7,000 books 80 periodicals media	librarian + 2 students	1980	48 hours
5. Kenosha, WI LRC	new facility	n/a	staff;packing; movers: transport	1972?	n/a
6. Yakima, Washington HS	new facility	11,589 volumes	students	196(8?)	1 day
7. Mercersburg (PA) Academy	new facility	10,000 volumes	library and academy staff, 450 students	1951?	1 hour, 10 minutes

Location	Type of container	Transport method	Special problems	Citation
1. Gay Memorial Junior High School (Harlinger TX)	carriers (book troughs)	within building		Stout (1997)
2. Austin, MN HS	none	book brigade		Cliff & Strom (1995)
3. Natick, MA private school	boxes	booktrucks, dollies	lack of resources, detailed logistical planning	Lambert (1992)
4. Monrovia, IN Jr/Sr HS	book shelves encased in trash bags	n/a	need for vermin-proof storage	Schick (1981)
5. Kenosha, WI LRC	box holding 25 books	n/a	merging two collections no elevator in one old facility	Burke (1973)
6. Yakima, Washington HS	n/a	walking in line		"Students..." (1968)
7. Mercersburg (PA) Academy	n/a	book brigade		Kulp (1952)

Archives (moves 1-8)

Location	Reason	Collection size	Moved by whom	Approx. date	Approx. duration
1. University of Colorado at Boulder, archives of the American Music Research Center	new facility	1,000 linear feet	n/a	2002 (planned)	n/a
2. Oklahoma State Archives and Records Management Divisions	expansion facility	archives: 27,000 cubic feet; records management: 40,000 cubic feet	n/a	July 2000; January 22-26 2001	10,730 cu ft: July 17-28; 8,000 boxes: Jan 22-26
3. Brigham Young University Special Collections	new facility	300,000 books, 10,000 manuscript collections, a million photographs & negatives, including some glass plates	student crews, supervised by Special Collections staff	Fall 1999	10 weeks
4. Dartmouth College Special Collections	new facility	6.5 million manuscripts; 500,000 photographs; 95,000 rare books	prof. library movers	late Oct. - Dec. 15, 1998	2,910 hours staff time planning; 3,120 hours staff time moving materials; 3,470 hours movers' time
5. University of Utah, Special Collections Dept	renovation & expansion	n/a, but moving into 42,000 sf	n/a	Spring 1998; Spring & Summer 1999	n/a
6. Colorado State University Archives	renovation & flood	10,000 rare books	archivist, with 4 black-belt karate colleagues	April 1997	1 day
7. Archives of the Redemptorists	consolidation & relocation	n/a	prof. movers	October 1996	n/a
8. Delaware Public Archives	moving part of the collection to a storage facility	23,000 cubic feet	prof. movers	1996	approx. 16 weeks

Archives (moves 1-8, continued)

Location	Type of container	Transport method	Special problems	Citation
1. University of Colorado at Boulder, archives of the American Music Research Center	n/a	n/a	move to a historic building, with floor loading, HVAC, asbestos, and alarm system issues	Volpe in Newman & Jones (2002)
2. Oklahoma State Archives and Records Management Divisions	boxed records placed on pallets and shrink-wrapped	forklifts and semi-trailers	moving from compact shelving; moving into 10' high shelving; working with lowest bidder; temporary chute constructed to overcome inadequate elevator	Harrington in Newman & Jones (2002)
3. Brigham Young University Special Collections	n/a	book trucks, shrink-wrapped	moving from half a dozen scattered facilities on- and off-campus, some with no direct elevator access; some book trucks unloaded out of order; some items missing after move; shelving cross-bracing hampered through-shelving	Taylor in Newman & Jones (2002)
4. Dartmouth College Special Collections	shelving units on wheels	n/a	pre-move inventory; high security; items cleaned	Cronenwett (1999)
5. University of Utah, Special Collections Dept	36" long book trucks; 24" book trucks	within building	mishandling of old, fragile, and rare material by untrained movers; disgruntled staff, dirty conditions; cleaning shelving	Jones in Newman & Jones (2002)
6. Colorado State University Archives	books in individual boxes	hand trucks and carts	professional movers were available and not used, based on observation of their techniques & level of care	Newman in Newman & Jones (2002)
7. Archives of the Redemptorists	boxes	trucks	long distance moves from Oakland, CA and Glenview, IL to Denver; over-reliance on mover's reputation; fragile material not packed as per librarian's direction; boxes packed carelessly in trucks; lengthy claim for damages; significant damage to collections and furniture	Kniffen in Newman & Jones (2002)
8. Delaware Public Archives	boxes, shrink-wrapped	trucks	need to change from series- to item- or container-level records, and to replace existing record containers; shrink-wrapping 46,000 items; poor handling techniques by movers	Mattern in Newman & Jones (2002)

Archives (moves 9-27)

Location	Reason	Collection size	Moved by whom	Approx. date	Approx. duration
9. Northwestern University Library Archives	internal space reallocation	10,000 cubic feet	3 crews of student assistants	January 1995	4 working days
10. National Archives	new facility	1.2 million cubic feet	prof. movers	1994/95	n/a
11. American Heritage Center University of Wyoming	new facility	70,000 cubic feet	"University's movers"	1992/93?	n/a
12. US NARA	new facility	500,000 cubic ft.	n/a	future	n/a
13. Rhode Island State Archives and Public Records Administration	emergency asbestos abatement following fire	50,000 cubic feet	n/a	June 9 - 23,1989	
14. US NARA	Reagan papers: end of administration	21,000 cubic ft.	n/a	(1989?)	n/a
15. Clemson, SC University special collections	new facility	5,000 cubic feet books, records, and manuscripts	library staff: packing prof.: transport	April 1989	move: 4 days
16. National Archives of Canada	interim storage	70,000 linear ft.	n/a	1988	n/a
17. Iowa State Archives		20,000 cubic ft. 2,000 vols. bd. newspapers	prof. movers	1988	n/a
18. Louisiana State Archives	new facility	14,000 cubic ft. records 45,000 cubic ft. temporary records	n/a	1987	n/a
19. AFL-CIO/Washington, DC	new facility	7,000 cubic ft.	n/a	1987	n/a
20. Maryland State Archives	new facility	63,000 cubic ft.	staff	1987	n/a
21. American Psychiatric Assoc. Washington, DC		800 cubic ft.	n/a	1982	n/a
22. LC Manuscript. Music Div.	new facility	200,000 archive boxes 1.3 million sound recordings 9,000 lin. ft. mss. 26,000 lin ft. from Motion Picture Div. 9 million photographs	own moving crew	1979-1984	18 months' moving time over four years
23. LC Map & Geography Division	new facility	5,299 map cases	own moving crew	1979-1984	n/a
24. British Public Records Office	new facility	219,817 lin. ft.	staff + prof. movers	1977	n/a
25. Massachusetts State Archives	new facility	n/a	prof. movers	1975-76	n/a
26. Northeast Regional Archives, NYC	consolidate 8 facilities	62,000 cubic feet	staff of 8	n/a	13 months
27. [Wisconsin] State Historical Society Library	new location	n/a	movers	January (1967?)	n/a

Archives (moves 9-27, continued)

Location	Type of container	Transport method	Special problems	Citation
9. Northwestern University Library Archives	n/a	25 book trucks	cleaning & respacing shelves; rehousing items in non-standard boxes	Quinn in Newman & Jones (2002)
10. National Archives	"housing capable of withstanding the move"	n/a	archival materials	Pilette (1995)
11. American Heritage Center University of Wyoming	archival containers custom boxes: glass negatives, audio tapes cabinet drawers: maps, flat filed materials telescoping boxes: phonograph records, 35 mm films artifacts: fabric storage boxes sculpture: crates, bubble wrap	wooden carriers, booktrucks, trucks	rare and fragile material	White & Cook (1994)
12. US NARA	n/a	n/a		Morrow (1990)
13. Rhode Island State Archives and Public Records Administration	n/a	'book brigade', then motorized conveyer	fire-caused water damage and asbestos contamination to collections	Wagner in Newman & Jones (2002)
14. US NARA	n/a	n/a		Morrow (1990)
15. Clemson, SC University special collections	boxes	n/a	tight time frame heat	Chepesiuk (1991)
16. National Archives of Canada	n/a	n/a		Morrow (1990)
17. Iowa State Archives	n/a	n/a		Morrow (1990)
18. Louisiana State Archives	n/a	n/a		Morrow (1990)
19. AFL-CIO/Washington, DC	40 mail carts	n/a		Morrow (1990)
20. Maryland State Archives	custom-constructed carts	van		Morrow (1990)
21. American Psychiatric Assoc. Washington, DC	n/a	n/a		Morrow (1990)
22. LC Manuscript, Music Div.	large canvas carts (similar to mail hampers; booktrucks	van		Morrow (1990)
23. LC Map & Geography Division	n/a	n/a		Morrow (1990)
24. British Public Records Office	custom-constructed containers	n/a		Morrow (1990)
25. Massachusetts State	n/a	n/a	fumigation	Morrow (1990)
26. Northeast Regional Archives, NYC	n/a	n/a	archival materials	Pilette (1995)
27. [Wisconsin] State Historical Society Library	n/a	semi-trailers	de facto inventory needed prior to move; missing records and series	Quinn in Newman & Jones (2002)

University and College (moves 1-10)

Location	Reason	Collection size	Moved by whom	Approx. date	Approx. duration
1. Louisiana State University, Chemistry Library	library closing	4,382 boxes of material, including 381 boxes holding 3,681 periodical volumes	University Transportation, augmented by special hires and student staff	Feb-May 2005	4 months
2. Valparaiso University, Indiana	new high-density, automated-retrieval facility	59,000 volumes, including periodicals, governement publications, selected reference and archival material	Circulation staff	2004, starting in early June	5 weeks
3. Bossier Parish (LA) Community College	new facility on new campus	35,000 items	library faculty and staff; college's movers	December 2004	3 days
4. University of Wisconsin-Madison	new facility	n/a	"standard moving company"	May-June 2004	4 weeks
5. Loyola University (New Orleans) music branch library	closing branch library; moving collection to main campus library	n/a	bound periodicals: library staff and students; rest of collection: professional movers	Nov-Dec 2003	bound periodicals: 2 weeks; rest of collection: 4 days
6. University of Arkansas, Fayetteville, Physics & Chemistry Library	renovation	36,000 volumes	staff	(Spring 2003?)	n/a
7. Dalton (GA) State College	expansion	114,000 volumes	library staff packed; outside laborers moved; specialist company moved fully loaded stacks	Fall 2001, April 2002	2 weeks, twice
8. University of Louisville (KY)	expansion into newly installed shelving	journals	n/a	2001	n/a
9. Brooklyn College (NY)	new library	more than 1.2 million volumes	n/a	July 23-October 27, 1999	3 months
10. Loyola University (New Orleans)	new building	235,000 circulating books; 60,000 bound periodicals; 100,000 government documents; 11,000 volumes in special collections; 3,000 reference volumes	professional movers (but not library movers)	Winter 1999	"seven days a week for almost a month"

APPENDIX B: TWO HUNDRED MOVES REPORTED IN THE LITERATURE

University and College (moves 1-10, continued)

Location	Type of container	Transport method	Special problems	Citation
1. Louisiana State University, Chemistry Library	boxes	n/a	changing location information; relabeling periodical volumes; providing access during move	Armstrong (2005)
2. Valparaiso University, Indiana	automated retrieval system bins	n/a	changing location information in library system; inventory problem resolution; new service model	Amrhein & Resetar (2004)
3. Bossier Parish (LA) Community College	n/a	n/a		Bryan & Brantley (2006)
4. University of Wisconsin-Madison	book carts	n/a	merging three health sciences libraries; correcting cataloging problems; reclassing and relabeling; binding/boxing fragile items	Hitchcock et al (2005)
5. Loyola University (New Orleans) music branch library	n/a	n/a	integrating periodicals in existing collection; risk of shelving instability	Gibson et al (2006)
6. University of Arkansas, Fayetteville , Physics & Chemistry Library	book carts	covered truck	temporary merger of two libraries; splitting collections based on usage	Johnson et al (2004)
7. Dalton (GA) State College	boxes	stack mover; method of moving boxes n/a	two separate moves, to accommodate building expansion; moving fully loaded stacks	Bagley (2003)
8. University of Louisville (KY)	n/a	n/a	using a spreadsheet to streamline detailed planning	Brinkman & Whiteside (2002)
9. Brooklyn College (NY)	n/a	n/a	elevator and shelving problems delayed completion by two months; paging material from temporary facilities during construction	Deutch (2001)
10. Loyola University (New Orleans)			inaccurate measurements; use of movers without substantial library experience; no elevators in old building; tangles in 50' 'magic string' to measure collections	Snow (2004)

University and College (moves 11-24)

Location	Reason	Collection size	Moved by whom	Approx. date	Approx. duration
11. Middlebury College (VT) map collection	new building	75,000 maps	professional library movers	August 1999	n/a
12. University of Colorado, Boulder	relieve overcrowding	325,000 volumes moved	n/a	March 1998 - December 1999	n/a
13. University of Kentucky	new building	2.1 million books	professional library movers	Summer 1998	
14. University of British Columbia	new building	500,000 volumes of 840,000 collection moved	n/a	December 1996	"over the holiday break"
15. University of Rhode Island College of Continuing Education	new building	50,000 volumes	Prison Industries of Rhode Island	January 1996	"twice as long as planned"
16. University of Kansas Map Library	new space	254 map cases	professional library movers	summer 1995	n/a
17. Rutgers University, Chemistry Library	integrate chemistry collection into main campus library	15,000 volumes	external contractors	1995	10 days
18. University of Pittsburg at Greensburg	new facility	73,000 volumes	library staff; 30 student hires, plus volunteers	1995	3 days
19. Florida Christian College Library	new building	30,000 volumes	library staff + 55 students, faculty, and administrators	(1995?)	n/a
20. Ohio State University, Biological Sciences and Pharmacy Libraries	merger	2600+ serial titles from four different buildings; 135,000 monographs, including 25,000 in book depository	staff; movers	August 1994	n/a
21. Moffitt Library, U. California, Berkeley	seismic strengthening	40,000 volumes 1,200 videos	n/a	1992	n/a
22. Pennsylvania State University	relieve overcrowding	47,000 brittle items	shrink-wrapped by 4 part-time staff; moved by professional movers	Fall 1991: shrink-wrapping	393 hours to shrink-wrap 47,000 in 8,341 packages
23. University of Arkansas, Fayetteville	remote storage	30,000 volumes 4,000 lin. ft. Special Coll.	prof. movers	1991	about 7 days
24. Sibley Music Library; University of new facility Rochester (NY)		500,000 items, including 50,000 fragile items	n/a	Christmas break 1988/89	

Location	Type of container	Transport method	Special problems	Citation
11. Middlebury College (VT) map collection	moved in old map cases	vans	new map cases; drawer-by-drawer labeling	S. Tucker (2000)
12. University of Colorado, Boulder	n/a	n/a	selection	Austin & Seaman (2002)
13. University of Kentucky	special book trucks		moving to compact shelving; resequencing 600,000 books reclassed from Dewey to LC	Bruns (1999)
14. University of British Columbia	n/a	n/a	new building held only 60% of collections; intensive selection undertaken; marking items to move; changing records	Godolphin (2001)
15. University of Rhode Island College of Continuing Education	book trucks; boxes (half the journal collection)	vans	short notice; snowstorm during scheduled move dates; staff illness; stacks set up without library oversight, creating code compliance issue; contractor coordination	Burkhardt (1998)
16. University of Kansas Map Library	maps moved in their cases	n/a	moving fully loaded map cases	Dienes (1995)
17. Rutgers University, Chemistry Library	n/a	n/a	user group representation on planning team; moving shelving; collection assessment before move; more books on shelf than shown in official holdings	Calderhead (1996)
18. University of Pittsburg at Greensburg	boxes, placed in hampers	trucks	balancing move staff in old and new buildings	Duck (2000)
19. Florida Christian College Library	trays	n/a	moving shelving and books	Stark (1995)
20. Ohio State University, Biological Sciences and Pharmacy Libraries	n/a	n/a	moving shelving and books; integrating journal collections; moving from remote depository; moving from compact shelving	Leach (1997)
21. Moffitt Library, U. California, Berkeley	extra-large booktrucks	n/a	dust and dirt	Meltzer (1993)
22. Pennsylvania State University	n/a	moving vans	smoke fumes from burning film found non-toxic but annoying; set off smoke detectors	Kellerman (1993)
23. University of Arkansas, Fayetteville	n/a	n/a		Mosby (1992)
24. Sibley Music Library; University of book carts	n/a	n/a	using shrink wrap to move unbound items, scrap books, 19th century quarter-leather items with red rot; unbound sheet music; catalog drawers	Hansen & Honea (1990)
24. Harding University, Searcy, Arkansas	boxes, 12" x 12" x 16"	forklift to move palletized groups of boxes	move to temporary location storage of 2/3 of collection	Spurrier (1990)

University and College (moves 25-40)

Location	Reason	Collection size	Moved by whom	Approx. date	Approx. duration
25. Harding University, Searcy, Arkansas	building renovation & expansion	12,000 boxes of books	library and university staff; student helpers	1989-1990	n/a
26. University of Louisville (KY)	library expansion; consolidation of science & engineering journals	journals	n/a	1989	n/a
27. Brenau College, Georgia	new facility	100,000 items	staff and volunteers;packing prof. movers: transportation	Aug.-Oct. 1988	n/a
28. Governors State University (IL)	recarpeting & stack respacing	serials, documents, A&I: 2,100 serial titles education collection	prof. movers	Spring 1988 Dec. 1988	n/a n/a
29. Texas A&M	relieve overcrowding; within-building storage	53,000 volumes	student assistants; staff	Spring 1988	15 days
30. Purdue University dept. library	new facility	20,000 volumes 15,000 microforms 180,000 maps	5 library staff: packing 6 Physical Plant staff: transport	Summer 1988	packing & moving: under 1 week storage: 10 weeks unpacking: 4 days map collection integration: 2 weeks
31. Georgia State U., Atlanta	expansion	1.5 million items	134 library staff	12/87 - 1/88	under 3 weeks
32. University of South Africa, Pretoria	new facility	100,000 volumes	2 teams of 43 each	late 1987	3-4 weeks
33. U. of Florida science library	new facility	n/a	prof. movers	February 1987	2 weeks
34. Ohio State University	relieve overcrowding; off-site storage	10,000 volumes	student assistants	1987	3 weeks; 450 student hours
35. U. Tennessee, Knoxville	new facility	1,500,000 volumes	200+ library, physical plant staff	1987	38 workdays
36. University of Miami	reclassification of abstract & index coll.	7,000 volumes	staff: 2 2-man crews 2 supervisors	June 1986	less than 4 days
37. University of North Carolina	new facility	1.7 million volumes 1.8 million documents 85,000 reels microfilm	prof. movers	1983	6-8 weeks (est.)
38. Niagara County (NY) Community College	respacing collection	1,120 shelves of material	student assistants	summer 198(3?)	42 hours' shifting
39. University of Louisville (KY)	merger of two science & engineering branches	all journals prior to 1965	n/a	1983	20+ hours' planning
40. Crerar Library, U. of Chicago	merger, new facility	770,000 vols. fr. Crerar 400,000 vols. fr. U. Chicago	prof. movers	1982-1984	n/a

334

University and College (moves 25–40, continued)

Location	Approx. duration	Type of container	Transport method	Special problems	Citation
25. Harding University, Searcy, Arkansas		boxes, 12" x 12" x 16"	forklift to move palletized groups of boxes	move to temporary location storage of 2/3 of collection	Spurrier (1990)
26. University of Louisville (KY)	n/a	n/a	n/a	precise planning for 8 years' growth resulted in accommodating growth for 10 years without shifting	Brinkman & Whiteside (2002)
27. Brenau College, Georgia	n/a	boxes	trucks		Bridges (1990)
28. Governors State University (IL)	n/a n/a	large cardboard boxes, dollies	moving truck	stack reassembly	Conant & Diodato (1990)
29. Texas A&M	15 days	booktrucks	within building		Gyeszly et al (1990)
30. Purdue University dept. library	packing & moving: under 1 week storage: 10 weeks unpacking: 4 days map collection integration: 2 weeks	2,000 boxes banded onto pallets in 3 layers of 9 boxes/layer	trucks	shelving setup delays storage of boxes	Laffoon et al (1991)
31. Georgia State U., Atlanta	under 3 weeks	carts	within building	26 planning scenarios	Cravey & Cravey (1991) Moreland et al. (1993)
32. University of South Africa, Pretoria	3-4 weeks	plastic containers with lids: "cheptainers"	4 10-ton trucks	temporary building access via roller bridges temporary slide constructed in stairwell to augment elevator capacity	DeJager & Malan (1989)
33. U. of Florida science library	2 weeks	n/a	n/a	integration of multiple collections	Battiste et al. (1989)
34. Ohio State University	3 weeks: 450 student hours	bookcarts; boxes	compact pickup truck	book carts too heavy to lift onto truck bed	Seaman & DeGeorge (1992)
35. U. Tennessee, Knoxville	38 workdays	bookcarts	van	collection integration two work shifts	Bayne (1990)
36. University of Miami	less than 4 days	n/a	n/a	rearrangement of occupied space	Seiler & Robar (1987)
37. University of North Carolina	6-8 weeks (est.)	n/a	n/a		"University..." (1983)
38. Niagara County (NY) Community College	42 hours' shifting 20+ hours' planning	n/a	within building		Faller (1984)
39. University of Louisville (KY)	n/a	n/a	n/a	planning "didn't consider differences in volume widths or the number of bound volumes per year... nor was space reserved for new titles"	Brinkman & Whiteside (2002)
40. Crerar Library, U. of Chicago	n/a	n/a	n/a	merger of two institutions	Swanson (1986)

University and College (moves 41-65)

Location	Reason	Collection size	Moved by whom	Approx. date	Approx. duration
41. (British) City University Business School	new facility	n/a	prof. movers, staff	1982	1 1/2 days
42. Sheridan College (WV)	new facility	75,000 volumes	library and maintenance personnel	1982(?)	3 weeks
43. Purdue University General Library	collection reorganization	250,000 monographs	experienced shelvers	May/June (1982?)	less than a month
44. U. Oklahoma	new addition	91,000 lin. ft.	staff, 65 student assistants; 15,850 hours' labor for entire project	summer 1982	n/a
45. Tasmanian College of Advanced Education	closure	23,000 titles in Phase I	n/a	1981	n/a
46. California State, Bakersfield	recarpeting	n/a	n/a	1980's	n/a
47. Virginia Polytech Institute and State University	off-site storage	160,000 volumes	2 crews of student assistants	late 1970's	16 working days
48. U. Massachusetts/Amherst	unsafe building conditions	150,000 monographs 75,000 periodical volumes	2 movers with a closed van	Fall 1979	about 2 months
49. Smith College Northampton, MA	new addition	682,810 volumes	student assistants	1978	1,291.5 man-hours
50. U. California, Santa Cruz	building addition	400,000 volumes moved	staff	Fall 1976	n/a
51. Illinois State University Library	new facility	700,000 volumes	prof. movers, library staff	1976	4 50-hour weeks
52. Ahmadu Bello University Zaria, Nigeria	new facility	150,000 volumes 3,000 periodicals	library and university staff	1976	transport: 2 weeks total: 6 weeks
53. Cornell Fine Arts Library	expansion	n/a	n/a	197?(?)	n/a
54. Central Washington State College Library map library	new facility	40,000+ maps in 24 5-drawer cases	student hires and library staff	summer 1975	1 1/2 days
55. Didsbury College of Education (UK)	new facility	66,000 books	prof. movers and staff	August 1973	3 1/2 days
56. Maui Community College	new facility	22,000 volumes	31 student volunteers, 5 student assts, staff, 3 drivers	1971(?)	12 hours
57. U. Chicago, Regenstein	new facility	1,800,000 volumes	prof. movers	1970	approx. 2 months
58. Tulane University	new building	750,000 volumes	75 library staff 100 student assistants scores of prof. movers	July-August 1968	56 days
59. University of Sydney (Australia)	new facility	500,000 volumes	students and library staff	12/66 - 1/67	approx. 50 days
60. Dutchess Community College Poughkeepsie, NY	new facility	21,000 volumes	92 student volunteers library staff	Spring 1966(?)	4 hours
61. University of Otago (New Zealand)	new facility	180,000 volumes 459 feet oversize newspapers 600 feet archives 30 boxes misc.	prof. movers, student hires, and library staff	Feb.-March 1965	14 1/2 days
62. Utah State University Library	new facility	400,000 volumes	staff, students	12/26/63 - 1/3/64	n/a
63. Auburn University	new facility	320,000 bound volumes	staff, students	1962-1963	n/a
64. St. Louis University	new facility	n/a	library staff, temporary staff	May 1959	n/a
65. Mississippi College	new facility	60,000 books	students, staff	1959	8 days

336

University and College (moves 41-65, continued)

Location	Type of container	Transport method	Special problems	Citation
41. (British) City University Business School	200 rented Giltspur Bullen crates	trucks	jumbling of packed crates	Baldwin (1982)
42. Sheridan College (WY)	rolling carts	n/a		Ryan (1982)
43. Purdue University General Library	booktrucks	within building	rearrangement of occupied area	Pinzelik (1983)
44. U. Oklahoma	boxes, booktrucks	within building	staff stress	Weaver-Meyers & Wasowski (1984)
45. Tasmanian College of Advanced Education	trolleys (booktrucks)	vans		Waters (1981)
46. California State, Bakersfield	cartons, 18" x 12" x 12", piled four high on handtrucks	within building	moving shelving without disassembly	Segesta (1986)
47. Virginia Polytech Institute and State University	booktrucks	moving van	maintaining access	Hubbard (1979)
48. U. Massachusetts/Amherst	n/a	n/a	safety issues	"Fast Response..." (1980)
49. Smith College Northampton, MA	booktrucks	within building		Kurkul (1983)
50. U. California, Santa Cruz	n/a	n/a		"UCSC..." (1977)
51. Illinois State University Library	120 custom-made metal bookcarts	van	bookcart breakdown collection integration shelving overruns	Townsend (1977)
52. Ahmadu Bello University Zaria, Nigeria	200 boxes, each 42" x 18" x 12"	2 6-ton trucks	inadequate number boxes truck breakdowns; rain and mud staff morale	Ifidon (1979)
53. Cornell Fine Arts Library	n/a	n/a	ongoing construction	Holiday (1976)
54. Central Washington State College Library map library	map drawers, loaded on dollies	truck		Langgaard, "Moving a Map Library..."
55. Didsbury College of Education (UK)	book trollies	small vans		Shercliff (1974)
56. Maui Community College	boxes	trucks		Hoefler (1971)
57. U. Chicago, Regenstein	cartons	vans	collection integration	Moran (1972)
58. Tulane University	booktrucks		use of wooden ramp	Gribben (1969)
59. University of Sydney (Australia)	booktrucks with safety straps	library van	occupancy delay, mid-move	Slight (1967)
60. Dutchess Community College Poughkeepsie, NY	bulk of materials: canvas bags remainder: liquor cartons	book brigade booktrucks		Feret (1967)
61. University of Otago (New Zealand)	cardboard cartons, human chain	printers' trollies, trucks, chutes		Hlavac (1965)
62. Utah State University Library	boxes and booktrucks	trucks	creation of four subject divisions	Chappell (1964)
63. Auburn University	cartons	trucks	lack of trucks after initial period	Szilassy (1964)
64. St. Louis University	4,000 beer cases	trucks	construction high-lift at old facility	Vollmar (1960)
65. Mississippi College	book troughs (3' long), cartons, hand-carrying	flat-bed trucks	rain	Landrum (1959)

337

University and College (moves 66-79)

Location	Reason	Collection size	Moved by whom	Approx. date	Approx. duration
41. (British) City University Business School	new facility	n/a	prof. movers, staff	1982	1 1/2 days
42. Sheridan College (WY)	new facility	75,000 volumes	library and maintenance personnel	198(2?)	3 weeks
43. Purdue University General Library	collection reorganization	250,000 monographs	experienced shelvers	May/June (1982?)	less than a month
44. U. Oklahoma	new addition	91,000 lin. ft.	staff, 65 student assistants; 15,850 hours' labor for entire project	summer 1982	n/a
45. Tasmanian College of Advanced Education	closure	23,000 titles in Phase I	n/a	1981	n/a
46. California State, Bakersfield	recarpeting	n/a	n/a	1980's	n/a
66. U. of Illinois	new addition	1,500,000 volumes	50 students @ 12-20 hrs/week 3 supervisors, half-time bookstack librarian	1958/59	4 months
67. USAF Academy	temporary, new facilities	65,000-70,000 items	staff: packing commercial movers: transport	1958-1959 in four phases	n/a
68. Pine Manor College Wellesley, MA	new facility	11,000 books	students: books prof. movers: reference, periodicals, furniture and equipment	March 1957	4 hours: books
69. U. of Idaho, Moscow	new facility	160,000 bound volumes 540,000 documents 62,000 maps	staff, temporary labor	Aug.-Oct. 195(6?)	3 weeks
70. University of Rochester	college merger	450,000 volumes	student and permanent staff	1954-55	shifting: 6 months move & integration: 1 month
71. Midland College Freemont, NE	new facility	27,000 books	260 students, plus library staff, faculty	Feb. 1954	5 hours
72. Wisconsin State College at Whitewater	new facility	50,000 books 10,000 pamphlets	2 librarians, 6 maintenance men students	Feb. (1954?)	5 days
73. Idaho State College	new facility	50,000 books 250,000 documents	61 library and buildings and grounds staff	April 1954	24 hours: move
74. College of Puget Sound Seattle	new facility	75,000 books half a million magazines and unbound documents	students	April 1954	24 hours: reshelving move: one day cleanup; approx. 2 weeks
75. Russell Sage College Troy, NY	new facility	55,000 volumes	500 students	May 1953	2 days: bulk of move 1 week: last 10%
76. Hillsdale College, Michigan	new facility	27,000 books 7,000 periodical volumes	students	May 1951	8 hours
77. Hollins College, FL	new facility	81,000 volumes	n/a (1,790 man-hours)	1951	26 working days
78. Kenka College Kenka Park, NY	new facility	38,000 books	300 college students	1951	8 hours
79. Mississippi State College	new facility	n/a	Utilities Dept. staff	Summer 195(0?)	4 weeks

University and College (moves 66-79, continued)

Location	Approx. duration	Type of container	Transport method	Special problems	Citation
41. (British) City University Business School	1 1/2 days	200 rented Gitspur Bullen crates	trucks	jumbling of packed crates	Baldwin (1982)
42. Sheridan College (WY)	3 weeks	rolling carts	n/a		Ryan (1982)
43. Purdue University General Library	less than a month	booktrucks	within building	rearrangement of occupied area	Pinzelik (1983)
44. U. Oklahoma	n/a	boxes, booktrucks	within building	staff stress	Weaver-Meyers & Wasowski (1984)
45. Tasmanian College of Advanced Education	n/a	trolleys (booktrucks)	vans		Waters (1981)
46. California State, Bakersfield	n/a	cartons, 18" x 12" x 12",	within building	moving shelving without disassembly	Segesta (1986)
66. U. of Illinois	4 months	n/a	within building		Hammer (1960)
67. USAF Academy	n/a	cardboard library tote boxes: 18" x 12" x 12 1/2"	moving vans	phased move	Fagan (1959)
68. Pine Manor College Wellesley, MA	4 hours: books	n/a	book brigade		Paragamian (1959)
69. U. of Idaho, Moscow	3 weeks	booktrucks	trucks	delay in stack installation	Zimmerman (1957, 1958)
70. University of Rochester	shifting: 6 months move & integration: 1 month	wooden boxes and cardboard cartons	trucks	collection integration delay in stack installation	"Moving 450,000..." (1956)
71. Midland College Freemont, NE	5 hours	n/a	book brigade		Stickney & Meinhold (1955)
72. Wisconsin State College at Whitewater	5 days	n/a	book brigade		Knilans (1954)
73. Idaho State College	24 hours: move 24 hours: reshelving	cardboard boxes (beer cartons, shelving cartons)	trucks	wooden chutes	Oboler (1954)
74. College of Puget Sound Seattle	move: one day cleanup; approx. 2 weeks	corrugated tomato boxes on bookcarts	bookcarts	steep ramp shelving mix-ups rambunctious students	Bauer (1954)
75. Russell Sage College Troy, NY	2 days: bulk of move 1 week: last 10%	n/a	book brigade	rain	Long & Meyer (1954)
76. Hillsdale College, Michigan	8 hours	n/a	book brigade	no elevator in old facility minor misshelvings	Fitch (1951)
77. Hollins College, FL	26 working days	orange crates	truck		Kruse (1951)
78. Keuka College Keuka Park, NY	8 hours		book brigade		Wilkins (1951)
79. Mississippi State College	4 weeks	150 boxes, 16" x 24" x 12"	truck		Peebles (1951)

University and College (moves 80-89)

Location	Reason	Collection size	Moved by whom	Approx. date	Approx. duration
80. California State Polytechnic College, San Luis Obispo	new facility	17,000 volumes	library staff, student hires	Summer 19(49?)	five days
81. U. Washington, Seattle	building addition	400,000 volumes	10 assistants	(1949?)	n/a
82. Firestone Library, Princeton	new facility	n/a	n/a	1948	about 2 months
83. Manhattanville College (NY)	new facility	50,000 volumes	students	194(2?)	less than 4 days
84. Pennsylvania State	new facility	n/a	grounds staff and student assistants	Summer 1940	3 weeks
85. Brown University	branch library consolidation	45,000 volumes	students	Sept. 1938	
	clear stack	35,000 volumes	janitors	Dec. 1938	
	renovations	470,000 volumes	students	Summer 1939	
	branch library consolidation	30,000 volumes	students	Summer 1940	
	branch library moves	35,000 volumes	students	Summer 1940	
86. Denison University Granville, OH	new facility	96,000	students	1938	n/a
87. St. Bonaventure College (NY)	new facility	35,000 volumes	students, seminarians	Spring 1938 (?)	one day
88. Cambridge University	new facility	n/a	staff: packing, unpacking professional movers: transport	Summer 1934	8 weeks
89. Yale University	new facility	n/a	student hires and library staff	July, Sept. 19(29?)	6 weeks

APPENDIX B: TWO HUNDRED MOVES REPORTED IN THE LITERATURE

University and College (moves 80-89, continued)

Location	Approx. duration	Type of container	Transport method	Special problems	Citation
80. California State Polytechnic College, San Luis Obispo	five days	10,000 corrugated boxes	trucks	modified forklift for second-floor access	Allen (1950)
81. U. Washington, Seattle	n/a	booktrucks	panel truck		Mostar (1950)
82. Firestone Library, Princeton	about 2 months	metal, wood booktrucks with safety straps	booktrucks	coordination with contractors	Lee (1950); "Princeton ..." (1948)
83. Manhattanville College (NY)	less than 4 days	by hand	book brigade		Buck (1943)
84. Pennsylvania State	3 weeks	boxes	trucks		Stokes & Knoll (1941)
85. Brown University		boxes, 3' x 1' x 1'; boxes, 3' x 1' x 1'; boxes, 1' x 1' x 8"; n/a; n/a	human chain, passing boxes; human chain, passing boxes; human chain, passing boxes; truck; no truck		Jesse (1941)
86. Denison University Granville, OH	n/a	wooden boxes	chutes, trucks	use of chutes, moving from multiple locations	Craigie (1938)
87. St. Bonaventure College (NY)	one day	by hand	book brigade	damage to books	Herscher (1938)
88. Cambridge University	8 weeks	boxes	horse-drawn lorries		Ansell (1935)
89. Yale University	6 weeks	1,000 reinforced fiber boxes, loaded on trollies	vans		"How ..." (1930)

341

ANNOTATED REFERENCES

Abbott, Christine. (1990). Using Excel at Aston University Library and Information Services: The application of spreadsheets to library stock management. *Program, 24*(3), 269–79. Detailed description of Excel spreadsheet used to calculate beginning and ending shelving locations for periodical titles, including growth space.

Adams, Cris. (1990). Moving experience. *Library Journal, 115*, 91–92. Planning and implementation of Hobbs (NM) Public Library's move to temporary quarters and back into its renovated facility. Practical tips on packing bound volumes into boxes. Suggestions on spacing collections to allow for growth lack detail, but might work for a very small collection.

Adams, Scott. (1954). Moving on wheels. *DC Libraries, 25*, 5–8. Planning and implementing move of the National Institute of Health Library, using book carts outfitted with safety straps. Detailed comparison of time studies of specific operations conducted in planning stage to actual amount of time actually required for same operations during the move. Detailed discussion of manpower allocations planned and actually needed. Practical advice on specific operational aspects of moving.

343

ANNOTATED REFERENCES

Allardyce, A. (1966). Walkie-talkie in the stacks. *Occasional Newsletter (National Central Library)*, 7, 6–7. Account of the British National Central Library's move of collections from Malet Place to Store Street, using staff, a moving company, and tiered baskets; walkie-talkie used to coordinate integration of collections into a no-growth stack area.

Allen, Emil W. (1955). Major book move: The move. *Library Journal*, 80(19), 2419–22. Management perspective on move described in Jewel Hardkopf's article, "Major book move: The time study."

Allen, Francis S. (1950). This California library found easy moving ways. *Library Journal*, 75, 724–26. News account of moving the California Polytechnic Institute's library to new quarters. Featured use of a modified forklift to remove material from the second floor of a building lacking an elevator.

Alley, Brian (1979). Utility book truck designed for moving library collections. *Library Acquisitions: Theory and Practice*, 3(1), 33–37. Design, construction, and use of a custom book truck for moving library collections. Plans included.

———. (1982). Moving steel stacks with a special dolly. *Library Acquisitions: Practice and Theory*, 6(3), 253–57. Description and plans for building a dolly to move assembled unloaded book stacks. See Segesta 1986 for a refinement to this design.

———. (1983). Discussion of Amodeo's "Helpful hints for moving or shifting collections." *College & Research Libraries News*, 44(6), 182. Further suggestions on design and construction of book trucks suitable for moving collections (as opposed to commercially available book trucks), and a device for moving fully loaded book stacks. References provided to two articles by Alley on these topics (both included in this bibliography).

Ames, Mark. (1973). How to move a library in one easy lesson; or, everything you always wanted to know about moving a library but were afraid to ask. *Michigan Librarian*, 39, 9–10. News account of moving part of a public library collection to a temporary location, using library staff and boxes. Discusses how moved items were selected, and public relations issues.

Ames, Neil. (1988). Details of a library move. *Law Library Lights*, 31(5), 12–13. Tips on moving a law library.

Amodeo, Anthony J. (1983). Helpful hints for moving or shifting collections. *College & Research Library News*, 44(3), 82–83. Useful, practical comments on preservation aspects of move operations, including economic impact of improper handling procedures, marking methods, removing bound volumes from the shelf, loading onto carts, conveying book carts, reshelving. Subsequent comments in *C&RL News*' Letters led Amodeo to modify his recommendation on order of book cart loading (bottom up is more stable than top down).

Amrhein, Rick, and Donna Resetar. (2004). Maximizing library storage with high-tech robotic shelving. *Computers in Libraries, 24*(10), 6–8, 51–56. Description of planning and implementing an ASRS high-density storage facility at Valparaiso University.

Anderson, Marvin Roger, and Emily J. Batista. (1984). Space requirement checklist for basic resources. *Legal Reference Services Quarterly, 4*(1), 65–71. Linear feet (rounded) and numbers of 3-foot shelves needed to house approximately 115 legal resources, including digests and indexes to multivolume sets, advance sheets, and pamphlets. See also similar articles by Blaustein and Matthews (1967); Chrisant (1982); Anderson and Golden (1985); and Golden (1989).

Anderson, Marvin Roger, and Barbara L. Golden. (1985). Space requirement checklist for basic resources update—1985. *Legal Reference Services Quarterly, 5*(4), 101–4. Update of Anderson and Batista's 1984 article. Additions are updated current shelf space requirements and projection of five-year shelving needs. Note that annual requirements are recorded in rounded linear feet.

Anderson, Mary Alice. (2007). Moving a boatload. *Multimedia & Internet@Schools, 14*(1), 31–33. Good practical advice on planning and executing a media center move using staff.

A-Nony-Mouse [Rust, M. E.] (1952). We moved—and how! *Wilson Library Bulletin, 26*, 458–59, 465. Humorous account of moving a library, written from a mouse's perspective.

Ansell, E. (1935). The move of the Cambridge University Library. *Library Association Record, 4th series, 2*, 92–96. Planning and executing a large move. Useful detail on labeling boxes and tracking lorry-loads and boxes of material, as well as using a color and numbering system to direct loads of material to specific entrances and elevators. Dated in description of transport methods (horse-drawn lorries were preferred to motor vans partly because they involved no risk of fire!), but not in describing basic planning issues.

Armstrong, William W. (2005). The closing of the LSU chemistry library. *Issues in Science and Technology Librarianship, 44*(Fall 2005), www.istl.org/o5–fall/article5.html. Describes in detail planning and carrying out the closure of a branch library. Covers collection assessment, OPAC record changes, moving collections in coordination with shelving, and follow-up. Move included relocating collections to a temporary location, and used student labor and in-house facilities/ transportation staff.

Atkins, Stephanie, and Jennifer Hain Teper. (2005). A survey of library practices in planning and managing temporary moves. *Collection Management*, 30(4), 59–79. Substantive article reviews literature on temporary moves and reports results of a survey completed by 82 ARL libraries on the characteristics of temporary relocations, including relocation frequency, number of volumes moved, the type of materials involved, length of relocation, transportation method, methods of storage and access, location selection criteria, and more.

Auld, Lawrence W. S. (1986). Estimating shelving capacity. In *Electronic spreadsheets for libraries*, ed. Lawrence W. S. Auld, 77–100. Oryx Press. Details the preparation and use of three spreadsheets. Shelving Capacity Variables Spreadsheet calculates items per square foot given use of varying shelves per section of shelving. Predicting Shelving Capacity Spreadsheet calculates shelving capacity in items for various stack layouts. Shelving Density by Shelf, Section, Range and Total Spreadsheet uses shelf-by-shelf estimated shelf occupancy combined with a standard books-per-linear-foot figure to calculate the approximate percentage of shelving capacity used, and the current and maximum total number of volumes accommodated. Neglects notion of working capacity.

———. (1993). Estimating shelving capacity. In *Computer Spreadsheets for Library Applications*, 2nd ed., ed. Lawrence W. S. Auld, 113–21. Oryx. Presents CASMS, Computer Assisted Shelf Management System, "adapted from a spreadsheet originally designed by Horman Holmes." Calculates percent of shelf spaced used and remaining; then adjusts this, using current year's acquisitions and items withdrawn. Doesn't take the next logical step of projecting years of growth remaining or number of volumes accommodated, but could be easily adapted to do this.

Austin, Brice, and Scott Seaman. (2002). Temporary remote book storage at the University of Colorado, Boulder Libraries: Facilities planning, materials preparation, selection, and retrieval. *Collection Management*, 27(1), 59–78. Describes planning and implementing a temporary off-site storage facility to hold 325,000 volumes, including criteria for selecting the facility and materials, moving, item retrieval, project cost, and lessons learned.

Babits, Ann, and Kurt Grice. (1987). Microcomputers in shelf space management. *Microcomputers for Information Management, 4*(2), 139–51. Detailed description of method used to calculate growth requirements for periodical titles and assign each title a specific shelving location. Calculations based on measurement of current holdings to the nearest quarter shelf, introducing imprecision. Good discussion of options for allocating growth space. Interesting method described for assigning specific shelf locations to specific titles.

Bagley, Elizabeth L. (2003). Re-building a learning community . . . or what to do when you face a library move. *Georgia Library Quarterly, 40*(1), 4–10. Detailed tips drawn from a move that included use of a stack-mover.

Baldwin, Lesley. (1982). How to move a library. *New Library World, 83,* 57–58. Moving the library for the (British) City University Business School into the Barbican Arts Centre. Useful comments on political/public relations aspect of collection fill ratio choice.

Balmforth, C. K. (1973). Measuring a library: A quantity surveyor's approach. In *The Art of the Librarian,* ed. Alan Jeffreys, 33–45. Newcastle-upon-Tyne: Oriel Press. Using a quantity surveying firm to count and measure a university library's collection, including comments on the expense of this approach and difficulties encountered. Includes comments useful to anyone undertaking a measurement project, on notices made to users before the start of the project, the difficulties of accurately measuring and counting a collection, and the impact of accuracy. Especially useful are the comments on the impact of apparently small percentage errors and apparently small differences in average volume widths in estimating the total extent of a collection.

Banks, J. (1990). Shelf-reading: A pilot study. *Collection Management, 13*(1/2), 39–46. Pilot study found that several incentives had no effect on shelf-reading speed, but did improve morale. Notes 67 percent of participants disliked shelf-reading, but 94 percent agreed it was important.

Banks, Joyce M. (1987). *Guidelines for preventive conservation,* rev. ed. Ottawa: Canadian Government Publishing Centre. The section on handling library materials is of particular interest.

Battiste, Anita L., et al. (1989). The University of Florida's moving experience. *College & Research Library News, 50*(6), 467–71. Consolidating branch staff and collections into a central science library at University of Florida. Describes two methods of proximately integrating collections. Notes that full item-by-item integration took 3 months for staff to complete after conclusion of the move proper.

Bauer, Harry C. (1954). Moving day. *Library Journal, 79,* 2384–86. Moving the College of Puget Sound (Seattle)'s library, using students, book carts, and tomato boxes. Notes problems with using student workers.

Baule, Steven M. (1999). *Facilities planning for school library media & technology centers.* Worthington, OH: Linworth Publishing. Of interest to a move planner: a section on shelving the collection (pp. 14–19), and Chapter 7, "Wrapping Up," which deals primarily with moving.

Baumann, Kari. (2006). Using a transition team to facilitate library building moves. *Colorado Libraries, 32*(1), 13–17. Focus is on organizational change involved in construction and renovation of several facilities in a public library district. Used a rented storage "box" (container) in the parking lot to temporarily house collections, instead of a remote facility.

Bayne, Pauline S. (1988). Moving a 1.5 million-volume library: A study of communication in project management. In *LAMA president's program papers: Communication and the language of leadership* (ERIC Document ED 305 149 microform). Chicago: American Library Association. Paper presented at Library Administration and Management Association's President's Program at the Annual Convention of the American Library Association (New Orleans, LA, July 10, 1988). Excellent analysis of communication in project management, with special reference to managing the move of library collections. Required reading for any library planning a large move.

———. (1990). The "do-it-yourself" move for a 1.5 million-volume library. *College & Research Libraries, 51*(1), 55–67. Excellent, detailed review of factors involved in planning and successfully executing a large, complex move without use of professional movers, illustrated with specifics from the University of Tennessee at Knoxville's 1987 move. Covers staffing allocation, organization, and training, including integration of library and physical plant staff; operational logistics, including balancing sending and receiving teams; collection integration strategy; description of three types of custom-constructed carts used to move books, card catalog units, and equipment; public relations rationale and effect; and a cost analysis. Required reading for anyone planning a large, complex move.

Benamati, Dennis C. (1988a). Moving a small- to medium-sized library: Part I, attention to some basic library operations. *Trends in Law Library Management and Technology, 1*(9), 1–3. Moving a law library: what to do 1–2 years in advance: inventory; weed; review collecting, format, arrangement and classification issues.

———. (1988b). Moving a small- to medium-sized library: Part II, getting the collection organized. *Trends in Law Library Management and Technology, 1(10)*, 3–5. Steps to take in the year before a law library move: identify, measure, and plan the arrangement of the collection.

———. (1988c). Moving a small- to medium-sized library: Part III, getting the collection there. *Trends in Law Library Management and Technology, 2(1)*, 4–6. Technique for integrating a collection dispersed among offices and multiple locations; suggests integrating materials on book carts at the starting location. Strongly advocates use of carts over boxing materials.

———. (1988d). Moving a small- to medium-sized library: Part IV, some final tips. *Trends in Law Library Management and Technology, 2(2)*, 7–8. Hiring assistants for a small do-it-yourself move; lessons learned.

Bendix, Caroline. (2005). *Packing and Moving Library and Archive Collections.* www.bl.uk/npo/pdf/moving.pdf. Well-done, point-by-point recommendations for packing and moving rare and fragile materials, with particular attention to environmental conditions.

Bennett, Margaret Johnson., David T. Buxton, and Ella Capriotti. (1979). Shelf-reading in a large, open-stack library. *Journal of Academic Librarianship, 5(1)*, 4–8. Describes project to determine optimum organization for shelf-reading at Princeton's Firestone Library. Interesting comments on selecting, training, scheduling, and managing student assistants for shelf-reading, and on patterns of misshelving in high- versus low-use collections.

Berry, Sara. (2004). "Get a move on!" or when your firm relocates. *Legal Information Management, 4(3)*, 154–56. Practical tips derived from moving a law firm's library.

Bing, Michelle. (1998). Surviving the library move. *Business Information Alert, 10(7)*, 1–3, 11–12. Summarizes steps in planning and moving into a new library.

Black, William K., and Joyce E. Bahrenfus. (1988). Planning for collection redistribution at the Iowa State University Library. *Iowa Library Quarterly, 25*, 37–48. Factors considered and methods used to plan the layout of collections at the Iowa State University Library. Good itemization of factors to consider in assessing areas where a collection may grow.

ANNOTATED REFERENCES

Blaustein, Albert P., and Matthews, Jessie L. (1967). Space for a periodical collection. *Law Library Journal*, 60(2), 147–61. Lists linear space required to house 501 legal periodicals' backfiles through 1965 at Rutgers–The State University, School of Law, Camden. Notes that measurements are based on local practice. See also similar articles by Chrisant (1982); Anderson and Batista (1984); Anderson and Golden (1985); and Golden (1989).

Boyajian, Barbara. (1986). Creating a new library facility for Ayerst Laboratories Research, Inc. *Science and Technology Libraries*, 7, 3–13. Includes brief description of move of collections from Montreal to Princeton, NJ.

Brawner, Lee B., and Donald K. Beck Jr. (1996). *Determining your public library's future size*. Chicago: American Library Association. Excellent work on the needs assessment process for public library facilities. Of particular interest to move planners is Appendix A, Table A.1: Space Allowances for Library Materials, which offers guidance in estimating the number of items per linear foot and number of items per square foot for a range of print and nonprint materials.

Breckbill, Anita, Paul Orkiszewski, and Alicia Hansen. (2006). *Music library facilities: A bibliography*. Available at musiclibraryassoc.org/association/committees/facilities/co_fac_bibliography.htm (accessed August 15, 2007). Compiled, updated, and annotated by members of the Music Library Association's Facilities Subcommittee; sections include music libraries (2 pages), libraries in general (6 pages), specific issues (accessibility, facilities for a digital age, interior design, preservation and disaster planning, safety, off-site storage, 5 pages).

Bridges, Elinor Folger Vaughan. (1990). Meeting the challenge: Moving the small college library. *Georgia Librarian*, 27, 95–98. Planning and moving collections into the new Trustee Library at Brenau College, using staff and student assistants to pack and unpack collections into boxes, and a professional moving company to transport the boxes.

Bright, Franklyn P. (1991). *Planning for a movable compact shelving system*. Chicago: American Library Association. Guide to the selection and installation of compact shelving. Sections include a description of structural requirements for the building, components, safety features, lighting, layout, and a model request for quotation.

Brinkman, Carol S., and Stephen W. Whiteside. (2002). Planning and space calculations needed to shift a journal collection. *Kentucky Libraries*, 66(1), 12–17. Reports on different methods used for three journal collection shifts in 1983, 1989, and 2001 at University of Louisville; emphasizes the value of precise advance planning.

Broaddus, Billie, and Alice Hurlebaus. (1981). Planning and implementing a major journal shift in a health sciences library. *Bulletin of the Medical Library Association*, 69(4), 395–96. Detailed description of a method for allocating growth space for journal titles, using estimates of current and future growth requirements rather than exact measurements.

Brogan, Linda L., and Carolyn E. Lipscomb. (1982). Moving the collections of an academic health sciences library. *Bulletin of the Medical Library Association*, 70(4), 374–79. Substantive discussion of University of North Carolina at Chapel Hill's Health Sciences Library's relocation of its collections to new stack floors. Detailed discussion of collection layout planning, including excellent spreadsheet methodology for planning journal space requirements and layout, taking into account ceased and on order titles. Good discussion of move operations, including use of checkpoints for making adjustments during collection reshelving.

Bruns, Adam. (1999). Moving day: An exercise in mind and matter. *American Libraries*, 30(4), 48–50. News report of University of Kentucky move of 2.1 million books to a new building, including relabeling and rearranging from Dewey to LC.

Bryan, Ginger, and Brenda Brantley. (2006). Bossier Parish Community College Library. *Louisiana Libraries*, 68(3), 49–51. News report on new library building, including brief mention of moving 35,000 collection items in three days.

Bryant, Darcel A. (2004). Louis Stokes Health Science Library: The Howard University move experience [electronic version]. *Journal of the Medical Library Association*, 92(2), 251–56. Available at pubmedcentral. nih.gov/articlerender.fcgi?artid=385307 (accessed July 7, 2007). Detailed account of planning and moving 169,000 books, including descriptions of crew size and roles, correcting fill rate problems, dealing with visitors, and a sample checklist for moving a library.

Buck, Gertrude. (1943). The Brady Memorial Library of Manhattanville College of the Sacred Heart. *Catholic Library World*, 14(8, pt. 2), 264–69, 277. News account of the new facility of Manhattanville College and using a bucket brigade to move into it.

Bugher, Kathryn M. (2006, August 28). Design Considerations for School Library Media Centers. Available at dpi.state.wi.us/imt/desgnlmc.html (accessed August 13, 2007). Includes planning calculations for shelving picture/thin, standard sized, and reference books, and displayed periodicals.

Burke, M. Nancy. (1973). Get ready! Get set! Go! Gateway's Racine LRC finds a home. *Wisconsin Library Bulletin, 69*(3), 153–54. News account of LRC move. Includes some detail on calculating number of boxes required to move a collection and on labeling and tracking boxes of materials.

Burkhardt, Joanna M. (1998). Do's and don'ts for moving a small academic library. *College & Research Libraries News, 49*(7), 499–503. Practical tips, based on the 1996 move of a 50,000-volume academic library using nonlibrary movers, including visiting the site while its under construction; planning the move when good weather is likely; staring early; allowing a flexible time frame; hiring movers with library experience and working closely with them; measuring and marking shelving before the move; and making communication a priority.

Calderhead, Veronica. (1996). An operations management approach to a chemistry library relocation: Measure often, move once. *Science & Technology Libraries, 16*(1), 61–80. Focuses on the rationale, planning, and relocation of a branch library collection to the main library. Good practical observations on shelving unit variations, collection measurement, use of uniform versus subject-specific growth rates, the value of conducting an inventory before planning the new collection layout, and the importance of (and time required to conduct) measurements and inventory.

Callinan, Ellen M. (1988). Crowell & Moring on the move. *Law Library Lights, 31*(5), 9–11. A law firm relocates. Good tips on maintaining morale and using T-shirts for identification.

Carlson, Barbara A. (1987). Using Lotus 1–2–3 to shift and maintain a serials collection. *Serials Librarian, 13*(4), 39–58. Detailed account of planning a serials collection shift using a spreadsheet. Good data collection form for shelf space inventory. Reasons detailed for using actual measurements rather than estimates in projecting serial space requirements.

Cash, Derek. (2001). Moving a library collection. *Public Library Quarterly, 20*(4), 17–28. Comparison of the 2000/2001 move of the Fort Smith Public Library, with advice on key points offered in six monographs on moving (including the first edition of *Moving Library Collections*); comments on difficulties with moving into an unfinished building, interbuilding communications, and shelf measurements.

ANNOTATED REFERENCES

Caywood, Carolyn. (1992). How to hire library shelvers. *School Library Journal*, 38(7), 35. Practical tips on interviewing and hiring library shelvers. Relevant to the selection of move workers.

Chappell, D. LaMont. (1964). Operation move. *Utah Libraries*, 7, 7–8, 18–19. Brief account of moving 400,000 volumes to the new Utah State University Library.

Chappell, Shirien. (2006, September 20). Moving library collections: Planning shifts of library collections. Available at libweb. uoregon.edu/acs_svc/shift/ (accessed July 7, 2007). This is a terrific Web site, full of practical how-tos and inspiration. Particularly notable are a detailed explanation, with photos, of how to measure collections via the string method; a description of how to do a paper move and why it's essential to do it; how to calculate the time required based on a test run; and using a "no-fault" approach to maintain morale.

Chepesiuk, Ron. (1991). An anatomy of a move: The Clemson University Library special collections. *Wilson Library Bulletin*, 65, 32–35, 155. Account of Clemson University Special Collections' move into new facility, including tight time deadlines imposed by a high-profile dedication attended by Vice President Dan Quayle. Negative impact of using an interior designer not familiar with library functions and shelving, impact of shelving installation delays, and other problems are discussed.

Chrisant, Rosemarie. (1982). Growth analysis of the major supplemented law books in a county law library. *Law Library Journal*, 75, 536–39. List of annual shelf space requirements for major sets supplemented or expanded by bound volumes or advance sheets in the Akron Law Library Association Law Library between October 1980 and October 1981. Calculations also provided for projected 5-year growth requirements, including a 10 percent allowance for increases in volume size. Se also similar articles by Blaustein and Matthews 1967; Anderson and Batista (1984); Anderson and Golden (1985); and Golden (1989).

Cliff, Barbara, and Randa Strom. (1995). A moving story with a mathematical twist. *School Librarian's Workshop*, 16, 7–8. Austin High School library's move to a newly renovated media center, using students to calculate the time required and to staff a book brigade. Calculations are based on average books/shelf, rather than total linear feet of materials in the collection, but otherwise a useful discussion of the methodology. Includes brief but practical discussion of issues in managing a student book brigade.

ANNOTATED REFERENCES

Clifton, A. (1971). Moving the JPL's serials and newspaper collection into a new stack. *South African Libraries, 39*(1), 56–59. Planning and executing move of the Johannesburg Public Library's serials and newspaper collections into a stack addition.

Conant, Barbara M., and Louise W. Diodato. (1990). Moving library collections: The Governors State University experience. *Collection Management, 12*(3/4), 135–43. Moving the serials and documents collection and the Education and Materials Center Library at Governors State University Library. Detailed discussion of method used to allocate growth space and to label expansion shelves.

Conversion factors derived from a count of the National Library's monograph collection. (1981). *National Library News, 13,* 12–14. Report of a study at the National Library of Canada to determine the average number of volumes per linear foot. Very good description of methodology used, factors affecting the outcome, and results. Reference to other studies.

Cooper, Michael D., and John Wolthausen. (1977). Misplacement of books on library shelves: A mathematical model. *Library Quarterly, 47*(1), 43–57. Study of misshelving; intended to determine the optimal interval for shelf-reading. Tangential findings included are that books are more likely to be misshelved on higher shelves than on lower shelves, within the same shelf than further away, and to the left of the proper location than to the right.

Craigie, Annie L. (1938). Moving day. *Library Journal, 63,* 388–89. Report of move in progress at Denison University, using student labor, specially constructed wooden boxes, and a chute to move boxes from upper stories of buildings.

Crampon, Jean E. (1994). Moving to storage: Balancing technical and public services needs. In *Preserving the past, looking to the future.* Proceedings of the 19th Annual Conference of the International Association of Aquatic and Marine Science Libraries and Information Centers. Reviews key questions to ask in moving materials to storage and uses them to review two collection moves and two moves to storage. Good practical observations.

Cravey, Pamela J., and G. Randall Cravey. (1991). Use of computer modeling to redistribute a library's collection. *Technical Services Quarterly, 8*(3), 25–33. Using computer modeling to examine collection layout options. Brief discussion of using library staff to execute a move.

Cronenwett, Philip N. (1999). Notes from the special collections: Moving a library [electronic version]. *Dartmouth College Library Bulletin*, 39. Available at www.dartmouth.edu/~library/Library_Bulletin/Apr1999/Cronenwett.html (accessed July 7, 2007). Description of planning and executing the well-done move of Dartmouth's large special collections library in 1998. Emphasizes security measures and collaboration with specialist library moves.

Cunningham, Everett V. (1988). How to survive moving a bookstore. *AB Bookman's Weekly*, *81*, 2194–97. Focuses on when to relocate a bookstore, with practical comments on packing and moving books.

Daehn, Ralph M. (1982a). The measurement and projection of shelf space. *Collection Management*, *4*(4), 25–39. Very useful, insightful, and detailed comments on measuring and projecting shelf space requirements. Topics addressed include achieving acceptable accuracy, timing, assessing nonprint materials' extent and stack capacity, allowing for materials not on the shelf (in circulation, at bindery) when the collection is measured, allowing for new acquisitions, and the development and use of holdings conversions factors.

————. (1982b). *Space for growth: The measurement and projection of shelf space at the University of Guelph Library*. Guelph: University of Guelph Library. Detailed report on the procedures, rationale, and results of a shelf space survey done at University of Guelph in 1981.

Dahlgren, Anders C., and Erla P. Heyns. (1995). *Planning library buildings: A select bibliography*. Chicago: American Library Association; Library Administration and Management Association. Pages 41 and 42 list resources on moving.

De Jager, Pieter J., and Dawie Malan. (1989). Unisa Library move in retrospect. *South African Journal of Information Science*, *57*(2), 115–24. Account of the planning and implementation of an academic library move. Detailed discussion of logistical planning, including formation of a move committee, selection of a moving company, selection of containers ("cheptainers," rented plastic box containers), measuring collections, labeling materials being moved and their destinations, moving furniture and equipment, move team sizes and responsibilities, alternate vertical transport, and building egress paths. Appendix 1 is "Points agreed upon with contractor re: library move." Methodology for allocation of growth space based on imprecise "increments."

Deutch, Miriam. (2001). Paging a library collection: The Brooklyn College Library experience. *Collection Building*, *20*(1), 25–31. Detailed descriptions of the rationale and method for retrieving books from closed storage during a renovation project.

Dienes, Jennie. (1995). Moving the University of Kansas map library. *Information Bulletin (Western Association of Map Libraries), 27(1),* 16–31. Brief article plus detailed photo essay showing method for moving a large collection of map cases.

Dimenstein, Catherine. (2004). Executing a library move. *Information Outlook, 8(1),* 37–38, 41–42. Good practical advice, including consideration of staging space, pre-move weeding, packing cartons, coordinating move routes, public access to the building, ergonomics; based on experience moving corporate libraries.

Don't return books, says moving library director. (1976). *American Libraries, 7(9),* 563. Brief news report of Bettendorf, IA Public Library's request that patrons check out books from old facility and return them to new, reducing the total to be moved by some 20,000 volumes (of a total of 65,000–70,000).

Ducas, Ada M. (1985). The planning, implementation and moving of a journal collection in a hospital library. *Argus, 14(3),* 75–79. Good, detailed, and practical account of planning and executing the move of a journal collection, including pre-move collection evaluation. Useful suggestions for calculating required space for each title and marking starting points for shelving title.

Duck, Patricia M. (2000). "Move" is not a four-letter word. *College & Undergraduate Libraries, 7(1),* 25–32. Good tips for a do-it-yourself move, based on the 1995 three-day move of 73,000 volumes to a new academic library, with an unfavorable move date driven by donors' availability for building dedication.

Duckworth, Alan. (1976). On the move. *New Library World, 77,* 9–10. Humorous, personality-focused account of moving a library into a renovated department store.

Ellis, Judith Compton. (1988). Planning and executing a major bookshift/move using an electronic spreadsheet. *College & Research Libraries News, 49(5),* 282–87. Very useful comments on planning and executing a collection move. Detailed discussion of a spreadsheet used to calculate sections of shelving and moving time required per class, and using this information in move planning and management. Practical suggestions for planning staff and equipment and maintaining staff morale during move operations. Very useful suggestions on developing a convenient collection ribbon.

ANNOTATED REFERENCES

Estes, Mark E. (1989). Moving—yet another story. *Trends in Law Library Management and Technology, 2*(9), 5–6. Advance planning for 36-inch-wide shelves has to be reworked when actual shelves are found to be 30 inches wide on day of move.

Evans, Bruce. (1996). Flood threat in Medicine Hat: Contents of public library's lower floor moved to main floor. *PNLA Quarterly, 60,* 14–15. Moving 80,000 volumes in 15 hours using library staff and 100 volunteers.

Fagan, George V. (1959). Moving the Air Force Academy library. *Mountain-Plains Library Quarterly, 3*(4), 13–14. General account of the four phases of moving the Air Force Academy Library from temporary to permanent quarters.

Faller, Martha Lewkus. (1984). Collection shifting . . . from crowding to user comfort. *New Library Scene, 3,* 9–10, 15–17. Describes an approach to respacing an existing collection to reallocate growth space. Bases calculations on subjective estimates of collections occupying each shelf, rather than precise measurements, so probably not suited to large collections. Useful range labeling system described, with sample illustrated. Worksheet could be adapted to use with precise measurements.

Fast response to library emergency. (1980). *College & Research Libraries News, 41*(3), 57–58. News report of moving collections out of the University of Massachusetts' main library due to safety issues.

Feret, Barbara L. (1967). Moving the library at Dutchess Community College. *American Library Association Bulletin, 61*(1), 68–71. Moving a 21,000-volume collection using a combination of methods, including a student book brigade. Features use of canvas carriers as book containers, and liquor boxes to hold materials for which there was no shelf space prior to the move.

Fitch, H. Glen. (1951). Moving the Hillsdale College library. *Michigan Librarian, 17,* 7–8. Account of moving a college library collection using a book brigade. Useful comments on average number of books one person can carry and effects of underestimating this on overall time required to complete the move.

Fitt, Stephen D. (1989). Moving fully-loaded stacks inexpensively. *College & Research Libraries News, 50*(1), 19–21. Describes benefits and method of using the Range Dolly to move fully loaded book stacks at San Diego State University Library. Developed by a retired manufacturing engineer, the device is described as working with Contemporary Ames library shelving, with modifications planned to allow its use with other types of steel shelving.

500 Pratt volunteers. (1966). *Kansas Library Bulletin, 35,* 30. Brief news account of a book brigade move conducted in two days for the Pratt (KS) Public Library.

Fling, Michael. (1991). Recordings, scores, square feet: Making it all add up. In *Space utilization in music libraries,* comp. J. P. Cassaro, 89–100. Canton, MA: Music Library Association. Summarizes key findings in his more comprehensive work, *Shelving capacity in the music library.*

Fling, Robert Michael. (1981). *Shelving capacity in the music library.* Philadelphia: Music Library Association. Based on careful measurements done at the Indiana University Music Library, Fling articulates shelving and space planning requirements for music scores and recordings, including the average width per item, the number of shelves per section of shelving, and shelf depth. Required reading for music library space planners.

Fowles, Charlotte. (2004). When your mission changes: Heave ho! It's time to reevaluate and move the collection. *Collection Management, 29(1),* 43–53. Describes weeding and rearrangement of the Idaho State Library collection in response to a change in mission. Useful observations on working with low-skill, low-literacy movers (Correctional Industries) and the practical benefit of making sure all staff understand the purpose of the project.

Fraley, Ruth A., and Carol Lee Anderson. (1990). *Library space planning: A how-to-do-it manual for assessing, allocating and reorganizing collections, Resources and Facilities.* New York: Neal-Schuman. Planning and executing a move in the context of managing space. Emphasis is on planning and executing a shelf-to-shelf move without a professional mover. Many useful and perceptive comments on topics not addressed in any depth elsewhere. Especially strong in the areas of publicity, library operations during the move, alternative workforce sources and management, practical aspects of move operations. Required reading for move planners.

French, Thomas R. (2006). Law librarians and library design, construction, and renovation: An annotated bibliography and review of the literature. *Law Library Journal, 98(1),* 99–155. Huge, usefully annotated bibliographic essay, addressing topics ranging from the library as place and the future of the physical library, the impact of technology, recent building projects, Web sites about specific projects, building design and construction, working with architects, post-occupancy evaluation, and lessons learned.

Galbraith, Betty. (1978). Planning for a grand opening. *Sourdough, 15,* 20–21. Brief article with lots of creative ideas for publicizing the opening of a new building; particularly applicable to public libraries.

Gertz, Janet. (1992). After the fall. *Conservation Administration News, 51,* 1–2, 30. Account of collection recovery after a stack collapse. Emphasis on insurance and preservation considerations.

Gibson, D. B. (1978). Planning and executing a library move: The experience of the Home Office library. *State Librarian, 26,* 9–10. General account of the (British) Home Office Library's 1973 move.

Gibson, Laurie Phillips, Alicia Hansen, and Deborah Poole. (2006). You can't hurry love: Patience, perseverance, and a positive attitude move a music library. *Notes 63(1),* 13–42. Detailed description of the consensus-building process used to successfully integrate the music library of Loyola University (New Orleans) into its main library.

Godolphin, Jocelyn. (2001). Moving or leaving: Defining the best partial collection for a new building. *Collection Management, 25(3),* 39–52. Detailed description of process used to split a collection in response to space constraints.

Golden, Barbara L. (1989). 1989 space requirements and price list. *Legal Reference Services Quarterly, 9(3/4),* 271–81. Update of 1985 Anderson and Golden listing.

Greenwood, Derek, and John Shawyer. (1993). Moving the British Library—the book control system. *Aslib Information, 21(1),* 28–31. Description of the book control system designed by Ernst & Young to move and consolidate 8 million books from multiple locations; system included data on the height, width, and depth of each bay of shelves in the St. Pancras location and in the sending locations. Stresses efficiency of presetting shelves to minimum possible heights and value of collecting book heights during planning phase.

Grey, Billie J. (1992). Making your move. *American Libraries, 23,* 330–31. Practical, detailed, management- and operational-level advice that will help prevent "unexpected" problems, communicated with humor and the voice of experience.

Gribbin, John H. (1969). Tulane library moves across the street. *Louisiana Library Journal, 32,* 26–30. Practical advice for planning and carrying out a large, complex move, drawn from experience of Tulane

University's move into the Howard-Tilton Library. Includes description of covered wooden ramp, 220 feet long, connecting old and new buildings, over which book trucks and moving carts were pushed.

Grimwood-Jones, Diana. (1993). A quick guide to moving your library. *Aslib Information, 21*, 17. Overview of potential library move problems, including issues involving staff (will there be retirements? layoffs?) and choosing a moving company.

Gyeszly, Suzanne D. (1990). Computer aided storage design. *Technical Services Quarterly, 8*(1), 51–59. Describes methodology used to plan shelving for journal storage by size, using dBase.

Gyeszly, Suzanne D., Marifran Bustion, and Jane Treadwell. (1990). Infrequently used serials: A space utilization project. *Collection Management, 12*(1), 109–23. Account of selecting and moving 53,000 serial volumes to a newly created, within-building, low-use storage area.

Hagloch, Susan B. (1994). *Library building projects: Tips for survival.* Englewood, CO: Libraries Unlimited. Brief discussion of moving-related issues on pages 26–27 and 65–69 offers practical tips, particularly on morale issues.

Haka, Cliff H., et al. (1983). Discussion of Amodeo's "Helpful hints for moving or shifting collections." *College & Research Library News, 44*(5), 153. Responses to Amodeo's article include Clifford Haka's recommendation to load book trucks from bottom to top for greater stability and fully loading one side before beginning to load the second side, for greater speed. Response by Amodeo agrees with bottom up loading, but argues alternate side loading, though slower, is preferable as it reduces the potential for tipping. Additional letters by Thomas Lindsey and Michael Kathman suggest, respectively, having new shelving installed with 12-inch spacing and checking whether the shelving as installed has sufficient stability to accept uneven loading without hazard of falling over.

Hall, M. (2004). Moving in and throwing a party: An insider's guide for the branch supervisor. *Unabashed Librarian,* (130), 8–11. Shelf-to-shelf move. Useful checklist of considerations for a building dedication party.

Hamilton, C. J. (1991). Moves, mergers & mayhem: Recent library developments in CAB International. *Aslib Proceedings, 43*(4), 109–14. Planning for merger of CABI and with IIE Library, and its move from London to Silwood. Useful comments on problems encountered with a moving company that did not fully understand the scope of work contemplated.

Hamilton, Patricia, and Pam Hindman. (1987). Moving a public library collection. *Public Libraries*, 26(1), 4–7. Describes Cedar Rapids Public Library's move using staff, volunteers, and professional movers. Good practical tips on recruitment and management of volunteers, overcoming logistical challenges, and integrating work performed by staff, volunteer, and professional movers.

Hammer, Donald P. (1960). Operation book shift. *College & Research Libraries*, 21(5), 393–94. Planning and implementing a move of 1.5 million volumes at the University of Illinois Library over a period of 4 months, using student labor. Describes simple but effective spacing device used to assure appropriate fill ratio used in reshelving.

Hansen, Charles, and Ted Honea. (1990). Shrink-wrapping for moving. *Abbey Newsletter*, 14(1), 17–19. Describes shrink-wrapping technique to protect physical integrity and stability of approximately 50,000 items, including rare books, special collections, cataloged music, and catalog drawers, as part of the move of the Sibley Music Library of the Eastman School of Music, University of Rochester (NY).

Hardkopf, Jewel. (1955). Major book move: The time study. *Library Journal*, 80(19), 2417–19. Describes time studies undertaken for planning a series of collection moves at the Brooklyn (NY) Public Library. Presupposes familiarity with 1950s time study processes, e.g., "following the established standard method it was determined," but still useful.

Harriss, Charlotte. (1990). A race against time: The California State Library's collection shift. *California State Library Foundation Bulletin*, 33, 11–15. Discusses preservation rationale for moving material into compact shelving at the California State Library.

Harvard law library moves 300,000 books. (1960). *Law Library Journal*, 53, 226–27. Reorganization and relocation of Harvard Law Library's foreign treatise collection by high school students over 5 months, using a book brigade method.

Harvey, Ross. (1993). *Preservation in libraries: Principles, strategies, and practices for librarians*. London: Bowker-Saur. Of particular interest is Chapter 5, "An Attitude of Respect: Careful Handling and the Education of Users and Librarians," on handling techniques for print and nonprint materials.

ANNOTATED REFERENCES

Hawthorne, Gadys. (1963). Library moving made easy. *American Library Association Bulletin*, *57*(7), 671. Brief description of method for shelf-to-shelf moving of materials, using a specially constructed frame and moving dollies.

Hazelton, Penny, and Jonathan Franklin. (2004). Moving a law library. *AALL Spectrum* (May), 22–23. Lessons learned from relocation of University of Washington Law Library, including coordination of moving both shelving and the books on it, moving from 22-inch stack aisles, and practical advice on maintaining staff morale.

Head, Anita K. (1987). Remodeling and expanding space: Library services during the construction period. *Law Library Journal*, *79*, 335–45. Good advice on coping with the change implicit in a move, along with general comments on planning a move. Collection layout planning advice covers direct shelf-to-shelf moves only (no provision for incorporating expansion space during the move). Very useful comments on psychological impact of moving on staff, and of the role of senior library management in easing the transition to a new facility. *Note:* Erratum, published in *Law Library Journal* 79 (Fall 1987): 845, corrects (reverses) lines 27–29 on page 536, from which a phrase was dropped. The correct text should read, "In other words, it is not possible to start out with a new and rational plan. It will be necessary to work around such factors as existing floors."

Heath, Margaret. (1988). Space: Planning and moving; preparation is essential. *Law Library Lights*, *31*(5). 1, 5. Advice on planning a law library move.

Henexson, Fay. (1995). Planning and moving a library: Don't panic—plan it. *Trends in Law Library Management and Technology*, *6*(5), 2–5. Practical tips based on a law library move. Suggests using a database to make shelf labels. Recommends that in earthquake country, shelving only be moved by shelving specialists, and that "recovery time" be planned to shelf-read, unpack offices, and check equipment before reopening.

Herscher, I. J. (1938). The New Friedsam Library of St. Bonaventure College. *Library Journal*, *63*, 45–349. Account of the new library at St. Bonaventure College and the move into it, using students and seminarians to form a book brigade. Useful comments on damage done to books through mishandling by book brigade members.

Hitchcock, Mary, Rhonda Sager, and Julie Schneider. (2005). And then there was one: Moving and merging three health science library collections [electronic version]. *Issues in Science and Technology*

Librarianship. Available at www.istl.org/05–fall/article3.html (accessed August 3, 2007). Detailed description of planning and executing the merger of three collections. Very useful detail on merging journal collections with differing classification and organizational schemes, collection assessment, and the amount of time required.

Hlavac, R. M. (1965). Removal of the University of Otago Library. *New Zealand Libraries, 28*(4), 73–82. Detailed account of planning and carrying out the move of the University of Otago Library in 1965, using a creative mix of professional movers, library staff, and student hires; boxes; printers' trolleys; trucks; slides; and a human chain.

Hoefler, Barbara Burton. (1971). Mini operation for a maxi move. *Hawaii Library Association Journal, 28*, 24–26. News account of moving the Maui Community College Library to new quarters using student volunteers, library staff, and others. Emphasizes need for detailed planning and instruction to volunteers as keys to success.

Hofstetter, Janet. (1993). Best laid plans & pitfalls. *Book Report, 11*, 13–15. Practical tips on planning and moving into a new library, written from the perspective of a school librarian. Includes useful comments on packing and labeling boxes.

Holab-Abelman, Robin. (2004). Letter to the editor [re Dimenstein, "Executing a library move . . . a planned approach to moving your library"]. *Information Outlook, 8*(3), 7. Substantive, very useful tips include how to estimate the number of carts or boxes needed, how to mark shelves to indicate fill ratio, caution on the weight of fully loaded moving book trucks, a toolkit for movers, and checking the shelf layout and setup, including shelf adjustment for oversized material.

Hole, Carol. (1988). Librarian has a ring-around-the-collar job. In *Alternative library literature, 1986/1987: A biennial anthology*, ed. Sanford Berman and James P. Danky, 2. Jefferson, NC: McFarland. Reprinted from *Gainesville Sun*, January 5, 1986, p. 5G. Brief, humorous piece on physical labor required in library work, including shifting collections.

Holiday, Judy. (1976). A "new" fine arts library. *Cornell University Library Bulletin, no. 199*, 9–10. Interview with Judy Holiday on the expansion of Cornell's Fine Arts Library. Brief discussion of problems of moving a collection while construction is still in progress.

Holt, Raymond M. (1989). *Planning library buildings and facilities: From concept to completion*. Metuchen, NJ: Scarecrow. Chapter 9, "Occupying the Building," discusses issues related to planning and making the move and to settling in.

Holt, Raymond M., and Anders C. Dahlgren. (1990). *Planning library buildings and facilities: From concept to completion.* 2nd ed., rev. Madison: Wisconsin Department of Public Instruction. Excellent survey of library building planning, construction, and occupancy issues. Chapter 13, "Occupying the New Facility" (pp. 171–75), touches on major choices in planning a move.

How the books were moved. (1930). *Yale University Gazette,* 5, 30–34. Detailed account of methods used for move into Yale's Sterling Memorial Library. Includes comments on box design and labeling, book trucks, work team composition, and operational logistics.

Hoxsey, Judith A. (1995). Estes Valley residents move their library. *Colorado Libraries,* 21, 27–28. Account of planning and carrying out the move of a collection of 30,000 volumes using volunteer labor, milk crates, and forklift trucks. Useful description of labor allocation and packing methods.

Hubbard, William J. (1979). Development and administration of a large off-campus shelving facility. In *New horizons for academic libraries: Papers presented at the first national conference of the Association of College and Research Libraries, Boston, Massachusetts, November 8–11, 1978,* ed. Robert D. Stueart and Richard D. Johnson, 550–55. New York: K.G. Saur Publishing. Account of Virginia Polytechnic Institute and State University's development of, move to, and operation of an off-site collection storage facility. Discussion of allowing for growth in collection layout planning, selection of book carts to move collections, sequencing moving crew operations.

———, ed. (1981). *Stack management: A practical guide to shelving and maintaining library collections.* Chicago: American Library Association. Of particular interest are Chapter 3, "Moving and Shifting Books," and Chapter 6, "Care of Books."

Huber, Tom. (2001). They're just plain big! Oversized shelving solutions at the Illinois State Library's map department. *Information Bulletin Western Association of Map Libraries,* 33(1), 26–29. Description and photos.

Ifidon, Sam E. (1979). Moving an academic library. *Journal of Academic Librarianship,* 4(6), 434–37. Planning and carrying out Ahmadu Bello University's move into a new main library.

Impact: Guidelines for North Carolina media and technology programs (2005). Public Schools of North Carolina. Available at www.ncwiseowl.org/IMPACT/docs/IMPACT.pdf (accessed August 14, 2007). Details educational specifications for various areas of the school library media center, and for furniture, shelving, and built-ins.

Iwaschkin, Ruth. (1982). Counter points. *New Library World, 82*, 82–83. Sampling of negative user reaction to the rearrangement of collections in a branch library. Useful in considering new collection layouts and in planning opening day publicity.

Jablonski, Barbara. (1993). On the move. *Indiana Media Journal, 15*(4), 73–75. Brief but useful advice on planning and executing a media center move. Suggests using a book cart brigade, a practical variation on the hand-passing book brigade, maintaining a stable core of volunteers to reduce the need for repeat instruction.

James, Katherine B. (1957). Hurried move in Louisiana. *Library Journal, 82*, 2109–11. News report of the Louisiana State Library's move, forced when their building was damaged by nearby construction and became unsafe for occupancy.

Jesse, William H. (1941). Moving books. *Library Quarterly, 11*, 328–33. Discussion of the cost and logistics of several moves carried out at Brown University in 1938 and 1939. Useful comments on efficient box sizing (What size box allows each individual to carry the greatest linear feet of material?) and move logistics (the rate of shelving drives the rate of the move).

Johnson, Donna, Caitlin Kennedy, and Usha Gupta. (2004). A do-it-yourself model: Relocation of a 36,000 volume chemistry library in three months. *Arkansas Libraries, 61*(3), 16–18. Describes decision criteria (including usage and availability in electronic format) used to assign items to multiple temporary locations during a renovation. Stresses value of communication and flexibility.

Johnson, Linda B. (1998). Moving a library—planning is key. *The Unabashed Librarian, 109*, 16–19. Brief article with several good tips, including making sure stacks are secured before loading, checking the accuracy of stack layouts before the move, and using the library's Web page for communicating move progress.

Johnson, Nancy P. (1980). Rearranging a law library: A case study. *Law Library Journal, 73*, 129–33. Planning and implementing reclassification and reorganization of a university law library of 320,000 volumes, within existing space, in two phases, using student help and library staff.

ANNOTATED REFERENCES

Jorgensen, William E. (1941). Rearranging a book collection. *Library Journal*, 66(12), 570–71. General account of planning for a stack shift at Oregon State College Library, necessitated by addition of an annex.

Josselyn, Lloyd W. (1933). Moving the Enoch Pratt Library. *Library Journal*, 58, 480–82. Detailed account of logistics for the 1933 move into Baltimore's Enoch Pratt Free Library.

Kallenberg, Polly. (1977). Does this sound familiar? *Sourdough*, 14, 6–7. Brief account of moving 12,000 volumes and shelving into a 400-square-foot expansion of the Chugiak-Eagle River branch of the Anchorage public library system, including using volunteer labor to assemble new shelving and relocate existing shelving.

Kathman, Michael D. (1983, May). Moving collections (letter). *C&RL News*, 44, 153. Discussion of Amodeo, "Helpful hints for moving or shifting collections."

Keck, Bruce L. (1994). Moving your library. In *Preserving the past, looking to the future: Proceedings of the 19th annual conference of the International Association of Aquatic and Marine Science Libraries and Information Centers*, 183–91. Detailed comments on planning and executing the move of the U.S. Geological Survey (USGS) Reston Library from off-site warehouse storage. Includes observations on working with a low bid mover, poor security, using a forklift to remove material from a mezzanine, moving loaded map cases, inaccurate building plans, and installation of compact shelving.

Keen, Eunice, and Virginia Thomason. (1952). Moving day for bookworms at Lakeland High School Library. *Florida Libraries*, 3, 12, 21. Brief, humorous account of a high school library's move, in the form of a play/dialog between two bookworms.

Kellerman, L. Suzanne. (1993). Moving fragile materials: Shrink-wrapping at Penn State. *Collection Management*, 18(1/2), 117–28. Decisions and process used to shrink-wrap 47,000 fragile and brittle items identified for movement to a remote storage facility.

Kelly, Robert Q. (1958). Moving your law library. *Law Library Journal*, 51, 34–36. Advice on moving a law library, based on experience of DePaul University Law Library's 1957 move.

Kelsey, Donald G. (1991). Movement of materials. In *The great divide: Challenges in remote storage*, ed. James R. Kennedy and Gloria Stockton, 49–62. Chicago: American Library Association. Well written and succinct, these pages provide a practical, detailed overview of packing options and differences between one-time and continuous collection moves.

————. (2005, August 9). *Collection move planning*. Available at donaldgkelsey.com/planning_corner_02.html (accessed December 27, 2007). Detailed description of how to measure collections using the "magic string" method, and its accuracy.

Kendrick, Curtis L. (1991). Performance measures of shelving accuracy. *Journal of Academic Librarianship, 17*(1), 16–18. Describes factors associated with establishing performance measures of shelving accuracy and method used for measuring shelving accuracy at State University of New York, Stony Brook.

Kephart, John E., ed. (1952). *Moving a library*. rev. ed. n.p.: University of Illinois Library School. Summarizes factors in planning and carrying out collection moves at 30 libraries, including plans of operations, manpower and methods of moving, and costs. Some broad conclusions are drawn, which are still relevant despite the passage of time (e.g., "The librarian who is planning to move must know his own situation thoroughly.") .

King, Marion M. (1959). Operation library at Lorain. *Wilson Library Bulletin, 33*, 42–743. Moving the Lorain (OH) Public Library into a new facility on an evening schedule using library staff, Jaycees, and a moving van.

Kinney, Lisa. (1981). Albany Co. Library on the move. *Wyoming Library Roundup, 37*, 1–3. Albany County (Wyoming) Library moves to a new building, using a human chain. Useful anecdotes illustrating some practical problems of using this method and volunteers.

Kinzer, Rose W. (1958). "Operation library" in Midland. *Texas Library Journal, 34*, 137. Midland County Library moves to a new facility using volunteer labor (Jaycees) to box and move books.

Kirby, Lynn. (1995). Door to door: How to get your library moving . . . painlessly. *School Library Journal, 41*(2), 26–27. Brief but useful general advice on planning and executing a move, including comments on choice of a coordinator, timing, weeding, staffing, labeling, cleaning, selection of move containers, and public relations.

Klasing, Jane P. (1991). *Designing and renovating school library media centers*. Chicago: American Library Association. Of particular interest is Appendix E, "General Information on Shelving and Layouts."

Knilans, Edith. (1954). Did you ever move a library? We did! *Wilson Library Bulletin, 28,* 791. Collections of Wisconsin State College at Whitewater move to a new facility using a student-staffed book brigade.

Kopecky, Linda A. (1989). Oversized publications in a U.S. federal depository collection: A space management study. *Illinois Libraries, 71,* 485–89. Detailed description of the height characteristics of federal depository publications held at a university library selecting over 90 percent of items offered. Includes table listing, by agency, the total inches of material considered over tall or over deep. Discusses implications for maximizing shelf space utilization.

Kozlowski, Ken. (2005). New digs for the Supreme Court of Ohio. *AALL Spectrum, 9(7),* 22–23. Problems resulting from a move of collections and shelving executed by separate companies, including coordination issues and poor performance by the movers.

Kruse, Paul. (1951). To build is to move. *Library Journal, 76(22),* 2044–45, 2089. Describes the new Hollins College library, and moving into it.

Kulp, Aimee K. (1952). We used the bucket brigade. *Wilson Library Bulletin, 26(6),* 456–57. The Mercersburg, PA, Academy Library moves, using students and faculty and the book brigade method.

Kurkul, Donna Lee. (1983). Planning, implementation, and movement of an academic library collection. *College & Research Libraries, 44(4),* 220–234. Comments on assessing layout options, growth space allocation, calculation of labor-hours required and of move duration, selection of student assistants. Brief review of literature. Describes phased move of Smith College's Neilsen Library collections.

Kurkul, Donna Lee and Charles H. Davis. (1983). Planning, implementation and movement of an academic library collection: Discussion. *College & Research Libraries, 44(6),* 486–87. Exchange of letters between Davis and Kurkul concerning Kurkul's inclusion of an appendix on basic algebraic principles.

Kurth, William H., and Ray W. Grim, eds. (1966). *Moving a library.* New York: Scarecrow. A classic. Detailed, analytical consideration of issues in planning and implementing a library move, using moves conducted at the National Library of Medicine and UCLA as examples. Particularly strong discussions of methods to assess the extent of current collections using sampling techniques, methods of merging collections, using ratios of book trucks to shelving units to achieve desired allocation of shelf space, impact of shelf spacing on stack capacity and usability. Sample move specifications and contracts, inventories of materials (e.g., furniture and equipment) to be moved. Required reading for the move planner.

Kurtz, Winifred M. (1988). Changes changes. *Illinois Libraries*, 70, 19–21. Reorganizing Youth Services Department of a public library, including stacks.

Ladley, Barbara. (1987). Questions to ask . . . . *Bottom Line*, 1(4), 8. Succinct list of important business questions relevant to selecting a library mover.

Laffoon, Carolyn J., Graham T. Richardson, and Wilton N. Melhorn. (1991). Relocating a science library: How to cope with plans gone awry! *Science and Technology Libraries*, 12(1), 91–97. Responses to problems with timing, transportation and storage of materials, shelving procurement and installation, in the relocation and expansion of the library of Purdue University's Department of Earth & Atmospheric Sciences.

Lamb, Kurt. (1991). A moving experience. *Show-Me Libraries*, 42, 21–22. Moving an entire historic Carnegie library building in Mexico, Missouri.

Lambert, Linda Stern. (1992). How to survive library renovation. *School Library Journal*, 38, 38–39. Describes renovation timeline for a private school library, including move into and out of temporary storage, and consequences of carrying out a move without a great deal of logistical planning.

Lancaster, Joan C. (1969). India Office records and the India Office library: The move to a new building. *Archives*, 9, 2–10. Planning a new facility for the British India Office Records and Library, with brief account of the move and of planning for it. Good description of detailed labeling used to bring together series shelved in multiple locations.

Landrum, Claudia S. (1959). Moving day at Mississippi College. *Mississippi Library News*, 23, 9. Brief account of Mississippi College's move into a new facility using three-foot-long book troughs, boxes, and hand-carrying methods.

Larsgaard, M. (1976). Moving a map library; or, How to keep your sanity while losing your grip. *SLA Geography and Map Division Bulletin*, no. 105, 20–24. Moving the map library at Central Washington State College Library, using staff and student help. Practical comments on moving maps in map case drawers, leveling map cases. Includes layouts of old and new facilities.

ANNOTATED REFERENCES

LC begins major books move, stacks cleaning program. (1972). *Library of Congress Information Bulletin, 31*(5), 280–81. News report of book and stack cleaning program to be undertaken at the Library of Congress. Brief description of procedures planned.

Leach, Bruce A. (1997). A simple program simplifies moving and integrating serial collections. *Serials Librarian, 32*(3/4), 93–105. Describes a QBASIC program used to generate exact shelf-by-shelf locations for a merged serials collection.

Leadley, Ian, Pam Airey, and Peter Wray. (1981). Stock move 1980 at the British Library Lending division. *Interlending Review, 9*(2), 60–61. Report on the 1980 move of the British Lending Library's move into a building addition, including planning for growth space, and move logistics.

Leary, Margaret A. (1982). Move of the University of Michigan law library. *Law Library Journal, 75*, 308–13. Planning and implementing a move of 300,000 volumes within a building using library staff and temporary employees. Useful comments on hiring, training, and assigning temporary employees; gross analysis of move logistics, including increasing the rate of vertical transport using wooden chutes. Describes custom-made boxes, design rationale, and move budget.

Lee, Lionel James. (1950). Always so much to move! *Library Journal, 75*, 534–37. Moving collections to Princeton's Firestone Library.

Leighton, Philip D., and David C. Weber. (1999). *Planning academic and research library buildings.* 3rd ed. Chicago: American Library Association. The encyclopedic resource on planning academic and library buildings. Of particular interest to the move planner are Chapter 16, "Activation," including section 16.6, "Moving In"; and tables in Appendix B.5, "Bookstack Capacity."

Library and media center facilities design—K–12. (2007). Available at edfacilities.org/rl/libraries.cfm (accessed August 13, 2007). Annotated bibliography of Web sites and print publications. Focus is on facility design.

Library facilities design—Higher education. (2007). Available at edfacilities. org/rl/LibrariesHE.cfm (accessed August 14, 2007). Annotated bibliography of Web sites and publications. Focus is on facilities planning; a few move-related citations.

Library move saves money and makes new friends. (1984). *Library Journal, 109*, 937. News report of moving the Reading, MA, Public Library using volunteers.

Library moves. (1979). *Texas Library Journal, 55*(2), 37. Report on a presentation to the Texas Library Association Annual Conference, 1979. Includes general tips on planning a move using a moving company.

Little, Gretchen D. (1955). "M-daze" in the Atlas library. *Special Libraries Council Philadelphia & Vicinity Bulletin, 22,* 2–5. Account of moving the Atlas Powder Company's library, using a professional moving company.

Long, Frances G., and Margaret R. Meyer. (1954). Library on the move. *Wilson Library Bulletin, 28*(9), 793–795. Describes Russell Sage College library's move to a new facility, using students to carry collections. Effects of rain on this type of move are described.

Lowenberg, Susan. (1989). A comprehensive shelf reading program. *Journal of Academic Librarianship, 15*(1), 24–27. Development and implementation of a shelf-reading program at California State University, Northridge, including a methodology for sampling stack areas to identify those most in need of shelf-reading, and identification of the range of annual shelving errors per section (EPS) found acceptable by this library's users.

Lumb, Audrey E. (1972). Moving an academic library: A case study. *Journal of Librarianship, 4*(4), 253–71. Excellent, well-written summary of factors to consider in planning a move, including timing, use of staff versus professional movers, bid preparation, contract conditions, and calculating shelving allocations. Lengthy bibliography.

Lumley, A., V. K. Datta, and J. A. Wright. (1991). Merging and moving—the NRI experience: An exercise in library integration and relocation. *Aslib Proceedings, 43*(4), 115–32. Merger and relocation of multiple separate library operations to form new Natural Resources Institute library. Focuses on merger of operations and staffs. Brief description of collection move.

Maine school library facilities handbook. (1999). Available at 130.111. 214.138/~masl//about/facilities/handbook.html (accessed August 13, 2007). Appendix B, "Calculating Shelving Requirements" includes useful information on selecting shelving for school library media centers and either calculating its capacity or calculating the amount needed to house a collection of a given size.

Manley, Kathy. (2003). 10 tips for surviving a knock-down, drag-out media center "renovation." *Library Media Connection, 21*(4), 50–51. Practical advice based on a school media center move, including checking building plans for accuracy, reading contracts, and taking digital pictures of the cable connections for computer and multimedia equipment.

Manzoor, Suhail. (1981). Uniformity in book sizes: A need of the hour. *Annals of Library Science and Documentation*, 28(1–4), 90–96. Argument in favor of standardizing book sizes to increase the efficiency of shelf space utilization in libraries. (Although the notion may seem whimsical, after dealing with shelf spacing and oversized material questions, move planners may agree with the author!)

Mareachen, Jo Ann. (1988). Asbestos removal steps. *Indiana Media Journal*, 10, 19–20. Practical advice for school media centers facing relocation due to asbestos removal, though there is little discussion of potential health and safety issues.

Martin, Jess A. (1968). Planning the new NIH research library. *Special Libraries*, 59(1), 30–38. General description of planning a new library facility. Discussion of the move focuses on general considerations and a day-by-day calendar of the NIH move.

Mason, Alexandra. (1983). Discussion of Amodeo "Helpful hints for moving or shifting collections." *College & Research Libraries News*, 44(7), 232–33. Additional suggestions are to construct a collection layout plan, load only one bookshelf's contents onto each book truck shelf, wrap book trucks to protect contents from falling off in transit; if two rows of materials are shelved on one book truck shelf, separate them.

Matthews, Fred W. (1987). Sorting a mountain of books. *Library Resources and Technical Services*, 31(1), 88–94. Description of computer-based method used to sort and make accessible prior to their reshelving materials removed from the Dalhousie University Law Library following fire and water damage.

McCarrier, Eileen. (1988). A retrospective look at moving a library. *Law Library Lights*, 31(9), 14–15. Lessons learned from a law library move.

McCaughan, Dave. (1991). Ingratiating yourself to all and sundry . . . or how I crawled my way to notoriety. *Special Libraries*, 83(2), 183–88. Detailed description of a special library's use of a post-move celebration to increase awareness and use of its services.

McDonald, Andrew. (1994). *Moving your library*. London: Aslib. Substantive 36-page guide to planning and executing a move. Detailed description of how to use a double-label book move control system to control "creep." British terminology; metric measurements.

Meinke, Darrel M. (1988). Pulling the rug out from under the stacks (revisited). *College & Research Libraries News, 49*(5), 288–89. Describes method and benefits of using a device to move fully loaded book stacks at Moorhead (MN) State University. Notes that it was used successfully with four manufacturers' steel shelving. Only a general description of the device is provided, as it is noted that the inventor planned to market it.

Meltzer, Ellen. (1993). Successfully moving the library—temporarily. *College & Research Libraries News, 54*(10), 557, 559–60. Account of planning and implementation of a temporary move of collections, staff, and operations, from University of California, Berkeley's Moffitt Library during a seismic strengthening renovation. Focus is on planning accommodations for staff and service during the relocation.

Merrill-Oldham, Jan. (2000, April 10). *General specifications for moving and cleaning library materials.* Available at preserve.harvard.edu/guidelines/cleaning.pdf (accessed July 7, 2007). Good model, from an authoritative author.

Messinger, Lucile. (1951). Quick work. *Wilson Library Bulletin, 25,* 760. Brief report of moving 17,000 books on short notice to a temporary location in advance of renovations at the Newark, NY, Free Public Library, using staff and volunteers.

Middlesex county library moved by book cart. (1967). *Ontario Library Review, 51*(3), 180. Brief news account of moving the Middlesex County Library.

Mier, Karen. (2005). Asking the questions. *Nebraska Library Association Quarterly, 36*(1), 12–14. Preparing to serve academic medical library clients while in a much smaller interim location. Stresses value of communicating with clients.

Miller, Richard T., Jr. (1982). Wolfner move: 166 tons and wha'd'ya get? *Show-Me Libraries, 33*(11), 24–27. Account of moving the collections, book stacks, furniture, and equipment of the Wolfner Memorial Library for the Blind and Physically Handicapped to a new facility using staff and pre-release prisoners. Describes extra space required to accommodate books and shelving, which was not set up until after all materials had been moved.

Miltner, Terrance C., and Gordon Flagg. (2004). 10,000 books found in abandoned East St. Louis Library. *American Libraries, 35*(9), 13. This is a cautionary tale: books were left behind because the old library wasn't inspected after move-out.

Minter, Sydney. (2007). On your mark, get set, move! *Library Media Connection*, 25(7), 44–46. Basic advice based on move from a school media center, including weeding and inventorying before moving, using carts rather than boxes, and getting and checking blueprints before the move.

Monk, Clare. (2005). "It's all gone Woolly." *Legal Information Management*, 5(1), 58–60. Report on the consolidation of a corporate law library's two locations.

Moran, Robert F., Jr. (1972). Moving a large library. *Special Libraries*, 63(4), 163–71. Planning and implementing University of Chicago's move into the Regenstein Library, using a moving company (Hallett). Detailed description of integrating multiple collections using the shelving increment method and a division of labor whereby movers placed related materials on adjacent shelves, and library staff were responsible for item-by-item interfiling. Brief discussion of preservation impact of moving bound volumes in boxes.

Moreland, Rachel S. (1987). Managing library stacks space with a microcomputer. *Small Computers in Libraries* 7(6), 38–41. Describes a SuperCalc spreadsheet devised to project where shelving space will be needed based on five years' growth data, and a second spreadsheet showing how shelf space is being used. Formulas are provided and could be adapted to use with any spreadsheet package.

Moreland, Virginia F., et al. (1991). *The "do-it-yourself" library move: Consequences for staff interactions and morale.* [ERIC Document ED 341 397 microform]. Similar to article by Moreland et al. in *Journal of Academic Librarianship*.

Moreland, Virginia F., Carolyn L. Robison, and Joan M. Stephens. (1993). Moving a library collection: Impact on staff morale. *Journal of Academic Librarianship*, 19(1), 8–11. Interesting and useful discussion of an important aspect of planning and implementing a do-it-yourself move. Includes comments on learning curve, group cohesiveness, status relationship reversals, sense of closure, ownership, and satisfaction.

Morrow, Mary Frances. (1990). Moving an archives. *American Archivist*, 53, 420–31. Reports on a survey of ten archives institutions' moves. Topics covered include planning considerations (shelf survey, allocation of records, labeling, shelving), unanticipated problems, containers, handling of bound volumes, use of a contractor rather than staff, maintenance of services, and special problems.

Mosby, Norma. (1992). University of Arkansas opts for remote storage. *Arkansas Libraries*, 49(1), 13–16. Describes selection and move of

30,000 volumes to an on-campus remote storage facility. Emphasis is on selection procedures.

Mostar, Roman W. (1950). Moving day didn't interrupt this university library's service. *Library Journal, 75,* 1226–27, 1230. Account of moving collections into a new addition at the University of Washington, Seattle.

Mount, Ellis. (1988). Moving the library. In *Creative planning of special library facilities,* ed. E. Mount, 35–40. New York: Haworth Press. Factors to consider in planning and implementing a move, including selection of a moving company, scheduling the move, pre-move preparations, working with movers, and post-move activities.

Move-in snapshots. (1995). *California State Library Foundation Bulletin, 50,* 24–26. Photographic essay illustrates use of a scissor lift to move the California State Library's Information File and card catalog cabinets.

Moving day. (1958). *Library Journal, 83,* 39–3340. News account describes Jaycees' role in moving Lorain, OH, public library.

Moving 450,000 books. (1956). *University of Rochester Library Bulletin, 11,* 22–24. Account of integrating a collection of 100,000 volumes into an existing collection of 350,000 volumes.

Moving libraries: ALA fact sheet number 14. (2002, March 22). Available at archive.ala.org/library/fact14.html (accessed July 7, 2007). Includes list of library movers, bibliography.

Moving specialists. (1965). *Library Journal, 90,* 5242. News report on Fisher & Bros. movers describes and pictures proprietary moving case on wheels, which "can be made to match library stacks shelf for shelf, simplifying packing procedures."

Multnomah on the move. (1995). *Library Journal, 120*(2), 20. News report on Multnomah County Library's move to a temporary facility.

Murray, Jennifer S. (2005). How to survive a library move: Control the move instead of it controlling you. *AALL Spectrum, 10(1),* 18–19, 33. Basic advice; stresses the value of getting full information, planning, and a positive attitude.

Myers, Charles. (1992). A mover that only moves libraries. *American Libraries, 23,* 332–33. Interview with principals of National Library Relocations. Includes practical tips on planning and executing a successful move; description of NLR's book bin.

Newman, John, and Walter Jones, eds. (2002). *Moving archives: The experience of eleven archivists*. Lanham, MD: Scarecrow Press. Eleven case studies of archives' moves covers a wide range of collection types, movers, methods, conditions, types of material, and administrative and facility issues. Reading the collected experience of this diverse group reveals a host of possible issues and practical solutions, as well as those issues that recur with regularity. A must-read for any archivist planning a move.

Nitecki, Danuta A., and Curtis L. Kendrick, eds. (2001). *Library off-site shelving: Guide for high-density facilities*. Englewood, CO: Libraries Unlimited. Comprehensive guide to all aspects of library off-site storage. Sections include governance issues and cost models; design, construction, and implementation; preservation issues; material selection issues; transferring items; systems; accessioning and management issues; services; special collections, and a bibliography. Chapter 12, "Preparation for Transfer," by Lee Anne George, and Chapter 13, "Transportation and Logistics," by Donald G. Kelsey and Curtis L. Kendrick, will be of particular interest to the move planner.

Oboler, Eli M. (1954). Chute the works! *Library Journal, 79*, 2387–89. Idaho State College Library's move to a new building. Notable features are use of two wooden chutes to convey cartons of books from the second and third floors of old building and use of shelving boxes and beer cartons to pack books.

Ogden, Sherelyn, ed. (1994). *Preservation of library & archival materials: A manual*. rev., exp. ed. Andover, MA: Northeast Document Conservation Center. Collection of well-written, authoritative technical leaflets on preservation matters. Of particular interest are "Storage Methods and Handling Practices" and "Cleaning Books and Shelves."

———. (2007). Storage and handling. *Preservation leaflets*. Available at www.nedcc.org/resources/leaflets/4Storage_and_Handling/01Storage Methods.php (accessed August 19, 2007). Part of an authoritative, detailed, and practical series of leaflets, available online. "4.1 Storage Methods and Handling Practices" addresses these issues for bound volumes, unbound flat paper, oversized materials, newsprint, pamphlets, scrapbooks and ephemera, and photographs. "4.3 Cleaning Books and Shelves" may also be of interest to the move planner.

Oliver, Maryann. (1974). Are you moving your library? *California School Libraries, 46*(1), 26–27. Describes book brigade technique for elementary school students.

ANNOTATED REFERENCES

Olsgaard, Jane K. (2000). Relocation, reorganization, and retrenchment. *Library Collections, Acquisitions, and Technical Services*, 24(3), 426–28. Report on a conference presentation sets expectation management guidelines for those about to be involved in a move.

Pannu, Gurdial S. (1967). "No problem"; or, a moving experience. *Ontario Library Review*, 51(2), 88–90. Humorous account of problems encountered and overcome in moving the University of Toronto's Library School to new quarters.

Paragamian, Helen. (1959). Our book parade. *Wilson Library Bulletin*, 33, 744–45. Account of moving book collections at Pine Manor College (Wellesley, MA) using a book brigade. Practical tips on the power of publicity and prizes to motivate, also on sizing armloads of books and instruction to participants.

Pascoe, Frank. (1984). State library moves to new building. *Show-Me Libraries*, 35, 16–18. Brief report of moving 300,000 items using a local mover and canvas postal service "tubs."

Pascoe, J. D. (1966). Move of the National Archives. *New Zealand Libraries*, 29, 195–99. General account of moving the New Zealand National Archives to temporary new quarters in July–August 1965.

Paulson, Arthur E., Jr., Beryl E. Hoyt, and Marion M. King. (1958). Moving made easier by "Operation Library." *ALA Bulletin*, 52, 627–29. Accounts of moving the Racine, WI, and Lorain, OH, public libraries, assisted by Jaycees.

Payne, Sherry. (1978). Management of student assistants. *West Virginia Libraries*, 31(4), 22–24. Practical tips for supervising student assistants. Applicable to management of student workers during a move.

Peacock, P.G. (1983). Measuring a library. *Aslib Proceedings*, 35(3), 152–55. Argument for estimating shelf occupancy to the nearest quarter shelf rather than measuring. Computer simulation used to demonstrate that cumulative error using this technique is very small (0.6%). Discussion of factors that may bias an estimate. Neglects variations in shelf size as a confounding factor. Doesn't discuss linear footage impact of even a very small error.

———. (1985). The management of shelf space. *Vine*, 58, 39–42. Describes the benefits of managing shelf space allocation using a computer program. Incomplete detail provided on the methodology, but useful to the spreadsheet-savvy.

ANNOTATED REFERENCES

Peasgood, Adrian, and Peter Stone. (1984). The model library: Planning reshelving on a spreadsheet. *Library Micromation News*, 5, 2. One-page description of calculations performed by an early spreadsheet for managing stack space.

Peebles, Margaret. (1951). And now we are in. *Library Journal*, 76(12), 1040–42. News account of the move into and description of Mississippi State College's new facility.

Perry, Alan. (1984). Packaging the problems in Kansas City. *Abbey Newsletter*, 8(2), 25–26. Describes shrink-wrapping procedure used as short- to medium-term preservation technique.

Pikul, Diane M. (2006). Moving libraries and shifting collections. *Catholic Library World*, 76(3), 212–15. Advises planning ahead, careful measurement of collections and shelving, selecting and then working with an experienced mover.

Pilette, Roberta. (1995). Moving archives: 10th Annual Preservation Conference, National Archives and Records Administration, Washington, D. C. *Conservation Administration News*, 61, 21–22. News report of conference on moving the National Archives. Includes listing of criteria for judging a collection housing appropriate for the move.

Pinzelik, Barbara P. (1983). Rearranging occupied space. *Collection Management*, 5(1/2), 89–103. Detailed planning procedures for moving collections within a reorganized stack area, including relocated stacks.

Prevailing in the interim, part I. (1990). *School Librarian's Workshop*, 10(6), 1–3. General discussion of problems in planning for a temporary school media center location, including use of a consultant to plan a move.

Prevailing in the interim, part II. (1990). *School Librarian's Workshop*, 10(7), 4–5. Concise, practical advice on selecting and boxing school media center materials for storage during (extended) renovation of facilities.

Princeton University moves into its new building. (1948). *Library Journal*, 73, 1210–12. Report on the move in progress at Princeton University from the Green and Pyne Libraries into the Firestone Library.

Ragsdale, Kate W., and Gayle Baker. (1990). Tapping the expertise of on-campus consultants. *College & Research Libraries News*, 51(8), 721–22. Approaches taken and recommendations made by teams of industrial engineering and library and information studies students asked to analyze the University of Alabama's planned move.

Interesting for both observations on the process used and different professions' perceptions of a move's most urgent problems.

Ramsey, Charles George, and Harold Reeve Sleeper. (1994). *Architectural graphic standards*. 9th ed. New York: John Wiley & Sons. Standard reference source for architectural design practices and data.

Rawlinson, Rochelle. (2005). Changing places. *Legal Information Management, 5(1)*, 54–57. Key tips: get project management training, minimize uncertainty but recognize it will occur, reduce materials before move, keep a record of all actions and decisions.

Reid, Elizabeth, and Kathryn A. Shaw. (1991). Moving the hospital library: A checklist. *Bibliotheca Medica Canadiana, 12(3)*, 155–59. Good basic checklist, equally applicable to any small library.

Roberts, Justine. (1984). Stack capacity in medical and science libraries. *College & Research Libraries, 45(4)*, 306–14. Report of a study conducted to determine the average volumes per linear foot (VLF) in five health sciences and two science libraries at the University of California. Detailed discussion of methodology. No significant difference was found among the libraries' monograph VLF averages; however, differences were found for serials. Interesting summary of book width estimates reported by several authors shows considerable variation in monograph and serial volume width estimates.

Roberts, Matt. (1966). Some ideas on moving a book collection. *College & Research Libraries, 27(2)*, 103–8, 119. Practical advice on planning a collection move. Includes arguments in favor of measuring instead of estimating extent of collections, leaving buffer space between major collection blocks, using library staff as move supervisors. Additional comments on cartons versus book trucks, differential learning curve management, integrating serials in monograph collections.

Robertson, Elizabeth. (1983). Moving the Wits Medical Library, November–December 1983. *Wits Journal of Librarianship and Information Science, 2*, 75–86. Weeding, cleaning, reclassification as part of a 100,000-volume hospital library move in South Africa, complicated by rainstorms and moving delays.

Robles, Patricia. A. (1996). Security upon moving into a new library building. *College & Research Libraries News, 57(7)*, 427–30. Useful discussion of planning and implementing security measures during a move, focusing on preventing materials loss and facility access by unauthorized individuals.

ANNOTATED REFERENCES

Rochford, Hilary. (1992). From basement blues to the upwardly mobile library: Planning a move. *Law Librarian, 23*(1), 2–6. Presented at a 1991 BIALL preconference workshop. General discussion of factors in planning and moving into a new library.

Roth, Britain G. (1985). Moving a medical center library. *Special Libraries, 76*, 31–34. Planning and implementation of double move of library at Geisinger Medical Center in Danville, PA, to temporary space and then to a new facility. Stresses need for library staff to supervise moving company staff without library moving expertise.

Ryan, Kevin. (1982). New home for Sheridan College Library. *Wyoming Library Roundup, 37*, 48–49. Describes Sheridan College's new library, with brief mention of the move into it.

Sapp, Gregg, and George Suttle. (1994). A method for measuring collection expansion rates and shelf space capacities. *Journal of Academic Librarianship, 20*(3), 156–61. Detailed description of methods used during "16 month project to measure existing space and growth rates, and provide predictive, quantitative data on growth capabilities throughout the building" at Montana State University-Bozeman's Renne Library.

Schabo, Pat, and Diana Breuer Baculis. (1989). Speed and accuracy for shelving. *Library Journal, 114*, 67–68. Methods used to select, train, and motivate high school student shelvers and achieve a drop in shelving errors from 10–16 percent to 0–3 percent at the Cedar Rapids (IA) Public Library.

Schick, Joan L. (1981). Bagging books helps school library move. *Unabashed Librarian, no. 41*, 4. Brief account of method for moving a school library collection.

Schlipf, Frederick A., and John A. Moorman (2002, November 13). *The public library construction process: From problem recognition to ribbon snipping.* Available at web.archive.org/web/20041212164726/urbanafree library.org/fredcons.htm (accessed August 13, 2007). Overview, with good advice. Section 14 addresses moving. Modified and expanded from the authors' presentation at 1999 PLA conference.

Schunk, Russell J. (1941). Librarian's nightmare. *Library Journal, 66*, 817–21. Planning and implementation of the Toledo (OH) Public Library's move into a new building.

Schuyler, Jane A. (1972). Library moving procedure. In *Planning the special library*, ed. E. Mount, 52–54. New York: Special Libraries Association.

Review of general considerations for move planning and implementation.

Schwartz, Joanne. (2004). Pack up all your cares . . . . *School Librarian's Workshop*, 24(10), 4–5. Practical advice, based on a school media center move, including securing high-value equipment, checking shelving dimensions, and checking the new facility carefully for punch list items before move-in.

Seaman, Scott, and Diana DeGeorge. (1992). Selecting and moving books to a remote depository: A case study. *Collection Management*, 16(1), 137–42. Describes selection and relocation to a remote depository of 10,000 fragile, old, and less-used volumes from the Ohio State University Libraries' Main Library. Focus is on selection criteria and procedures.

Segesta, James. (1986). Pulling the rug out from under the stacks. *College & Research Libraries News*, 47(7), 441–44. Moving unloaded stacks and collections to permit recarpeting stack areas at California State College, Bakersfield. Advises checking with shelving manufacturer to ensure shelving will not be damaged by process. Describes use of a custom-built device, based on Alley's description in "Moving Steel Stacks with a Special Dolly," with a design refinement to avoid ranges slipping down.

Seiler, Susan L., and Terri J. Robar. (1987). Reference service vs. work crews: Meeting the needs of both during a collection shift. *Reference Librarian*, 19, 327–39. Detailed account of planning and executing the reorganization of a reference abstract and index collection while maintaining public and staff access. Detailed procedures for reorganizing a serial collection and for reorganizing a collection within the same set of stacks.

Sell, Violet. (1954). Moving can be fun! *Wilson Library Bulletin*, 28(9), 792, 795. Account of moving a branch of the Long Beach Public Library using giant book troughs, "designed by a staff brother-in-law." Not addressed are securing books from falling out of the troughs, difficulty of maneuvering a 6-foot-long trough, stabilizing the trough atop a book truck (described as the method for moving the trough), comparative capacity of the trough versus either a book truck or a carton.

Sexton, Kathryn. (1968). Moving into the new San Antonio public library. *Texas Library Journal*, 44(1), 69–70. News report of San Antonio Public Library's move to new building, using a moving company, and beer cartons as containers.

ANNOTATED REFERENCES

Shanahan, Thomas J. (1950). Moving a library. *Minnesota Libraries, 16*(5), 131–32. Moving the library at St. Paul Seminary in St. Paul, MN, using a modified book brigade method. Individuals carried books on a carrying tray designed to hold the number of books to be placed on one shelf in the new facility. Good descriptions of logistics, division of labor, and a system for numbering individual members of the brigade to ensure their loads were reshelved in the correct order.

Sheetz, A. Coleman. (1932). The journey of the 360,000. *Pennsylvania Library Notes, 13,* 133–36. Using staff, professional movers, and packing boxes to move the Pennsylvania State Library to a new facility.

Shercliff, W. H. (1974). Removing a college of education library: A case study of the removal of 70,000 books. *Education Libraries Bulletin, 17,* 15–27. Excellent, detailed account of planning and execution of the move of Didsbury College of Education's 1973 move of about 66,000 volumes in three and a half days using professional movers and library staff. Cogent comments on the rationale for various decisions, on timing, on use of a professional mover, use of book carts rather than cartons, and so forth. Very useful comments on move operations, including loading book trucks, securing their contents, team sequencing.

Shields, Gerald R. (1994). Recycling buildings for libraries: A moving account. *Public Libraries, 33*(2), 93–95. Moving a historic Carnegie building in Mexico, Missouri.

Simon, Rose. (1987). Computer tells books where to go: A BASIC program for shifting collections. *North Carolina Libraries, 45,* 36–37. Description and code for a BASIC program written on an Apple II+ to determine "(1) the approximate number of inches to be filled with books in each new shelf [location], and (2) the current location of the book which should be the last one place in a face . . . of new shelving."

Slight, Owen E. (1967). Sydney University Library moves its research collections. *Australian Library Journal, 16,* 240–44. Planning and implementing a move of book stacks and 500,000 volumes using primarily student workers. Detailed discussion of using book trucks with safety straps to move bound volumes and methods used for dismantling and moving steel shelving. Discusses impact on schedule of occupancy delays. Detailed discussion of staffing assignments.

Smallwood, Carol. (1995). A do-it-yourself, low-cost move to a new library. *Book Report, 13,* 25–27. General advice on planning and executing school media center move using donated boxes and volunteer student labor.

Smith, Debbi A. (2007). Creating stack floor plans and signage: Excel as a collection management tool. *Technical Services Quarterly*, *24(3)*, 29–39. Creative planning for a time-pressed merger of collections in the absence of blueprints or accurate collection linear footage measurements. In retrospect, the author observes that a merger should not be attempted "without first completely understanding [the] size requirements [of the collections], and whether the area they were to be moved to could contain them."

Smith, N. R. (1990). A shelf-management model implemented on Multiplan. *Information Technology and Libraries*, *9*, 66–73. Detailed description of an early spreadsheet model for calculating percent occupancy of an area of shelving.

Snow, Richard. (2004). How not to move a library: Misadventures in moving. *Collection Management 29(2)*, 53–67. Humorous, very informative look at the reality of moving collections, with insider lessons about how people act during a move. Required reading for anyone planning or contemplating coordinating a move.

Snyder, Nancy. (1976). How to move a 60,000 volume public library for $1,000 (or enlist the National Guard). *Unabashed Librarian, no. 21*, 1, 3–4. Vineland, NJ, public library's move to a new building using volunteers, the National Guard, and the Red Cross, including recruiting and scheduling issues, color-coding collection measuring, packing, use of a conveyer system, and corrugated boxes.

Spurrier, Suzanne. (1990). To build or remodel? That was the question . . . . *Arkansas Libraries*, *47(3)*, 16–18. Report of planning for and move into a new facility. Emphasis on planning for a new building.

Spyers-Duran, Peter. (1964). *Moving library materials*. Milwaukee, WI: Library Associates of UW-M. Brief, but important. One of the basic works on moving library collections; required reading for anyone planning a move. Major sections are planning the move, moving methods, and specifications and contract forms. Very useful section on the use and conduct of time and motion studies, the merits of various move methods and containers, and the use of volunteers. Sample instructions for moving, bid specification, and contract. Chart summarizing characteristics of twenty-nine library moves conducted in the late 1950s and early 1960s. Good bibliography.

ANNOTATED REFERENCES

———. (1965). *Moving library materials*. rev. ed. Chicago: American Library Association. Slightly revised version of 1964 edition. Format somewhat easier to read, but content is essentially the same.

Stankus, Tony, and Kevin Rosseel. (1988). Estimation of shelving needs: Selection of equipment. In *Creative planning of special library facilities*, ed. E. Mount, 81–98. New York: Haworth Press. Focus is on selection of shelving. Cursory discussion of estimating shelving needs, but reviews several methods for estimating the extent of current holdings.

Stark, Linda. (1995). Florida Christian College Library. *Christian Librarian*, 38(1), 105–6. Brief description of moving 30,000 volumes plus reused shelving using library staff, along with students, faculty, and staff; stresses value of planning.

Stebbins, Howard L. (1941). Moving day. *Wilson Library Bulletin*, 15(5), 425. Brief but detailed account of the Social Law Library (Boston)'s 1939–1940 move.

Steele, Thomas M., Miriam A. Murphy, and Martha E. Thomas. (1994). *A law library move: Planning, preparation, and execution*. [n.p.]: Glanville Publishers. Detailed guide to moving a library. Chapters include general considerations, organizing the staff, preparing the old facility, selecting a mover and move method, executing the move, and post-move considerations. Written for law libraries, but applicable to libraries of all types.

Stephenson, Mary Sue. (1990). *Planning library facilities: A selected, annotated bibliography*. Metuchen, NJ: Scarecrow. Section 2.7 includes eighteen annotated entries on moving libraries.

Stickney, Edith P., and Janet Larsen Meinhold. (1955). Operation big switch. *Wilson Library Bulletin*, 30(3), 253–55. Moving Midland College's book collections using book brigade. Practical advice on briefing and managing student workers, rationale for differentiating book brigade "loaders" from "carriers."

Stoddart, Helen, and Lesley Hughes. (1984). Library removal—it could happen to you. *New Zealand Libraries*, 44(5), 83–84. Account of planning and implementation of the New Zealand Ministry of Agriculture and Fisheries' Central Library's move to a new facility. Detailed discussion of labeling system used to space out holdings to allow for growth.

Stokes, Katherine M., and Margaret F. Knoll. (1941). Moving the Pennsylvania State College Library. *Wilson Library Bulletin*, 16, 230–38. Detailed account of planning and carrying out move logistics for a large academic library collection, using university grounds staff and student library assistants.

Stout, Betty. (1997). Managing a move, without a hitch [electronic version]. *Book Report, 15*(4). Available at http://0-web.ebscohost.com.ilsprod. lib.neu.edu/ehost/detail?vid=3&hid=103&sid=3db891b9-37c1-4d84-9af8-1d4c8bee19a8%40sessionmgr110&bdata=JnNpdGU9ZWhvc3 QtbGl2ZQ%3d%3d#db=aph&AN=9707086160 (accessed August 3, 2007). Librarian successfully completes a shelf-to-shelf school library move in one day, using 200 physical education students, custom-built book troughs, and a triplicate index card system to identify shelf locations.

Students pitch-in to move Yakima school library. (1968). *Library News Bulletin, 35*, 36. News report of moving Davis High School's (Yakima, Washington) 11,589 volumes using students walking in line.

Surles, Richard H., and Jatin N. Mukerji, eds. and comps. (1977). *Legal periodical management data, Volume 1, 1977.* Buffalo, NY: William S. Hein. Listing of subscription price, frequency, starting and ending dates of available indexing; shelf space (in inches) required for specified back files; and annual growth for legal periodicals in the 1977 catalog of William S. Hein & Co.

Suvak, Daniel. (1982, October). Opening day: What to expect in a new library. *Wilson Library Bulletin, 57*, 140–41, 190. Impact of a new library on service and staff.

Suzuki, Takao. (1963). Removal of the National Diet Library of Japan. *Unesco Bulletin for Libraries, 17*(3), 175–77. Planning and executing the move of the National Diet Library of Japan's collection of over two million volumes from five separate locations to a new facility in 1961.

Swanepoel, Adrian. (2002). Moving a small library in an African setting. *African Journal of Library, Archives & Information Science, 12*(1), 27–38. Suggests planning collection layout by drawing a front view of every section of shelving. Several good practical tips at end of article.

Swanson, Patricia K. (1986). The John Crerar Library of the University of Chicago. *Science and Technology Libraries, 7*, 31–41. Merger of the John Crerar Library with the University of Chicago, including a brief description of the move into their new facility.

Swartzburg, Susan G. (1995). *Preserving library materials: A manual.* 2nd ed. Metuchen, NJ: Scarecrow Press. Of particular interest are comments in Chapter 3, "Collection Management, the Care and Preservation of Library Materials," on shelving and packing books.

ANNOTATED REFERENCES

Sweetland, James H. (1988). Time required for shelf reading—a case study. *College & Research Libraries, 49(1)*, 75–78. Review of literature related to rate of shelf-reading, and report on a shelf-reading project undertaken by students at the School of Library and Information Science at the University of Wisconsin-Milwaukee. Shelf-reading, reshelving, shifting as needed, and simple weeding were done by trained, motivated volunteers at an average rate of 583 volumes per hour.

Szilassy, Sandor S. (1964). Moving to a new library. *Alabama Librarian, 15,* 24–26. Moving the Auburn University Library into a new facility in 1962–1963; examples of the results of inadequate planning for periodical titles, sets cited.

Tatterton, E., and A. Braid. (1973). A moving story: The transfer of material to phase I of the NLL's new building. *NLL Review, 2,* 145–53. Detailed account of planning the move of the British National Lending Library's materials to a new building. Very useful analysis of constraint-driven planning: deriving the required rates of materials transfer to meet a set timetable and accessibility requirement, then deriving the labor and materials needed given additional facility constraints (elevator capacity, stack aisle size), to achieve those requirements.

Taylor, Gil. (2005, April 20). *Moving libraries and archives: A selected bibliography.* Available at www.sil.si.edu/silpublications/Moving LibrariesBib.pdf (accessed August 2007). Adapted, expanded, and revised from ALA *Library Fact Sheet Number 14.* Four pages.

Taylor-Christopher, Freda. (1997). *Relocating libraries and collections: A selective bibliography.* Canadian Libraries and Librarianship, Bibliography Series 5. Last updated , May 27, 2003. Available at www.collectionscanada.ca/6/7/s7–2601–e.html (accessed August 19, 2007). Five pages of citations covering relocations of academic, public, school, and special libraries.

Teper, Jennifer Hain, and Stephanie Atkins. (2003). Time and cost analysis of preparing and processing materials for off-site shelving at the University of Illinois at Urbana-Champaign Library. *Collection Management, 28(4),* 43–65. Detailed description of steps taken to select, prepare, and move 700,000 monograph and journal volumes to permanent high-density shelving, including bar-coding and updating bibliographic records; condition assessment and stabilization; transferring materials; unpacking, cleaning, and accessing materials; cost analysis; percentage of materials needing each process.

ANNOTATED REFERENCES

Tessmer, Julie. (2002). *Moving a library's collection.* Paper presented at the Wisconsin Library Association, 2002 Annual Conference. Available at www.wla.lib.wi.us/conferences/2002/postconf/moving.ppt (accessed January 20, 2008). PowerPoint slides. Notes the value of regular e-mail updates to staff, "not to exceed" statement in mover's bid, working with the mover; includes list of move tools, what to carry with you on move day, dos and don'ts. Based on move of Wisconsin State Law Library.

Tetro, Robert, and Kathie Callahan. (2002). *Stacks domino: Stacks management during renovation or construction.* Workshop presentation given April 27, 2002. Describes the use of DuPont's "Liftman" system to move fully loaded stacks during the eight-month move of Renne Library at Montana State University-Bozeman. Outlines pros and cons of range-mover versus traditional methods and provides a good, succinct comparison of time, labor, and cost to move using range-mover versus traditional means. Concludes that the range-mover cost was less than 50 percent as expensive and took 1.25 days versus 25 days required for the traditional method. Photographs illustrate the process.

Theilig, Richard. (1997). Remote possibilities. *Library Mosaics* 8(6), 14–15. Good description of selection rationale, marking, and moving of pre-1966 journals to remote storage.

Thorne, Marco. (1955). Two moves to home. *Library Journal,* 80, 840–44. Account of the San Diego Public Library's moves to temporary quarters and then to a new building.

Townsend, Robert B. (1977). Moving the Illinois State University library. *Illinois Libraries,* 59, 295–99. Account of moving, merging, and reorganizing a collection of 700,000 volumes. Useful comments on sampling versus measuring, reserving space for sets in collection mergers, shelf height spacing, correcting fill rates as a move progresses, and the time required to correct for shelving overruns.

Tucker, Dennis C. (1987). *From here to there: Moving a library.* Bristol, IN: Wyndham Hall Press. General comments on factors to consider in planning and executing a move. Useful comments on security, comparison of labor options, especially on the use of volunteers.

———. (1999). *Library relocations and collection shifts.* Medford, NJ: Information Today. Breezy guide to moving and carrying out a move. Includes sections on fumigation and deacidification. Revision of 1987 *From here to there: Moving a library.*

ANNOTATED REFERENCES

Tucker, Susan W. (2000). Moving the Middlebury map collection. *Information Bulletin (Western Association of Map Libraries)*, *32(1)*, 26–32. Describes reorganization and relocation of a map collection by professional movers and rationale for selection of new map cases.

Tunstall, Patricia. (2001). Let's move: How to move your collection without hiring movers (and without spending a fortune!). *Unabashed librarian*, *120*, 8–13. Good, brief step-by-step advice on planning a do-it-yourself move, including measuring collections, planning collection space, tagging the collection, reusing shelving, renting heavy-duty book trucks, staffing, tagging shelves, maintaining morale, and having a backup move coordinator.

UCSC library starts move into new addition. (1977). *College & Research Libraries News*, *38(1)*, 32–33. News report of move into addition at University of California, Santa Cruz.

University of North Carolina faces huge moving operation. (1983). *Library Journal*, *108*, 1420. University of North Carolina's planned move of 1.7 million volumes, 1.8 million documents, 85,000 reels of microfilm, and staff effects from the Wilson Library to the new Davis Library, using a professional moving company. Interesting comment on the amount of volunteer labor that would be needed to execute the move.

Uzelac, Constance. (1969). Moving a fragmented collection. *Special Libraries*, *60(7)*, 457–58. Moving from several locations and integrating the University of Southern California School of Medicine Library's serials collections. Useful comments on estimating annual inches of growth per title for material that is not physically accessible.

Vollmar, E. R. (1960). Operation beer case. *Library Journal*, *85*, 46–48. Moving St. Louis University's library to a new building. Features use of beer cases to pack books and a construction high-lift to compensate for lack of an elevator.

Waldron, Helen J. (1958). How to move documents. *Special Libraries*, *49(6)*, 266–67. Planning and implementing transfer of documents from file cabinets to open shelving.

Wallace, Mary. (1970). Time-space and the music library. *Notes (second series)*, *27(1)*, 12–18. Comments on space planning and equipment selection issues unique to music libraries, including observations on selection of shelving for scores of various sizes.

Wallace, Patricia M. (1990). Predicting future shelving needs. *Collection Management*, *12(1/2)*, 95–107. Outlines imprecise method for predicting shelving needs, based on estimating shelving utilization to the nearest one-quarter shelf, estimating number of volumes based on a small sample, and then using these data to project the exact number of volumes and capacity to the nearest percentage for various LC subclasses.

Waters, David. (1981). Problems of merging libraries. *Australian Academic and Research Libraries, 12*, 167–73. Account of transferring collections from the Tasmanian College of Advanced Education (TCAE) at Mt. Nelson (Hobart, Australia) to the University of Tasmania upon the closing of TCAE. Article focuses on selection of materials for transfer, control, and access issues. Brief discussion of the move.

Weaver-Meyers, Pat, and Dale Francis Wasowski. (1984). A committee approach to moving a library: Planning, personnel, and stress. *Journal of Library Administration, 5*(4), 21–32. Account of planning and implementing expansion into a new wing at the University of Oklahoma's Bizzell Library using library staff and student assistants. Focus is on role of the committee responsible for planning and supervising the move, including its value in informal communication with staff, leadership, stress reduction, and providing expertise in diverse areas. Important comments on the short- and long-term impact of stress on staff asked to maintain normal responsibilities while taking on significant move responsibilities.

Wells, Dorothy D. (1957). One-day move in Toledo. *Library Journal, 82*(21), 3046–47. Move into and new facility of the Sigmond Sanger branch library in Toledo, OH.

Wells, Marianna, and Rosemary Young. (1994). Making your move and getting it right. *Special Libraries, 85*(3), 145–53. General comments on successfully planning and implementing a move.

———. (1997). *Moving and reorganizing a library*. Brookfield, VT: Gower. Well-written, accessible overview. Includes considerable useful material on planning collection space and carrying out a collection move.

White, Kris A., and Glenn S. Cook. (1994). Round 'em up, move 'em out: How to move & preserve archive materials. *Conservation Administration News, 57*, 16–17. Packing and moving techniques for archival material, including selection of storage boxes; design of a box for moving glass plate negatives; and boxing methods for phonograph records, artifacts, large volumes. Also discussed is handling methods for map case drawers and flat storage case drawers.

Whiteway, Frances. (1966). Middlesex book transfusion supplies new for old at Glencoe. *Ontario Library Review, 50*(3), 171–73. Account of the full replacement of Glencoe, ON, public library's collection of 4,000 books with newer material from its county library.

Wiegandt-Sakoun, Carolyn, and Catherine Gunet. (1990). Moving the library: The INIST experience. *Interlending and Document Supply, 18*(3), 101–5. Planning and implementing move of the Institute de l'Information Scientifique et Technique (INIST) from Paris to Nancy. Includes detail on collection evaluation and deselection prior to move, selection of a moving company, and logistics.

Wilkins, Betty. (1967). Book brigade shifts library. *Law Library Journal, 60*, 283. Brief news report of a stack shift conducted at the Gould Law School, University of Southern California, by 100 students.

Wilkins, Frances Vroman. (1951). Moving à la Tom Sawyer. *Wilson Library Bulletin, 25*, 758–59. News account of moving the Keuka College library's 38,000 books using a student book brigade. Useful tips on sizing the number of books each person can carry, maintaining morale, briefing participants, routes.

Williams, Joan. (1998). Old books in new buildings: The new library building at Hereford Cathedral. *Library History, 14*(1), 17–22. Includes a brief description of techniques used to move the Chained Library.

Williams, Robert W. (1991). Computer-assisted instruction for student book shelvers using dBase III+. *Library Software Review, 10*(1), 35–36. Describes a program to teach proper call number sequencing.

Willis, Jean L., and Amy Hale-Janeke. (2003). Some cheese with your whine: San Diego Library keeps patrons, staff happy during remodeling closure. *AALL Spectrum 7*(8), 26–27, 31. Staff involvement led to critical contributions and good morale while the San Diego County Public Law Library maintained services during remodeling.

Wilsted, Thomas P. (2007). *Planning new and remodeled archival facilities.* Chicago: Society of American Archivists. Attractive and well written, this volume pulls together in one place many considerations related to planning an archives facility. Pages 116–23 address the unique collection storage issues for archives, and chapter 10 deals with moving archives' collections, with detail on the additional lead time required to prepare archives' collections and collection records for a move; handling fragile material; collection security; bar-coding; handling map cases, flat files, and glass negatives; and archives-related special factors to consider in selecting and working with a moving company.

Wittenborg, Karen, and John F. Camp. (1977). *Shelf space projection survey.* n.p.: SUNY Council of Head Librarians. [ERIC Document ED 156

140; IR 006 071]. Survey of SUNY libraries, reporting dates on which they were expected to reach maximum working capacity. Describes survey methods and reports results. Text reports that "7.5 volumes per linear foot was found to be a convenient and reasonably accurate estimate of shelf capacity" (3), however, Table 3 (14) reports the average volumes per foot calculated for forty SUNY libraries, ranging from 14.83 volumes/foot in the SUNY Buffalo Music Library to 2.73 volumes/foot in the SUNY Buffalo Library Studies Library.

Wolf, Edwin, II. (1966). A 235-year-old library moves 235,000 books. *Bibliographic Society of America Papers*, 60, 166–75. Library Company of Philadelphia's 1966 move from old building at Broad and Christian Streets to 1314 Locust Street, under less than ideal circumstances and conditions. Includes descriptions of local classification and shelving arrangements, shelf location coding, considerations in selecting a moving company, design of book carts constructed for the move, moving from a building without elevators, overcoming operational difficulties.

Woodward, Jeannette. (2000). *Countdown to a new library: Managing the building project*. Chicago: American Library Association. Chapter 10, "Moving and Getting Settled," offers commonsense guidance for move planning.

Woodward, W. B. (1977). Laughing all the way to the stack. *Library Association Record*, 79(7), 365. Brief, illustrated description of a system for visually presenting instructions for relocating books. Useful for moving small quantities of materials.

Wright, Shirley Louise. (1955). N.J. Library lightens move. *Library Journal*, 80, 1662–63. News account of Westfield (NJ) Free Public Library's move: 10,000 books were moved by asking public to check out twice their normal number; 35,000 books were moved by professional movers, using a product manufactured by a city councilman's firm, in addition to standard moving equipment.

Wyatt, Quanta, ed. (2001). Q&A: moving libraries. *Arkansas Libraries*, 58(3), 22–23. Advice drawn from seven Arkansas libraries that had recently moved includes start planning early, visualize the move to discover missing details, and make sure the labeling system works for all types of collections.

Zimmerman, Lee. (1957). On moving a library. *Bookmark*, 10, 42–45. Moving the University of Idaho (Moscow) library, using library and university staff, and a small pool of additional labor, book trucks, and university trucks. Impact of stack installation delays, difficulties in hiring labor discussed.

———. (1958). On moving a library. *Idaho Librarian, 10*, 10–14. Account of planning for and moving a college library using book trucks. Abridged version of article in *Bookmark* (December 1957).

INDEX

INDEX

INDEX

INDEX

INDEX

INDEX

ABOUT THE AUTHOR, CONTRIBUTORS, AND AUTHOR OF THE FOREWORD

Elizabeth Chamberlain Habich is Administrative Operations Manager for the Northeastern University Libraries, where she is responsible for budget, facilities, and personnel issues. Earlier, as its Building Projects Officer, she led the Libraries' planning for Snell Library, a new central library that opened in 1990, including the move into that building. The move brought together collections and services from the old main Dodge library, three science branch libraries, and a storage facility; incorporated reorganization of the serials collection in a new classification scheme; and separation of lesser-used material into compact shelving. Before coming to Northeastern as Head, Reserve Services, Habich served as Reference Librarian at the Saugus (MA) Public Library, and worked in preprofessional positions at MIT's Rotch Library and the Hingham (MA) Public Library. Habich is an active member of the Library Leadership Administration and Management Association (LLAMA). She has served as chair of its Buildings and Equipment Section (BES) and of several committees. She has written and spoken on topics including assessment, facilities design, workstation ergonomics, and adaptive access, and consults on library design issues. Habich holds an MBA from Northeastern University, an MS in Library and Information Science from Simmons College, and a BA from Wellesley College.

The late **Lee B. Brawner** was Executive Director of Oklahoma County's Metropolitan Library System from 1971 to 1999. Long recognized for his expertise in planning and building libraries, Lee contributed to the planning of well in excess of 100 libraries through his work as principal in Brawner Associates, LLC, provided an influential model through his planning for Oklahoma City's state-of-the-art Ronald J. Norick Downtown Library, which opened in 2004, and shared his expertise and mentored many in the library building planning community through his activities in LLAMA. Among many other awards, Lee was awarded the 1998 Hugh M. Hefner First Amendment Award in recognition of his uncompromising belief in intellectual freedom and the founding Lifetime Achievement Award from the (Oklahoma) Metropolitan Library System's Endowment Trust, which named the award after him. Lee Brawner died in 2006.

Michael J. Kent is Vice President, Library Relocation Division, William B. Meyer, Inc., of Stratford, Connecticut. Over the past twenty-five years, Mike has been involved in developing move plans for libraries of all sizes and types throughout the country. He has developed a library move team that has handled some of the largest and most difficult projects known. Their reputation for excellent service has placed the Meyer team at the top of its industry. A graduate of Villanova University, Mike has been in the moving industry since 1970.

The late **Joyce Frank Watson** was Building Planning Coordinator at the University of Hawaii Library for many years, where she coordinated planning for the second (1970–1979) and third (1990–2001) additions to Hamilton Library. Other library responsibilities included space analysis, building management, and a variety of special projects. In between library jobs, she coauthored a psychology textbook and edited *Ideafisher*, a computer software package designed to increase users' creativity. In her spare time she was a serious backyard gardener and a Scottish country dancer. Joyce held a BLS from the University of Toronto. Joyce Watson died in 2001.